Although historians of the French Revolution have paid it little attention, the French navy provides a striking illustration of the impact of the new ideology of Popular Sovereignty. This book examines the navy's involvement in political conflict from 1789 to 1794 and charts the evolution of a struggle between opposing definitions of authority in France. The fleet depended on the support of executive power. In 1789 royal government collapsed in the face of defiance from the National Assembly, but Popular Sovereignty was not confined to the legislature. The struggle between competing claims to represent the Nation's Will lay behind the fleet's surrender at Toulon in 1793 and the mutiny at Quiberon Bay. Sent to Brest to save the Republic's navy, Jeanbon Saint-André sought to restrict Popular Sovereignty in the context of the Terror. Thus this study presents a revisionist interpretation of the nature of Revolutionary politics.

REVOLUTION AND POLITICAL CONFLICT
IN THE FRENCH NAVY
1789–1794

REVOLUTION AND POLITICAL CONFLICT IN THE FRENCH NAVY

1789–1794

William S. Cormack

CAMBRIDGE
UNIVERSITY PRESS

Published by the Press Syndicate of the University of Cambridge
The Pitt Building, Trumpington Street, Cambridge, CB2 1RP
40 West 20th Street, New York, NY 10011-4211, USA
10 Stamford Road, Oakleigh, Melbourne 3166, Australia

First published 1995

Printed in Great Britain at the University Press, Cambridge

A catalogue record for this book is available from the British Library

Library of Congress cataloguing in publication data
Cormack, William S.
Revolution and political conflict in the French Navy, 1789–1794 /
William S. Cormack.
p.   cm.
Includes bibliographical references and index.
ISBN 0 521 47209 1
1. France – History, Naval – 18th century. 2. France. Marine – Officers – Political
activity. 3. France – History – Revolution, 1789–1799 – Influence. 4. Toulon
(France) – History – Siege, 1793.
I. Title.
DC153.C66   1995
944.04′1 – dc20   94-17249   CIP

ISBN 0 521 47209 1 hardback

CONTENTS

Contents

ILLUSTRATIONS

MAPS

All maps were drawn by Mr. Ross Hough of the
Department of Geography, Queen's University at Kingston, Ontario. Each map was adapted and modified
from the sources listed in the captions.

ACKNOWLEDGEMENTS

This book is a revised version of a doctoral thesis accepted by Queen's University at Kingston, Ontario, in 1992. Thus the people who assisted and supported me in that project have also contributed to this one. First among these, I would like to thank James Leith. Not only did Professor Leith supervise the writing of the thesis, but his support for its transformation into a book included locating illustrations and providing financial assistance for the preparation of the maps. There are two other people to whom I owe a great deal. James Pritchard, also of Queen's, generously shared his expertise in naval history and gave me the benefit of his critical assessment of draft chapters, but I am most grateful for his constant encouragement. Michael Sydenham, of Carleton University in Ottawa, has been my sternest critic but also my most staunch supporter, and I am deeply indebted to him for his advice and guidance.

My research in France was made possible by assistance from the staffs of the Archives Nationales and Bibliothèque Nationale in Paris, the Archives Départementales du Finistère in Quimper, and the Archives Municipales in Toulon. I would like to acknowledge in particular the help and kindness I received from the personnel of the Service Historique de la Marine: at Brest I benefitted immensely from the assistance of the Conservateur, M. Philippe Henwood, and his staff, especially Capitaine de vaisseau (en retraite) Daguzan; at Toulon the Conservateur, Mme. Madeline Astorkia, smoothed my way and her entire staff, especially Mme. Baronti of the Bibliothèque de la Marine, was very helpful. Here in Kingston, the staffs of Queen's University Libraries and of Massey Library at the Royal Military College of Canada have always been most cooperative.

I wish to express special appreciation for the efforts of several other people as well. I benefitted greatly from a conversation with M. Antoine

Tramoni, of the Service éducatif des Archives in Toulon, regarding the Revolution in Toulon. Clarke Garrett and Mary Kimbrough kindly sent me copies of their papers. Stewart Webster steered me towards some valuable material. Paul Christianson, Anne Godlewska, and Colin Duncan read various draft chapters and made valuable suggestions. Martin Nicolai gave me a copy of his biographical article on Bougainville and shared many references and sources. Ross Hough did an excellent job of drawing the maps based on my sketches and copies. Jim Burant of the National Archives of Canada, Visual and Sound Archives Division, located the book's cover illustration. Ian Germani reassured me of the feasibility and value of this topic at a crucial moment, and helped me to survive the Archives' initial broadsides.

The Social Sciences and Humanities Research Council of Canada provided me with financial assistance in the form of two doctoral fellowships. I also received a travel grant from Queen's University, Office of Research Services, which helped with the expenses of my trip to France.

Richard Fisher of Cambridge University Press has been helpful and considerate. I must also thank the three anonymous readers selected by the Press for their careful reading of my typescript and for their insightful comments. Their suggestions have improved the book immensely.

Finally, I would like to acknowledge the support and encouragement I received from my family and friends, for which I am most grateful. Above all, I wish to express my gratitude to my wife, Penny, who endured Revolution and mutiny without murmur, and who never complained when a promised holiday by the sea turned out to be on the wind-swept coast of Brittany rather than on the Côte-d'Azur. Her contribution has been the greatest of all.

Kingston, Ontario

ABBREVIATIONS

AD Finistère	Archives Départementales du Finistère, Quimper
AN	Archives Nationales, Paris
AP	*Archives Parlementaires de 1787 à 1860.* Paris, 1875–1987
BN	Bibliothèque Nationale, Paris
Brest	Service Historique de la Marine, Archives et Bibliothèque, Brest
Marine	Archives de la Marine, Paris
Moniteur	*Réimpression de l'Ancien Moniteur.* Paris, 1840–1854
Toulon	Service Historique de la Marine, Archives et Bibliothèque, Toulon

CHAPTER

1

THE FRENCH NAVY, THE REVOLUTION, AND THE HISTORIANS

The history of the French navy during the crucial years of 1789–1794 has been largely ignored by historians of the French Revolution. While every textbook or survey of the period describes developments in the French army, discussion of the navy is limited to passing references to the loss of the Mediterranean fleet at Toulon or the sinking of *Le Vengeur*.[1] There are several detailed studies of the army which deal with the interaction between the Revolution and the troops, rather than campaigns or strategy,[2] but the situation of the fleet has been left to

[1] In Georges Lefebvre, *The French Revolution: From Its Origins to 1793*, trans. E. M. Evanson (1962; repr. New York: Columbia University Press, 1967) and *The French Revolution: From 1793 to 1799*, trans. J. H. Stewart and J. Friguglietti (1964; repr. New York: Columbia University Press, 1967), a great number of pages are dedicated to the army of the Revolution, but almost none to the navy. Indeed, in the second volume, a section entitled "Maritime and Colonial Warfare," pp. 17–21, concerns the British navy exclusively: the state of the French navy is given in one sentence. Similarly, Albert Soboul, *The French Revolution, 1787–1799*, trans. A. Forest and C. Jones (Paris, 1962; repr. New York: Vintage Books, 1975), contains nothing on the Revolutionary navy, while devoting much space to the army. Two recent surveys in English show similar disparity: D. M. G. Sutherland, *France 1789–1815. Revolution and Counterrevolution* (London: Fontana Press, 1985); William Doyle, *The Oxford History of the French Revolution* (Oxford: Clarendon Press, 1989), has a good page on the pre-Revolutionary navy, p. 32, but little on developments after 1789. J. M. Thompson, *The French Revolution* (1943; repr. New York: Oxford University Press, 1966), is perhaps unique in featuring two entire pages on the naval situation, pp. 466–468, although he too says far more about developments in the army.
[2] See for example: Albert Soboul, *Les Soldats de l'an II* (Paris: le club français du livre, 1959); Samuel F. Scott, *The Response of the Royal Army to the French Revolution: The Role and Development of the Line Army, 1789–1793* (Oxford: Oxford University Press, 1978); John A. Lynn, *The Bayonets of the Republic: Motivation and Tactics in the Army of Revolutionary France, 1791–1794* (Chicago and Urbana: University of Illinois Press, 1984); Jean-Paul Bertaud, *The Army of the French Revolution. From Citizen-Soldiers to Instrument of Power*, trans. R. R. Palmer (Paris, 1979; repr. Princeton: Princeton University Press, 1988); Alan Forrest, *The Soldiers of the French Revolution* (Durham: Duke University Press, 1989).

1

strictly naval history. Thus the period of the Revolutionary wars, 1793–1815, is placed within the broader context of the maritime rivalry between France and Great Britain throughout the eighteenth century, the "Second Hundred Years' War."[3] The focus of the existing literature, therefore, is to explain the French fleet's ineffectiveness up to its final disaster at Trafalgar, or why the French Revolutionary navy failed.

In his excellent study of the naval officer corps between the World Wars, Ronald Chalmers Hood described the burden of history which has weighed upon the French navy: "Its officers shared a generally pessimistic view of history, and they strove to prevent repeating it. At the heart of their soul searching was the quest for a way to avoid the recurring problem of losing their fleet just on the eve of some great successful venture."[4] This attitude has also characterized the historians who studied the French navy, most of them serving or retired naval officers themselves. Their explanations for the fleet's failure between 1793 and 1815 have depicted the French Revolution as a catastrophe which destroyed the superb service bequeathed to France by Louis XVI. This historiographical tradition began in the nineteenth century with Jean-Pierre-Edmond Jurien de La Gravière, who wrote history while actively serving in the French fleet. Son of an Admiral who served during the Revolution, Jurien de La Gravière had a distinguished naval career which included action during the Crimean War and culminated in his promotion to Vice-Admiral in 1862.[5] His *Guerres Maritimes sous la République et l'Empire* was the first history of the French navy during the Revolutionary period and it was written to persuade his own generation of the need to revitalize France's naval power.[6]

---

[3] For discussions of 1793–1815 within this context, see Theodore Ropp, *The Development of a Modern Navy. French Naval Policy, 1871–1904*, ed. Stephen S. Roberts (Annapolis: Naval Institute Press, 1987), pp. 1–5, and Paul M. Kennedy, *The Rise and Fall of British Naval Mastery* (London: Allen Lane, 1976), pp. 123–147.

[4] Ronald Chalmers Hood, III, *Royal Republicans: The French Naval Dynasties Between the World Wars* (Baton Route and London: Louisiana State University Press, 1985), p. 7; see also pp. 7–16. The French Revolution is seen by the officers in this study as probably the worst of the successive disasters to befall the French fleet, and this view partly explains their animosity towards the Third Republic.

[5] Etienne Taillemite, *Dictionnaire des marins français* (Paris: Editions Maritimes et d'Outre-Mer, 1982), p. 177. As well as writing history, Jurien de La Gravière published the memoirs of his father, Pierre-Roch Jurien de La Gravière, *Souvenirs d'un Amiral*, 2 vols. (Paris: Hachette, 1860).

[6] Jean-Pierre-Edmond Jurien de La Gravière, *Guerres Maritimes sous la République et l'Empire*, 2 vols. (Paris: Charpentier, 1847); see esp. II, pp. 236–292.

2

Jurien de La Gravière explained the ultimate destruction of the French navy at Trafalgar by a strategic revolution in the British navy personified by Horatio Nelson, whose papers were a major source for his history. Nelson's audacity and rejection of traditionally cautious tactics were justified because the French navy was no longer equal to the British navy, as it had been during the War of American Independence.[7] This disequilibrium dated from 1793, according to Jurien de La Gravière, and stemmed partly from the dilapidation of naval material, but more importantly from the disorganization of personnel. The Revolution's erosion of all social bonds destroyed passive obedience and subordination in the fleet, and rebellious sailors had to be replaced by levies of fishermen and inexperienced conscripts. Worse was the imprisonment and execution of the noble officers of the *Grand Corps* during the Terror.[8]

Jurien de La Gravière was interested primarily in the maritime war with Great Britain and he gave few details on the navy's situation from 1789 to 1793. Historians who followed him, however, would stress those early years of the Revolution as the period which assured subsequent decay and defeat. Léon Guérin, in his massive maritime history of France published in the 1850s, argued that the Revolution had inherited an excellent fleet and quickly began to destroy it by unleashing popular violence against its commanders. The National Assembly's failure to punish the perpetrators of such attacks was a signal for the collapse of discipline and the dissolution of the officer corps.[9] When insubordination became general during the mutiny at Brest in 1790, "France was already defeated at sea"[10] long before the declaration of war. Yet Guérin condemned Revolutionary politicians for more than condoning destructive anarchy. While chaos prevailed in the ports, the Constituent Assembly considered proposals to reorganize the navy, and Guérin portrayed these debates as both unnecessarily divisive and utterly naive. This, he thought, was particularly true of the suggestions to assimilate the fighting navy with the merchant marine.[11] For Guérin,

---

[7] Ibid., I, pp. 2–10; esp. p. 9.
[8] Ibid., I, pp. 52–55.
[9] Léon Guérin, *Histoire maritime de France*, 6 vols. (Paris: Dufour, Mulat et Boulanger, 1851–1856), V, p. 234.
[10] Ibid., V, p. 268.
[11] Ibid., V, pp. 277–278, 281–290.

such ideas were in direct opposition with naval realities. Indeed, he saw the Assembly's new organization of the navy as symbolizing the decline of French naval power.

Guérin's distrust and disdain for the meddling of politicians in naval affairs became a hallmark for future histories of this subject, as did his defence of naval professionalism. This theme was further developed by Troude, the successor to Guérin and Jurien de La Gravière, in his *Batailles navales de la France*.[12] Troude described the navy as an institution as well as a battle fleet. In this context, all French naval disasters were attributed to "vices of organization."[13] If the exclusivism of the officer corps of the Old Regime had encouraged disobedience to higher authority, Troude thought the egalitarianism of the Revolution had similarly damaging effects on naval discipline. Like Guérin, Troude believed that the promotion of merchant officers to command units of the fleet by virtue of their Revolutionary *civisme* was the "height of blindness."[14] The elimination of "independence," the cause of past defeats, required the organization of a professional naval officer corps which was well trained but also highly disciplined. Such a development had only begun, according to Troude, under Louis XVI and was brought to an abrupt end by Revolutionary reforms.

Naval historians who followed Troude would repeat that the Revolutionary Assemblies were in grave error when they tried to dispense with professional officers. None would state this argument more categorically than American Alfred Thayer Mahan. Where Troude stressed the need to uphold successful organization, Mahan condemned French governments during the Revolutionary period for ignoring the "immutable principles of sea power."[15] The British navy and its success in the Revolutionary wars demonstrated these principles or laws of sea power, but Mahan used French history as an effective foil. Thus, Mahan argued, the attempts to replace naval professionals with merchant captains or, worse still, with elected officers could only have proved disastrous. The

---

[12] O. Troude, *Batailles navales de la France*, 4 vols. (Paris: Challamel, 1867–1868), II, p. 273.
[13] Ibid., II, pp. 247–252.
[14] Ibid., II, p. 263.
[15] Alfred Thayer Mahan, *The Influence of Sea Power upon the French Revolution and Empire, 1793–1812*, 2 vols. (Boston: Little, Brown and Co., 1898), I, esp. pp. 35–41, 49–64. For a discussion of Mahan's positivism, see Donald M. Schurman, *The Education of a Navy: The Development of British Naval Strategic Thought, 1867–1914* (London: Cassell, 1965), pp. 60–82.

application of theory by the Revolutionaries with "no appreciation of the factors conditioning efficiency at sea,"[16] also extended to the Convention's elimination of the corps of trained sea-gunners and its failure to preserve discipline among crews. Mahan certainly disapproved of the insubordination in French squadrons and ports, but his most damning criticism of the Revolution was for its amateur interference with a professional navy.

These major themes regarding the Revolution's impact on the navy were reiterated throughout the nineteenth century and, taken together, characterize a pattern of interpretation. This is not to say that the naval historians who followed, and drew heavily upon, Jurien de La Gravière, Guérin and Troude did not vary in their approach to the subject or their emphasis on certain aspects. Charles Rouvier was far more sympathetic to the Republican regime than his predecessors. The avowed purpose of his *Histoire des marins français sous la République* was not to lay blame for disaster, but to exonerate those sailors, officers and Revolutionary administrators who made heroic efforts under difficult circumstances.[17] Edouard Chevalier, however, had little sympathy for the Revolutionaries in his *Histoire de la marine française sous la première République*, which is perhaps the standard work on this subject. Chevalier's main concern was naval operations, but he argued that political struggles in the ports and the activities of the Jacobin Clubs affected the situation of the fleet profoundly.[18] Maurice Loir wrote several essays on the navy during the Revolution and contributed a valuable work on the state of the French navy in 1789.[19] Many of these writers shared an unfortunate predilection to blame supposed English espionage and treachery for contributing to the disintegration, rather than defeat, of the French fleet: "Perfidious Albion" was denounced with particular vehemence in relation to the disaster at Toulon in 1793.[20] French naval historians were united fundamentally, however, in

---

[16] Mahan, *Influence of Sea Power upon the French Revolution*, I, p. 37.

[17] Charles Rouvier, *Histoire des marins français sous la République (de 1789 à 1803)* (Paris: Arthus Bertrand, 1868), esp. pp. 1–3.

[18] Edouard Chevalier, *Histoire de la marine française sous la première République* (Paris: Hachette, 1886), see esp. pp. 66–72, 95–108.

[19] Maurice Loir, *Etudes d'histoire maritime. Révolution – Restauration – Empire* (Paris and Nancy: Berger-Levrault, 1901); *La Marine royale en 1789* (Paris: Armand Colin, 1892). The latter study fits the larger interpretative pattern by describing the superb fleet on the eve of its destruction.

[20] For general hostility and suspicion towards the English enemy, see, for example: Guérin, V, pp. 218, 237, 273, 327; Rouvier, pp. 25, 100–102, 113–114. Regarding

their indictment of the Revolution for interfering with naval organization, stimulating insubordination, and for persecuting professional sea officers.

What is particularly striking about this interpretation is its resiliency. Although the pattern was formulated in the mid-nineteenth century, more recent French studies of the Revolutionary navy have, in general, restated the traditional position. Joannès Tramond's maritime history of France, published in 1916 under the direction of the *Service historique de l'Etat-Major de la Marine*, included a scholarly and thoughtful section on the Revolution, but one which was hardly new in its explanation of the fall of French naval power.[21] René Jouan's history of the French navy, which appeared in 1950, conformed even more closely to the views of nineteenth-century naval historians.[22] Jouan's repetition of old arguments was hardly surprising given his reliance upon secondary sources. The same certainly cannot be said of Etienne Taillemite's recent publication, *L'Histoire ignorée de la marine française*. Taillemite, former Inspector-General of the French Archives, has unmatched knowledge of the Marine Series and this excellent survey was grounded firmly upon those collections. The book argued that French governments and society have been historically ignorant of maritime affairs and their importance, and it discussed the Revolution's effect on the navy in this context.[23] Taillemite's interpretation showed a sophisticated understanding of economic forces, social conditions, and the structures of naval organization, yet in the end his conclusions were those of his prede-

Toulon, Paul Cottin, *Toulon et les Anglais en 1793* (Paris: P. Ollendorff, 1898), esp. pp. 397–410, shows how the nationalist "Perfidious Albion" theme could encompass both pro-Revolutionary sentiment and sympathy for French rebels at the same time: the English are damned for gaining control of Toulon by treachery and for their cruelty in abandoning their French allies. The constant was the supposedly implacable English hostility to the French navy. For a recent example of this view, see Jacques Ferrier, "L'événement de Toulon du 28 août 1793," *Bulletin de l'Académie du Var* (1985), esp. pp. 150, 170–171. The theme is also important in the historiography of Counter-Revolution. Maurice Hutt, *Chouannerie and Counter-Revolution. Puisaye, the Princes and the British Government in the 1790s* (Cambridge: Cambridge University Press, 1983), p. 325 notes that the disastrous Quiberon landing of 1795 is seen by some French writers as a sequel to Toulon in England's plot to cripple France and mutilate her navy.

[21] Joannès Tramond, *Manuel d'histoire maritime de la France des origines à 1815* (Paris, 1916; repr. Société d'Editions Géographiques, Maritimes et Coloniales, 1947), pp. 549–580.

[22] René Jouan, *Histoire de la marine française* (Paris: Payot, 1950), pp. 173–236.

[23] Etienne Taillemite, *L'Histoire ignorée de la marine française* (Paris: Librairie Académique Perrin, 1988), pp. 279–291.

6

cessors: the Revolution destroyed the French navy at its apogee by sanctioning indiscipline, alienating professional officers, and by overturning the existing institutions. The publication of Taillemite's survey was followed closely by the appearance of Joseph Martray's *La destruction de la marine française par la Révolution*. This work was not one of research but, in the author's words, one of "reflection": it is highly derivative of Taillemite, although lacking his depth and accuracy. Martray's major argument was that ideological sectarianism destroyed the navy, yet he provided no real analysis of Revolutionary ideology and its impact on naval personnel.[24] Martray may have aspired to provocative reinterpretation, but, in reality, he has merely reiterated nineteenth-century wisdom.

A notable exception to this pattern is *Marines et Révolution*, by Martine Acerra and Jean Meyer, which goes far beyond the restatement of traditional arguments. In the preface, the authors presented their naval history as one which does not focus on battles, but on the relatively unknown human, financial, and logistical factors.[25] They placed the Revolutionary naval war in an international perspective, not only as the turning point in the "Second Hundred Years' War" but as the culmination of a European naval arms race during the 1780s. Considerable technological progress accompanied this rearmament phenomenon, which stemmed largely from rivalry over international commerce.[26] Despite discussion of all European naval powers, however, the book is primarily an examination of the French navy during the Revolutionary period. Acerra and Meyer broke with previous studies by arguing that the navy in 1789 suffered from important structural weaknesses. These included tensions within the officer corps, an inadequate reserve of trained seamen, insufficient supplies of timber and other primary resources, and the French state's financial weakness.[27] These structural problems made the Revolutionary navy terribly fragile. Acerra and Meyer emphasized that the larger financial and economic situations following 1789 affected naval construction and mobilization profoundly.[28] Similarly the authors examined radicalization of the naval ports, which

[24] Joseph Martray, *La destruction de la marine française par la Révolution* (Paris: Editions France Empire, 1988), see esp. pp. 12–17, 57–71, 231–243.
[25] Martine Acerra and Jean Meyer, *Marines et Révolution* (Rennes: Editions Ouest-France, 1988), p. 7.
[26] Ibid., see esp. pp. 11–27, 55–80, 134–139.
[27] Ibid., see esp. pp. 90–93.
[28] Ibid., see esp. pp. 152–154, 165–169.

influenced insubordination and officer emigration, in the light of the most recent social and demographic studies.[29] *Marines et Révolution*, unlike traditional treatments of this subject, does not remove the navy from its social and economic context. Acerra and Meyer suggested that the Battle of the Nile in 1798, not Trafalgar, was the disaster from which the French navy could not recover, and the central theme of the book is to explain the underlying factors which led to this defeat. Thus, despite the authors' novel examination of the topic, this valuable study reiterates the question which dominates naval histories: why did the French Revolutionary navy fail?

A recent article by Jonathan Dull exposed the problematic assumptions underlying this standard question.[30] The French navy's defeats between 1793 and 1815 were in keeping with the pattern of the entire eighteenth century, with the exception of the American War of Independence. French maritime success in that conflict, Dull argued, can be attributed to alliances which enabled France to overcome British superiority in number of ships and overall naval resources. In February 1793, however, the French navy faced its stronger British opponent without allies and the quantitative obstacles became insurmountable after the loss of the Mediterranean fleet: according to Dull, the effects of the Revolution on the officer corps or naval organization were largely irrelevant to the question of the navy's failure. Moreover, the concept of failure is itself misleading. Naval war is too often seen only in terms of ship losses incurred in battle, rather than in terms of the state's greater interests. Dull argued that the French navy did, in fact, contribute to the achievement of France's major war aims between 1793 and 1801, chiefly by enduring. By continuing to pose a threat, the French fleet forced Britain to expend energy and resources, creating enormous expenses which helped prevent a conclusion to the war reflective of the British navy's triumphs in battle.

One might also argue that a victorious navy was simply not essential to French national survival in the way it was to Great Britain's, and that the demands and expectations placed upon the two fleets were markedly different. The question of the French navy's relative success or failure during this period is thus more complicated than some historians have suggested. These complex issues of naval strategy and

[29] Ibid., see esp. pp. 104–113, 120–126, 132–133.
[30] Jonathan R. Dull, "Why did the French Revolutionary Navy Fail?," *The Consortium on Revolutionary Europe, 1750–1850. Proceedings* 18: 2 (1989), 121–137.

foreign policy will not be discussed in depth, however, because they lie outside the specific focus of this study. The history of the navy during the Revolution need not be restricted to strictly military concerns. In an article on the Constituent Assembly's Marine Committee, Norman Hampson stated:

There is a sense in which all naval history is general history, since the structure and preoccupations of a state influence both the services which it demands of its fleets and the type of naval organization appropriate to their performance. This relationship is most obvious in periods of social and political revolution when the navy, like other institutions, finds itself out of harmony with the principles of the new order.[31]

As Hampson argued, navies reflect the states which build them and the societies which surround them. The value of examining the interaction between fleets and revolutionary upheavals has been demonstrated by studies such as Norman Saul's insightful discussion of the Russian Baltic Fleet in 1917, or Bernard Capp's recent history of the English navy from 1648 to 1660.[32] Thus the history of the French navy between 1789 and 1794 has significance far beyond battles and strategy; it could shed light on the fundamental nature of the Revolution itself.

This survey began with the suggestion that historians of the Revolution have shown little interest in the navy. Three important exceptions to this rule should be noted which belong outside the edifice of naval history discussed above. Unlike those whose primary concern was the navy, for whom the Revolution was only important as its destroyer, these historians were interested chiefly in the Revolutionary struggle and used naval affairs as illustrations of the larger issues at stake. While the French naval historians often wished to influence contemporary naval policy, Oscar Havard and Léon Lévy-Schneider were deeply concerned with the uncertain French politics of their own day and, although of diametrically opposing views, both used history to support political positions bearing on the future of the Third Republic.

---

[31] Norman Hampson, "The 'Comité de Marine' of the Constituent Assembly," *The Historical Journal*, 2 (1959), 130.
[32] Norman Saul, *Sailors in Revolt: The Russian Baltic Fleet in 1917* (Laurence: Regents Press of Kansas, 1978); Bernard Capp, *Cromwell's Navy: The Fleet and the English Revolution 1648–1660* (Oxford: Clarendon Press, 1989). See also: Daniel Horn, *Mutiny on the High Seas: The Imperial German Naval Mutinies of World War One* (London: Leslie Frewin, 1973); Hood, *Royal Republicans*, esp. pp. 148–183.

Havard's *Histoire de la Révolution dans les ports de guerre* is a unique study of the events of the Revolution which occurred in the naval ports: one volume concerned Toulon and the second the Atlantic ports, principally Brest. Although published in 1911–1913, Havard's work remains useful as a source of otherwise unpublished documentary material. The study was, however, the product of strong political prejudice and the analysis of the naval situation was subordinated to a vitriolic condemnation of every aspect of the Revolution. Havard was a ferocious defender of "Throne and Altar" and his interpretation can best be termed ultra-royalist. He viewed the Revolution's changes to naval organization as only part of a deadly and unjust assault on the institution of the monarchy, and he linked the persecution of naval officers led by popular societies in the ports to a vast masonic and anti-French conspiracy.[33] His evaluation of Jeanbon Saint-André, the Revolutionary leader most closely associated with the fate of the navy, illustrates the extremity of Havard's interpretation. This bizarre portrayal brought together Havard's antipathy for Protestants and his profound suspicion of the English. Havard, relying upon dubious evidence, claimed that Jeanbon plotted to deliver Brest to the British: while he concealed the true motives for his severity against the officer corps behind a mask of fierce Republicanism, Jeanbon, the former Huguenot pastor, sought to destroy the navy as personal revenge against Catholic France.[34]

Lévy-Schneider's massive biography of Jeanbon Saint-André countered this image of an insidious conspirator effectively. This study depicted the *conventionnel* as a patriotic and dedicated servant of France and the Republic, particularly because of his heroic efforts to revitalize the fleet during his missions to Brest.[35] Jeanbon, member of the Committee of Public Safety, was the Montagnards' naval expert and his biographer was much concerned with the changing situation of the navy throughout the Revolution. The book was based upon thorough and painstaking primary research and has been the best source for the

[33] Oscar Havard, *Histoire de la Révolution dans les ports de guerre*, 2 vols. (Paris: Nouvelle Librairie Nationale, 1911–1913), II, pp. 52–59, 82, 164, passim.
[34] Ibid., II, pp. 292–303, 307–308, 311–314. Havard's only evidence of Jeanbon's plot is the *mémoires* of Lieutenant Louis Besson, a naval officer who speculated that only a treacherous arrangement with the British could explain the persecution and dismissal of talented commanders, and a quotation by Admiral Truguet in a 1797 issue of *Républicain français*.
[35] Léon Lévy-Schneider, *Le conventionnel Jeanbon Saint-André*, 2 vols. (Paris: Felix Alcan, 1901), I, pp. 476–581, 623–661; II, pp. 705–794.

10

impact of political strife on the navy during the Terror. The study was certainly more subtle than Havard's, but it also reflected the pronounced political commitments of its author. Lévy-Schneider wrote in the Republican tradition of Revolutionary historiography established by Alphonse Aulard and, thus, he viewed the efforts of Jeanbon and his Montagnard colleagues as part of the struggle to ensure the victory of democracy. This victory required, according to Lévy-Schneider, the suppression of all political dissidence and he argued that opposition to the Revolutionary Government in the ports and in the squadrons was anti-democratic by definition and inevitably linked to Counter-Revolution.[36]

The interpretations of the French Revolution evident in the work of Lévy-Schneider and Havard were influenced heavily by French politics at the beginning of the twentieth century. This was not the case in the third study of the Revolutionary navy, Norman Hampson's *La Marine de l'an II*. Published in 1959, this excellent book examined the mobilization of the Atlantic fleet under the Jacobin Republic as a relatively unknown aspect of the Revolutionary war effort, rather than as traditional naval history. Hampson outlined the poor state of the French fleet on the eve of war,[37] and described the ambitious strategy imposed on the navy by the Revolutionary Government which required unprecedented construction and outfitting of warships, as well as the requisition of vast amounts of material and the levy of great numbers of seamen.[38] The study was a triumph of archival research and Hampson's analysis of the complexity of this mobilization, and the obstacles to its success, was astute and cogent.

Despite its obvious merits, *La Marine de l'an II* should not be considered the final word on the interaction between the Revolution and the navy. The study is limited to 1793–1794, with earlier developments presented only in outline. Hampson recognized the existence of complex political divisions in French society, yet he implied that quarrels and distrust between naval officers and Revolutionary politicians were explicable by the supposed royalism of the former: this dialectic reflected the accusations of the Revolutionaries and the interpretations of previous historians. The book's central theme was that the French navy in 1793–1794 was in a vulnerable transition between an out-dated, hierarchical

---

[36] See for example Lévy-Schneider, I, p. 517.
[37] Norman Hampson, *La Marine de l'an II: Mobilisation de la Flotte de l'Océan, 1793–1794* (Paris: Librairie Marcel Rivière, 1959), pp. 18–65.
[38] Ibid., pp. 82–93.

11

institution and a modern, democratic one.[39] Hampson's principal argument, that the creation of a Republican navy required the imposition of unity and firm central control,[40] echoed the solution advocated by the Montagnards themselves: ultimately, his vision of the Revolution conformed to the then-predominant interpretation which combined the Republican tradition with the Marxist paradigm of class struggle.

This "Classical Theory" of the French Revolution, which explains 1789 as the political advent of the bourgeoisie, was the accepted scholarly consensus when Hampson wrote his history of the Revolutionary navy. In subsequent decades, however, this interpretation came under increasing attack. In 1985 Donald Sutherland was able to write that "the whole idea of the class origins of the Revolution has collapsed, probably forever."[41] If liberal empiricists who demonstrated that the theory of Bourgeois Revolution was not supported by the evidence undermined the old paradigm initially, the latest wave of revisionism has sought to break with the old quarrels over social origins and outcomes in order to shed new light on the meaning of the Revolutionary experience. These efforts to create an entirely new historical framework have centered on analysis of language and of symbols, and the interaction of these with political action and ideas. François Furet began this new critique in a series of provocative essays. He insisted that the interpretation of the Bourgeois Revolution merely expressed the logic of the Revolution's own consciousness, a retrospective illusion of inevitable change. This arose from the Revolutionaries' endeavours to forge a new society through language, and it was the evolution of a "Revolutionary Discourse," the substitution of language for power, which represented the true break with the past.[42] Furet's thesis influenced Lynn Hunt, who also suggested that the French Revolution was fundamentally a political phenomenon in which politics became the instrument to regenerate

[39] Ibid., p. 65, passim.
[40] Ibid., p. 95, passim.
[41] Sutherland, *France 1789–1815*, p. 12. For an overview of the debate between Marxist Orthodoxy and revisionism, see William Doyle, *Origins of the French Revolution* (1980; 2nd edn, Oxford: Oxford University Press, 1989), Part I, "A Consensus and Its Collapse," pp. 7–40. See also Jacques Solé, *La Révolution en questions* (Paris: Editions du Seuil, 1988), esp. pp. 19–99.
[42] François Furet, *Interpreting the French Revolution*, trans. E. Forster (Paris, 1978; repr. Cambridge Univeristy Press, 1985), see esp. "The French Revolution is Over," pp. 1–80. See also François Furet and Mona Ozouf (eds.), *A Critical Dictionary of the French Revolution*, trans. Arthur Goldhammer (Cambridge, Mass.: Belknap Press of Harvard University Press, 1989).

society. A new "Revolutionary Political Culture" emerged with the collapse of Old Regime political culture and through the competition for political space which accompanied this collapse. For Hunt the new political culture comprised both Revolutionary rhetoric, the linguistic reconstitution of the social and political world, and symbolic forms of political practice, the notion that Revolutionary symbols were not metaphors of power but the means and ends of power itself.[43] Keith Baker concurred that political authority during the Revolution was equivalent to linguistic authority, but he argued that this did not distinguish the Revolutionary period from the years which preceded it. To understand Revolutionary political culture, according to Baker, one must examine its invention during the Old Regime by the competition of different political discourses.[44]

The effect of this new historical framework, put very simply, has been to change the focus of scholarship on the French Revolution from social approaches to political ones. Despite the new emphasis on language, symbols, and their deconstruction, these revisionist studies reassert the notion that changing concepts of authority and conflicting ideas of governance were at the heart of the Revolutionary struggle. These issues were central to the experience of the navy. Yet the new literature tends to concentrate on the evolution of ideas rather than upon their application, and discussions of political culture have often remained detached from any narrative of the political events of the Revolution, particularly those in the provinces. An examination of political conflict in the fleet, which would explore the actual impact of Revolutionary ideology on a major arm of the French state, could fill this gap and thus make a strong contribution to the most recent debates on the French Revolution.

Further reference should be made to the work of Baker and Furet to clarify how recent literature revives older theory of Revolutionary

---

[43] Lynn Hunt, *Politics, Culture and Class in the French Revolution* (Los Angeles and Berkeley: University of California Press, 1984), see esp. pp. 213–236. Hunt criticized Furet for failing to give the notion of Revolutionary discourse any social context and she suggests, ambiguously, that the creation of a new political culture was accompanied by the rise of a new "Political Class"; see pp. 149–179.
[44] Keith Michael Baker, *Inventing the French Revolution* (Cambridge: Cambridge University Press, 1990), see esp. 4–10, 12–27, 203–223. The influence of Baker's arguments can be seen in the renewed interest in French political ideology before 1789; see for example the essays in Keith Michael Baker (ed.), *The Political Culture of the Old Regime* (Oxford: Pergamon Press, 1987).

ideology: theory which is more easily applicable to a narrative of naval politics, but which is in keeping with the thrust of revisionism. The late eighteenth century saw the evolution of a new concept of sovereignty in France which transferred absolute authority from the king to the nation. The nation, however, was an abstraction and the location of its will remained ambiguous. Keith Baker linked this ambiguity to the problem of defining representation in 1789. In *The Social Contract* and other works, Rousseau argued that political freedom required the transfer of sovereignty from the monarch to the body of citizens as a whole. Subjection to particular wills would be eliminated by subjection to the General Will. The sovereignty created by this social contract, according to Rousseau, could neither be eliminated nor represented. Baker emphasized the problem this created for the revolutionaries of 1789 who embraced the principle of sovereignty inherent in Rousseau's notion of the General Will, yet fell back on the practice of representation which he had repudiated. The deputies of the Third Estate claimed to represent a unitary national will, while seeking to legitimate a revolution which had carried them far beyond the mandates they had received from their constituents.[45]

The question of representation was bound up with that of the constitution. Baker pointed out that the Tennis Court Oath of June 20, 1789, in which the deputies swore to "fix" the French constitution, did not clarify whether an existing constitution was to be reformed or whether a constitution was to be created entirely anew on the basis of Revolutionary principles. During the crucial constitutional debates of August and September 1789 the deputies rejected a proposed balance of powers under a tempered historical monarchy, as well as Sieyès' arguments that the true expression of the General Will was located only in the rational deliberations of a unitary legislature. Instead the Assembly opted to create a radical new constitution based on the principle of national sovereignty. National sovereignty, according to this discourse, resided directly and inalienably in the General Will but could be reconciled with the practice of representation through a suspensive royal veto on disputed legislation to be followed by a direct appeal to the people in the primary assemblies. The deputies accepted the institution of a constitution by an act of sovereign will, but did not confine national sovereignty to a representative body. Baker argued that they had thus

[45] Baker, pp. 224–251.

chosen the most unstable combination of the theory of an inalienable General Will and the practice of representation. By institutionalizing competing claims to represent the General Will, the Assembly opened conceptual space between the notion of revolution and that of the constitution which made the establishment of the latter impossible.[46]

Baker's careful analysis of the language of constitutional debates reinforced Furet's more abstract discussion. Furet argued that the instability inherent in Revolutionary politics resulted from the replacement of the normal conflict of interests for power with a competition of discourses for the appropriation of legitimacy. This substitution was driven by the perception that executive power was secretive and corrupt, while language was open to scrutiny and would always belong to the "People." Thus Revolutionary Discourse, according to Furet, gave legitimacy to those who symbolically embodied the "People's Will" and could monopolize the appeal to it.[47] Alfred Cobban suggested the implications of this legitimacy eighteen years earlier. Cobban argued that although the French Revolution was shaped by multiple and complex factors, it was also the embodiment of a powerful idea: Popular Sovereignty. This idea, that those who exercise political power are identical to those over whom it is exercised, represented for Cobban both the break with Enlightenment liberalism and the fundamental explanation for Revolutionary war and tyranny:

The identification [of rulers with ruled] is, . . . in practice impossible; but the mere belief in such an identification makes any constitutional device for attempting to control or limit government unnecessary and irrelevant. A Government has only to assert that it is the Government of the people to be automatically emancipated from all restraints. Whoever lifts a finger against it, or utters a word of criticism, is an enemy of the people.[48]

This equivalence between People and Government enabled those who could embody the "People's Will," who could master Furet's Revolutionary Discourse, to destroy those who could not. The Terror thus represented the complete identification of Popular Will with the government of the state.

---

[46] Ibid., pp. 252–305.
[47] Furet, pp. 47–49.
[48] Alfred Cobban, *In Search of Humanity: The Role of the Enlightenment in Modern History* (London: Jonathan Cape, 1960), p. 190; see pp. 181–193.

15

Other historians have also referred to the ideology of Popular Sovereignty to account for the Terror, and to explain why stable authority eluded Revolutionary Assemblies and the executive ministries before 1793. Jack Censer discussed the dynamic of Popular Sovereignty prior to the advent of the Republic in his astute study of the Parisian radical press. Censer defined it as the belief that the populace was itself sovereign and must never surrender its ultimate prerogative to any authority, elected or not, and he argued that this was the guiding principle of all radical agitation from 1789 to 1791.[49] These political inclinations are very similar to those which Albert Soboul attributed to the Parisian *Sans-Culottes* of 1793–1794.[50] Popular Sovereignty, thus defined by Censer, Cobban, and others,[51] was antithetical to the practice of representative government, as well as to the principle of executive authority. Its ramifications can be illustrated in the experience of the navy as a national institution. Although the pages which follow will refer more frequently to the ideology of Popular Sovereignty than to Revolutionary Discourse, it is hoped that this discussion will contribute to the development of the new interpretative paradigm suggested by Furet, Baker, and others which has restored the importance of ideas to the meaning of the French Revolution.

This study will examine the impact of the Revolution on the French navy from 1789 to 1794. Rather than seeking an explanation for naval defeats, the analysis of conflict in the squadrons and arsenals which follows is intended to shed light on the complex interplay of social tensions, factional strife, and ideological struggle which lay behind

[49] Jack Richard Censer, *Prelude to Power: The Parisian Radical Press, 1789–1791* (Baltimore and London: Johns Hopkins University Press, 1976), see esp. pp. 1–12, 37–72. Censer contends that the ideology of Popular Sovereignty incorporated a Manichean view of the virtuous *peuple* in conflict with the demonic *aristocratie*. This is similar to Furet's emphasis on the aristocratic plot, the constant denunciation of which allowed rival Revolutionaries to continually raise the ideological stakes; Furet, esp. pp. 55–56.
[50] Albert Soboul, *The Sans-Culottes: The Popular Movement and Revolutionary Government, 1793–1794*, trans. Rémy Inglis Hall (Paris, 1965; Princeton: Princeton University Press, 1980), pp. 95–221; see esp. p. 95 for a definition of Popular Sovereignty as the *Sans-Culottes'* basic political principle, and pp. 128–134 for a discussion of insurrection as the ultimate recourse of Popular Sovereignty.
[51] See also Eric Thompson, *Popular Sovereignty and the French Constituent Assembly, 1789–91* (Manchester: Manchester University Press, 1952), esp. pp. 153–157, and M. J. Sydenham, *The French Revolution* (London, 1965; repr. Westport, Conn.: Greenwood Press, 1985), esp. pp. 64–65.

16

Revolutionary politics. Furthermore, the study of the fleet and naval ports is intended to provide a balance between provincial and national perspectives often lacking in monographs dealing specifically with local or parliamentary developments. Above all, this study will chart the evolution of conflict between authority based ambiguously on the "Sovereign People" and naval authority based on executive power. Despite this emphasis on political ideology, room will also be left for the role of individuals because events of significance were shaped by the will and personality of particular actors. In short, the situation of the French navy from 1789 to 1794 is not of interest only to military historians: conflict in the navy was a microcosm of the Revolution throughout France.

THE FRENCH NAVY ON THE EVE OF REVOLUTION

The state of the French navy on the eve of the Revolution has been misunderstood. According to contemporaries and naval historians, the service reached its apogee in the final years of the Old Regime.[1] This image of excellence reflected the glory won by the fleet during the American Revolutionary War, when the French navy played a major role in achieving American Independence. The relative success in that conflict, however, obscured serious institutional deficiencies which Martine Acerra and Jean Meyer refer to as structural weaknesses.[2] Disruptive antagonisms existed within the officer corps. The navy had not solved its longstanding difficulty in manning its warships. Much of the material required to build these ships had to be imported from outside France's borders. Naval construction, the payment of personnel, and the functioning of a large and complex administration required vast sums of money: thus the strength and effectiveness of the fleet was limited by the financial weakness of the French Crown. These problems existed long before 1789 and should not be attributed to the effect of the Revolution.

The Revolution's major impact on the French navy was to undermine executive authority. The navy, even more so than the army, was dependent upon royal government. This included more than the infusion of state capital. The fleet's continued existence demanded the control and

---

[1] For the contemporary view, see the *Mémoire* addressed to the king by the comte de La Luzerne, 23 October 1790, AN Colonies F 3/138, ff. 522–549; cited in Taillemite, *L'Histoire ignorée*, pp. 279–281. For the traditional judgement of naval historians, see for example: Chevalier, p. 24; Jouan, p. 173; Taillemite, *L'Histoire ignorée*, pp. 177–199.

[2] Acerra and Meyer, p. 90.

coordination of diverse and widespread operations. The naval ports, especially Brest and Toulon, were far from Versailles in provinces where the acceptance of central control was hardly complete. The authority of naval Commandants and Intendants, itself based on royal authority, was secure only so long as the central government was strong and respected. An examination of the navy's organization will illustrate its extreme vulnerability to the political upheaval which lay on the horizon.

Just as it was dependent on the state which created it, the navy was a reflection of the society which surrounded it. Like all institutions of eighteenth-century France, a privileged aristocracy dominated the fleet. This explained, in part, the intense suspicion with which Revolutionaries regarded the naval officer corps. Yet Revolutionary rhetoric should not be accepted without qualification. Naval authority was more paternalistic than despotic, and the navy was a traditional defender of its workers and sailors. Moreover, the French navy at the end of the Old Regime, like the monarchy itself, was undergoing significant reform. This was epitomized by the "Code de Castries," a series of ordinances and regulations which modernized the fleet and introduced reforms in keeping with the ideals of 1789.

The War of American Independence has great importance in the history of the French navy: for the first time, the fleet was the principal instrument of French foreign policy. Moreover, the navy's prominent role during the conflict followed a period of remarkable recovery. The disasters of the Seven Years' War brought about the virtual elimination of French sea power. Yet naval revival began under the leadership of Etienne-François, duc de Choiseul even before the war ended.[3] The extent to which Choiseul initiated real reform of naval organization is questionable,[4] but his plans for a war of revenge against Great Britain included a powerful navy and he made its restoration into a great

---

[3] Choiseul became Minister of Marine and of War in 1761. With his cousin, Choiseul-Praslin, holding the office of Foreign Affairs, Choiseul was able to provide France with something akin to a united government; see Alfred Cobban, *A History of Modern France. Volume I: 1715–1799* (London: Penguin, 1957; repr. 1979), pp. 90–92.
[4] James Pritchard, *Louis XV's Navy, 1748–1762. A Study of Organization and Administration* (Kingston and Montreal: McGill–Queen's University Press, 1987), pp. 212–214. Pritchard argues that Choiseul's reforms to organization, contained in the ordinance of 1765, were less significant than changes which had occurred since 1748, and that Choiseul failed utterly to reform naval finances which were at the root of French naval weakness.

patriotic cause. Antoine-Gabriel de Sartine, however, was the Minister of Marine[5] most responsible for rebuilding the fleet. Sartine, appointed by Louis XVI in 1774, had been lieutenant-general of police in Paris and he proved to be a highly capable and efficient administrator despite his lack of maritime experience. He reformed naval administration and implemented a massive program of naval construction.[6] Sartine's policy was only possible because of a vast increase to the Marine budget, which was due in part to the efforts of the Minister of Foreign Affairs, Charles-Gravier, comte de Vergennes. Vergennes was the new champion of a war of revenge and he steered France towards involvement in the American Revolution. Naval rearmament and the outbreak of war with Great Britain were related: Jonathan Dull argued that the progress of work in the dockyards was a greater influence on the French decision to abandon neutrality in 1778 than the American victory at Saratoga.[7]

The French navy's first real test of the war came at the Battle of Ouessant on July 27, 1778, when a fleet commanded by Louis-Guillouet, comte d'Orvilliers fought the British under Admiral Keppel.[8] The outcome was indecisive and this relative success led to plans for an invasion of England. Yet France required naval reinforcement for such a major operation, and this became available only with Spain's declaration of war against Great Britain in 1779.[9] A combined Franco-Spanish

[5] Technically, the position was *Secrétaire d'Etat à la Marine* and its holder was not necessarily a Minister, which implied membership on the Royal Council of State. Pritchard, pp. 3–18 discusses the problems during the Seven Years' War when various Secretaries of State for the navy were not Ministers.
[6] See Georges Lacour-Gayet, *La Marine militaire de la France sous le règne de Louis XVI* (Paris: Honoré Champion, 1905), pp. 26–63, esp. 52–57, and Taillemite, *L'Histoire ignorée*, pp. 178–184. For a recent detailed examination of Sartine's contribution, see Jacques Michel, *Du Paris de Louis XV à la marine de Louis XVI. L'oeuvre de M. de Sartine*, Vol. II: *La Reconquête de la liberté des mers* (Paris, 1984).
[7] Jonathan R. Dull, *The French Navy and American Independence: A Study of Arms and Diplomacy, 1774–1787* (Princeton: Princeton University Press, 1975), p. 90. Dull suggests that Vergennes' seeming moderation in foreign policy before 1778 was motivated partly by fear of a dangerously short war, but that he also supported a period of limited intervention on behalf of the Americans because it provided time for rearmament: Vergennes' and Sartine's policies were mutually reinforcing; pp. 30–33, 49–55.
[8] For accounts of the battle, see Lacour-Gayet, pp. 125–134 and Alfred Thayer Mahan, *The Influence of Sea Power upon History, 1660–1783* (Boston: Little, Brown and Co., 1890; repr. 1918), pp. 350–353.
[9] Dull, *French Navy and American Independence*, pp. 126–146. The desire of the French government and navy for the Spanish alliance, and its importance to overall war strategy, are central themes of Dull's study.

fleet gained command of the English Channel in August 1779; the British navy declined battle, but epidemics decimated the Allied crews and the invasion was aborted.[10] The major strategic theatre for the French navy, however, lay across the Atlantic. French squadrons under Charles-Henri, comte d'Estaing and Luc-Urbain de Bouexic, comte de Guichen achieved some success in the Caribbean,[11] but an effective offensive strategy was not implemented until Charles-Eugène de La Croix, marquis de Castries replaced Sartine as Minister of Marine in October 1780.[12] In March 1781 Castries sent a fleet under the command of François-Joseph, comte de Grasse-Tilly to the West Indies. Admiral de Grasse received news in July that Washington and the French expeditionary force under Rochambeau were poised to attack the British army at Yorktown, and he sailed immediately from Saint-Domingue for the Chesapeake Bay. The French fleet arrived at the end of August to land troops and to blockade Cornwallis, the British commander, from possible rescue. On September 5, 1781, a British fleet under Admiral Graves reached the Chesapeake and de Grasse's victory in the subsequent battle rendered the surrender of Yorktown, and the independence of the United States, inevitable.[13]

[10] Patrick Villiers, "La stratégie de la marine française de l'arrivée de Sartine à la victoire de la Chesapeake," in Martine Acerra, José Merino, and Jean Meyer (eds.), *Les Marines de Guerre Européennes, XVII–XVIIIe siècles* (Paris: Presses de l'Université de Paris – Sorbonne, 1985), pp. 208–213. See also Lacour-Gayet, pp. 231–294. For a detailed study of the Allied operation, see Alfred Temple Patterson, *The Other Armada: The Franco-Spanish Attempt to Invade Britain in 1779* (Manchester: Manchester University Press, 1960).
[11] Admiral d'Estaing captured Grenada in July 1779, but failed at Savanah, while Guichen out-manoeuvred Rodney and Hood in three indecisive battles in 1780. See Lacour-Gayet, pp. 138–230, 332–345, and Taillemite, *L'Histoire ignorée*, pp. 186–188, 203–206.
[12] Dull, *French Navy and American Independence*, p. 202 argues that Sartine was sacrificed to appease the Spanish and to conciliate domestic opponents of the French Royal Council. Castries was seen as a compromise candidate, acceptable to diverse factions. See also René de La Croix, duc de Castries, *Le maréchal de Castries (1727–1800)* (Paris: Flammarion, 1956), pp. 74–79, and Lacour-Gayet, pp. 58–63, 553–555. According to Villiers, "La stratégie . . .," pp. 215–220 Castries abandoned Sartine's cautious emphasis on the European theater and gave the initiative to bold commanders for distant operations, specifically de Grasse in America and Suffren in India. See also Taillemite, *L'Histoire ignorée*, pp. 188–189.
[13] It should be noted that the victory did not include the capture or destruction of any ships, but merely the denial of Chesapeake Bay to the British fleet. For a classic discussion of the strategic implications of the battle, see Mahan, *Influence of Sea Power upon History*, pp. 387–400. See also Villiers, "La stratégie . . .," pp. 230–231, and Taillemite, *L'Histoire ignorée*, pp. 189–190. Dull, *French Navy and American*

The Indian Ocean was the other theater in which the French navy performed well. The same month that de Grasse sailed for the West Indies, Castries dispatched Pierre-André de Suffren de Saint-Tropez to India in command of a small squadron. His audacity was shown in his attack on a British squadron anchored in the Cape Verdes Islands, and he fought an extensive campaign in the Indian Ocean during 1782–1783 with little support.[14] Suffren's exploits, however, did not include a true victory at sea. In American waters, the French plan to capture Jamaica failed and the British defeated de Grasse at the Battle of the Saints on April 12, 1782.[15] Thus the War of American Independence was hardly an unmitigated triumph, despite its portrayal in French naval histories.[16]

The navy continued to grow after the war. Castries did not believe that the Peace signed in 1783 would last, and his series of ordinances from 1781 to 1786 were intended to improve the fleet for a new confrontation.[17] Moreover, Castries proposed expanding the navy from its traditional strength of sixty ships of the line to a permanent fleet of eighty battleships.[18] This tremendous naval construction effort continued under Castries' successor, César-Henri, comte La Luzerne.[19] According

Independence, pp. 238–249 presents the battle and the surrender of Yorktown as the victory of French diplomacy.

[14] See Taillemite, *L'Histoire ignorée*, pp. 210–233, and Lacour-Gayet, pp. 476–552.

[15] The British fleet under Rodney captured five French ships, including de Grasse's flagship; see Mahan, *Influence of Sea Power upon History*, pp. 487–489, and Lacour-Gayet, pp. 425–434.

[16] This portrayal sometimes involves omission of the defeats. See for example Martray, pp. 21–37, whose chapter on the American War makes no reference to the Battle of the Saints.

[17] Taillemite, *L'Histoire ignorée*, pp. 177–178, 191.

[18] Loire, *La Marine royale en 1789*, p. 1 gives *l'effectif* fixed in 1786, which was not yet attained in 1789: 81 ships of the line; 81 frigates; etc. Dull, *French Navy and American Independence*, pp. 337–338 traces this new level to Castries' proposals of 1781. According to Dull, maintaining a permanent fleet of 60–65 ships of the line was reasonable in terms of available manpower and of what would not be provocative to Britain; a fleet of 80 battleships, however, could not be manned and the necessary growth of the naval budget would lead to a dangerous arms race with the British. Acerra and Meyer, pp. 58–59 suggest that naval rearmament occurred throughout Europe in the 1780s, not only in France.

[19] A lieutenant-general in the army, La Luzerne was governor of Saint-Dominigue when appointed Minister of Marine. Although an intelligent and well-intentioned administrator, he is generally considered a lesser figure than his predecessors; Guérin, V, pp. 190–191; Loir, *La Marine royale en 1789*, pp. 66–67; Taillemite, *L'Histoire ignorée*, p. 196. Castries resigned in 1787 after quarrels with *controleur-général* Calonne, who saw the increase in Marine budgets as a major source of the Royal deficit; Castries, pp. 145–152.

22

to La Luzerne's *mémoire* of December 14, 1788, the fleet's effective strength in 1789 would include sixty-four ships of the line and sixty-four frigates.[20] This made France the world's second greatest naval power in 1789.[21] The quality of French ships, long considered superior to those built on the other side of the Channel,[22] also improved with the standardization and perfection of warship types. The construction of ships of the line, formerly of several rates, was confined to three uniform designs based on the number of guns: 118s, 80s, and 74s.[23] Frigates were also standardized, and British technical innovations were incorporated into French warships: copper-sheathed hulls, which gave increased speed and provided protection from marine parasites; carronades, weapons of short range but devastating effect.[24]

Yet the expansion of the 1780s did not solve serious problems within the structure of the French navy. Shipbuilding consumed huge amounts of material; principally timber, but also hemp for rope-making, linen for sail-cloth, iron and copper.[25] The increased rhythm of construction caused supplies in France to dwindle and exposed the navy's reliance on overseas sources.[26] Arsenals could stockpile reserves, but the difficulties

---

[20] Loire, *La Marine royale en 1789*, p. 2. See also Taillemite, *L'Histoire ignorée*, p. 198 for an estimate of the fleet's total strength at the end of 1789, and pp. 279–280 for a comparison of the *chiffres* for 1788 and 1790 which indicate the fleet's growth during 1789. Acerra and Meyer, p. 56 state that the French navy in 1789 included 73 ships of the line and 63 frigates, but several of these were under construction and far from being outfitted.

[21] Great Britain had the largest navy, followed by those of France, Spain, Russia and Holland respectively. See Acerra and Meyer, p. 60 for tables giving the relative strengths of the European navies in 1790.

[22] Pritchard, p. 126.

[23] Hampson, *La marine de l'an II*, pp. 23–28; Acerra and Meyer, pp. 66–70. For a recent and detailed analysis of the ships of the French navy before the Revolution see Patrick Villiers, *La Marine de Louis XVI; de Choiseul à Sartine* (Grenoble: J. P. Debbane, 1985). This is the first of four volumes, each of which will include a collection of ships' plans and the service histories of these vessels.

[24] Loir, *La Marine royale en 1789*, pp. 204–206, 189–190; Acerra and Meyer, pp. 64–66, 77–79. For a discussion of the standardization of French naval artillery after the American War, see Jean Boudriot, "France 17e–18e Siècles: Artillerie et vaisseaux royaux," in Acerra, Merino, and Meyer (eds.), pp. 99–101.

[25] Jean Boudriot, *The Seventy-Four Gun Ship: A Practical Treatise on the Art of Naval Architecture*, trans. David H. Roberts, 4 vols. (Paris, 1973; repr. Annapolis: Naval Institute Press, 1986), I, pp. 50–61.

[26] Despite the Royal forests reserved for the navy, the Atlantic dockyards depended heavily on Baltic timber while Toulon relied upon timber from Corsica and Italy; Acerra and Meyer, pp. 80–90. For a detailed analysis of the French navy's traditional difficulties in obtaining adequate timber supplies, see Paul Walden Bamford, *Forests*

of the Revolutionary navy, forced by enemy blockade to rely on French resources, showed the continuity of an Old Regime problem. Similarly, the effectiveness of the fleet was limited absolutely by the financial weakness of the French state. As Acerra and Meyer put it, there was a major contradiction between French naval rearmament and the practical impossibility of using the fleet.[27] The monarchy's inability to raise sufficient funds to pay for war, a major cause of the financial collapse which led to the Revolution,[28] would prevent even an expanded French navy from challenging British supremacy without the support of allies.[29]

Even if a fleet of eighty or more capital ships could be built, it could not be manned. The navy's failure to obtain sufficient numbers of sailors did not arise with the expansion of the 1780s, but had been a constant problem throughout the eighteenth century. Colbert established the method of recruitment for the fleet, and it was more or less maintained throughout the eighteenth century.[30] All men in coastal towns and parishes were compelled to register on the *rôle des gens de mer* and were divided into *classes*, each of which was required to serve a year in the navy every three, four or five years depending on the size of the district. The navy maintained seamen not needed to commission warships during their year of service, theoretically, on half-pay; however, they were forbidden to sign on merchant ships. The Crown

and French Sea Power, 1660–1789 (Toronto: University of Toronto Press, 1956), see esp. pp. 206–211.

[27] Acerra and Meyer, p. 92 refer to the example of the Nootka Sound crisis in 1790, when the French government recoiled from the prospect of a maritime war for which Castries and La Luzerne had been preparing: the cost of any major naval operation was insupportable.

[28] Regarding the relationship between the financial crisis and the origins of the Revolution, see Doyle, *Origins*, esp. pp. 43–52. See also Paul Kennedy, *The Rise and Fall of the Great Powers. Economic Change and Military Conflict from 1500 to 2000* (London: Unwin Hyman, 1988), pp. 79–85, and J. F. Bosher, *French Finances 1770–1795, From Business to Bureaucracy* (Cambridge: Cambridge University Press, 1970). For conflicting views of the extent to which expenditures on the American War, and specifically the increases to the Marine budget, were responsible for the Crown's crippling deficit see Robert D. Harris, "French Finances and the American War, 1777–1783," *Journal of Modern History*, 48 (June 1976), 233–258, and Dull, *French Navy and American Independence*, pp. 344–350.

[29] Acerra and Meyer, p. 92. See also Dull, "French Revolutionary Navy," pp. 121–137.

[30] Pritchard, pp. 72–73 argues that the "Tour of Duty" replaced the *classes* as the guiding principle of conscription in the 1720s under Maurepas, and that by 1750 the *classes* existed only as a means of registering seamen.

gave "classed" men various privileges in return for this perpetual commitment: exemption from certain taxes, including the *corvée* and the burden of lodging soldiers; eligibility to receive money from the *Caisse des invalides*, a royal fund for invalid seamen or the families of those lost at sea.[31] The system of classes was intended to place all of the maritime population at the navy's disposal, yet it was constantly unable to supply crews needed for the commissioning of warships.

Contemporaries and historians have suggested various explanations. Pierre-Victor Malouet, the naval Intendant at Toulon before the Revolution, believed that France had neither encouraged nor protected merchant navigation and fishing adequately, and thus failed to assure a thriving population of seamen which was the foundation of naval power.[32] According to T. J. A. Le Goff, the leading authority on this subject, the number of professional French sailors at the end of the Old Regime did not exceed 60,000.[33] The size of France's maritime population was inferior to Britain's, but the real issue was the formation of an adequate reserve of seamen for the fleet. Acerra and Meyer suggest several factors which undermined this reserve throughout the eighteenth century:[34] recruitment by privateers took sailors away from the navy; the capture of ships during wartime constituted a significant drain on manpower;[35] the mortality of seamen was high on all long voyages. The manning problem was not, however, simply one of numbers. Figures from the navy's central *Bureau des classes* show great numbers of sailors on the rolls during periods when the fleet was desperate for men.[36]

---

[31] Acerra and Meyer, pp. 30–32; Loir, *La Marine royale en 1789*, pp. 28–32.
[32] Pierre-Victor Malouet, *Mémoires de Malouet*, 2 vols. (Paris: Didier, 1868), I, p. 198.
[33] T. J. A. Le Goff, "Les origines sociales des gens de mer français au XVIIIe siècle," *La France d'Ancien Régime: Etudes réunies en l'honneur de Pierre Goubert* (1985), p. 368. According to Le Goff, the size of the seafaring population was relatively stable, but the demand for seamen rose during the eighteenth century due to the expansion of French commerce and the growth of naval forces. Technical developments such as the simplification of rigging allowed ships to sail with smaller crews, but increasing numbers of novices were recruited; see T. J. A. Le Goff, "Offre et productivité de la main d'oeuvre dans les armements français aux XVIIIe siècle," *Histoire, economie et société*, 2 (1983), 457–473, and "Naval Recruitment and Labour Supply in the French War Effort, 1755–59," *Naval History Symposium* (Annapolis, 1981).
[34] Acerra and Meyer, pp. 32–36.
[35] See T. J. A. Le Goff, "L'impact des prises effectuées par les Anglais sur la capacité en hommes de la marine française au XVIIIe Siècle," in Acerra, Merino, and Meyer (eds.), pp. 103–122. This loss of seamen was often permanent because of the high mortality in English prisons.
[36] Pritchard, pp. 73–76.

25

James Pritchard, in his study of Louis XV's navy, suggests that it was less a matter of poor administration than of uncertain finances: the French navy was constantly unable to pay its crews and, consequently, seamen did all they could to resist conscription or to desert.[37] The system of classes was certainly resented in the maritime provinces.[38] Naval service, more than commerce or the fisheries, meant economic deprivation for a sailor's family. As the demand for seamen rose during the eighteenth century, peasants were just as reluctant to serve in the fleet as men with seafaring backgrounds.[39] This resistance was based also on the harsh conditions and high mortality experienced in the fleet. Sailors were not issued with a uniform and often went to sea without proper clothing. Crews had an inadequate diet which made them more susceptible to the disease-ridden environment in which they found themselves.[40] Appalling hygiene, poor ventilation below decks, the conservation of drinking water in wooden casks prone to spoilage, and inadequate medical care made warships prime breeding grounds for epidemics of scurvy, typhoid, and typhus.[41]

[37] Ibid., pp. 71, 77–80.
[38] For a study of the problem at the beginning of the eighteenth century, see Eugene L. Asher, *The Resistance to the Maritime Classes: The Survival of Feudalism in the France of Colbert* (Berkeley and Los Angeles: University of California Press, 1960). Alain Cabantous, *La Vergue et les fers: Mutins et déserteurs dans la marine de l'ancienne France (XVIIe–XVIIIe Siècles)* (Paris: Tallandier, 1984), pp. 84–90, stresses that the resistance to the *classes* was rarely expressed collectively beyond the support of communities for those who fled or evaded the system; the prevalent resistance was individual desertion. See also T. J. A. Le Goff, "Les gens de mer devant la système des classes (1755–1763): résistance ou passivité?" in A. Lottin, J. Hocquet, and S. Lebecq (eds.), "Les hommes et la mer dans l'Europe du Nord–Ouest de l'Antiquité à nos jours," *Revue du Nord* (extra number) 1986. However as the Revolutionary and Napoleonic Wars dragged on, registration in the *classes* became a refuge for young men seeking to avoid military conscription; Alan Forrest, *Conscripts and Deserters: The Army and French Society during the Revolution and Empire* (Oxford and New York: Oxford University Press, 1989), pp. 56–57.
[39] Le Goff, "Origines sociales," pp. 370–372. Le Goff suggests that about 50 percent of the navy's sailors at the end of the Old Regime, based on his analysis of "la revue général de 1785-6" and other sources, were first generation seamen; their fathers had non-maritime vocations. A relatively low proportion of these outsiders, however, came from the peasantry; ibid., pp. 367–379.
[40] Cabantous, *La Vergue et les fers*, pp. 47–49 suggests that the well-known lack of vitamin C, which made scurvy the scourge of the maritime world, was only one of the deficiencies in the sailor's diet which also lacked adequate vitamin B.
[41] Pritchard, pp. 83–84 documents the appalling typhus epidemic of 1757–1758 which ravaged Dubois de la Motte's squadron and went on to devastate Brittany. Regarding the impact of scurvy, and efforts by the British and French navies to deal with the

It should be noted that the living conditions in the navy were not enormously different from those prevailing elsewhere in the maritime world. Sailors in the fleet, however, were subjected to a regime of severe discipline. Naval officers, whose authority was backed by garrisons of marine troops, had recourse to a number of brutal punishments to maintain this discipline. A captain could order a stoppage of wine or a short imprisonment in the hold for minor offenses, but he could also condemn the transgressor to be put in irons on a diet of bread and water. Sailors were lashed and, for serious crimes, forced to run a gauntlet of petty officers armed with ropes' ends. The most infamous punishment was the "cale," often misinterpreted as keel-hauling, which involved hauling the bound prisoner up to a yard and then dropping him repeatedly into the water on the end of a line.[42]

Given its chronic shortage of seamen, the navy was particularly concerned with discouraging desertion. Deserters could be condemned to life in the galleys, "the living death," or be sentenced to summary execution. Yet the application of punishment was far from systematic. The practice of simply withholding deserters' pay and prize money was common enough that the *Fonds des déserteurs* was an established source of aid for maritime families.[43] Many officers and administrators felt that the full weight of punishment could hardly be imposed on seamen who did not receive regular pay.[44] More fundamentally, the indulgence often shown to deserters reflected the ambiguous position of the navy towards its crews: a system of repression was maintained to uphold royal authority, but this authority was the traditional defender of sailors who were not easily replaced.[45] This same ambiguity existed in regard to the crime of mutiny, ranging from simple disobedience

disease during Pacific exploration, see O. H. K. Spate, *Paradise Found and Lost. The Pacific since Magellan, Volume III* (Minneapolis: University of Minnesota Press, 1988), pp. 191–196. There were French efforts during the eighteenth century to improve naval hygiene and medicine. See Taillemite, *L'Histoire ignorée*, pp. 268–269, and P. Pluchon (ed.), *Histoire des médecins et pharmaciens de marine et des colonies* (Toulouse, 1985).
[42] Cabantous, *La Vergue et les fers*, pp. 114–115.
[43] Ibid., p. 119.
[44] Pritchard, p. 87. In 1783 Malouet was so moved by the fate of unpaid sailors demobilized at Toulon, six of whom were driven to highway-robbery and executed at Aix, that he borrowed funds in Marseilles on his own authority to pay off crews. See Malouet, *Mémoires*, I, p. 216, and Vincent-Félix Brun, *Guerres maritimes de la France: Port de Toulon. Ses armements, son administration, depuis son origine jusqu'à nos jours*, 2 vols. (Paris: Henri Plon, 1861), II, p. 69.
[45] Cabantous, *La Vergue et les fers*, pp. 124, 130–132.

to general uprisings. In theory the king's wrath against mutineers would be terrible, but in practice the navy tended to limit its reaction to making examples of ring-leaders in serious affairs. Small numbers of those convicted for mutiny were sent to the galleys, but most were pardoned to a life of service in the fleet.[46]

Mutiny became almost constant in the French navy with the coming of the Revolution. Revolutionary mutinies, which will be discussed in subsequent chapters, had a strong political or ideological character, and were thus quite different from the traditional pattern of maritime disobedience. A recent study by Alain Cabantous linked mutiny and desertion as the collective and individual manifestations of rebellion by seamen against the "hierarchical structure of maritime society," and the contestation of the order, authority and technical knowledge implicit in that hierarchy.[47] Cabantous suggests that mutiny was rare in the French navy before the Revolution not only because of the force of authority, but also because desertion offered an important safety valve.[48] An eighteenth-century ship was an "accentuated reflection of traditional social hierarchy,"[49] but mutiny should not be seen as an expression of class conflict. The causes of revolt were often related to the dangers of navigation, but mutiny was less a reaction against poor conditions than an attempt to restore the accepted margin of safety.[50] According to Cabantous, mutinies were directed against the captain as the defender of sailors' interests, rather than against officers in general. The captain represented technical competence and therefore merited obedience and respect. If incorrect orders, personal failings, or bad conduct destroyed this image, seamen felt that rebellion was justified.[51]

This discussion of mutiny illustrates the relationship between men and authority in the navy before the Revolution. French society tended to view its navy as a floating prison, a perception made worse by "enlightened" attempts to embark undesirables,[52] but sailors were

---

[46] Ibid., pp. 120–122.
[47] Ibid., p. 10. Cabantous' study deals with the entire range of French maritime activity during the eighteenth century, and not the navy exclusively.
[48] "Elle [desertion] offrait alors aux individus insatisfais une sortie sans risque et donnait aux officiers la possibilité de se séparer au meilleur compte de marins qui auraient pu cristalliser autour d'eux une contestation plus violente;" ibid., p. 11.
[49] Ibid., p. 138.
[50] Ibid., pp. 57–58.
[51] Ibid., pp. 141–143.
[52] In September 1790 the Mayor of Paris proposed embarking the city's vagabonds on naval ships; Marine BB 2/1, f. 273. Michael L. Kennedy, *The Jacobin Clubs in the*

neither criminals nor perpetual rebels.[53] Ships of war could not be run as floating concentration camps. As N. A. M. Rodger argued in his study of the eighteenth-century British navy, officers needed the willing cooperation of their crew and sailors knew they were a precious commodity.[54] A community of interests existed between officers and men in the French navy despite the social gulf between them.[55] This broke down after 1789 under the impact of Revolutionary politics, not simply because of resentment against the traditional rigours of naval service.

The operation of ships at sea was only a small component of naval organization. The Ministry of Marine was a major branch of royal government and was responsible for all French maritime and overseas activity. The central administration of the Ministry at Versailles was divided between various *bureaux*: Ports and Arsenals; Colonies; Classes; Finances.[56] The Minister, with the assistance of his staff, exercised central control over the navy, but the fleet was administered directly from the naval ports. The three major naval bases were Brest, Toulon, and Rochefort, with the first two being the largest and most important. These ports were the sites of the arsenals or naval dockyards for the construction and maintenance of warships, and squadrons were assembled in their roadsteads. The navy also maintained limited facilities in at least six other French ports: Lorient, Dunkirk, Le Havre, Bordeaux, Bayonne, and Marseilles. Of these only Lorient, transferred to the Crown from the *Compagnie des Indes* in 1770, possessed an arsenal and it was used to build frigates and ships of the line during the Revolution.[57] The navy lacked a major port on the English Channel

French Revolution: The First Years (Princeton: Princeton University Press, 1982), p. 203 cites a Nantes merchant who defended the slave trade in 1790 by suggesting that slaves were treated no worse than sailors aboard frigates.

[53] Cabantous, *La Vergue et les fers*, pp. 145–154.

[54] N. A. M. Rodger, *The Wooden World: An Anatomy of the Georgian Navy* (London: Collins, 1986; repr. Fontana, 1988), esp. pp. 344–346.

[55] Acerra and Meyer, pp. 53–54 suggest that this was often based on regional solidarity.

[56] See Loir, *La Marine royale en 1789*, pp. 67–68 and H. Fontaine de Resbecq, "L'Administration Centrale de la marine avant 1793," *Revue maritime et coloniale*, 61 (1879), 148–154. In 1789 Charles-Pierre Claret, comte de Fleurieu, who would become Minister of Marine in 1790, was the *premier commis* in charge of Ports and Arsenals. For a detailed discussion of the limitations on the efficiency of the navy's central *bureaux*, see Pritchard, pp. 19–36.

[57] Loir, *La Marine royale en 1789*, pp. 159–160. Regarding the emergence of Lorient as a naval port, see Jakez Cornou and Bruno Jonin, *L'Odyssée du Vaisseau "Droits de l'homme" et l'expédition d'Irlande de 1796* (Quimper: Editions DUFA, 1988), pp. 19–20.

and began construction on an artificial harbour at Cherbourg in 1783; the project was abandoned in 1789 due to lack of funds.[58] The administration of naval ports was complex. Colbert had vested supreme authority in each port in the naval Intendant, but after 1776 it was embodied in the *Commandant de la marine*, a senior naval officer who had served in the fleet.[59] Two separate organizational structures lay under the Commandant's control: one was responsible for work in the dockyards and reported directly to the Commandant; the other was responsible for accounting and general administration, and reported indirectly through the Intendant. Sea-going naval officers, the "officers of the sword," supervised arsenal work in three departments: shipbuilding, port, and ordnance. A corps of commissioners and clerks, the "officers of the pen," carried out administration in five offices: central stores; shipyards and workshops; pay and establishment; ship's stores and victualling; hospitals and forced labour.[60] A naval council, presided over by the Commandant, met once every two weeks to coordinate the port's diverse activities.[61]

The traditional hostility between the sword and the pen was a major obstacle to such coordination.[62] This rivalry should not be seen as one

---

[58] See Loir, *La Marine royale en 1789*, p. 161 and Castries, pp. 125–127. For a description of Louis XVI's visit to Cherbourg in June 1786 to view the new harbour, see Simon Schama, *Citizens. A Chronicle of the French Revolution* (Toronto: Random House, 1989), pp. 56–60.

[59] Loir, *La Marine royale en 1789*, pp. 162–166, and Pritchard, pp. 37–38.

[60] Each Department was headed by a Director, usually a *capitaine de vaisseau*, and all were under the supervision of the Director General. There was a Commissioner in charge of each *bureau* and they worked under the Commissioner General. An independent Comptroller supervised all accounting. See Boudriot, *Seventy-Four Gun Ship*, I, pp. 10–11. On the division of duties between the Intendant and the Commandant, see Loir, *La Marine royale en 1789*, pp. 165–168.

[61] Sartine established the *Conseil de marine* which was composed of: the Intendant; the Director General; the Commissioner General; the *Major de la marine*, who was the Commandant's aide responsible for his secretariat; the Comptroller, who functioned as secretary to the Council. For a table of the Naval Council listing all officers of each Department and Bureau, and their responsibilities, see Boudriot, *Seventy-Four Gun Ship*, I, pp. 14–15. See also Loir, *La Marine royale en 1789*, pp. 170–171. Brun, II, p. 42 states that Castries reemphasized the importance of the Council as a coordinating body, and introduced the practice of sending common correspondence to the Commandant and Intendant, expecting joint replies. In 1788 La Luzerne established a national *Conseil de marine*, presided over by the Minister, on which sat naval officers, engineers, and administrators; Lacour-Gayet, pp. 581–583.

[62] For a discussion of this rivalry at mid-century, see Pritchard, pp. 49–53. See also Loir, *La Marine royale en 1789*, pp. 163–167. François Bluche, *La vie Quotidienne de la Noblesse Française au XVIIIe siècle* (Paris: Hachette Littérature, 1973), p. 164

between administrators and sailors, or between civilians and the military. The pen was a corps, with a uniform and sense of group identity, and was an arm of royal government like the Intendant.[63] The pen saw the sea-officers as incompetent, and the sword viewed the clerks as social inferiors.[64] Sartine's regulations of 1776, which assured the domination of the sword, defined the limits of responsibilities in order to end the rivalry. The example of Intendant Malouet's quarrels with Commandant de Fabry in Toulon suggests that the conflict was not resolved so easily.[65] Malouet, however, had an excellent relationship with de Fabry's successor, the comte d'Albert de Rioms, and it seems that a sense of devotion to naval service beyond group interests was emerging on the eve of the Revolution.

The focus of port administration was the dockyards. Naval arsenals were huge establishments and their concentration of labour and capital was rare for the eighteenth century.[66] Along with the actual yards where warship hulls were assembled, arsenals included numerous workshops, storage magazines, and specialized facilities including dry-docks, mast wells, ropeyards, sail lofts, and smitheries. The navy developed sophisticated equipment for warship construction such as the "masting machine" which enabled workers to fit masts into floating hulls.[67] Despite the obvious complexity and scale of these operations, eighteenth-century

documents various scuffles between *gardes de la marine* and officers of the pen at Brest.

[63] Pritchard, pp. 37–40.

[64] Loir, *La Marine royale en 1789*, p. 220 refers to the rivalry as "une lutte de caste."

[65] The chevalier de Fabry attempted to block Malouet's efforts to establish a needed hospital for the navy in Toulon's *Maison de Jésuits*, suggesting that the Intendant's own country house would be more suitable. After Castries supported Malouet's proposal in 1785, de Fabry tried unsuccessfully to poison the relations between the Intendant and all the port's naval officers; Malouet, *Mémoires*, I, pp. 214–217. See also John Charles While, *Pierre Victor Malouet: Administrator and Legislator (1740–1792)* (Ph.D. Thesis, Duke University, 1964), pp. 80–91.

[66] Armel de Wismes, *La vie quotidienne dans les Ports Bretons aux XVIIe et XVIIIe siècles (Nantes, Brest, Saint-Malo, Lorient)* (Paris: Hachette, 1973), p. 76. See also Malcolm Crook, *Toulon in war and revolution: From the ancien régime to the Restoration, 1750–1820* (Manchester and New York: Manchester University Press, 1991), pp. 13–14, and Acerra and Meyer, pp. 87–88.

[67] For a brief description of the launching, mast fitting, and general outfitting of *Le Droits de l'homme* (74), completed in May 1794 at Lorient, see Cornou and Jonin, pp. 25–31. For a detailed discussion of the construction of a French ship of the line, see Boudriot, *Seventy-Four Gun Ship*, I for various chapters on the assembly of the hull; II for chapters on hull-fittings, internal arrangements, ballast, and stowage, and the equipment carried aboard ship.

31

Map 1. The naval ports of France, c. 1789. *After* "Ancien-Régime France" in Simon Schama, *Citizens* (Toronto: Vintage Books, 1989), p. xii and "Pre-revolutionary France" in William Doyle, *Oxford History of the French Revolution* (Oxford: Clarendon Press, 1989), p. 3.

arsenals belonged to a pre-industrial world. Each was a self-sufficient unit by geographic necessity. Production was not organized rationally in a factory system, but carried out by traditional craftsmen.[68] The workers were divided among the various skills required: carpenters, caulkers, drillers, sawyers, and sailmakers; but their handicraft labour limited the number of men who could be employed effectively on any one task, or hull, thus limiting the overall speed of production.[69]

The nature of the dockyards' labour force was even less modern. Little is known of the lives of arsenal workers or of the nature of their vocation, but a petition from the drillers of Brest in September 1793 indicates the harsh physical demands and potential danger of the work.[70] Maritime workers were a self-recruiting group and it was customary for the sons of workers to be put on arsenal payrolls in order to perpetuate a skilled workforce.[71] Workers held a number of traditional privileges, such as the right to collect wood chips from the dockyards for fuel, and valued these as much as their formal wages which were regularly in arrears.[72] The navy of the Old Regime recognized these traditions and even the Revolutionaries seemed reluctant, even powerless, to alter them.[73] Only the permanent high-skilled workers, the *entretenus*, enjoyed these privileges. Classed workers, conscripted during wartime, were also paid less and lacked any security of employment.[74] The final element in the arsenal's labour force was the chain-gang of

---

[68] Pritchard, p. 89. Wismes, p. 76 also remarks on the juxtaposition of industrial and premodern features in the eighteenth-century naval arsenal.

[69] Pritchard, pp. 115–116.

[70] Marine BB 3/38, ff. 353–355. The *perceurs*, or drillers, called their jobs "les plus rudes, les plus pénibles, et les plus dangereux." These workers also complained that their wages did not compensate for the great expense of providing their own tools, which was probably not unique to this trade.

[71] Brun, II, p. 103. See also Wismes, p. 76.

[72] Pritchard, p. 118 suggests that the failure to pay workers, due mostly to the lack of funds in naval treasuries, was also related to discipline: port authorities believed that delays in payment would keep workers in the arsenal. Regarding the workers' privileges, see Norman Hampson, "Les Ouvriers des arsenaux de la marine au cours de la Révolution française (1789–1794)," *Revue d'histoire économique et sociale*, 39 (1961), 292–293. See also Crook, *Toulon*, pp. 45–46.

[73] Despite the abuse of the workers' privilege of chip removal at Brest, Jeanbon Saint-André attempted only to control rather than abolish the practice in 1794: "Arrêté le 13 Nivôse an II," and "Arrêté le 6 Floréal an II;" Brest "Fonds Levot" 1965. Jeanbon's *arrêtés* demonstrate that formal discipline in the arsenal was not accomplished easily: incentives appeared more effective than threats of punishment.

[74] Hampson, "Ouvriers," pp. 288–293 suggests that the conscription infused the arsenals with a mass of discontented and geographically heterogeneous workers.

"galley-slaves," the convicts used as port workers after the suppression of the Galley Corps in 1748.[75]

Arsenals operated under a regime of strict discipline, but the control of workers was no more absolute than that of sailors aboard warships. In both cases, the navy relied as much upon social deference and personal appeal as upon effective coercion. Naval authority, however, extended beyond the arsenals and roadsteads. Naval bases were outposts of royal authority in the maritime provinces. Eighteenth-century France was not a modern centralized state and naval Intendants, like other servants of the Crown, were not simply administrators. They possessed judicial and political authority within their jurisdictions[76] which often clashed with the power of local corporate bodies. Malouet collided with the Parlement of Aix, the *Chambre des comptes*, and the *Etats-de-Provence* in 1783 over Toulon's bread toll: when his demands were ignored for the repeal of the tax, which encouraged bakers to use substandard flour in the bread for three thousand arsenal workers, the Intendant opened the royal magazines to feed the arsenal with supplies exempt from taxation. The local sovereign courts were enraged at this cancellation of municipal prerogative, but Malouet was prepared to use armed force to repel local troops if necessary.[77] The Intendant's action is an example of the navy's paternalistic efforts to protect its labour force.[78] More

[75] Paul W. Bamford, *Fighting Ships and Prisons: The Mediterranean Galleys of France in the Age of Louis XIV* (Minneapolis: University of Minneapolis Press, 1973), pp. 281–297. See also: Pritchard, pp. 108–109; Wismes, p. 208; Malouet, *Mémoires*, I, pp. 236–242. For a recent analysis of the social origins of prisoners condemned to the galleys in 1748, see André Zysberg, "Galley Rowers in the Mid-Eighteenth Century," in Orest Ranum and Robert Forster (eds.), *Deviants and the Abandoned in French Society: Selections from the Annales ESC* (Baltimore: Johns Hopkins University Press, 1978), pp. 83–110. The use of convicts in the arsenals expanded after the American War. Malouet objected to this in 1785 on both pragmatic and humanitarian grounds. The cost of supervising convicts was high, they posed a security risk in the arsenal, and funds would be better spent giving employment to indigent day labourers: Brun, II, pp. 117–118.
[76] Pritchard, pp. 38–39, 42–44.
[77] Malouet, *Mémoires*, I, pp. 208–212. See also White, *Malouet*, pp. 75–77, and Crook, *Toulon*, pp. 58–60.
[78] The navy's lack of funds had become so extreme by 1790 that La Luzerne urged his Commandants and Intendants to employ a minimum of workers in the arsenals. However Commandant Hector and Intendant Redon de Beaupréau at Brest admitted more workers within the arsenal to save them from starvation, and the Intendant defended their actions stating, "motives of humanity, more than the advantages of the service, were often the basis of our conduct;" Marine BB 3/2, f. 71. See also Marine BB 2/1, f. 71; BB 3/2, ff. 39–40. Lorient experienced a similar social crisis in 1790

importantly, the incident illustrates why naval authority was often resented in the port cities as the local manifestation of executive power. The political context changed during the Revolution, but the navy continued to represent a distant and distrusted central government.

Naval authority and aristocratic privilege were embodied in the fleet's professional sea-officers, known collectively as the *Grand Corps*. Historians have not defined this eighteenth-century term uniformly. Michel Vergé-Franceschi, in his master's thesis, stated that the *Grand Corps* comprised all military officers paid by the Crown who sailed on king's ships; it did not include merchant officers, those of the *Compagnie des Indes*, or officers of the Galley Corps.[79] Maurice Loir defined the *Grand Corps* more exclusively, however, to include only general-grade officers (*vice-amiral, lieutenant-général, chef d'escadre*), and the ranks of *capitaine de vaisseau, lieutenant de vaisseau* and *enseigne de vaisseau*. This excludes the intermediate grades of *capitaine de frégate, capitaine de brûlot, lieutenant de frégate* and *capitaine de flûte* which formed the navy's *Petit Corps*.[80] The distinction between the corps was based upon different recruitment, and thus to a large degree on social origin. Entry to the *Grand Corps* was through the companies of *gardes de la marine* and *gardes du pavillon*, and the *gardes* were exclusively of noble birth.[81] More was required than aristocratic pedigree, however. The potential *garde* needed a letter of appointment and this favoured the sons of naval families who could solicit the assistance of Intendants and Commandants.[82] The parents also had to provide the new *garde* with a hefty allowance, and

and Intendant Poulletier believed it was his responsibility to secure bread for his workers; Marine BB 3/2, ff. 200–202.

[79] Michel Vergé-Franceschi, *Les officiers de Marine d'origine Provençale à Toulon au XVIIIème siècle* (Mémoire de la maîtrise, Nice, 1973), p. 16. Vergé-Franceschi does not include in his definition the *grades intermédiaires*, but neither does he explain the differences which set them outside the *Grand Corps*. This lack of clarity, common to most discussions of the subject, is emphasized by the title which appears on the outside cover of his thesis, "Les officiers du Grand-Corps à Toulon au XVIIIe siècle," implying that *Grand Corps* and *officiers de marine* are synonomous expressions.

[80] Loir, *La Marine royale en 1789*, p. 24. Officers of these ranks, as the titles imply, commanded auxiliary vessels. They could stand watch aboard, but never command, a large warship.

[81] Vergé-Franceschi, *Les officiers . . . Provençale*, pp. 31–32, 35, 55. The *gardes de la marine* at Brest, Rochefort, and Toulon were established under Colbert, while the *gardes du pavillon amiral*, only at Toulon and Brest, were formed in 1716 to serve as honorary aides to the Admiral of France. Although there may have been social distinction attached to the latter group, there was no difference in rank.

[82] Ibid., pp. 61–63. Pritchard, p. 63 suggests local nobility were at an advantage because a *garde*'s seniority dated from the registry of the *certificat* in the port.

this often prevented more than one son of poor noble families from pursuing naval careers.[83]

The education and character of the *gardes* represented the formation of France's naval officers. The curriculum followed in the ports stressed mathematics, but the *gardes* also studied hydrography, naval architecture, English, and Spanish: no history, naval or otherwise, was taught. Time was alloted daily for dancing and fencing. Although these officer candidates advanced eventually to the study of navigation and seamanship aboard ship,[84] the emphasis on theoretical education over practical training was in sharp contrast to the formation of midshipmen in the British navy.[85] Furthermore, the *gardes* had a reputation for insubordination, rowdiness, and violence. Imbued with a sense of social superiority, these young noblemen were difficult for their commanders to control and quarreled frequently with officers of the pen and with civilians.[86] In 1774 a senior naval administrator summed up the increasing dissatisfaction with the *gardes* as the foundation of the officer corps:

The spirit of independence, of contrariness, of egotism which has long distinguished the different classes of naval officers, which is so opposed to the good of the King's service, certainly is born in the companies of the *gardes de la marine* and *du pavillon*; they perpetuate it in carrying it with them to all ranks. Daily experience and the public voice announce as clearly that this disorder will be replaced only when one will have the courage to attack it at its known source and tear it out forever.[87]

[83] Jacques Aman, *Les Officiers Bleus dans la marine française au XVIIIe siècle* (Geneva: Librairie Droz, 1976), p. 47. See also Vergé-Franceschi, *Les officiers . . . Provençale*, pp. 55–56, and Loir, *La Marine royale en 1789*, p. 17. This may have explained the myth that only the younger sons of the aristocracy entered the navy.
[84] See César-Auguste de Lannoy, "Mémorial de M. de Lannoy (1763–1793): Notes de voyage d'un officier de marine de l'ancien régime," *Carnet de la Sabretache: Revue militaire retrospective*, Whole series, vol. 13, 2nd series, 3 (1904), pp. 682–683. See also Bluche, pp. 161–163, and Vergé-Franceschi, *Les officiers . . . Provençale*, pp. 66–78.
[85] Rodger, pp. 259–260 states, "The quality which above all determined an officer's fortunes in the [British] Navy, and marked it out from other professions, was his practical ability as a seaman. The capacity, not merely to command and to navigate, but to hand, reef and steer, was the basic requirement for an officer." This contrast between the scientific education of French officers and the superior seamanship of their British counterparts is referred to by Acerra and Meyer, p. 50.
[86] Vergé-Franceschi, *Les officiers . . . Provençale*, pp. 79–84. Pritchard, p. 66 suggests that "all efforts were directed to turn gentlemen into sailors and no attempt was made in the opposite direction."
[87] "Mémoire du 27 septembre 1774," attributed to Truguet, *premier commis de la marine*; cited in Loir, *La Marine royale en 1789*, p. 12.

It should be noted, however, that a large number of non-nobles did serve as naval officers throughout the eighteenth century.[88] This was particularly true during the War of American Independence when the naval establishment was unable to provide sufficient officers for the expansion of France's maritime war effort. The fleet had to use a great number of auxiliary officers, most of whom came from the merchant service and held temporary appointments as naval officers of intermediate grade.[89] Many of these men distinguished themselves during the American War and a significant number became Revolutionary naval commanders.

The auxiliary officers, along with the entire *Petit Corps* of intermediate grades, are often considered to be equivalent to the eighteenth-century term *officiers bleus*, implying simply non-noble officers serving in the fleet.[90] The situation was far more complex. Jacques Aman suggested that the *bleus* served voluntarily and in a temporary capacity, unlike career officers of intermediate grade, while the auxiliaries of 1778–1783 received a level of pay closer to permanent officers.[91] While most of the *bleus* were recruited from the merchant service or from among the navy's petty officers,[92] Aman found that a significant twentieth of them were noble.[93] Thus the hostility of members of the *Grand Corps*, the

[88] It was not uncommon for merchant officers and the commanders of privateers to serve in Louis XIV's navy as volunteers. This became rare after 1715, but Choiseul revived the concept as an alternative to the *gardes*. His ordinance of 1764 allowed "young men of good family" (i.e. non-noble), as well as aristocrats not among the fixed number of *gardes*, to be admitted as volunteer officers. Most would be promoted to intermediate grades, but the possibility of attaining rank in the *Grand Corps* was not excluded. See: Aman, pp. 41–43, 153–156; Loir, *La Marine royale en 1789*, pp. 22–23; Vergé-Franceschi, *Les officiers . . . Provençale*, pp. 31–34.

[89] Aman, pp. 135–136, 143–144.

[90] According to such a definition, the *bleus'* plebeian origins were the root of the disdain and hostility shown them by the aristocratic *Grand Corps*, the so-called *rouges*. See Loir, *La Marine royale en 1789*, pp. 23, 24, 117–118, and Marcel Guyon, "Les Officiers de la marine royale et la Révolution," *Revue maritime* (Octobre 1922), 446, 448. See also Aman, pp. 1–4 for an overview of the confusion in historical definitions of *officiers bleus*. Aman, pp. 5–7, 96–100 dispenses with the myth that the term *bleus* originated in an all-blue uniform required of commoners to set them apart from *garde*-officers. Such an origin or explanation is also dismissed by Armand Hayet, "Officiers Rouges, Officiers Bleus," *Revue maritime* (Avril 1960), 453–454.

[91] Aman, pp. 16–17, 77–87, 135–145. Despite their temporary appointments, it was not unknown for *bleus* to be promoted into the *Grand Corps* during the Old Regime; pp. 4–5.

[92] Ibid., pp. 31–41. Some naval service was a requirement for candidates seeking merchant commands.

[93] Ibid., pp. 41–55. It is interesting to note that Aman states that nobles sometimes sought appointment as *bleus* as a path to merchant commands, an involvement in the world of commerce for which they would not suffer derogation. On this point see

officiers rouges, towards the *bleus* was not based wholly on social prejudice.[94] The hostility also arose from the discontent of professionals who
feared an amateur reserve depriving them of their exclusive privilege
to command the king's ships.[95]

The *Grand Corps'* arrogance towards non-*gardes*, however, was infamous.[96] The treatment of the *bleus* was only part of sea-officers' general
hostility towards all outsiders. The *Grand Corps* has been described as
a naval caste, both in terms of its self-recruitment and its jealous
oppositon to any penetration or imposition on the group's prerogatives.
The rivalry with officers of the pen supports this description. The
Grand Corps showed similar antipathy for officers who entered the fleet
after serving in the army: such men were referred to pejoratively as
intrus and the fact that many were from the high nobility was irrelevant.[97]
In 1771 officers of the then-defunct *Compagnie des Indes* expressed the
extent of the feeling against outsiders:

an excellent subject, gentleman or bourgeois, who has not come from the grade
of *garde de la marine* will indubitably become the victim of what happens so
often. Monsieur le comte d'Estaing, known by all of France for his birth, his
titles, his rank, his capacity and the reputation which he acquired by his actions
on land and sea, is not safe from this dangerous prejudice. How would simple
gentlemen and others of known and well-connected families, who have only
virtues and estimable talents to speak for them, protect themselves from this?[98]

Jean Meyer, *La Noblesse Bretonne au XVIIIe siècle* (Paris: S.E.V.P.E.N., 1966), I, pp.
151–153.
[94] Aman, p. 20 calls this conclusion, "a simplistic generalization." See also Acerra and
Meyer, pp. 46–47.
[95] Aman, pp. 28, 30. Hayet, p. 455 argues that the true division among naval officers
was not between nobles and commoners, or between the *Grand Corps* and the
intermediate grades, but between permanent officers and temporary reserves. The
gardes could not supply sufficient officers for the navy's wartime needs, and
traditionally the gap was filled by *bleus*. Both Choiseul and Sartine, however, hoped to
create an expanded and permanent reserve corps; Aman, pp. 26–28, 154–160.
[96] Loir, *La Marine royale en 1789*, pp. 89–95, 114–119. Loir suggests that this
arrogance continued towards the *sous-lieutenants* created by Castries in 1786, "L'esprit
de caste aveuglait donc le grand corps, quand il affectait une si dédaigneuse
indifférence vis-à-vis de ceux qui ne provenaient pas de la pepinière aristocratique des
gardes ou des élèves;" p. 117.
[97] Loir, *La Marine royale en 1789*, p. 21 suggests that officers from the *Compagnie des
Indes* were also classified as *intrus*, as does Aman, pp. 24–25. See also Vergé-
Franceschi, *Les officiers . . . Provençale*, pp. 250–252.
[98] *Mémoire* of 16 June 1771 to Minister of Marine de Boynes, AN Colonies C 2/271;
cited in Aman, p. 26. The disasters of the Seven Years' War were often blamed on
the inadequacies of the *gardes*. Choiseul seems to have contemplated abolishing the

This caste spirit seems to have developed since the Regency (1715–1723). In his doctoral thesis on the navy's general-grade officers from 1715 to 1774, Vergé-Franceschi stressed the importance of family networks, what he called family clans, in shaping the nature and advancement of naval officers.[99] This family tradition did not exist in Louis XIV's navy. Colbert promoted officers to flag-rank for their loyalty and influence, and he chose them from all regions of France and from a wide social spectrum which included Court aristocracy as well as non-nobles of proven competence.[100] This heterogenous richness was lost, and later in the eighteenth century senior officers were recruited almost exclusively from naval families in the maritime provinces of Provence or Brittany.[101] According to Vergé-Franceschi, this self-recruitment marginalized the navy under Louis XV and isolated the officer corps from Paris and the Court.[102] The development of an introverted naval caste, however, did not prevent antagonisms within its own ranks. The divisions were often geographic: Breton officers felt little in common with their peers from Provence, who in turn preferred to serve in squadrons based at Toulon.[103] Another cause of friction was the relative poverty of many officers in the *Grand Corps*. Bitter conflicts for favour, and therefore

companies, and de Boynes tried, unsuccessfully, to suppress the *gardes* in 1772; Aman, pp. 154–158. See also Pritchard, pp. 55, 69, and Loir, *La Marine royale en 1789*, p. 12.

[99] Michel Vergé-Franceschi, *Les Officiers généraux de la marine royale (1715–1774). Origines – condition – services* (Thèse en vue de l'obtention du Doctorat d'Etat Paris, 1987), see esp. Introduction, pp. 8–18.

[100] Ibid., pp. 2417–2446.

[101] This conclusion seems in direct contradiction to the results of Vergé-Franceschi's research on officers from Provence, *Les officiers . . . Provençale*, pp. 37–46, which contended that most of these men were not *"enfants du corps."* Naval officers were more likely, according to the earlier work, to be children of robe or other provincial noble families than the sons of naval officers. Perhaps the pattern for general-grade officers was vastly different, but this contradiction is confusing.

[102] Vergé-Franceschi, *Les Officiers généraux*, pp. 2579–2580.

[103] Vergé-Franceschi, *Les officiers . . . Provençale*, pp. 246–248 argues that hostility existed between officers from the three major ports, but adds that conflicts remained between those of Toulon. On the antagonism between Bretons and Provençaux, see also Acerra and Meyer, p. 53. The nobility of Provence and Languedoc had provided most of the officers for the Galley Corps, while Brittany supplied the lion's share of those for the sailing navy; see Meyer, *Noblesse Bretonne*, II, pp. 1124–25, 1128; esp. p. 1134, Table: "Récrutement des officiers de la marine militaire royale par province." The naval officer corps was unified after the abolition of the Galley Corps in 1748, but its members continued to remain distinct from each other in attitudes and loyalties. Regarding interservice rivalry before 1748, see Bamford, *Fighting Ships and Prisons*, pp. 53, 105–106.

advancement, were exacerbated by the navy's irregular payment of salaries which left officers frequently in debt.[104] Whatever their causes, jealousies and factionalism among French naval officers resulted in flagrant insubordination and outright disobedience which compromised the fleet's effectiveness.[105]

This disunity was related to problems with the navy's high command. The Admiral of France, a purely honorific position, had not been made a focus of loyalty and the entire *Grand Corps* lacked strong direction and unifying leadership from its senior officers.[106] Taillemite argued that the French navy emphasized administration over the fleet's military role, and that it lacked an effective command structure.[107] There was no high echelon body to define strategy, to direct naval operations, and to instill order in the officer corps: there was no equivalent to the British Admiralty.[108] Moreover, the same developments which fostered a caste spirit had created a "gerontocracy" of general-grade officers. In Louis XIV's navy officers were named to flag-rank on the basis of distinguished service and fitness to command at sea. After 1715, however, promotions to *vice-amiral* and *lieutenant-général* became retirement honours rather than indications of leadership.[109] Too often fleet com-

[104] Loir, *La Marine royale en 1789*, pp. 86–87, 99–105. See also Vergé-Franceschi, *Les officiers . . . Provençale*, pp. 121, 154–185, 234–235.

[105] An often cited example of the deleterious effects of the officer indiscipline on French naval operations is Suffren's Indian campaign; see for example Taillemite, *L'Histoire ignorée*, pp. 216, 224–229, and Lacour-Gayet, p. 599, who states that Suffren did not know Nelson's happiness to command a "Band of Brothers." For further examples of this problem in the 1780s, see Lacour-Gayet, pp. 598–601.

[106] Loir, *La Marine royale en 1789*, p. 74 calls the Admiral of France a figurehead position which constituted a profitable sinecure for a Prince of the Blood, the duc de Penthièvre in 1789; he refers to the *vice-amiraux* as "offices rather than ranks," p. 78. Pritchard, pp. 57–58 suggests that the navy's failure to develop group cohesion among its officers resulted from the lack of focus for their loyalty. This was not helped by the fact that many naval officers were also Knights of Malta and saw their obligations to the Order of Saint John as equal to their duty in the fleet; see Bluche, pp. 169–172 and Bamford, *Fighting Ships and Prisons*, pp. 101–104.

[107] Etienne Taillemite, "Le Haut-Commandement de la marine française de Colbert à la Révolution," in Acerra, Merino, and Meyer (eds.), pp. 249–260.

[108] Ibid., p. 246. Taillemite contends that La Luzerne's *Conseil de Marine* of 1788 was paradoxical. To an extent it prefigured the nineteenth-century "Conseil Supérieur de la Marine," but it also demonstrated the extent to which the navy at the end of the Old Regime remained the prisoner of a predominantly administrative vision, p. 260.

[109] Ibid., pp. 260–264. Only three of twenty-two *vice-amiraux* promoted between 1715 and 1789 had commanded fleets at sea; only eighteen of sixty-eight *lieutenants-généraux* named between 1720 and 1784 had held such commands. Loir, *La Marine royale en 1789*, pp. 81–82 argues that flag-officers in the navy were free from the taint of Court

mands were given to aged and unfit flag-officers, and the death of many heroes of the American War before the Revolution was less the result of fate than of an unhealthy system.

The lack of cohesion and leadership in the officer corps was a serious problem in the French navy. Yet the *Grand Corps* should not be caricatured as an arrogant caste of insubordinate provincial reactionaries. These men lived by a chivalric code which demanded high standards of personal bravery, honourable conduct towards enemies, and paternalistic concern for those beneath them in the military and social hierarchy.[110] Growing professionalism accompanied these traditional values in the late eighteenth century. Following the American Revolutionary War, the need to develop skills at sea and to practice fleet manoeuvres inspired the outfitting of *escadres d'évolutions*, or training squadrons, to exercise both officers and crews in seamanship, gunnery, and battle tactics.[111] Alongside military professionalism were tremendous developments in navigation, particularly the perfection of longitudinal calculation, which demanded a highly educated officer corps.[112] Sophisticated navigational training was only one element of a larger scientific movement in the navy which saw similar strides in hydrography, naval architecture, and cartography.[113] The *Académie Royale de la Marine*,

intrigue, but he admits that birth took precedence over experience in their promotions. See also Taillemite, *L'Histoire ignorée*, pp. 162–172, and Michel Vergé-Franceschi, "Les Officers Généraux de la Marine Royale en 1715," *Revue historique*, 273: 1 (1985), pp. 131–157.

[110] "Enfin l'officier fait souvent figure de ces seigneurs moyenâgeux; peut-être leur fonction militaire fait-elle revivre en eux l'idéal chevaleresque des anciens soldats, pieux et charitables, dévoués protecteurs de leur ville, des petites gens et des pauvres;" Vergé-Franceschi, *Les officiers . . . Provençale*, p. 256.

[111] Loir, *La Marine royale en 1789*, p. 110; Brun, II, pp. 110, 125, 132–133; Lannoy, p. 760. Lacour-Gayet, p. 591 stresses the research and training in tactics and strategy promoted under Castries: "Ces discussions scientifiques entre officiers supérieurs étaient la preuve du travail intellectuel qui se faisait dans les états-majors et la condition même du progrès."

[112] Taillemite, *L'Histoire ignorée*, p. 265. Loir, pp. 108–109 states that the increased study of navigation by officers reduced the importance of *pilotes*, petty officer navigators equivalent to English Sailing Masters. Such men continued to be important in the education of officers, however, as shown in the recent biography by Amiral Maurice Dupont, *L'Amiral Willaumez* (Paris: Editions Tallandier, 1987), pp. 91–94 which describes the future Admiral, then *aide-pilot*, training officer candidates in scientific navigation at sea in 1786.

[113] Taillemite, *L'Histoire ignorée*, pp. 263–267. Taillemite entitles this section: "Les marines centres de recherche scientifiques." See also Loir, *La Marine royale en 1789*, pp. 105–107. There is debate as to the level of scientific education which most officers actually received. The argument that officers were imbued with the spirit of scientific inquiry is supported by Roger Hahn, "L'Enseignement scientifique des gardes de la marine en XVIIIe siècle," in R. Taton (ed.), *Enseignement et diffusion des sciences en*

founded at Brest in 1752, sought to encourage the spirit of scientific inquiry in officers, many of whom participated in the renewed exploration of the eighteenth century. Alongside the name of James Cook should be placed those of several French naval explorers: Louis-Antoine, comte de Bougainville, whose scientific voyage circled the earth in 1767–1768; Yves-Joseph de Kerguelen de Trémarec, who explored the southern Indian Ocean in 1771–1774; Jean-François de Galaup, comte de Lapérouse, whose famous expedition disappeared in the South Seas in 1788.[114]

Thus far from being ignorant *hobéraux*, naval officers were highly educated professionals and some of them belonged to an international scientific elite.[115] Although isolated from Parisian culture, officers had direct contact with the world beyond France through their service in the fleet. This included involvement in the American Revolution. Captain de Granchain served in American waters during the war and he expressed enthusiasm for the founding of the United States:

I do not know if this people has, to become free, all the political and natural titles they claim, but I know that the epoch of their liberty will be one of the most interesting in human history, and I am glad to have been witness to it and to have cooperated in its affirmation.[116]

It is unclear whether such sentiment was widely held, but it is unlikely that the *Grand Corps* was untouched by the currents of liberalism in French society at the end of the Old Regime.[117] A negative

---

France au XVIIIe siècle (Paris: Hermann, 1964), pp. 547–558. However Pritchard, p. 65, questions the amount of scientific knowledge most officers possessed: "The scientific accomplishments of the few were exceptions to the general indifference and ignorance of the many."

[114] For general discussions of the explorations of these three officers, see Spate, pp. 76, 95–98, 155–160 and Taillemite, *L'Histoire ignorée*, pp. 235–237, 263, 239–242. A scientific expedition was mounted under the command of Joseph-Antoine Bruny d'Entrecasteaux to search for Lapérouse in 1791. The search was a failure and the expedition was torn with political strife between scientists and naval officers. See: Taillemite, *L'Histoire ignorée*, pp. 242–243; Spate, pp. 161–165; Dupont, pp. 122–219. For a recent detailed study of the expedition and its scientific work, see Hélène Richard, *Une grande expédition scientifique au temps de la Révolution française: Le Voyage de d'Entrecasteaux à la recherche de Lapérouse* (Paris: Editions du Comité des Travaux historiques et scientifiques, 1986).

[115] Acerra and Meyer, p. 103.

[116] Quotation cited in Guyon, p. 449.

[117] Most naval officers were nobles and the traditional assumptions regarding the ideological position of the French nobility on the eve of the Revoution have been challenged recently. Guy Chaussinand-Nogaret, *The French Nobility in the Eighteenth Century: From Feudalism to Enlightenment*, trans. William Doyle (Cambridge: Cambridge University Press, 1985), esp. pp. 11–42, 65–83 argues that the nobility was

reaction to Revolutionary ideals was not predetermined among naval officers.[118] Whatever the ambiguity of its members, the French naval officer corps was undergoing significant reform at the end of the Old Regime. In 1786 Castries abolished the *gardes de la marine*, long perceived as the root of arrogance and insubordination within the *Grand Corps*, and replaced them with *élèves de la marine* as the basis of officer recruitment. These officer candidates began as *aspirants* in two naval colleges at Vannes and Alais where they studied mathematics and technical subjects; however, following the completion of examinations, there was new emphasis on practical training at sea.[119] Boys required proof of nobility to become *élèves-aspirants*, but there was to be more competition for places based on academic ability and the Crown would support the candidate and remove the financial burden from his family.[120] Moreover, Castries created a parallel recruitment stream, the *volontaires*, which followed the same training pattern. Volunteers needed no proof of nobility, although the Minister's ordinance indicated that they were to come from a social élite.[121]

a rejuvenated élite, rather than a declining social group, and that its massive penetration by members of the Third Estate caused it to question the justification of hereditary superiority in favour of personal merit. Thus the nobility played a prominent role in the culture of the Enlightenment and the criticism of the old order. Chaussinand-Nogaret demonstrates the degree to which the notion of merit had penetrated noble ideology by examining the Second Estate's *cahiers* of 1789, pp. 145–165. Regarding the intellectual interests of naval officers, see Vergé-Franceschi, *Les officiers . . . Provençale*, pp. 236–246 who suggests that officers read widely and enjoyed cultural activities, but were more oriented towards science than literature.

[118] See for example Tramond, pp. 550–551 who characterizes the officer corps in 1789 as essentially professional, even liberal, and certainly not intrinsically reactionary. See also Acerra and Meyer, pp. 114–115.

[119] See: Loir, *La Marine royale en 1789*, pp. 14–15; Vergé-Franceschi, *Les officiers . . . Provençale*, p. 78; Rouvier, p. 7.

[120] See: Loir, *La Marine royale en 1789*, pp. 13–16; Vergé-Franceschi, *Les officiers . . . Provençale*, pp. 34, 63; Castries, p. 119; Acerra and Meyer, pp. 49–50. Loir suggests that the proof of nobility required by the navy was far less restrictive than that required by the army's Ségur ordinance, yet it could be argued that both represented attempts to foster professionalism by preserving the military as a career for poor provincial nobles; see S. F. Scott, pp. 24–31. The Ségur ordinance has been seen in the context of a widespread aristocratic reaction, but it can also be argued that it was in keeping with traditional principles in that it resulted from division within the nobility; see David Bien, "La Réaction aristocratique avant 1789: l'exemple de l'armée," *Annales. Economies, Sociétés, Civilisations*, 39 (1974), 23–48, and William Doyle, "Was there an Aristocratic Reaction in Pre-Revolutionary France?," *Past and Present*, 57 (November 1972), 97–122.

[121] The *ordonnance* stated that *volontaires* would be chosen from "fils de gentilshommes, ou de sous-lieutenants de vaisseau ou de port, et les fils de négociants en gros,

These changes in recruitment were linked directly to reform of officer hierarchy. Castries suppressed the old intermediate grades, as well as the rank of *enseigne*, and created the new grade of *sous-lieutenant de vaisseau*. These sub-lieutenants were to be recruited primarily from the new volunteers[122] and would be ranked directly beneath the *lieutenants de vaisseau* within the *Grand Corps*. Thus the Minister of Marine had deliberately opened the aristocratic naval officer corps to non-nobles.[123] This was done partly to ensure a stable officer reserve for the navy. *Sous-lieutenants* would command small warships during hostilities, but could sail in the merchant service during peacetime and receive half-pay from the navy. The possiblity of promotion to full lieutenant, codified in the ordinance, made them full members of the officer corps so that the grade of *sous-lieutenant* constituted a situation of honour as well as security.[124] These junior officers would also have played more than a reserve role, given the projected expansion of the fleet and the limited number of *élèves*, had Castries' organization survived.[125] Resentment of the reform certainly existed within the *Grand Corps*, but there were also liberals such as Albert de Rioms who defended the sub-lieutenants as valuable additions.[126] There is also evidence that friendships developed between officers from the different recruiting streams, although there was often contradiction between the high esteem expressed for individuals and group hostility on principle.[127] Before the Revolution, nevertheless, the French navy

armateurs, capitaines marchands, et gens vivant noblement;" cited in Vergé-Franceschi, *Les officiers . . . Provençale*, p. 34.
[122] The regulations also made provision for the direct nomination to *sous-lieutenant* of merchant captains and naval petty officers; Aman, pp. 148–150.
[123] Loir, *La Marine royale en 1789*, pp. 26–27.
[124] Aman, pp. 145–151. Aman suggests that the creation of this true officer reserve, fully assimilated to the navy, heralded the end of the traditional *officiers bleus*.
[125] See the fixed number of officers at the various grades in the *Etat-major de l'armée navale* for 1789, in Loir, *La Marine royale en 1789*, p. 85. According to these figures there were 840 *sous-lieutenants*, but only 500 *élèves* in 1789. See also "Appendice IV: Liste des officiers de la Marine royale au 1er janvier 1787;" in Lacour-Gayet, pp. 662–672.
[126] Brun, II, p. 435. Crook, *Toulon*, p. 58 acknowledges that a sense of loyalty to the service, which united all ranks and branches of the navy, was emerging in the 1780s.
[127] See the synopsis of letters between two young naval officers, the vicomte de La Porte and the Huguenot *sous-lieutenant* Luther Martin, in 1789; Ferdinand Des Robert, "Correspondance de deux officiers de Marine en 1789," *Académie de Stanislas: Mémoires*, série 5, Tom. 9 (1892), 191–239. Aman, pp. 89–92 suggests the contradiction between attitudes towards individuals and the principle of group hostility in regard to the hostility toward the *officiers bleus*. This points to the more

was moving towards the selection of its officers on the basis of merit as well as privilege.[128] These reforms to the officer corps were included within a series of ordinances introduced by Castries between 1781 and 1786. These culminated in a comprehensive set of regulations published in January 1786, the "Code de Castries," which Loir called "the testament of the Old Regime's navy."[129] The suggestion that these new regulations perfected the French fleet must be qualified, but the Code did represent the Minister's efforts to modernize the navy and to address the deficiencies exposed by the American War. Castries organized the expanded fleet into nine permanent squadrons which would be based in different naval ports.[130] The Minister established the *canonniers-matelots* to provide the navy with a corps of professional gunners and marine troops.[131] Port administration was altered slightly,[132] but changes to the payment of arsenal workers affected

fundamental problem of finding the norm in the highly idiosyncratic social behavior of the Old Regime.

[128] Castries, p. 119 suggests that Castries believed in the new notion of merit and that his establishment of the *volontaires* was intended as a step towards the full assimilation of non-nobles into the officer corps. Regarding the competition for places as *élèves*, La Luzerne asked Louis XVI not to limit his selection to aristocrats: "Votre Majesté sait que le temps présent ne change point mon opinion à cet égard; que plusieurs fois avant que les changements actuels puissent être prévus, j'ai insisté fortement auprès d'Elle, et de son Conseil sur la nécessité de considérer, non ce que les hommes étaient nés, mais ce qu'ils étaient lorsqu'il s'agissait de distribuer entre eux des emplois importants . . .," cited in Acerra and Meyer, p. 48.

[129] Loir, *La Marine royale en 1789*, p. xvi. See also Taillemite, *L'Histoire ignorée*, pp. 177–178, 191 who contends that Castries' regulations honed the fleet to a new state of excellence, and Lacour-Gayet, pp. 577–579 who suggests that only the impending financial collapse and political upheaval prevented Castries from perfecting the navy. For a different view, see Guérin, V, p. 147 who argues that Castries, whom he calls "Necker's creature," was an inferior minister to Sartine and was responsible for the defeat at The Saints.

[130] Five squadrons would be based at Brest, two at Rochefort and two at Toulon, although the number of ships in the Toulon squadrons would be slightly higher. See: Loir, *La Marine royale en 1789*, p. 55; Lacour-Gayet, p. 568; Castries, p. 118.

[131] See: Loir, *La Marine royale en 1789*, pp. 149–158; Lacour-Gayet, pp. 572–573; Castries, p. 118. Choiseul had suppressed the companies of the old *troupes franches* in 1762, forcing warships to rely on garrisons of regular infantry. Few in the navy were pleased with Choiseul's action, but naval officers did not welcome the establishment of the new *Canonniers-matelots* since they had come to believe that sailors should serve the guns as in the British fleet. Nevertheless, in 1789 the *Canonniers-matelots* represented the navy's élite troops, both afloat and ashore, and they were missed following their abolition under the Convention.

[132] Castries sought to improve the situation in the ports by striking a better balance between pen and sword; Taillemite, *L'Histoire ignorée*, p. 195. Loir, *La Marine royale*

the naval bases more significantly. In 1785 Castries abolished the traditonal system of day wages, *à la journée*, and established payment by contract or piece work, *à l'entreprise*.[133] Although some tasks had often been contracted, the plan to have this system applied to all work in the arsenals was an innovation made in the name of needed economy and increased efficiency. Workers, who feared a loss of income, resisted its implementation and the reform contributed to tensions in the arsenals on the eve of the Revolution.[134]

Several of Castries' most important ordinances concerned sailors. Administrators like Malouet had objected to the conscription system as an unjust yoke on the seafaring population,[135] and the Minister's efforts to reform the *classes* reflected this concern. He modified the lifetime obligation so that men could renounce the sea at eighteen or, given sufficient notice, could remove themselves from the *classes* later in life. Members of the same family would not follow each other on the roll to avoid being called in the same levy, sons could replace fathers, and the navy was to rely more upon single than married men. The geographic organization of the system was rationalized and its supervision was placed in the hands of retired naval officers to ensure justice.[136] Castries also sought to improve conditions for seamen within the navy. He ordered the construction of barracks for sailors waiting to join ships, demanded that they be provided with uniforms, and sought to provide

en 1789, pp. 212–217 disputes the existence of any true balance and emphasizes the complete domination of the sword and the limitations of a system in which administrators had no real power to regulate expenses or to limit consumption. This impotence, according to Loir, extended to the *Conseils de marine*. However, Castries also took responsibility for naval construction, artillery, and *mouvements du port* away from sea-officers and returned it to technical experts, in the persons of the revived *officiers du port*; Loir, *La Marine royale en 1789*, pp. 168–169. *Officiers du port* should be seen as distinct from those of the pen since the former were part of the naval officer corps; see Pritchard, p. 62.

[133] Brun, II, pp. 101–102. See also Hampson, "Ouvriers," pp. 290–292.

[134] Loir, *La Marine royale en 1789*, p. 175. The navy's severe shortage of funds forced naval authorities at Toulon in October 1788 to the desperate decision of closing the arsenal gates two days per week. The resulting economic deprivation aroused such discontent among the workers, who faced spiralling bread prices, that the dockyards were returned to full work in November; Brun, II, pp. 130, 133 and White, *Malouet*, p. 95. See also Crook, *Toulon*, pp. 46–47, 72–73.

[135] Malouet, *Mémoires*, I, p. 197; Brun, II, p. 54.

[136] See: Loir, *La Marine royale en 1789*, pp. 41–45; Brun, II, pp. 94–96; Castries pp. 116–117. Malouet wrote to the Minister to express his approval: "Les gens de mer et la nation même vous doivent des remerciements d'avoir amélioré le sort des hommes classés;" cited in Lacour-Gayet, pp. 567–568.

better rations.[137] The Minister was particularly concerned with the health of naval crews. He introduced the practice of airing, washing, and fumigating the holds of ships which had experienced epidemics, and he wished to improve the navy's hospitals.[138] Castries' reforms demonstrate that the navy on the eve of the Revolution had embraced attitudes of utility and humanitarianism which were in keeping with the spirit of much of the Constituent Assembly's early legislation.[139]

Castries' ordinances did not put an end to the navy's structural weaknesses. Despite reforms to make naval conscription more effective and humane, the fleet continued to have great difficulty manning its ships after 1789. The ports and arsenals were upgraded, but the navy still relied upon overseas sources for its stores and construction material. Castries and La Luzerne pushed forward a system of officer selection which eroded privilege in favour of personal merit. This was not welcomed universally and disruptive antagonisms continued within the officer corps, although a sense of loyalty to the service and to the state had emerged among naval officers and administrators in the 1780s. The most serious structural weakness was financial, and all of Castries' progressive reforms could not mitigate the limitations placed on the fleet by the French Crown's inability to raise sufficient revenue.

The problem of finances demonstrates the navy's fundamental nature as a national institution which was absolutely dependent upon government support. The operation of its dockyards and of all the other organizational structures required state capital, but it also needed executive authority. Tied to isolated bases, the navy was terribly vulnerable to political upheaval which weakened the authority and control of the

---

[137] Loir, *La Marine royale en 1789*, pp. 123, 129–130, and Wismes, p. 63. Before the construction of barracks, conscripts arriving in naval ports were totally at the mercy of shady inn keepers and other land sharks. A reform of 1786 declared that the navy would provide its crews with uniforms, but French sailors continued to sail without adequate clothing during the Revolution. Regarding naval rations, Castries was most concerned to eradicate the speculation among suppliers and pursers which deprived crews of regulation quantities and quality of food.

[138] Loir, *La Marine royale en 1789*, pp. 127–130 and Castries, pp. 116, 120–121.

[139] John Charles White, "Aspects of Reform of the French Navy under Castries: A Case for Humanity and Justice," *The Consortium on Revolutionary Europe, 1750–1850. Proceedings*, 4 (1975), 59–67. Lacour-Gayet, p. 565 emphasizes that Castries was advised on his reforms by many naval officers and administrators, including the comte d'Hector and Captain Latouche-Tréville.

Plate 1. Charles-Eugène de La Croix, marquis de Castries.
Engraving by J. Perin (Phot. Bibl. Nat. Paris)

central government. The Revolution of 1789 was a direct assault on
the legitimacy and authority of royal government, and thus had a
profound impact on the French navy. This was illustrated most clearly
by events in Toulon.

THE REVOLUTION BEGINS: THE TOULON
AFFAIR OF 1789

On December 1, 1789 local civil authorities at Toulon imprisoned Commandant Albert de Rioms following a major riot in the port. This attack on a senior officer of the Crown, and the reluctance of the central government to intervene, illustrates the collapse of executive power in 1789 and its effect on the French navy. This collapse was linked to the establishment of the National Assembly and the emergence of a new definition of sovereignty. Patriots within the Estates General, primarily though not exclusively from the third estate, declared themselves to be the representatives of the nation, and thus to represent authority superior to that of the king. The National Assembly's triumph, which was assured only by popular insurrection in Paris, led to the preparation of a new constitution and the regeneration of French institutions.[1] Louis XVI continued to reign, but royal executive authority was widely discredited and distrusted.

Provincial developments were both the cause and the reflection of the paralysis of central government which accompanied the rise of the nation. Municipal revolutions occurred throughout France during 1789 and permanent committees of third-estate electors replaced existing urban governments and ousted royal officials. These Revolutionary municipalities formed companies of citizen militia, the nascent National Guard, and exercised uncontrolled local power.[2] Every military outpost

[1] The classic discussion of the events of 1789 is Georges Lefebvre's *The Coming of the French Revolution*, trans. R. R. Palmer (Paris, 1939; Princeton: Princeton University press, 1947; repr. 1979), esp. pp. 41–128, 155–181. Doyle, *Origins*, pp. 168–203 argues that the Revolution of 1789 was the unforeseen result of a political struggle which followed the collapse of the Old Regime, and not the inevitable advent of the "bourgeoisie."

[2] Lefebvre, *Coming*, pp. 123–128, Doyle, *Origins*, p. 190. A recent survey which emphasizes the collapse of government is Guy Chaussinand-Nogaret, *La Bastille est prise. La Révolution française commence* (Paris: Editions Complexe, 1988), see esp. p. 113. For a detailed discussion of the municipal revolution in the provinces, see

in the provinces seemed a potential Bastille, and the new municipalities in the port cities viewed naval commanders with deep suspicion. These Revolutionaries took advantage of the economic discontent of sailors and arsenal workers to undermine the officers' authority, and there were several confrontations. The navy's calls for support from the National Assembly went unanswered. The ideology of Popular Sovereignty prevented the deputies from supporting agents of royal executive power over those who appealed to the legitimacy of the People's Will. The impact upon the navy of this conflict between popular and executive authority in 1789, and its implications for the years ahead, is best illustrated in what became known as the "Toulon Affair."

The spring of 1789 was a time of political excitement and growing social crisis in Toulon. Throughout France members of the three estates elected deputies to the Estates General, which was to begin its session at Versailles in May, and drafted the *cahiers de doléances*. They carried out these activities in a spirit of high expectation, but also against a background of economic anxiety due to the poor harvest of 1788.[3] Representatives of the third estate met at Toulon's *Hôtel de Ville* on March 23 to name commissioners to examine draft *cahiers*, but the proceedings were interrupted by an outburst of popular violence. An angry crowd surrounded the *Hôtel de Ville* and demanded the deliverance of Lantier de Villebranche, a former municipal consul, and Beaudin, the former archivist. The crowd blamed these two for the hated *droit de piquet*, the tax imposed on grain reentering Toulon from mills outside the city, which was pushing up the price of bread to unacceptable levels. Officials would not surrender the men and the crowd attacked Beaudin's house, then invaded the bishop's residence, seized a carriage and hurled it into the harbour. The following day arsenal workers and elements of the city's lower classes pillaged Lantier's house and attacked the custom post.[4]

Georges Lefebvre, *The Great Fear of 1789: Rural Panic in Revolutionary France*, trans. Joan White (Princeton: Princeton University press, 1973; repr. 1982), pp. 75–90. See also Lynn Hunt, *Revolution and Urban Politics in Provincial France: Troyes and Reims, 1786–1790* (Stanford: Stanford University Press, 1978), esp. pp. 3–5, 141–142.
[3] Regarding the general economic crisis which arose during the winter of 1788–1789, see Doyle, *Origins*, pp. 158–167. According to Michel Vovelle, "Une champ de bataille de la Révolution (1789–1815)," in Maurice Agulhon (ed.), *Histoire de Toulon* (Toulouse: Privat, 1980), p. 167, the crisis in Toulon was the product of high grain prices combined with the new system of payment for arsenal workers.
[4] See D. M. J. Henry, *Histoire de Toulon depuis 1789 jusqu'au Consulat, d'après les documents de ses archives*, 2 vols. (Toulon: Eugène Aurel, 1855), I, pp. 43–47. Henry

The naval Commandant at Toulon, the comte d'Albert de Rioms,[5] attributed this riot to popular anger at the municipal authorities, but believed that more was to be feared from the discontent of unpaid arsenal workers.[6] The naval treasury at Toulon had been unable to pay these workers for several months and many of them refused to enter the dockyards on March 24, and instead marched through the city demanding their wages. The wealthy printer Mallard presented a loan to acting intendant Possel, which allowed the distribution of one month's pay, and calm was restored.[7] Albert de Rioms doubted that the situation in Toulon would remain peaceful. The municipality quieted the crowd by announcing that the price of bread would be lowered from five to three *sols* per pound, but the Commandant wondered who was going to furnish it at the reduced rate.[8]

Albert de Rioms emphasized the theme of impending social crisis more explicitly in his subsequent correspondence to the Minister of Marine. "Misery is extreme," he wrote, yet it was clear that naval authorities could not alleviate the suffering. Indeed, as he informed La Luzerne, the navy's own financial difficulties could worsen the situation: "We are going to be forced, by the economic arrangements we must take, consequent to your orders, on the proportion of expenditures for the current year, to open the arsenal only four days per week. You are aware, Sir, how much this measure must cost me in the present

cites the *Procès-verbal* of Toulon's *consuls*, the official account of the riot, which was requested by the Aix Parlement. See also Brun, II, p. 141 and Acerra and Meyer, p. 111. Vovelle, pp. 167–168 suggests that the riot represented a contestation of Toulon's social structure, but the event seems in keeping with the pattern of traditional bread riots. See Crook, *Toulon*, pp. 80–83.

[5] François-Hector, comte d'Albert de Rioms was born in 1728 at Avignon, and entered the navy as a *garde de la marine* at the age of fifteen. Named *enseigne de vaisseau* in 1748, he served in Dubois de La Motte's ill-fated Louisbourg expedition in 1757 and was taken prisoner following the capture of *L'Espérance*. He became a prisoner of war again in 1758 as a result of *Le Foudroyant*'s action off Carthagena. He was promoted to *Capitaine de vaisseau* in 1772 and served with distinction under d'Estaing and de Grasse during the War of American Independence, commanding *Le Pluton* (74) at the Battles of Chesapeake Bay and The Saints. In 1784 he was promoted to *chef d'escadre* and commanded the squadron which staged a mock battle for Louis XVI at Cherbourg in 1786. Albert de Rioms was named Commandant at Toulon in 1785; Taillemite, *Dictionnaire*, p. 12.

[6] See his letter of March 24, 1789 to La Luzerne, in comte d'Albert de Rioms, *Mémoire historique et justificatif de M. le comte D'Albert de Rioms sur l'affaire de Toulon* (Paris: Desenne, 1790), p. 11 [BN 8 Lb39 2826].

[7] Henry, I, pp. 56–57, 342–343. See also Brun, II, p. 142.

[8] Albert de Rioms, *Mémoire . . . justificatif*, p. 11.

circumstances . . ."[9] The Commandant believed that the troubles in Toulon were caused not only by economic hardship, but also by the passivity of royal troops which encouraged anarchy. If the government waited too long to act, he warned La Luzerne, the "revolt against nobles will become general" and the populace would treat all men of wealth as enemies.[10] The Toulonnais were taking advantage of social unrest to throw off the yoke of Old Regime officials, according to Albert de Rioms, and economic vulnerability made sailors and workers prone to disorder.[11] In order to avert disaster, the Commandant believed that workers and demobilized sailors had to be paid punctually for their labour; moreover, the arsenal's permanent workers needed to be given jobs: "above all to those with wives and children; those put outside the arsenal at this moment would be condemned to die of starvation, and you realize that this extremity can lead them to hopelessness."[12] The Commandant's "General Instruction for the arsenal service in case of alert," issued on April 10, indicates the level of tension in Toulon created by the social crisis.[13] This order called for increased vigilance, not only in the arsenal but aboard the ships in the roadsteads, and warned expressly against possible sedition.

Social unrest in the naval base was hardly a new phenomenon. The economic position of arsenal workers and of demobilized seamen was precarious throughout the eighteenth century due to the navy's frequent inability to pay their wages. This had always been a cause of great concern, but the situation facing naval authorities in 1789 was different, and far more dangerous, because of the highly charged political atmosphere. Albert de Rioms perceived that a revolution was unfolding in Toulon: the "bourgeoisie" were endeavoring to overthrow the local royal administration and, in the context of the elections for the Estates General, were appealing to the lower classes for support.[14] Municipal

---

[9] See letter of March 26, 1789 to La Luzerne, in Albert de Rioms, *Mémoire . . . justificatif*, pp. 15–16. Regarding the larger dilemma for naval authorities in 1789 between the desperate need for measures of economy and the paternalistic concern for arsenal workers, see Acerra and Meyer, pp. 106–110.
[10] Albert de Rioms, *Mémoire . . . justificatif*, pp. 17–18.
[11] Ibid., pp. 18–22. See also Acerra and Meyer, pp. 104–105.
[12] Ibid., p. 23.
[13] "Instruction Générale pour le Service de l'arsenal en cas d'alerte, 10 Avril 1789"; Toulon 4 A 1/259.
[14] See the letter of March 29, 1789 to La Luzerne, in Albert de Rioms, *Mémoire . . . justificatif*, pp. 18–22. This letter is reprinted in Brun, II, pp. 148–151. Vovelle, pp. 169–170 suggests that the radicalization of a segment of the Toulonnais bourgeoisie began shortly after the March riot, and the support of the "popular masses" was a

officers had announced lower bread prices under the threat of continued rioting, but they also took up the arsenal workers' grievance against the relatively new piece-work system of payment and demanded a return to the traditional day wages.[15] Even if Albert de Rioms had agreed that such a reversal was warranted, he did not have the authority to contravene ministerial directives. Nonetheless local Revolutionaries claimed that they, rather than the Commandant, were concerned with the workers' welfare.

Still more significant was the growing conflict between Albert de Rioms and Toulon's municipality over the employment of force and the need to punish agitators. Ever since the March 23 riot, the Commandant had condemned the failure of royal troops to quell violent uprisings and had warned the Minister of the danger of their inactivity. In his letter of April 2, which described the *fête* held in Toulon to celebrate the unity of the three estates and the nomination of electors, Albert de Rioms tempered the optimistic signs of reconciliation with a call for an end to the perception that the government supported disorder and a warning that "just severity" had to be restored.[16] Events in April indeed led the navy to stage a show of force in support of order in Toulon. An uprising occurred in the neighbouring village of la Seyne on April 14, over the reimposition of the grain tax, which resulted in an armed confrontation between rioters and troops. Rumours suggested that the prison would be stormed to release fourteen peasants and sailors who had been arrested. Albert de Rioms proposed that General de Coincy, the local military commander, transfer the prisoners to the imposing harbour fortress of la Grosse Tour in armed boats under the guard of marine troops. Anonymous letters threatened extreme actions, but the transfer was accomplished on April 15 without incident.[17]

The Commandant argued that this proved the value of showing strong military authority. He was just as convinced, however, that Toulon's municipality should not use the restoration of order to reimpose the hated grain tax. Setting the price of bread proportional to that of grain

---

key factor in gaining municipal power. In contrast, Crook, *Toulon*, pp. 84–85 emphasizes continuing tension between the notables and lower classes.

[15] Albert de Rioms, *Mémoire . . . justificatif*, pp. 23–24. See also the proposals regarding naval affairs submitted by the *sénéchaussée* of Toulon to the general assembly of the third estate, March 28, 1789, which include the demand for an end to "*entreprises et prix-faits*" in the arsenal; cited in Henry, I, pp. 30–31. See also Crook, *Toulon*, p. 83 and Acerra and Meyer, pp. 109–110.

[16] Albert de Rioms, *Mémoire . . . justificatif*, pp. 125–127.

[17] Ibid., pp. 27–30. See also Brun, II, pp. 144–145.

was one thing, but Albert de Rioms felt that it was unwise and unjust to reestablish the *droit de piquet* at a time of acute shortage.[18] These criticisms of municipal policy were accompanied by a growing political quarrel. The Commandant claimed that the municipal officers' official account of the March 23 riot was inaccurate and unjust in its description of his role.[19] He also accused the consuls of inciting disorder in the arsenal by exciting the workers with notions of direct democracy; this ferment, he claimed, was only dissipated by his personal appearance to give an example of severity.[20]

Collisions between naval authority and the power of local bodies were common throughout the eighteenth century. Naval administration represented intrusive monarchical centralism, and third-estate notables often resented the *Grand Corps*. The Revolution, however, provided a new political context. The Commandant recognized that social peace in the naval base required the protection of the arsenal's workforce, and the port's lower classes in general, from the worst effects of the economic crisis. He was also uncompromising in his insistence on order, and the success of his show of force in transferring prisoners marked him as a dangerous opponent of popular effervesence. The navy in Toulon, like army garrisons elsewhere, represented military force which the royal government might use to crush the Revolution. Moreover the Commandant's control of the arsenal, with its great number of workers and sailors, was based on executive power which did not acknowledge the legitimacy of public opinion or the pressure of popular agitation. The conflict between Albert de Rioms and local Revolutionaries which developed during 1789 was a conflict between two dramatically different conceptions of authority.

The Commandant's authority over his workers remained solid during the summer of 1789. According to Vincent-Félix Brun, continued lack of funds forced naval authorities, beginning in May, to close the arsenal

[18] See letter of April 15, 1789 to La Luzerne, in Albert de Rioms, *Mémoire . . . justificatif*, pp. 31–32. Albert de Rioms probably included this letter, which documented his opposition to the tax, in his *Mémoire justificatif* to increase his credibility in the aftermath of the "Toulon Affair"; he certainly gained no political advantage from his stance at the time.
[19] Ibid., pp. 34–37.
[20] Ibid., pp. 37–38. Albert de Rioms wrote that the ferment in the arsenal "ne fut point occasionnée par la menace du rétablissement du piquet, ni appaisée par la publication de votre déclaration, sa véritable cause fut l'importance que vous aviez cru devoir donner aux ouvriers dans vos délibérations, et le droit qu'ils crurent avoir de révoquer le Député qu'ils avaient choisi."

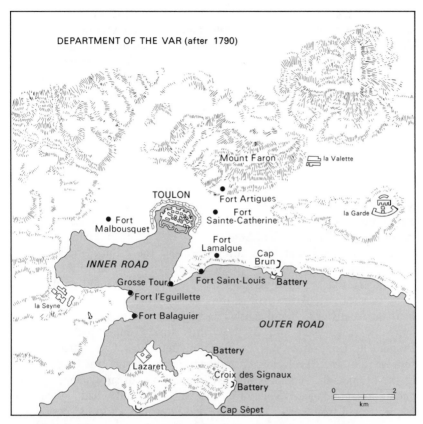

DEPARTMENT OF THE VAR (after 1790)

Mount Faron — la Valette

TOULON — Fort Artigues

Fort Malbousquet — Fort Sainte-Catherine — la Garde

Fort Lamalgue

INNER ROAD — Cap Brun

Grosse Tour — Fort Saint-Louis — Battery

la Seyne — Fort l'Eguillette

Fort Balaguier

OUTER ROAD

Battery

Lazaret — Croix des Signaux — Battery

Cap Sépet

0 ___ 2
km

Map 2. The port and roadsteads of Toulon and surrounding area. After "The Defence of Toulon, 1793" in J. Holland Rose, *Lord Hood and the Defence of Toulon* (Cambridge: Cambridge University Press, 1922), Appendix.

on Mondays. Little outcry from the workers occurred before August when Albert de Rioms consented to listen to a worker deputation which demanded a renewal of Monday operations, along with a return to day wages, exact pay at the end of every month, and the opening of the dockyards to all who lacked employment. Albert de Rioms agreed only to the reopening of the arsenal, remaining firm that all else was outside the scope of his authority as Commandant.[21] Albert de Rioms' own

[21] Brun, II, pp. 146–147.

55

version of his relations with the workers during the summer of 1789 suggested that many of them sought nightly shelter within the arsenal, along with their families, as a refuge from the terrors and ferment which haunted Toulon. At one point excited workers demanded to be armed, but Albert de Rioms claimed that he addressed them, unarmed and vulnerable, and was able to calm their fears and to flatter them with his trust.[22] Naval officers were traditionally the paternal protectors of their men, and maintained discipline through a combination of personal appeal and coercive force. This account shows that the Commandant believed this would continue, despite the political upheaval.

Although naval authority seemed secure within the arsenal's gates, the Revolution in Toulon escalated during the summer. Events at Versailles and Paris, where the fall of the Bastille indicated that the Revolution was a national *fait accompli*, had great effect on the situation in provincial France. On August 10, 1789 a triumphant National Assembly decreed that local authorities and the military must take a civic oath, swearing allegiance to the new regime. In Toulon the municipal officers and the marquis du Luc, the new commander of the local army garrison,[23] took the oath on the Place d'Armes in a public ceremony held on August 23. Significantly, naval personnel took the oath separately on August 24 and 25.[24] By this time Toulon had formed a Permanent Committee on the Paris model. This Committee, which represented new Revolutionary authority in the port,[25] was independent of the municipality and was divided into *bureaux* of subsistence, police, and correspondence. Roubaud, the third consul, had apparently requested aid from such a committee and he would act as its president.[26]

[22] Albert de Rioms, *Mémoire . . . justificatif*, pp. 52–57.
[23] Du Luc had succeeded the comte de Béthisy, discredited by a confrontation between soldiers and Toulonnais in July, as "*commandant de la 8e division militaire de Provence.*" Béthisy had replaced de Coincy in June, 1789. See Henry, I, pp. 77–78.
[24] Ibid., I, pp. 68–69. See also the exchange of letters between the consuls and *major-général* Bonneval, August 26 and 27; Toulon 4 A 1/364.
[25] Vovelle, p. 170; see also Acerra and Meyer, p. 112. Crook, *Toulon*, pp. 86–87 suggests that the formation of the Permanent Committee, which was separate initially from the municipal council but had merged with it into a single administration by December, represented a setback for the city's notables, who were forced to share power with artisans and shopkeepers.
[26] Henry, I, pp. 66–67. The other two consuls at Toulon no longer held their positions as Crown-appointed officers by August 23, 1789: Eynaud, the first consul, had resigned under the pressure of public animosity; Meyfrun, the former second consul, had been elected as a deputy to the Estates General.

Another imitation of the Paris Revolution was the formal integration of Toulon's citizen militia, which had been operating since March, into the National Guard on August 23. The military commander du Luc supported this formation, but its troops were to be controlled by the Permanent Committee.[27]

The establishment of the Permanent Committee and the National Guard confirmed Revolutionary authority in Toulon. The old royal-appointed municipal officers had either abdicated power or had been absorbed by the new regime. Such developments occurred throughout the country. In theory all authorities in France were now reconciled in subordination to the Nation, but in fact the position of agents of executive power remained dangerously ambiguous. There was, as yet, no constitution to clarify the relationship between the central government and local assemblies[28] or to indicate which authority represented the Nation's Will. The Revolution had forced the resignation of military commanders in many provincial cities, yet Albert de Rioms continued to run his naval base with little acknowledgement of the new civil power in Toulon. There had thus been no reconciliation between popular authority, based in the Permanent Committee, and royal executive authority, personified by the naval Commandant. Personal animosities aggravated this conflict. Albert de Rioms made no gesture of cooperation and, in his *Mémoire justificatif*, referred to the hostility of a particular member of the Permanent Committee, the former *procureur* Barthélemy: "I have reason to believe by his readiness to seize occasions to do me injury, that he holds the greatest resentment for me."[29] He criticized the Committee for admitting someone of such questionable reputation: "Barthélemy, *procureur* known to be of most dangerous character, has

---

[27] Henry, I, pp. 69–70. See also Vovelle, p. 170: "On comprend que la révolution municipale tourne autour de la formation de la garde nationale."

[28] See Alfred Cobban, "Local Government During the French Revolution," in *Aspects of the French Revolution* (London, 1968; repr. Frogmore: Paladin, 1973), pp. 115–118.

[29] See the footnote to his letter of April 16, 1789, in Albert de Rioms, *Mémoire . . . justificatif*, p. 37. Jean-Sébastien Barthélemy had been a lawyer and royal prosecutor, and became the secretary to the Permanent Committee's bureau of correspondence in 1789. He became a municipal officer in 1790 and was one of Toulon's most prominent Revolutionary extremists; see editorial footnote in Louis Richaud, *Mémoires de Louis Richaud sur la Révolte de Toulon et l'Emigration*, edited by R. Busquet, B. Roberty, and A. J. Parès (1809; repr. Paris: Les Editions Rieder, 1930), p. 27. Crook, *Toulon*, p. 87 suggests that Barthélemy joined the Committee as part of a radical faction which was emerging within Toulon's old elite.

become the arbiter and organ of this council;" and suggested that the man's conduct since March 23 had revealed his jealousy of the Commandant's authority.[30]

The "Toulon Affair" of December 1789 represents the culmination of the struggle between the two authorities. In immediate terms, the incident arose from the interlocking issues of the wearing of the national cockade, the tricolour which had become the symbol of the Revolution and of Popular Sovereignty, and of recruitment for the National Guard. The Commandant's position on both issues made him into an object of popular hostility in Toulon and led to a direct confrontation between Revolutionary and naval authority. Albert de Rioms wrote that his initial refusal to allow the cockade to be worn in the arsenal reflected the lack of general acceptance of the tricolour, which thus could be regarded only as a sign of particular association. When asked directly by a municipal deputation, early in August, he consented to allow workers to wear the cockade. This coincided with news that naval commanders at Brest and other ports had permitted the wearing of the tricolour.[31] Albert de Rioms disapproved of the display of what he considered partisan affiliation, but would tolerate it in concert with the navy's other senior officers. This stance reveals his desire to follow central direction, but it also suggests the vast difference between the Commandant's attitude and the Revolutionary outlook.

Albert de Rioms' consent to the tricolour was given only on the understanding that no one would be forced to wear the symbol, and that he and his officers would don the badge only after formal orders to that effect.[32] On October 14, however, Toulon's municipality requested that all citizens, especially those in the militia, wear the national cockade.[33] Despite assurances from the marquis du Luc to Albert de Rioms that both services would act in unison, many army officers began conforming with Revolutionary fashion before any such orders were issued. This exposed their naval counterparts to popular harassment.[34] Yet the first major tumult over the issue concerned an army officer of the Dauphiné regiment. The National Guard stopped Dauville at the gates of Toulon on November 13 for wearing a black

[30] Albert de Rioms, *Mémoire . . . justificatif*, p. 58.
[31] Brun, II, p. 147.
[32] Albert de Rioms, *Mémoire . . . justificatif*, pp. 48–51.
[33] Henry, I, p. 84.
[34] Albert de Rioms, *Mémoire . . . justificatif*, pp. 51–52.

cockade, commonly regarded as symbolic of Counter-Revolutionary sentiment, and imprisoned him following an altercation.[35] Reaction to Dauville's arrest revealed hostility within the regular military toward the National Guard, but it also demonstrates that subordinates were aware of the clash of competing authorities. In support of protests registered by army officers,[36] the petty officers of the navy's *canonniers-matelots* presented a declaration to Toulon's Permanent Committee on November 14 which stated their loyalty to the king and to their commanders, for whom they demanded respect. Having sworn to uphold security and public tranquility, the marine soldiers demanded: "this tranquility for military personnel and principally for the citizens of the city, continually tormented by the sentries of the national militia."[37]

This declaration suggests that the situation in Toulon was becoming explosive, and Albert de Rioms did little to defuse it. The Commandant inquired whether his gunners had presented their protest with due respect, but he supported their condemnation of the National Guard and reminded the municipality of its assurance that citizens would be free in their decision regarding the cockade. The continuation of such harassment would lead to conflict between the militia and regular troops which, Albert de Rioms warned, was to be feared above all.[38] The response by municipal officers was conciliatory, however, and they praised the conduct of the marine troops and claimed that the arrest of Dauville reflected merely the over-enthusiasm of individuals.[39] The evidence suggests that Roubaud, the consul who had become president of the Permanent Committee, wanted to avoid a confrontation between the Revolutionary municipality and the navy, and thus tried to conceal

[35] Ibid., p. 61. Henry, I, pp. 84–85 states that the officer was not arrested immediately, but only later when fears arose for his safety and for public order. Dauville (or d'Auville) was released on November 16, 1789.
[36] Henry, I, p. 85 states that army officers from Toulon sent a deputation to Paris to contradict the report to the National Assembly on the incident by a deputation from the National Guard. This dispatch of deputation and counter-deputation reveals the respect for the National Assembly by both sides in Toulon's conflict, but also illustrates the confusion regarding who represented the Nation's authority in the port.
[37] "Extrait d'une Déclaration présentée le 14 novembre 1789 par les Bas officiers du Corps Royal des Canonniers-matelots des 6e et 7e Divisions, au Conseil permanent établie à la municipalité de Toulon"; Toulon 4 A 1/364.
[38] Letter of November 15, 1789 from Albert de Rioms to the mayor and consuls of Toulon; Toulon 4 A 1/364. This is reprinted in Henry, I, pp. 347–348; see also pp. 85–86.
[39] Response of mayor and consuls to Albert de Rioms' letter of November 15, 1789; Toulon 4 A 1/364.

the gunners' declaration from the National Guard.[40] However the nature of the conflict between executive power and popular authority in Toulon, indeed the ideology of Popular Sovereignty itself, was not conducive to compromise. Roubaud's colleagues did not share his sentiments and informed the militia of the marine troops' criticism.

A volatile crowd of two hundred volunteer guardsmen invaded naval headquarters on November 17. The volunteers demanded that the Commandant recall the declaration and denounce his subordinates for making it. By Albert de Rioms' own account, he agreed to take back the declaration if the result would be civic peace, and this response appeared to satisfy the crowd.[41] The conflict intensified on November 19, however, when the Permanent Committee and the National Guard decided to send a deputation to the National Assembly with serious complaints against Commandant Albert de Rioms.[42]

This direct appeal to the National Assembly was characteristic of Revolutionary politics, and the dispatch of rival deputations demonstrates that the conflict in Toulon concerned which local power represented national authority. Naval officers at Toulon countered the municipal deputation with a letter to the Minister of Marine, which informed La Luzerne that they would be sending Captain de Costebelle to respond to any charges brought against their Commandant.[43] The petty officers of the *canonniers-matelots* also sent a declaration of loyalty to Albert de Rioms.[44] The marine troops stated their devotion, and denounced insinuations that their declaration of November 14 had been "foreign inspired."[45] Both of these documents suggest that many naval

[40] A deputation from Toulon presented a number of documents to the National Assembly and these were read by Hébrard, in the name of the *Comité des Rapports*, on December 7, 1789. See the summary in AP, vol. 10, p. 418.
[41] Albert de Rioms, *Mémoire . . . justificatif*, pp. 68–73. Albert de Rioms wrote to municipal officers on November 18, 1789 to appease any remaining anger, and he blamed the failure to achieve lasting reconciliation on the fiery volunteer guardsmen who refused to listen to the entreaties for calm from their officers. Henry, I, pp. 86–87 suggests that, despite his good intentions, Albert de Rioms' manner was provocative: "Le commandant de la marine était brusque et sévère, mais il n'était pas méchant, et dans plus d'une occasion il avait donné des preuves de ses bons sentiments en faveur de ses subordonnés et de la population même de la ville."
[42] For a summary of the documents brought by this deputation, presented by Hébrard on December 7, 1789, see AP, vol. 10, pp. 417–418. See also Henry, I, p. 87.
[43] "Copie de la lettre de MM. les officiers de la marine du Département de Toulon, écrite à M. le Cte. de La Luzerne, 20 novembre 1789"; Toulon 4 A 1/364.
[44] "Copie d'une Déclaration faite par les Bas officiers des 6e et 7e Divisions à M. le Cte. d'Albert, Commandant la Marine, 20 novembre 1789"; Toulon 4 A 1/364.
[45] Malouet alluded to Revolutionary accusations that the navy was somehow involved in foreign conspiracies in a speech to the National Assembly on December 14, 1789.

officers had as little inclination to avoid a direct confrontation as members of Toulon's Permanent Committee.

Among the complaints against Albert de Rioms brought before the National Assembly were charges that he prevented arsenal workers from wearing the tricolour, and that he had shown contempt for volunteer National Guardsmen.[46] Albert de Rioms claimed that he had never opposed the establishment of a militia, provided that it was "well-composed," but that he had criticized the National Guard for opening its volunteers to all, including former criminals, which made it an unstable and dangerous force.[47] The Commandant's major concern, however, was the enlistment of arsenal workers in the National Guard. Given the demonstrated hostility of the militia toward naval authority, Albert de Rioms saw the inclusion of his own workers within its ranks as posing a real threat to the security of the dockyards. Such enlistment represented a clear conflict of loyalties which he would not allow. Therefore the Commandant forbid workers from wearing the *pouf*, not the tricolour, which was a distinctive Provençal sign of military bearing and would indicate enrolment in the Guard. Any worker disobeying this order was to be driven from the arsenal.[48] On November 30, Albert de Rioms banished two petty officers from the dockyards on this charge. Roubaud and the army garrison commander visited him that evening, and pleaded with him to pardon the two men in order to prevent dangerous unrest in Toulon, but the Commandant remained firm in his conviction not to compromise his authority.[49]

He stated that part of the reason that naval officers were arrested on December 1 in Toulon was the false rumour of a conspiracy to deliver the port to a combined Anglo-Dutch fleet; AP, vol. 10, p. 572. Havard, II, pp. 52–54 claims that the rumour of a similar plot at Brest, which aroused hostility against Breton aristocrats and naval officers, was spread by the English ambassador, the Duke of Dorset, during the summer of 1789.

[46] Hébrard, in summarizing the charges, said that Albert de Rioms had treated the volunteers as "gens de la lie du peuple"; AP, vol. 10, p. 418.

[47] Albert de Rioms, *Mémoire . . . justificatif*, pp. 50, 57, 59–60. In a letter to André, the deputy of the National Assembly sent as *Commissaire du Roi* to Provence, Albert de Rioms wrote: "Croyez, Monsieur, que je ne m'abuse point en regardant la Milice de Toulon telle qu'elle est aujourd'hui, comme une troupe dangereuse par son insubordination et sa mauvaise composition"; p. 74.

[48] Ibid., pp. 75, 79–80. See also Brun, II, p. 149.

[49] Albert de Rioms, *Mémoire . . . justificatif*, pp. 81–84. Albert de Rioms justified banishing the two *maîtres de manoeuvre non-entretenus*, Causse and Ganivet, not only for their enrolment in the National Guard, but also because both had displayed bad conduct for months. Vovelle, p. 170 admits that the men were militant Revolutionaries, but suggests that the Commandant objected to worker enlistment in the militia because it would ensure popular power. This interpretation is sound, so

Albert de Rioms' resolve to exclude the two workers from the arsenal was not based only on maintaining naval authority against the incursion of the Permanent Committee. He claimed later that he had feared a workers' insurrection for some time, and believed that making an example of the two malefactors could head off such an event;[50] yet he also implied that he would welcome a confrontation to crush insubordination.[51] The banishment did produce a riot, but the arsenal's labour force was involved indirectly with the events of primary significance in Toulon on December 1, 1789. The popular turmoil, although serious, only provided the context for the clash between Revolutionary and naval authorities.

On the morning of December 1, most workers refused to enter the arsenal and gathered outside the gates or in nearby streets. A deputation from the Permanent Committee arrived at the naval base to discuss the situation with Albert de Rioms, but demanded that such a meeting be held at naval headquarters. The passage of the municipal representatives and the Commandant, escorted by naval officers, drew shouted threats and insults from the crowds. Some of the officers were attacked; a mob assaulted *major de vaisseau* Saint-Julien in particular and broke his sword.[52] Inside naval headquarters Roubaud and Barthélemy demanded that Albert de Rioms pardon the two workers, but he again refused.[53]

long as popular power is defined in terms of conflicting authorities rather than class interests. See also Cottin, pp. 19–20.

[50] Albert de Rioms, *Mémoire . . . justificatif*, pp. 80–81. Albert also cites letters to the comte de Caraman, the Governor of Provence, in which he requests additional troops be sent to Toulon for naval service, pp. 75–77. Henry, I, p. 89 states that the Commandant believed he had to make an example of the two men: "[il] crut devoir faire un exemple en les congédiant: cet acte fut la mêche qui mit le feu aux poudres."

[51] Albert de Rioms wrote that, on the night of November 30, 1789, he told Roubaud "que les ouvriers de l'arsenal avaient depuis peu pris avec leurs officiers un ton d'insubordination qu'il fallait leur faire quitter, et que j'étais bien aise d'avoir une occasion de leur montrer que je voulais et pouvais être le maître de me faire obéir par eux"; *Mémoire que M. le comte d'Albert de Rioms a fait dans la prison où il est détenu. Détail de ce qui s'est passé lundi 30 novembre, & le lendemain mardi 1er décembre* (1789), p. 1 [BN 4 Lb39 2615].

[52] Albert de Rioms, *Mémoire . . . justificatif*, p. 85, and *Mémoire . . . dans la prison*, p. 2 claims that Saint-Julien was attacked while defending the Commandant outside the *Hôtel de la Marine*. However in the account of events given by la Roque-Dourdan in his December 2, 1789 letter to La Luzerne, printed in AP, vol. 10, pp. 416–417, Saint-Julien was assaulted later in the day while carrying orders from naval headquarters to the arsenal. Albert de Rioms, *Mémoire . . . dans la prison*, p. 3 states that this was a second attack on the same officer. See also Havard, I, p. 49.

[53] Henry, I, p. 90 again suggests that Albert de Rioms' uncompromising manner aggravated the situation: "le général se montra inflexible, démontrant le danger qui

The Permanent Committee's *procès-verbal* of these events recorded a speech supposedly made by Barthélemy to the Commandant which illustrates that popular authority in Toulon claimed superiority over the navy by virtue of being the local representation of the Nation:

What! You have the power to refuse the commune a pardon which can restore calm to the city and prevent a general insurrection. We kneel before you and you refuse us that which is demanded in the King's name, of whom the mayor is the image at this moment, and in the name of the Nation, of which the Permanent Council is the organ in this case?[54]

While this exchange occurred, one hundred armed marine troops mustered on the nearby Place d'Armes for possible defence of naval headquarters.[55] Their position rapidly became untenable. As a large and hostile crowd converged on the square, the officer in charge of the troops, *major de vaisseau* de Brovès, appeared to panic. Whether or not he ordered the *canonniers-matelots* to load and open fire, or only to shoulder arms, remains unclear, but the troops dropped their weapons and the contingent made an undignified retreat, leaving the crowd in possession of the Place d'Armes.[56]

Whatever the intentions behind the deployment of these troops, naval authority no longer had recourse to armed force.[57] Very likely it was

résulterait pour la discipline d'une telle condescendance, et il employa encore, dans ce moment, quelques expressions peu flatteuses pour l'ensemble de la milice tracassière; expressions que trop de personnes avaient entendues pour qu'elles ne fussent pas répétées au milieu de la population déjà dans un état d'exaspération qu'il aurait fallu calmer au lieu de l'aigrir."

[54] "Procès-verbal dressé sur les événements du 1er décembre, relatifs à la marine," in Henry, I, p. 92. This account also records Roubaud's criticism of Albert de Rioms for deploying troops without the permission of the acting *commandant de la place*.

[55] Albert de Rioms, *Mémoire . . . justificatif*, p. 84 states that two detachments of fifty men each had been in a state of combat readiness since early that morning, and that the officers of the *canonniers-matelots* spent the previous night in the barracks.

[56] The Permanent Committee's "Procès-verbal" states that one of the municipal delegation heard the officer give the order to load from the balcony of the *Hôtel de la Marine*; in Henry, I, p. 93. La Roque-Dourdan claimed that de Brovès put his hand on his sword, ordering his men to raise arms, but never issued the order to load; AP, vol. 10, p. 416. Albert de Rioms, *Mémoire . . . dans la prison*, p. 4 denies the accusation that de Brovès ordered the troops to fire on the crowd, stating that their weapons were unloaded. Brun, II, pp. 150–151 states that the crowd misheard the order to shoulder arms as one to load and fire; however he maintains that this reflected the harsh resolutions made by Albert de Rioms since April 14. Regarding de Brovès, see Havard, I, pp. 47–48.

[57] Vovelle, p. 171 suggests that the refusal of marine troops to open fire represented the collapse of military power in Toulon.

this defection which persuaded Albert de Rioms to concede, and the Permanent Committee's announcement that the two workers had been pardoned did much to pacify the crowds outside the naval head-quarters.[58] The situation remained unstable, however, and the Commandant demanded that the municipality declare a state of martial law to guarantee security for himself and his subordinates and to restore order. The Committee refused and instead informed him that the National Guard would provide all the protection for naval officers, without recourse to regular troops. The arrival of militia columns, which surrounded naval headquarters and kept back the crowds, did restore calm. Later that afternoon, however, the guardsmen presented the naval officers with a warrant for the arrest of de Brovès who was charged with ordering his men to fire on unarmed citizens. Albert de Rioms was indignant, but de Brovès surrendered himself to avoid violence. When Albert de Rioms requested pickets of regular troops to supplement the militia who had retired, the National Guard volunteers stormed naval headquarters, seized the Commandant along with at least three other senior officers: the marquis de Castellet, the comte de Bonneval, and Commander de Villages. The National Guardsmen dragged Albert de Rioms and his men through the streets to the *Palais de Justice* and threw them into cells as prisoners.[59]

The National Assembly first learned of an insurrection at Toulon on December 7 when the Minister of Marine informed the deputies of the arrest of the naval officers and stressed the potential threat to the fleet: "I will limit myself to reminding you that at this moment twenty ships of the line, more than a quarter of our forces, of our naval munitions, and of our provisions of all kinds find themselves assembled in the

---

[58] "Procès-verbal"; in Henry, I, p. 93.
[59] Albert de Rioms, *Mémoire . . . dans la prison*, pp. 4–8. See also la Roque-Dourdan's account in AP, vol. 10, p. 417. For the version of events given by the Permanent Committee, see the addition to the "Procès-verbal"; in Henry, I, p. 95. Brun, II, p. 153 follows his account of the seizure of the officers by a discussion of the dual motives professed by the municipality: the officers were arrested to protect them from violence; but the commune also justified the arrests, claiming they were not forced by the populace or the National Guard, because of the officers' crimes. See the municipality's letter of December 15, 1789 to the National Assembly which announces the officers' release; AP, vol. 10, p. 692. Crook, *Toulon*, p. 88 states that, after the Commandant's inflexibility provoked the riot, it was left to the militia to "save the day" by taking the officers into protective custody. See also: Richaud, p. 6; Havard, I, pp. 50–55; Vovelle, p. 171.

port, arsenal, and magazines of Toulon."[60] Details of the events of December 1 came from a letter to the Minister from the marquis de la Roque-Dourdan, who found himself acting-commandant following Albert de Rioms' imprisonment. This letter included an account of the expulsion of the two arsenal workers and its effect in arousing hostility, a description of the confrontation between marine troops and the crowd: La Roque-Dourdan insisted that de Brovès had given no order to fire; and it portrayed Albert de Rioms and his officers as victims of grave injustice, placing blame squarely on the actions of the National Guard.[61] The impact of this account on the Assembly was conditioned, however, by the immediate presentation of a report by the deputation sent from Toulon on November 19. From the outset, therefore, discussion of the detentions was linked to the incident of the black cockade and to the complaints of Toulon's Permanent Committee and National Guard against Albert de Rioms: his support for the declaration made by marine troops; his own contempt for volunteer guardsmen; his supposed prevention of arsenal workers from wearing the national cockade.[62]

Pierre-Victor Malouet, the former naval Intendant, demanded the immediate release of the Commandant and his subordinates, and the punishment of those responsible. The marquis de Vaudreuil and the abbé de Bonneval, brother of the officer imprisoned at Toulon, seconded the motion. However Ricard de Séalt, a deputy from Toulon, countered by insisting that no decision be made until the municipality's version had been heard. Charles de Lameth supported this delay and proclaimed that the wearing of the black cockade indicated the existence of a Counter-Revolutionary conspiracy.[63] It should be noted that only two months had passed since the October Days, the insurrection which moved both Louis XVI and the Assembly from Versailles to Paris, which had been triggered partly by news that army officers wearing the black cockade had desecrated the tricolour.[64] Independent of any circumstances, however, vague allusions to plots and hidden enemies

---

[60] "Copie de la lettre de M. le comte de La Luzerne, ministre de la marine, à M. le garde des sceaux, en date du 6 décembre 1789"; AP, vol. 10, p. 416.
[61] "Copie de la lettre de M. de la Roque-Dourdan à le comte de La Luzerne, en date du 2 décembre 1789"; AP, vol. 10, pp. 416–417.
[62] AP, vol. 10, pp. 417–418.
[63] Ibid., p. 418.
[64] See for example Lefebvre, *Coming*, pp. 198–205, Sydenham, *French Revolution*, pp. 59–62, and Doyle, *Oxford History*, pp. 121–123.

were fundamental components of Revolutionary language and denunciation.[65]

Yet in the most important speech of this first round of debate on the "Toulon Affair," Malouet reversed the usual implications of who such "enemies" were and argued that the collapse of law and order posed the real threat to the Revolution. In defence of the naval officers, Malouet demanded to know: "What has become of Government, the authority of Law, on what foundations rests Public Liberty, and what or who rules in this Empire? Who must obey, who has the right to give orders, what is the authority which protects us, what are the means, forces which protect and what are those which threaten us?"[66] The only crime that Albert de Rioms and his officers had committed was to try to maintain discipline and to preserve the naval forces entrusted to them. The "enemies of the Nation," for Malouet, were those who persuaded the arsenal workers that "it is up to them to make the law; that all authority is henceforth an injustice; that all discipline is an insult to the People's rights. . ."[67] He placed this denunciation of such agitators, and the call for their punishment, in a broad political context. "Liberty," Malouet stated, "exists only when there is Government," and "liberty of outrage and violence is a kind of servitude which corrupts all we want to regenerate."[68] He concluded with a decree proposal which stated, above all, that the supreme executive authority was vested by the constitution in the king, and that those in whom he entrusted his authority need answer only to the legislature and to the monarch himself. Therefore, all municipalities and corps of armed citizens must be forbidden to intervene in acts of royal government, and any armed insurrection against the king's officers or administrators must be punished with the full rigour of the law.[69] Despite some support for Malouet's position,[70] the session of December 7 adjourned with only the promise that the king would be asked to order the officers' provisional release, and that the Assembly would delay pronouncing on the issue until a thorough report was prepared.

[65] See Furet, esp. pp. 53–56.
[66] Pierre-Victor Malouet, *Opinion de M. Malouet sur l'affaire de M. le comte d'Albert* (1789), p. 4 [BN 8 Le29 360]. See also AP, vol. 10, pp. 418–420.
[67] Malouet, *Opinion*, p. 6.
[68] Ibid., p. 9.
[69] Ibid., pp. 11–12.
[70] Notably, support came from the vicomte de Mirabeau whose lengthy, and less moderate, speech was also subsequently published, *Opinion du vicomte de Mirabeau, membre de l'Assemblée nationale, dans l'affaire de Toulon* (1789) [BN 8 Le29 359]; see also AP, vol. 10, pp. 420–422.

Malouet's speeches throughout the debates on the "Toulon Affair" illustrate his more fundamental attitude towards the Revolution and the conflict between different notions of authority. Malouet personified the *monarchiens* in the Constituent Assembly, according to Robert Griffiths, a group which should be seen as neither moderates lacking a definite position nor constitutional monarchists in general. *Monarchiens* was a term of abuse used by both the Jacobins and the far Right, but Griffiths used it to define a group which fought for strong, popular monarchical authority in opposition to reactionary desires for the pre-Revolution status quo and to the efforts of advanced constitutionalists to make the king a mere servant of the National Assembly.[71] Malouet had been elected as a deputy for the third estate of Rioms, but had little sympathy with the localism of his constituents in the Auvergne.[72] He envisaged a Revolution carried out by a reformist central government, ruling by consensus, which would rationalize French institutions and abolish aristocratic privilege.[73] Malouet supported the resistance of the third estate following the disappointing Royal Session of June 23, 1789,[74] but he opposed the Patriots' insistence that ultimate authority resided in the National Assembly rather than the king. During the summer and fall of 1789, Malouet and other *monarchiens* supported Jean-Joseph Mounier's constitutional proposals for an absolute royal veto and a two-chamber legislature.[75] Deputies rejected these in September and Mounier deserted the Assembly. Malouet remained, however, and continued to fight to strengthen royal executive power.[76]

---

[71] Robert Griffiths, *Le Centre Perdu. Malouet et les "monarchiens" dans la Révolution française* (Grenoble: Presses Universitaires de Grenoble, 1988), pp. 9–19, 55; see also Chapter 5, "L'identité des monarchiens, 1789–1791," pp. 105–128. E. Thompson, pp. 10–13 places Malouet somewhat less precisely within the "Right Centre" of the Constituent Assembly, but his analysis of this constitutional position is similar.
[72] Griffiths, pp. 28–45. See also Malouet, *Mémoires*, I, pp. 243–308 and White, *Malouet*, pp. 130–156.
[73] Griffiths, pp. 32–36, 45–53.
[74] Ibid., pp. 58–59. See also "The *Séance Royale* of 23 June," in John Hardman (ed.), *The French Revolution: The Fall of the Ancien Régime to the Thermidorian Reaction, 1785–1795* (London: Edward Arnold, 1981), pp. 98–101 and Doyle, *Origins*, pp. 174–177.
[75] Griffiths, pp. 62–80 suggests that the alliance behind Mounier's proposals for an absolute veto and a two-chamber legislature was based on expediency rather than a homogeneous position, and the resulting ambiguity during debate contributed to the defeat of the proposals. See also Baker, pp. 273–278 and E. Thompson, pp. 72–85.
[76] Griffiths, pp. 81–86 suggests that Mounier's efforts to encourage provincial revolt appalled Malouet, who instead founded the *Club des Impartiaux* to identify the cause

Malouet's political philosophy reflected his long service as a servant of the Crown,[77] and the former Intendant appreciated the navy's dependence on executive power from personal experience. His position on the "Toulon Affair" was based on more than a belief in law and order, or a conviction that the Revolution required royal leadership: if central government ceased to control the navy, according to Malouet, the consequences would be disastrous. On December 14 Malouet told the Constituent Assembly that arsenal workers were demanding an end to the piece-work system of payment and a return to the old day wages in Toulon. The old system had proven much less efficient, but according to Malouet the real danger would be to acquiesce to such demands under the prevailing circumstances. He moved that the President inform Toulon's municipality that petitions from arsenal workers would be addressed only when calm had been reestablished.[78] Robespierre's stinging rejoinder demonstrates the ideological opposition to Malouet's support for executive authority:

The letter proposed to you contains blame against the People and punishment against the workers;. . . You have seen or you should have seen the most insulting scorn for the sign of national liberty; you have seen that Toulon's Commandant has supported his soldiers with audacity, that he wanted to arm them against the defenders of *la patrie*,. . . I conclude that his [Malouet's] motion merits no consideration;[79]

Malouet renewed his insistence on December 15 that the President demand a restoration of subordination in Toulon. Ricard de Séalt challenged him on this occasion and reasserted the connection between the events of November in Toulon and the detention of the officers. Ricard stated that Toulon, like all military cities, was divided and that those who supported the Revolution were more numerous than those who opposed it. His implication was that military officers in general, those of the navy in particular, were Counter-Revolutionary by definition. Ricard went on to suggest that, if the Assembly was truly concerned for the security of Toulon's arsenal, three measures should be taken: the king should be asked to dismiss the naval officers presently

of the monarchy with the Revolution and to organize opposition to the growing influence of the Jacobins.
[77] Ibid., pp. 19–22. See also White, *Malouet*, p. 226.
[78] AP, vol. 10, pp. 572–573.
[79] Ibid., p. 573.

Plate 2. Pierre-Victor Malouet.
Engraving by Bonneville (Phot. Bibl. Nat. Paris)

serving there; these officers should be replaced with men not "suspected by the People"; and, more generally, confidence should be shown in "a generous people, avid for liberty."[80] For Ricard, as for Robespierre, Popular Sovereignty demanded support for Toulon's Permanent Committee over agents of the central government.

[80] Ibid., p. 589.

Toulon informed the Constituent Assembly on December 21 that the naval Commandant and his subordinates had been released and, at their request, had been issued passports to travel to Marseilles.[81] Their fate was still in doubt since no pronouncement had yet been made on their conduct and, given Ricard's speech, they had reason to fear condemnation and dismissal. Albert de Rioms made the long journey to Paris to defend himself and his officers, but the Assembly denied his request to speak at its bar on December 28.[82] The long-awaited report on the "Toulon Affair" from the *Comité de rapports* was even more ominous for the naval officers because it implied that Albert de Rioms was guilty of the charges made against him by the Permanent Committee. Nompère de Champagny denied such a conclusion vehemently on January 15, 1790. He argued that the accusations were based on misunderstanding and exaggeration, and he moved that the Commandant be declared exempt from all guilt. Nompère de Champagny also issued a warning: "If the Assembly does not show that it disapproves of the conduct of the National Guard, the city of Toulon will have imitators. . ."[83]

Ricard responded to this speech by again insisting that popular authority must prevail over that of king's officers. He proclaimed that the origins of the "Affair" went beyond the incidents of November, as did Albert de Rioms' imprudence and culpable "determination to be inexorable." Ricard countered any appeals to the Commandant's naval record: "I would like to be able to justify his conduct by his exploits, but when I cannot find the citizen within the hero, I will always abandon him to the law. . ."[84] Having damned Albert de Rioms, Ricard became the benevolent legislator and proposed a compromise by which the conduct of Toulon's municipality and National Guard would be declared satisfactory, but the faults of the naval officers would be excused by virtue of their past service and future loyalty.[85]

---

[81] Letter of December 15, 1789 to the National Assembly from the President and representatives of the commune of Toulon; AP, vol. 10, p. 692. It is significant that the prisoners were only released on December 15 following the reception of an order from the National Assembly. The municipality had received an earlier letter from Saint-Priest, Minister of the King's Household, which ordered the officers' release. However the Toulonnais decided that since the order did not have "the certain will of the King," and because Albert de Rioms had been arrested at the public clamour, they would await the decision of the National Assembly; AP, vol. 10, p. 638.

[82] AP, vol. 11, p. 30.

[83] Ibid., p. 190.

[84] Ibid., p. 190.

[85] Ibid., p. 191.

On January 16 the final session of debate on the "Toulon Affair" displayed the full range of attitudes in the Constituent Assembly, and reveals that fundamental notions of governance were at stake. The duc de Liancourt began by suggesting that difficulties and uncertainties during a great Revolution caused reprehensible actions to result from the best of intentions. While he insisted that Albert de Rioms' conduct had been based on his desire to preserve the naval base, the Commandant had spoken immoderately and had forgotten that the Revolution demanded a new form of command.[86] If this rationale excused the naval officers, it exonerated the Permanent Committee and the National Guard. The guardsmen may have been deceived, but "the People can never conceive of committing crime. . .," and Liancourt proposed that the Assembly render justice to the patriotic intentions of Toulon's municipality and declare the naval officers free of guilt.[87] Robespierre rejected such equivocation utterly. Nothing would be so unjust or so impolitic, he argued, as to bestow praise or absolution upon Albert de Rioms, who had manifested Counter-Revolutionary principles, or to place any hint of blame on the Toulonnais, whose conduct had followed only legitimate resistance to oppression. Robespierre declared: "Above all, I fear to see a decree of the National Assembly which discourages patriotism and encourages the enemies of liberty."[88]

Malouet also opposed an ambiguous pronouncement: his conviction that executive authority must be upheld was as strong as Robespierre's belief that it could not be trusted. Malouet saw the Commandant and his officers as the innocent victims of intrigue and violence.[89] In a long but cogent speech, he analyzed the charges against Albert de Rioms and argued that official complaints emerged only after December 1, when those who had violated the officers' rights needed justification for their actions.[90] Yet the guilty party was neither Toulon's municipality,

---

[86] "Si l'habitude d'un commandement sans opposition, d'une autorité sans bornes, tel que le service de la mer rend nécessaire, lui a paru quelquefois faire oublier, en 1789, que la révolution, désirée par toute la nation, et dont chaque jour augmentait l'influence, exigeait d'autres formes"; AP, vol. 11, p. 210. Liancourt gives no indication of what these "other forms" would be, and he seems to imply that strong naval authority was necessary at sea but not ashore.

[87] AP, vol. 11, p. 211.

[88] Ibid.

[89] Pierre-Victor Malouet, *Défense du commandant et des officiers de la marine, prisonniers à Toulon. Deuxième opinion de M. Malouet* (1790) [BN 8 Le29 361]. See also AP, vol. 11, pp. 211–221.

[90] Malouet, *Défense*, pp. 2–15.

71

which had been unable to act freely, nor the People, who had been excited by vicious rumours. The true criminals, according to Malouet, were those who instigated the riot, and the National Guard volunteers who stormed naval headquarters.[91] Malouet then examined the individual depositions in the report prepared for the Assembly, and rejected them in terms of their irrelevance and contradiction.[92] The naval officers were innocent by virtue of the evidence, and thus deserved justice. Malouet went beyond the "Affair" to plead for an end to calumny, universal agitation, and violence: "The destruction of all authorities prepares a return to despotism."[93]

The Decree of January 16 on the "Toulon Affair," foreshadowed in the proposals of Ricard and Liancourt, proclaimed that none of those involved were guilty: "The National Assembly, presuming the motives to have been favorable which animated Monsieur d'Albert de Rioms, the other naval officers implicated in this affair, the Municipal Officers and National Guard of Toulon, declares that there is no grounds for inculpation."[94] The Commandant and his subordinates were thus cleared of any charges, but the Decree had serious ramifications for the fate of the navy under the Revolution. The Constituent Assembly would not support naval officers, whom many deputies saw as politically suspect aristocrats, if those who challenged or defied them appealed to the legitimacy of the "People's Will." The majority of the deputies considered the navy's autonomy from local interference less vital than acknowledging popular authority to be superior to executive power.

Naval officers at Toulon were well aware that any pronouncement made by the Constituent Assembly on the events of December 1 would have tremendous significance. Albert de Rioms and the others who had been imprisoned were most concerned that their conduct be vindicated.[95] The officer corps at Toulon appealed to both the king and the Minister of Marine to influence the Assembly's decision. In a joint letter to the

---

[91] Ibid., pp. 14–17.
[92] Ibid., pp. 18–25.
[93] Ibid., p. 30. See also the summary of the fifteen principles of the *Club des Impartiaux*, in Griffiths, pp. 86–88.
[94] AP, vol. 11, p. 222. See also Toulon 4 A 1/364.
[95] See: "Déclaration du Cte de Bonneval, Major-Général de la Marine, sur les Evénements qui lui sont relatifs, passés à Toulon du 1er au 15 décembre 1789"; and "Copie de la lettre de M. le Cte de Bonneval à Mm. le Marquis de Vaudreuil, Malouet, De Virieu, Vt de Mirabeau, abbé de Bonneval; en leur envoyant sa Déclaration. A Toulon le 15 décembre 1789"; Toulon 4 A 1/364.

king, the officers swore that they had received no orders from their Commandant which threatened the life or liberty of their fellow citizens, and that he had given them an example of outstanding civic virtue.[96] They repeated the request that Albert de Rioms and the others be returned to their posts in a letter to La Luzerne, but this time with direct reference to the discussions in the National Assembly and the need to justify the officers' conduct.[97] These expressions of solidarity, while motivated by personal loyalty, indicate a growing conviction that the fate of the navy in Toulon would be determined by whether or not the government in Paris would assert itself against the authority of the municipality.

Such concern was not confined to Toulon, and it was widely perceived that the outcome of the "Affair" would have grave implications for the entire fleet. Naval officers at Brest were quick to show support for those who had been detained, and to warn that they could face a similar fate.[98] They expressed their concern in a letter to the king which stated that, having endured difficult circumstances at Brest for six months, the officers were now forced to break their silence over the events of December 1. Naval officers would become powerless if municipalities and the National Guard had the right to arrest, imprison, and judge those entrusted with the king's authority. The officers of Brest echoed Albert de Rioms' objection to volunteer guardsmen and argued that respect and subordination would only suffer if members of the militia in naval ports, most of whom were directly or indirectly in the service of the fleet, could contribute to the humiliation of officers ashore.[99] This appeal to the king was sent in care of the Minister, and the officers informed La Luzerne that they had no objections to legal punishment for the abuse of authority: "but it is important that any commanding officer have assured authority; the good of the state wants it, the success of our fleets depends upon it."[100]

---

[96] "Copie de la lettre du Corps des officiers de la marine du Département de Toulon, écrite au Roi. Du 1er janvier 1790"; Toulon 4 A 1/364.
[97] "Copie de la lettre du Corps des officiers de la marine du Département de Toulon, écrite à M. le Cte de La Luzerne. 1 janvier 1790"; Toulon 4 A 1/364.
[98] "Copie de la lettre de M. le Vte de Marigny à M. le Cte de Bonneval, chef de division, Major-Général de la Marine. Récu 30 décembre 1789"; Toulon 4 A 1/364.
[99] "Copie de la lettre du Corps de la Marine du Département de Brest, au Roi [no date]"; Toulon 4 A 1/364.
[100] "Copie de la lettre du Corps de la Marine du Département de Brest, au Ministre de la Marine [no date]"; Toulon 4 A 1/364.

This concern for the maintenance of naval authority in the face of aggressive local administrations reinforced fears that the arrest of Albert de Rioms, if not punished, would encourage the spread of defiance. The naval officers of Rochefort expressed this sentiment in a powerful letter to La Luzerne. They asked the Minister to solicit the Representatives of the Nation to make a severe example of those guilty of insubordination and assault against the commanders at Toulon:

if they do not take this indispensable measure all discipline will be destroyed, the multitude will henceforth make the law. The ports, the ships of war, and even merchantmen, will be exposed to mutinies and insurrections. Beyond this imminent danger to the State, naval officers envisage a particular danger to themselves; their honour, more dear than their lives, will depend upon the caprice of vicious persons who will be able to seduce and lead crews astray, since a prejudicial impunity in these circumstances will authorize them to commit disorders from which they believe they can derive advantage.[101]

Thus there was anxiety throughout the navy that the "Toulon Affair" could herald the collapse of discipline if the assault on naval authority, itself a reflection of royal executive power, was permitted.

The reaction to the Decree of January 16 was bitter, particularly in Toulon. The officers who had been imprisoned protested that the Decree, which presumed no guilt, did not constitute a judgement, and they feared deadly effects to public order, military discipline, and subordination, all so necessary to the security of arsenals and operation of naval forces.[102] The entire officer corps at Toulon submitted a collective letter, almost a petition, to the President of the National Assembly which expressed great disappointment. The deputies had failed to give justice to the Commandant for the shameful treatment he had suffered and the Decree offered a dangerous example by exonerating the National Guardsmen, many of whom belonged to the naval

[101] "Copie de la lettre écrite par les officiers de la Marine Royale de Rochefort, à M. le Cte de La Luzerne, 24 décembre 1789"; Toulon 4 A 1/364.
[102] "Copie de la lettre au Roi par MM. le Cte d'Albert de Rioms, le marquis de Castellet, le Cte de Bonneval, le commandeur du Villages, Gautier, et Cte de Brovès [no date]"; Toulon 4 A 1/364. Albert de Rioms sent his own message to the President of the Constituent Assembly which, under the veneer of respectful acceptance of the Decree, criticized the substitution of praise for justice and pleaded for an end to disorder and the implementation of the rule of law: "Copie de la lettre de M. le Cte d'Albert de Rioms à M. le Président de l'assemblée nationale, 22 janvier 1790"; Toulon 4 A 1/364.

service.[103] The Minister of Marine could only advise the naval officers to abstain from further protests, despite his sympathy with their position. La Luzerne warned the new Commandant at Toulon, Glandevès, to prevent his subordinates from reviving the memory of the recent events which could only reignite animosities.[104] Clearly the Minister could not affect the decision reached by the National Assembly, and it seems that he could do little to support the navy against local pressures.[105]

Despite the manifestations of solidarity and the collective protests over the "Toulon Affair," not all naval officers expressed vehement opposition to the emergence of popular authority. The bitter quarrel between Albert de Rioms and Joseph, marquis de Flotte[106] reveals two very different responses to the Revolution. Flotte was one of the senior officers at Toulon in 1789, but he was not arrested on December 1 despite being present at naval headquarters. Flotte attempted to justify his conduct on the fateful day in a letter to Albert de Rioms, and to defend himself against accusations of cowardice. He admitted retiring to the apartment where Albert de Rioms' family had taken refuge, but claimed that the Commandant had ordered him not to venture outside. Flotte later fled to Marseilles where he adopted an alias; he argued that these precautions had been necessary given the manner in which the officer corps had been compromised.[107] Albert de Rioms' reply was a

[103] "Copie de la lettre de MM. les officiers de la marine du Département de Toulon, écrite à M. le Président de l'assemblée Nationale. A Toulon, 26 janvier 1790"; Toulon 4 A 1/364.
[104] "Copie de la lettre du Ministre à M. le Commandant de Glandevès en réponse à celle que les officiers de la Marine du Département de Toulon écrite le 26 janvier 1790. Paris, le 4 février 1790"; Toulon 4 A 1/364.
[105] See also the Minister's reply to the Rochefort letter in which he states that his influence is limited in regard to the debates in the Assembly, and he recommends that the navy maintain good relations with civil authorities in Rochefort: "Copie de la lettre du Ministre écrite à M. le Vte de Vaudreuil en reponse à cette écrite au Roi et à M. le Cte de La Luzerne par Mm. les officiers de la marine du département de Rochefort le 24 décembre 1789. A Paris le 31 décembre 1789"; Toulon 4 A 1/364.
[106] Joseph, marquis de Flotte, or "Flottes," was born in 1734 at Saint-Pierre-d'Argençon (Hautes-Alpes) and joined the navy as a *garde de la marine* in 1754. Following service in both the Seven Years' War and War of American Independence, Flotte was promoted to *chef de division* in 1786 and carried out a diplomatic mission on the Guinea coast prior to the Revolution. See: Taillemite, *Dictionnaire*, pp. 121–122; Georges Six, *Dictionnaire biographique des généraux et amiraux français de la Révolution et de l'Empire (1792–1814)*, 2 vols. (Paris: Georges Saffroy, 1934), I, pp. 454–455.
[107] "Copie de la lettre de M. le Cte de Flotte à M. le Cte d'Albert, Commandant de la marine. Toulon, 21 janvier 1790"; Toulon 4 A 1/364.

scathing condemnation of Flotte for hiding when he had not been among those proscribed by the militia. Not only had he hidden, but he had been the last to leave naval headquarters and, unlike the other officers who were not arrested, he left under disguise. Even more reprehensible for Albert de Rioms was Flotte's failure immediately to take up command in Toulon, a duty demanded by Flotte's seniority. Albert de Rioms dismissed Flotte's justifications for leaving his post and concluded on a tone of pure contempt: "dissatisfied with your conduct during my detention, I must say that I was happy during such cruel and critical moments to have had only you to complain of."[108]

The conflict between these two men went beyond personal animosity arising from charges of cowardly behavior. Flotte refused to sign a declaration prepared by other officers in support of Albert de Rioms, and he defended his actions in terms of reaching an understanding with local civil authority: "I had offered words of peace to the municipality that the good of the state and public security rendered indispensable from a leader. I was unable, therefore, to give my adhesion to a document which could only perpetuate troubles without adding anything to the cause of our generals and other officers."[109] This notion that a commander's duty was to achieve peaceful coexistence with a Revolutionary municipality, by making concessions if necessary, is a striking contrast to the sentiments shown by Albert de Rioms less than two months before. It was probably no coincidence that Flotte signed a declaration to the National Assembly of December 17 which stressed the virtue of armed forces remaining within the letter of the law.[110] Flotte challenged his Commandant's right to criticize his conduct, and stated that the Minister of Marine and the citizens of Toulon would judge whether or not he had proved useful since Albert de Rioms' departure. Albert de Rioms replied that the Minister and the officer corps would make an account of Flotte's faults.

It is unclear how many other officers were prepared to adopt Flotte's stance towards the developments of 1789. It would appear that most

[108] "Copie de la lettre de M. le Cte d'Albert à M. le Cte de Flotte, capitaine de vaisseau. Paris, 2 février 1790"; Toulon 4 A 1/364.
[109] "Flotte à . . . d'Albert . . ., 21 janvier 1790"; Toulon 4 A 1/364.
[110] Ricard de Séalt read this declaration from naval officers at Toulon in the Constituent Assembly on January 2, 1790. The declaration defended the Barrois and Dauphiné regiments, which had not intervened on December 1, 1789, on the grounds that they were obliged to hold their positions because martial law had not been proclaimed; AP, vol. 11, p. 63.

continued to serve in the fleet and ports with the conviction that naval authority should remain above political turmoil. Historians of the French navy, however, identified the imprisonment of Albert de Rioms and the Assembly's response as an ominous turning point. Mahan's statement is typical of this interpretation: "The Toulon affair was the signal for the spread of mutiny among the crews and the breaking-up of the corps of commissioned sea-officers."[111] It is accurate that insubordination became rampant in 1790 and discipline collapsed throughout the fleet. These developments reflected the "Toulon Affair," but were not simply the results of the failure to punish those who arrested Albert de Rioms.

A struggle between competing authorities developed in Toulon during 1789. The naval Commandant, whose authority was a reflection of royal executive power, resisted the incursions of popular authority based in the Permanent Committee. As the economic situation in the port deteriorated, Albert de Rioms remained uncompromising in his insistence on order and he forbade naval personnel from enlisting in the National Guard. The struggle reached a climax when a riot by arsenal workers presented the opportunity for Revolutionaries to challenge naval authority directly and to arrest the Commandant. The navy appealed to the National Assembly, but the deputies would not support officers of the king over a Revolutionary commune. Yet the "Toulon Affair" involved issues more fundamental than the illegal imprisonment of the Commandant, or even the precedent of violent defiance. At stake was the continued authority of central government in France if Popular Sovereignty was not to be confined to the legislation of the National Assembly. This would render the maintenance of any naval authority and the autonomy of the fleet from local interference impossible. As Malouet put it, "no administrator or public officer can fulfil his duties . . . when each part of the People believes itself to be the Nation and authorizes itself to exercise sovereignty . . ."[112]

---

[111] Mahan, *Influence of Sea Power upon the French Revolution*, I, p. 44. See also: Guérin, V, p. 234; Chevalier, pp. 11–12; Tramond, pp. 552–553; Martray, p. 62.
[112] Malouet, *Opinion*, p. 9.

NAVAL REORGANIZATION AND THE MUTINY AT BREST, 1790–1791

In October 1789 the Constituent Assembly appointed a Marine Committee to reorganize the navy according to Revolutionary principles. The work of this committee, and the debates on its proposals, occurred in the shadow of a great mutiny which paralyzed the Atlantic fleet at Brest for several months in 1790–1791. Any assessment of Revolutionary naval reform must also examine this insurrection, which both reflected and influenced developments in Paris. Historians of the French navy have condemned the Assembly's reorganization as strongly as they deplored the collapse of discipline in the fleet. Léon Guérin, and those who followed him, claimed that the Constituent Assembly destroyed the professional officer corps through the disastrous assimilation of the fighting navy with the merchant service.[1] Yet this interpretation exaggerates the nature of the Marine Committee's reforms and their impact on the fleet. Despite the criticism of aristocratic privilege in the navy, Norman Hampson argued that the Assembly's reorganization did not weaken the position of officers from the *Grand Corps*.[2] The struggle between popular and executive authority affected the navy far more than any specific legislation.

The mutiny at Brest coincided with the climax of a conflict between naval commanders and the port's Commune. While distrusting officers as aristocrats, Brest's municipality challenged their authority as king's officers by claiming to be the local embodiment of the nation. Yet expressions of the "People's Will" were not confined to the Revolutionary Commune. The Brest mutiny reveals that the struggle between

---

[1] Guérin, V, p. 292. See also: Chevalier, pp. 24–27; Mahan, *Influence of Sea Power upon the French Revolution*, I, pp. 51–54; Tramond, pp. 557–558; Taillemite, *L'Histoire ignorée*, pp. 281–282; Martray, pp. 65–67.
[2] Hampson, "Comité de Marine," esp. p. 147.

competing notions of authority had begun to politicize the sailors, and crews justified insubordination as political protest. Brest's Commune was prepared to support mutiny, to some degree, in order to assert the power of popular authority against that of naval commanders. The Constituent Assembly's vindication of this local interference, as well as of the mutineers, signalled the central government's abandonment of the navy.

Two months before Albert de Rioms was imprisoned in Toulon, the Constituent Assembly established its Marine Committee. The marquis de Vaudreuil, one of its members, stated the Committee's objectives on April 15, 1790:

your committee has occupied itself in preparing the elements of a maritime constitution which, subordinate to the principles of the national constitution and joined with it by its primary connections, can at last acquire this desirable stability which characterizes institutions founded on reason. To examine to what degree of strength the French navy should be brought within the political system of Europe to conserve an advantageous equilibrium, without augmenting our means beyond our needs; to fix, according to the results of this examination, the expenses that this demands; to submit the several systems of administration which have followed one another in the course of a century to a severe analysis; to interrogate, at the same time, the maritime constitutions of foreigners: such is the plan that your committee has embraced.[3]

The Marine Committee was to consider the future of French naval power within the larger context of national regeneration undertaken by the Constituent Assembly. Given its privileged officer corps, the fleet seemed a prime target for Revolutionary reform. The Committee included twelve members elected on October 13.[4] Initially they were divided evenly between the nobility and the third estate, and five of the nobles were or had been naval officers: the marquis de Vaudreuil, the comte de Latouche-Tréville, the chevalier de Loynes de La Coudraye, Nompère de Champagny, and the marquis de La Poype-Vertrieux.[5]

---

[3] "le Marquis de Vaudreuil, au nom du comité de marine, présente un Rapport sur les classes de la marine, 15 avril 1790"; AP, vol. 13, p. 45.
[4] For the creation of the Committee on October 6, 1789, see AP, vol. 9, pp. 354–355; for the election of its members, see pp. 414–415.
[5] Regarding their backgrounds and service records, see: Taillemite, *Dictionnaire*, pp. 60–61, 186–187, 199–200, 335; Six, *Dictionnaire biographique*, pp. 66–68; Guérin, V, p. 275.

The deputies of the third estate included Malouet, and four men with direct connections to merchant shipping and commerce: Bégouen, Paul Nairac, de Curt, La Ville-Leroux.[6] Hampson described this membership in terms of a division between aristocratic naval officers and mercantile or colonial interests, as well as an uneasy balance between the political "Right" and "Left." He suggested that the conflict of interests and principles meant that the consideration of options for naval reorganization led to constant political quarrels.[7] This connection between social origins and political commitment should not be overstated, and the conflicts, both inside the Committee and on the floor of the Assembly, were not confined to issues of privilege or professionalism: maintaining central control of the navy deeply concerned Malouet and other deputies.

The plans for reforming the navy included the need to stabilize naval finances and maintain an effective but affordable fleet.[8] These issues were not particularly contentious, but controversy existed over the administration of ports and arsenals. In April 1790, Malouet proposed transferring control of dockyard operations from the Commandant to the naval Intendant.[9] This represented a reversal of Castries' ordinance of 1786, which guaranteed the ascendancy of the sword over the pen, and it aroused opposition from sea-officers in the Assembly.[10] The Constituent Assembly returned the Bill to the Committee and the issue of port administration was not settled until 1791. In July of that year Defermon proposed that naval ports and the arsenals should be firmly in civilian control.[11] All work in the dockyards was to be placed under the direction of a new naval *ordonnateur*, later called the *ordonnateur*

---

[6] The other noble was the army officer de Vialis, and the final member of the third estate was Alquier, a lawyer from La Rochelle. Six other members were added in June 1790: the comte de Rochegude, a noble and naval officer; Defermon, Legendre, and Poulain de Corbion who were Breton lawyers; Ledean, a merchant, and La Borde de Méréville, a banker. See Hampson, "Comité de Marine," p. 136.

[7] Hampson, "Comité de Marine," esp. pp. 130–133.

[8] See for example, "Rapport fait à l'Assemblée nationale sur les dépenses et le régime économique de la marine, par M. Malouet, membre du comité de la marine, 19 avril 1790"; AP, vol. 13, pp. 121–132, 133–143.

[9] Ibid., p. 133.

[10] See Hampson, "Comité de Marine," p. 135, and Guérin, V, pp. 274–277.

[11] "M. Defermon, au nom du comité de la marine, présente un projet de décret sur l'administration de la marine, 17 juillet 1791"; AP, vol. 28, pp. 381–384. The second article of the *projet de décret* stated: "L'administration des ports sera civile; elle sera incompatible avec toutes fonctions militaires"; p. 381.

civil.[12] Historians have represented this as a triumph for the pen,[13] but the decree adopted on September 21, 1791 stated that retired naval Commandants would be eligible for the post.[14] The reduction of the Commandant's authority indicates distrust of the *Grand Corps*, but the fact that the Assembly did not simply reinvest full control in the Intendants suggests a desire to separate naval administration from all former agents of royal executive power, both of the pen and the sword.

Reform of naval recruitment also provoked conflict within the Marine Committee. Pouget, the Intendant-general of naval *classes*, submitted an important report on this problem to the Committee.[15] Because a state's naval strength lay in the number of trained sailors it could mobilize, Pouget insisted that the French navy would be destroyed if the seaman's profession did not carry some obligation to military service. He argued that the existing system of *classes* was the superior means of manning the fleet, and of conserving sailors' liberty to work in commerce and the fisheries. The Committee was united in agreeing that the *classes*, as reformed by Castries' ordinance of 1784, should be retained as the basis of naval recruitment, but it was divided over how the system should be administered. Pouget defended the 1784 solution whereby retired naval officers resident in the various *quartiers* checked

---

[12] The third article of Defermon's *projet de décret* stated: "La direction générale de tous les travaux et approvisionnements, de la compatibilité, de toutes les dépenses de la police générale et des classes du ressort, sera confiée, dans chaque grand port, à un administrateur unique, sous le titre d'ordonnateur"; AP, vol. 28, p. 381. *Ordonnateur* was the title given to administrative officers in the dockyards long before the Revolution, but those created in 1791 replaced the Intendants as well as taking over the jurisdiction passed to the Commandants since 1776. See Rouvier, p. 14.
[13] Hampson, "Comité de Marine," p. 147 states that the Bill implied such a reversal, and argues that it received little opposition in the Assembly because the "Right" had boycotted debate following the Flight to Varennes. Taillemite, *L'Histoire ignorée*, p. 285 states that the *ordonnateurs civils* returned naval administration to Colbert's system, and he claims Malouet inspired their creation: in fact Malouet wanted serious amendments to the proposal, but did not receive support.
[14] "M. Defermon, au nom du comité de la marine, présente ensuite un projet de décret d'application pour l'administration de la marine, 21 septembre 1791"; AP, vol. 31, pp. 140–144. In its original form the *projet de décret* stated that *ordonnateurs* would be chosen by the king from among Intendants, *commissaires-généraux*, *ingénieurs-généraux* and *ingénieurs-directeurs*. It was amended to include "*anciens commandants des ports*" in this list before being adopted; p. 140.
[15] "Mémoire sur les classes de la marine, lu au comité de la marine de l'Assemblée nationale, le 11 février 1790, par M. Pouget, intendant-général des classes"; AP, vol. 11, pp. 557–574.

81

the authority of the *commissaires des classes*. He claimed that the inspection of the levies by these officers, whom the seamen knew and trusted, prevented abuses and increased the efficiency and humanity of the system. Despite these arguments, the majority of the Marine Committee believed that sailors should be treated as citizens when ashore and therefore were entitled to be governed by their own representatives. On April 15, 1790 the Committee proposed that authority over the administration of the *classes* be given to *syndics* elected by the seamen of each *quartier*.[16] Vaudreuil introduced this majority proposal, but stated his own opposition, and that of other members of the Committee, in a minority report advocating the status quo of 1784. Vaudreuil and La Coudraye insisted that control of the *classes*, and the agents who administered them, must remain with the executive power because only central authority could grasp the overall needs of the fleet.[17] The debate thus reveals fundamental differences in the conception of the navy's relationship to political authority, not merely technical disagreement. The question reverted to the Committee until December 31, 1790 when the deputies adopted a new proposal for the election of *syndics*.[18] The Assembly thus removed authority from the navy's traditional commanders, and it entrusted the *classes* to local democratic supervision rather than executive control.

Reform of the officer corps was the issue of most political significance for the Marine Committee, and of greatest potential consequence for the fleet. Despite Castries' creation of the *sous-lieutenants*, the *Grand Corps* remained essentially aristocratic and thus challenged the Revolutionary ideal of equality. Hereditary nobility was abolished in June 1790,[19] and the Constituent Assembly could hardly leave the naval officer corps unreformed. Moreover, the deputies faced considerable

---

[16] "Rapport et projet de décret sur les classes de la marine, 15 avril 1790"; AP, vol. 13, pp. 45–50.
[17] "Observations et projet de décret sur les classes de la marine, par MM. le marquis de Vaudreuil, lieutenant-général des armées navales, deputé de Castelnaudary, et le chevalier de La Coudraye, ancien lieutenant de vaisseau, deputé du Poitou, l'un et l'autre membres du comité de marine, 19 avril 1790"; AP, vol. 13, pp. 117–120. For a summary of the debates on naval conscription, see Hampson, "Comité de Marine," pp. 134–135.
[18] "M. Defermon présente un rapport du comité de la marine sur les classes des gens de mer, 31 décembre 1790"; AP, vol. 21, pp. 735–739.
[19] See "Decree Abolishing Hereditary Nobility and Titles, 19 June 1790," in John Hall Stewart (ed.), *A Documentary Survey of the French Revolution* (New York: Macmillan, 1951; repr. 1963), pp. 142–143.

public pressure in this regard. Several third estate *cahiers de doléances* of 1789 demanded equality between nobles and non-nobles in the navy, and some complained specifically against regulations which prevented merchant officers from obtaining rank within the *Grand Corps*.[20] In 1789 *sous-lieutenants* petitioned the National Assembly to protest their perpetually inferior status,[21] and naval petty officers also demanded that their opportunities for advancement not be limited to the grade of *sous-lieutenant*.[22] It was not surprising that reform of the officer corps was the principal element of naval reorganization considered by the Marine Committee.

Yet such reform took place in a broad context of institutional regeneration. On June 26, 1790, de Curt presented a Bill which defined the constitutional principles of the navy. These were intended to be the foundation of naval reorganization, just as the Declaration of the Rights of Man and Citizen were to be the basis of France's new Constitution. De Curt's opening remarks, as well as the *projet de décret*, made it clear that the fleet's primary role should be the protection of French commerce and colonies, rather than upholding the honour of the flag.[23] This suggestion reflected mercantile resentment of the aloof navy, a sentiment which was ardent in some port chambers of commerce. Yet more significantly, the Bill insisted that the navy was to be firmly in the hands of the nation. The king would continue to be Commander-in-Chief, but the National Assembly would approve naval credits annually and determine conditions for promotions, recognizing all citizens as eligible to obtain the highest rank in the officer corps.

The Committee's determination to prevent the navy from becoming a weapon of Counter-Revolution is even more revealing. One article of the Bill forbade foreign naval forces from entering French ports or from being employed by the state without the assent of the legislature,

---

[20] See examples cited in Lévy-Schneider, I, pp. 298–300.
[21] Letter of comte de Bonneval to Marigny, major-general at Brest, August 30, 1789; Toulon 4 A 1/364. See also Guyon, pp. 448, 455.
[22] *Réclamations des maîtres, seconds-maîtres, contre-maîtres & quartier-maîtres d'équipage du Port de Brest; présentées au Conseil général & permanent de cette ville* (Brest: Malassis, 1789); Brest "Fonds Levot" 1988 [7].
[23] "Rapport et projet de décret du comité de la marine sur les principes constitutionnels de la marine, 26 juin 1790"; AP, vol. 16, pp. 468–470. See also Rouvier, p. 10. Hampson, "Comité de la Marine," p. 136 sees the emphasis on commerce protection as an indication that the mercantile interests had gained the balance of power in the Committee following the election of new members on June 14, 1790.

and another forbade French warships from transporting foreign troops. Furthermore, all naval personnel were to swear an oath of loyalty which included the obligation to: "lend assistance requistioned by administrative corps and civil or municipal officers, and never to employ those under their orders against any citizen if this action is not by such requisition, which will always be read to the assembled troops."[24] The military's obedience to the legislature was essential to the establishment of political liberty, and it was necessary to limit executive prerogatives regarding the armed forces. The emigration and open hostility towards the Revolution of prominent military aristocrats, the Prince de Condé in particular, seemed to substantiate some deputies' suspicions of all king's officers.[25] Yet it was the Assembly's distrust of executive power generally which prevented it from perceiving any danger to the nation's naval forces from the interference of local civil administrations.

An international crisis which threatened to involve France in a maritime war underscored the urgency of consolidating national control of the navy. In May 1790 the Nootka Sound controversy, a bitter dispute between Britain and Spain over the right to colonize the Pacific coast of North America, led the Spanish government to invoke the Family Compact and to demand a firm statement of alliance from the Constituent Assembly. The British government sought to keep France neutral, but began to prepare for war.[26] Although generally sympathetic to Spain, the Assembly responded to the situation by declaring its refusal to participate in wars of aggression.[27] These pacific principles were sincere, but a naval war was unthinkable given the financial situation.[28] Nevertheless the French navy had every reason to believe that war was

[24] AP, vol. 16, p. 470. Compare this oath to that of August 1789 which army officers were required to swear, in L. G. Wickham Legg (ed.), *Select Documents Illustrative of the History of the French Revolution. The Constituent Assembly*, 2 vols. (Oxford: Oxford University Press, 1905), I, p. 205. See also S. F. Scott, pp. 73–74, 151.
[25] Regarding the early Counter-Revolutionary activities of the duc d'Artois and the Prince de Condé, see: Doyle, *Oxford History*, pp. 146–148, 298–301; Sutherland, *France 1789–1815*, pp. 107–108; Sydenham, *French Revolution*, p. 79.
[26] See Doyle, *Oxford History*, pp. 164–165, and Mahan, *Influence of Sea Power upon the French Revolution*, I, pp. 44–45. Regarding the British diplomatic efforts to keep France neutral, see H. V. Evans, "The Nootka Sound Controversy in Anglo-French Diplomacy – 1790," *Journal of Modern History*, 46 (1974), 609–640.
[27] See for example J. M. Thompson, p. 271.
[28] Acerra and Meyer, p. 92. See La Luzerne's letter of May 27, 1790 to the President of the National Assembly, which estimated the cost of outfitting the squadron of 14 ships of the line and 14 frigates at 2,036,045 *livres* for the first month, with an additional 500,000 *livres* for payment of officers and crews; AP, vol. 15, pp. 705–706.

imminent,[29] and La Luzerne ordered fourteen ships of the line fitted out at Brest to counter the English threat. The Minister of Marine appointed Albert de Rioms to command this squadron.[30] It remains unclear whether or not La Luzerne anticipated that this nomination would be unpopular, but the transfer of Albert de Rioms to Brest coincided with a new collision between naval and popular authority. On this occasion, however, national legislation provoked the crisis.

On August 21, 1790 the Constituent Assembly adopted a new Penal Code for the navy, which encompassed both regulations for Courts Martial and a list of offences and the punishments to be awarded. When introducing the Bill for the Marine Committee, Nompère de Champagny reported that it was imperative to end excessive severity against seamen who committed minor transgressions by introducing a gradation of punishments. The award of penalties should no longer be arbitrary: sailors, as French citizens, had the right to be tried by their peers.[31] Nompère de Champagny admitted the proposal was imperfect, but insisted that a new Penal Code was needed immediately. Such sentiment reflected pressure from the navy to clarify marine justice quickly to prevent the breakdown of discipline.[32] The new Penal Code introduced the reform of trial by jury for certain crimes, but retained many traditionally harsh punishments. "Keel-hauling," flogging, and running the gauntlet were maintained, and seamen could be sentenced to ride a capstan bar, to be tied to the mast, or to be clapped in leg-irons for minor offenses.[33] Despite the spirit of reform in which they were introduced, the announcement of these new laws provoked mutiny in the Atlantic fleet.

The Assembly first received news of mutiny at Brest on September 23, 1790 when the Minister of Marine informed the deputies that,

---

[29] See the apprehensive reports of British mobilization and fleet movements in the English Channel from May to July 1790: Marine BB 3/1, ff. 3–13 (Dunkerque); ff. 47–60 (Le Havre); f. 102 (Cherbourg); ff. 128–146 (St Malo).
[30] See: Dupont, p. 112; Guérin, V, p. 236; Rouvier, p. 26.
[31] "Nompère de Champagny présente un rapport du comité de marine sur les peines à infliger dans l'armée navale, 16 août 1790"; AP, vol. 18, pp. 94–97.
[32] Marine BB 4/1, f. 48. See aso La Luzerne's letter of August 5, 1790 to the President of the Assembly which reported on dangerous fermentation on the ships of both the Levant and West Indies stations and the necessity of reestablishing discipline in the navy; AP, vol. 17, pp. 626–627.
[33] "Code pénal pour être exécuté sur les vaisseaux, escadres et armées navales, et dans les ports et arsenaux, Annexe à la séance du 21 août 1790"; AP, vol. 18, pp. 207–212.

following demonstrations on September 1, an uprising had occurred
aboard warships in the roadstead on September 6. Sailors defied their
officers and went ashore to demand that Brest's municipality obtain the
suspension of the new Penal Code.[34] The crews resented the use of
humiliating physical punishments: sailors considered leg-irons with trai-
ling chains particularly offensive because they resembled the treatment
of convict labourers, the "galley-slaves," in the arsenal.[35] In the Marine
Committee's report on the insurrection, Defermon assured the Assembly
that the sailors could be shown that the analogy with convicts was false
and that the new Penal Code was both benevolent and humane. The
danger of the mutiny was thus minimized. Despite Albert de Rioms'
plea that either the squadron should be demobilized or commissioners
should be sent to restore the men to obedience, the Assembly merely
voted to disregard the crews' demands.[36]

Meanwhile the crisis at Brest escalated. The Minister had ordered a
division of eight ships under the command of the chevalier de Rivière
to sail for the West Indies as part of the government's effort to contain
growing rebellion in the colonies. On September 11 the crew of Captain
de Rivière's own ship, *Le Ferme* (74), refused to weigh anchor and get
under way, and demanded two months worth of advance pay.[37] This
open defiance shocked naval commanders, but they might have contained
the mutiny and persuaded the sailors to return to duty had it not been
for the unexpected arrival of *Le Léopard* (74) on September 14. This
ship had been stationed off Saint-Domingue when her crew mutinied,
abandoned Captain de La Galissonnière and most of his officers ashore,
and embarked eighty-five deputies of the colony's rebel assembly, *l'Assemblée de Saint-Marc*. Also coming aboard as passengers were troops

---

[34] "Lettre de M. de La Luzerne, 13 septembre 1790"; AP, vol. 18, p. 729. The other
grievance voiced by the sailors was that the decree raising their pay had neglected
several classes of seamen. Acerra and Meyer, p. 122 point out that it remains unclear
how much of the fleet actually participated in this first phase of the mutiny, although
it is usually claimed that 2,000 sailors went ashore. See also Philippe Henwood and
Edmond Monage, *Brest. Un port en Révolution, 1789–1799* (Rennes: Editions
Ouest-France, 1989), p. 115.
[35] "Rapport sur l'insurrection à Brest, 15 septembre 1790"; AP, vol. 18, p. 766. It
should be noted that the form of corporal punishment in the Penal Code was not the
subject of significant debate in the Assembly. Robespierre spoke against the Code, but
on the grounds that for the same crime a sailor could be keel-hauled while an officer
would be dismissed; AP, vol. 18, pp. 163–164.
[36] AP, vol. 18, pp. 766–767.
[37] Marine BB 3/2, ff. 126–129. See also Dupont, p. 115.

of the Port au Prince regiment who had thrown in their lot with the rebels. *Le Léopard* sailed for France on August 8 and upon arrival at Brest the former second-in-command, Lieutenant Santo-Domingo, reported to the municipality rather than to the Commandant or the senior flag officer.[38] The Brest Commune welcomed the mutineers and the colonial rebels as heroes of the Revolution, and there were exchanges of fraternity and support.[39] The arrival of *Le Léopard* infused an already tense situation with all of the passion of the conflict raging in the West Indies. The ship's passengers and crew aroused hostility towards naval officers by claiming that some of them had orders to crush the patriots in the colonies. In order to prevent any such Counter-Revolution, Brest's municipality prohibited *Le Ferme* and its division from sailing and demanded that Commandant Hector, Albert de Rioms, and other naval commanders submit their correspondence for examination.[40] This contravened orders from the Minister and was flagrant interference in naval operations. Popular authority in Brest thus took advantage of the spreading mutiny to challenge executive power directly.

Like the "Toulon Affair," the municipality's defiance of naval authority in Brest was the culmination of a conflict which developed since the beginning of the Revolution. In July 1789 popular pressure forced Brest's urban authorities to unite with the city's third estate electors in a General Council of the Commune.[41] This new body quickly assumed

[38] Marine BB 3/2, f. 130; BB 4/3, ff. 100–147, 150–185. See also La Luzerne's letter of September 17, 1790, and "Copie de la lettre de M. de Santo-Domingo à M. de La Luzerne"; AP, vol. 19, pp. 47–48. Regarding the struggle in Saint-Domingue and *Le Léopard*'s alliance with the colonial rebels, see: J. Saintoyant, *La Colonisation française pendant la Révolution (1789–1799)*, 2 vols. (Paris: La Renaissance du Livre, 1930), II, pp. 22–33; Herbert Elmer Mills, *The Early Years of the Revolution in San Domingo* (Ph.D. Thesis. Cornell University, 1889), pp. 70–73; Havard, II, pp. 96–97, 100–102; Guérin, V, pp. 254–256, 266–267.

[39] See *Lettre de MM. de la Municipalité de Brest à MM. les Membres de l'Assemblée Générale de Saint-Domingue à Paris. Brest, le 27 septembre 1790*, and *Réponse de l'Assemblée Générale de la partie française de Saint-Domingue à MM. les Maire et officiers de la Municipalité de Brest. Paris, le 2 octobre 1790*; Brest "Fonds Levot" 1991 [14] and [15]. See also Mills, p. 74–75. Dupont, p. 116 points out the irony of this alliance: "la municipalité de Brest, champion de la nation une et indivisible ainsi que des Droits de l'homme, accueille triomphalement des séparatistes, opposés par ailleurs à l'attribution de droits politiques aux hommes de couleur et à la libération des esclaves!"

[40] AP, vol. 19, p. 47. See also: Hampson, "Comité de Marine," p. 138; Dupont, p. 117; Havard, II, p. 110.

[41] Yves Le Gallo (ed.), *Histoire de Brest* (Toulouse: Privat, 1976), pp. 150–153. See also Henwood and Monage, pp. 55–63.

control of the militia, and demanded that the commander of the port's army garrison, the comte de Murinais, and the naval Commandant, Charles-Jean, comte d'Hector,[42] don the tricolour cockade to show their loyalty to the nation and their acceptance of the municipal revolution. Although deeply worried by developments in Brest, Hector complied and he also swore an oath of Federation drafted by the Commune on August 4.[43] Despite this submission to popular authority, naval commanders were regarded with suspicion in Brest: the General Council requested that Admiral d'Estaing, known to be an opponent of the *Grand Corps* and thus assumed to be a friend of the Revolution, be named Commandant.[44] The hostility towards noble officers may have originated from deep-rooted social antagonism,[45] but it was given a powerful focus in June 1790 with the founding of Brest's Jacobin Club.[46] The Club portrayed aristocrats as enemies of the Revolution, and Hector's refusal to allow the navy to participate in the *Fête de la Fédération* of July 14, 1790[47] supplied local Jacobins with ammunition to use against the *Grand Corps*.[48]

[42] Charles-Jean, comte d'Hector was born in 1722 at Fontenay-le-Comte (Vendée) and entered the *gardes de la marine* in 1741. He served during the War of Austrian Succession and the Seven Years' War, and was promoted *capitaine de vaisseau* following his contribution to the return of six ships to Brest which had been trapped in the River Vilaine following the Battle of Quiberon Bay in 1759. He commanded *L'Orient* (74) at the Battle of Ouessant in 1778, and was made Commandant at Brest in 1781. Promoted *lieutenant-général* in 1782, Hector influenced Castries during the Minister's reform of the navy; Taillemite, *Dictionnaire*, p. 159. See also Alain Boulaire, "Le Comte Hector, commandant de la Marine à Brest en 1789," *Les Cahiers de L'Iroise*, 35e Année – No. 3 (Nouvelle série) (Messidor 1988), 134–137.
[43] In a letter to La Luzerne of July 27, 1789, Hector wrote: "J'aimerais mieux faire dix campagnes de guerre que d'entretenir dix jours d'une pareille paix"; cited in Henwood and Monage, p. 67; see also pp. 64–67. Regarding Hector's submission to the municipality, see also Acerra and Meyer, pp. 119–120.
[44] See Henwood and Monage, pp. 67–68, and Le Gallo (ed.), p. 153.
[45] This claim is made by Henwood and Monage, pp. 26–27, 97–98, but it is based largely on quarrels between the pen and the sword. Merchant hostility toward the *Grand Corps* may have been more significant.
[46] See "Règlement adopté par la Société des Amis de la Constitution, 14 juin 1790"; printed in Henwood and Monage, pp. 89–92. See also Le Gallo (ed.), pp. 157–158.
[47] Commandant Hector refused to participate in the celebrations, or allow warships to fire salutes, since he had received no Ministerial order to do so: Le Gallo (ed.), p. 161; Henwood and Monage, p. 101. This reaction was not universal within the navy, as shown by Commandant Thévenard's description to the Minister of the full and enthusiastic participation of the navy at Lorient; Marine BB 3/2, f. 192.
[48] The Brest Jacobin Club's description of the navy's failure to celebrate July 14, 1790, and its denunciation of naval officers, was reported by *Révolutions de Paris* (7–14

The municipality's primary conflict with the navy, however, concerned different conceptions of authority. Naval commanders were agents of executive power and, as such, posed a threat to Popular Sovereignty embodied in the Commune.[49] The disputed jurisdiction over the *Salle du Comédie*, a theatre built by the Ministry of Marine, illustrates the nature of this conflict.[50] In April 1790 the municipality declared that it possessed police powers over the theatre, by virtue of the National Assembly's decree on public performances. Hector disputed this claim.[51] He doubted the municipality's ability to maintain order and, more importantly, he opposed its arrogation of control over naval property by virtue of its claim to represent the nation.[52] When the Commandant conceded jurisdiction over the theatre, the Commune requisitioned marine troops to carry out the policing.[53] This trend worried the Minister of Marine, who believed that his officers held the arsenal and naval forces at Brest in trust for the entire realm, and he saw the growing encroachment of the civil administration as the intrusion of private

août 1790), vol. 5, no. 57: "Dans un port, où le capitaine de la moindre gabare ne donnait pas la plus petite fête à son bord, sans la marquer par de coups de canons, plusieurs fois réitérés, un silence morne régnoit sur les vaisseaux de roi. Ils étaient étrangers à leur patrie. A qui donc confiera-t-elle ses vaisseaux, si jamais elle attaquée? Par quelles marques de patriotisme ces officiers ont-ils mérité notre confiance? Ce contraste entre leur conduite et celle des autres citoyens est plus expressif que tout ce qu'on pourrait dire d'une conduite aussi scandaleuse"; p. 244. Camille Desmoulins, in his *Révolutions de France et Brabant*, no. 45 (4 octobre 1790), claimed that the navy's non-participation on July 14 was made far worse by its solemn celebration of the king's birthday on August 25. See also M. Kennedy, *Jacobin Clubs . . . The First Years*, p. 199.

[49] The municipal revolution in Brest was consolidated in law by the spring of 1790: the National Guard was formalized, and the municipal elections of March rejected men of the Old Regime and vindicated those of the Commune; Henwood and Monage, pp. 68–82. Nevertheless the navy was still perceived as a potential threat to the gains of 1789.

[50] The *Salle du Comédie* was built in Brest to compensate public servants for the lack of other cultural facilities at the "extremity of France"; Marine BB 3/2, f. 84. Des Robert, pp. 191–239 suggests that naval officers took great interest in theatre.

[51] Marine BB 3/2, ff. 6–10, 13, 15, 84. The naval Intendant at Brest, Redon de Beaupréau, was more careful not to commit himself to a position opposing the municipality, but he was anxious for direction from the Minister; Marine BB 3/2, f. 74.

[52] Marine BB 3/2, f. 10. La Luzerne supported this position and feared that the municipality would next seek to gain control over the arsenal itself; Marine BB 2/1, ff. 47–49.

[53] Marine BB 2/1, ff. 49, 58; BB 3/2, 16–17, 19–22.

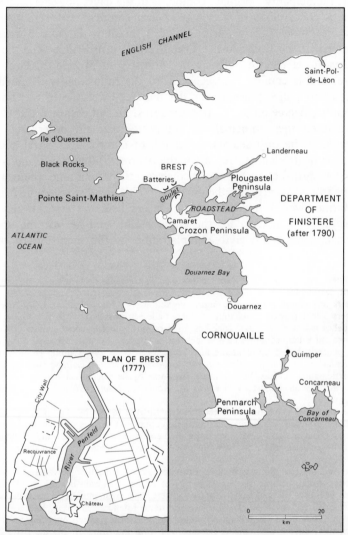

Map 3. The port and roadstead of Brest and surrounding area. *After* [*Main Map*] "Principal Sights" in *Michelin Tourist Guide to Brittany* (Harrow: Michelin Tyre Public Limited Company, 1987), pp. 5–8 and [*Insert*: Plan of Brest (1777)] "Plan de la ville de Brest en 1777" in Philippe Henwood and Edmond Monage, *Brest. Un port en Révolution, 1789–1799* (Rennes: Editions Ouest-France, 1989), p. 12.

interest. La Luzerne's only direction to Hector, however, was to maintain good relations with the municipality, even at the price of acceding to its will.[54] Brest's municipality also pressured the navy over the corvettes designated for training officer cadets, claiming that too few non-noble volunteers had been embarked, and it opposed the manufacture of grapeshot in the arsenal.[55] Civil–military relations worsened in May with the arrest of Lieutenant-Colonel de Martinais of the Beauce regiment, who had criticized a new oath imposed by the Commune.[56] Hector communicated his grave concern to the Minister, and reported that the incessant conflict with the municipality hindered naval commissioning.[57] On May 24 he asked to be replaced, claiming that his authority as Commandant had been nullified.[58]

The months of struggle between popular and naval authority in Brest did not merely dishearten commanders: it politicized the sailors. French seamen were neither the natural allies of local civil administrations, nor inevitably hostile towards their own officers.[59] The Jacobins' rhetoric helped to drive a wedge between officers and men,[60] and propaganda from *Le Léopard* whipped up suspicion and animosity.[61] Yet above all, it was the Commune's defiance of executive authority which transformed the mutiny from a protest over the Penal Code into a revolt against the *Grand Corps*.[62] On September 15 a drunken sailor from *Le Léopard* insulted *major de vaisseau* Huon de Kermadec aboard *Le Patriote* (74).

---

[54] Marine BB 2/1, f. 65.
[55] Marine BB 3/2, ff. 31–33, 53.
[56] Ibid., ff. 43, 48–49. The Beauce regiment had celebrated a *Pacte fédératif* in April with the Brest National Guard which undermined the authority of regular officers; Le Gallo (ed.), p. 161. See also Henwood and Monage, p. 101.
[57] Marine BB 3/2, f. 41.
[58] Ibid., ff. 50–51.
[59] Cabantous, *La Vergue et les fers*, esp. pp. 23–24, 141–143. See also Acerra and Meyer, pp. 53–54.
[60] In his letter to the Minister of August 2, 1790, Albert de Rioms reported that the Club was causing uneasiness in the squadron, as well as infringing upon his authority; Marine BB 4/1, f. 50.
[61] *Révolutions de Paris*, vol. 5, no. 63 (18–25 septembre 1790), pp. 524–531 reported that the mutiny could have ended with the promises to amend the Penal Code, except for the influence of *Le Léopard* and its passengers, "les aristocrates de Saint-Domingue." The journal condemned the colonial rebels, but it supported the grievances of the mutinous sailors against their aristocratic commanders: "il n'y aura point de révolution, tant que les forces actives de l'empire seront dirigées par des chefs connus ou soupçonnés d'être les ennemis de la liberté publique"; p. 530.
[62] See for example Henwood and Monage, p. 115.

The incident became a crisis when *Le Patriote*'s crew and garrison prevented the offender's arrest. Captain Entrecasteaux told his ship's company that he would resign if disorder continued, but was met with cries of: *"Tant mieux, vive la nation! les aristocrates à la lanterne!"* Albert de Rioms went aboard *Le Patriote* the following day and tried to regain control through a personal appeal. The sailors were silent when the squadron commander asked if they had any complaints against their officers, their captain, or against himself, but they also refused to release the outlaw.[63] General insurrection spread to Albert de Rioms' flagship, *Le Majestueux* (110), and throughout the squadron and arsenal.[64] As a threat and a macabre gesture of defiance, mutineers erected a gallows outside the home of the vicomte de Marigny, Hector's second in command, because of a rumour that he was to be sent to crush rebellion in the West Indies.[65] According to the report in *Révolutions de Paris*, sailors justified their insubordination in terms of Popular Sovereignty: "When the officers reminded the mutineers of the oath of loyalty and obedience which they had sworn, they responded that they had taken no oath, that they were the strongest and that they would make the law."[66]

Having failed to quell the mutiny by the strength of his personality, Albert de Rioms attempted to end it by resigning his command on October 2, despite the protests of his captains.[67] The venerable squadron commander explained that he could do nothing else: "I am convinced of the impossibility of reestablishing order myself, therefore I must ask the King if His Majesty would be so kind as to relieve me of the authority with which he entrusted me. He who will replace me will not have more zeal, but perhaps will be happier . . ."[68] The stigma of the "Toulon Affair" made Albert de Rioms a target for Revolutionary

---

[63] See the letter from Albert de Rioms to La Luzerne, September 16, 1790; AP, vol. 19, p. 92. See also Rouvier, pp. 26–27.
[64] For a detailed account, see Guérin, V, pp. 266–270.
[65] AP, vol. 19, p. 92. See also Havard, II, pp. 104–105.
[66] *Révolutions de Paris*, vol. 5, no. 63 (18–25 septembre 1790), p. 527. According to the letter of October 20, 1790 from the vicomte de Souillac to the Minister, mutinous sailors had compared themselves to the soldiers of the Châteauvieux Regiment at Nancy which indicates a high level of politicization; Marine BB 4/1, f. 96.
[67] "Copie de la lettre de M. d'Albert, chef d'escadre, à MM. les Capitaines. 3 octobre 1790," and "Copie de la lettre des capitaines de l'escadre à M. d'Albert, 8 octobre 1790"; Brest 1 A 127.
[68] Letter of Albert de Rioms to the President of the National Assembly, read during the session of 8 October 1790; AP, vol. 19, p. 509.

hostility. Yet he did not provoke the mutiny at Brest and his resignation had little effect. The same day that Albert de Rioms announced he was resigning his command, over seven hundred sailors from the port's barracks brawled with marine troops commanded by Marigny.[69] "The horror of the situation for naval officers stationed at the Port of Brest worsens daily. . .," wrote Commandant Hector in a letter which informed the Minister of seditious pamphlets circulating in the city.[70] The new commander of the squadron, the vicomte de Souillac, reported on October 18 that the mutiny continued, as did the cries of "*les aristocrates à la lanterne!*" in the arsenal.[71]

Fears that the fleet's *sous-lieutenants de vaisseau* were in sympathy with the mutiny heightened anxiety within the *Grand Corps*.[72] These were dispelled on October 13 when an assembly of *sous-lieutenants*, along with some lieutenants who had risen from the intermediate rank of *capitaine de brûlot*, gathered at naval headquarters to deliberate and to draft a public statement. Intended to disavow insinuations that they had fomented dissension among the crews in order to take officers' places, this document also demonstrated their willingness to cooperate fully in restoring order.[73] Addressing the sailors, the *sous-lieutenants* argued that the Revolutionary principle of equality should not make officers suspect, and they warned crews that a cabal of "false patriots" was misleading them and maligning virtuous men such as Albert de Rioms.[74] The significance of this address lies in its demonstration that non-noble naval officers united with those of the *Grand Corps* to condemn the mutiny. If resentment of aristocratic exclusivism was current in 1790, there also remained a community of interest among professional officers of different social origins who saw the service threatened by a collapse of discipline.[75] The key issue was not privilege, but the maintenance of naval authority.

---

[69] Henwood and Monage, p. 116.
[70] Letter of Hector to Minister of Marine, 4 October 1790; Brest 1 A 127. See also "Lettre des officiers de Brest au ministre de la Marine, 18 septembre 1790"; printed in Henwood and Monage, p. 112.
[71] Marine BB 4/1, f. 90.
[72] Letter of Hector to Minister of Marine, 22 September 1790; Brest 1 A 127.
[73] Letter of Hector to Minister of Marine, 13 October 1790; Brest 1 A 127.
[74] *Séance de MM. les officiers des grades intermédiaires de la Marine, assemblés extraordinairement à l'hôtel du Commandant, le 13 octobre 1790*; Brest "Fonds Levot" 1991 [16].
[75] According to Dupont, p. 116 this community of interest extended to petty officers like the *premier-pilote* Willaumez.

The Constituent Assembly reacted slowly to the burgeoning crisis in the Atlantic fleet. On September 18 the Minister of Marine informed the deputies of *Le Léopard*'s arrival in Brest and of the detention of *Le Ferme*, but the Assembly merely ordered the ship's release.[76] Two days later the obvious seriousness of the spreading mutiny prompted de Curt, in the name of the Marine Committee, to call for the punishment of the authors of the insurrection and to demand that the commander of *Le Léopard* and the members of the Saint-Domingue Assembly be brought to Paris. He also proposed that the king be asked to dispatch two commissioners to Brest to expedite these measures and to restore subordination in the squadron.[77] The dispatch of commissioners demonstrates a degree of cooperation between the legislature and the executive. The deputies Borie and Gandon were appointed for this task and arrived in Brest on September 27, where they united with two officers of the municipality in keeping with their instructions.[78] It was quickly apparent, however, that the presence of the king's commissioners was insufficient to quell the mutiny and they acknowledged their need for local assistance, which came from Brest's Jacobin Club.[79]

On October 14, the Club resolved to form a deputation to visit the ships and the barracks ashore in order to convince sailors to end their revolt. Although made in concert with the Commune, the initiative for this decision came from the Jacobins and the deputation included citizens from all classes.[80] Club members drafted an address which appealed to the sailors' patriotism and stressed the benefits of the new era ushered in by the Revolution. Chief among these was equality which had ended any obstacles of birth between the rank of able seaman and that of admiral. The Clubists also hailed the end of arbitrary authority which meant that naval commanders were accountable to the law and held their power only in the name of the nation.[81] Armed with this

---

[76] AP, vol. 19, p. 48.
[77] Ibid., p. 93.
[78] Marine BB 3/2, f. 136. Havard, II, p. 115 regarded the two, Malassis and Dovesnel, as spies and their attachment to the commissioners as a sign of submission to the "new power."
[79] *Lettre des Commissaires envoyés à Brest par le roi, sur la demande de l'Assemblée Nationale, pour rétablir l'ordre dans l'Escadre* (Paris: Imprimerie Nationale, 1790); Brest "Fonds Levot" 1991 [18]. See also Marine BB 3/2, f. 143.
[80] "Extrait du procès-verbal de la séance de la Société des Amis de la Constitution établie à Brest, 14 Octobre 1790"; Marine BB 4/1, f. 92.
[81] *Adresse de la Société des Amis de la Constitution, établie à Brest, aux citoyens, composant les équipages de l'Armée navale* (Brest: Malassis, 1790); Marine BB 4/1, ff. 93–95, or Brest "Fonds Levot" 1991 [16].

address, the deputation began its visit to the squadron on October 19 and rowed out to the anchored flagship *L'Auguste* (80). By the Club's own account, the initial reading of the address had no effect and it was only after hours of speeches and meetings that the crew promised to submit to the law.[82] Accompanied by five men from *L'Auguste*, the Jacobins moved on to another vessel and during the next two days toured all the warships in the roadstead. All crews agreed to return to duty, although aboard a few ships, such as *L'Apollon* (74), the mutiny had been very limited, leaving officers and men still united.[83] Within its account of the deputation's success, however, the Club admitted that the major factor in gaining sailors' confidence had been a promise to communicate their protests against the Penal Code to the king's commissioners.[84]

On October 22 Hector and the vicomte de Souillac acknowledged the assistance of the Jacobins in recalling the fleet to subordination, and the Club's president responded that the Society "was well persuaded that the commanders, seconded by their subordinates, would put all their efforts towards consolidating the work of the Friends of the Constitution and of all citizens of the city of Brest."[85] The Jacobins deserved credit for restoring order, but their promise to the sailors had imposed a solution on the commissioners. Borie and Gandon wrote to the Constituent Assembly that the abolition of certain punishments was the price of obedience and order in the squadron. The commissioners not only vindicated the mutineers, but praised the municipality and the patriotic citizens of Brest.[86] They made no mention of the detention of *Le Ferme* or the reception given to *Le Léopard*. Thus elected representatives of national government conformed entirely to the advice and interpretation of local Jacobins.

The same day that the Constituent Assembly ordered the two commissioners sent to Brest, it called for a joint report on the situation from its Marine, Colonial, and Diplomatic Committees. Menou presented this report on October 19. The Committees took the firm stance that the Penal Code should not be modified and the sailors should be consoled

---

[82] *Extrait du Procès-verbal de la séance de la Société des Amis de la Constitution à Brest, du 22 octobre 1790* (Paris: l'Imprimerie Nationale, 1790); Brest "Fonds Levot" 1991 [17].
[83] *Lettre des Commissaires envoyés à Brest . . .*; Brest "Fonds Levot" 1991 [18].
[84] *Extrait du Procès-verbal de la séance . . . du 22 octobre 1790*; Brest "Fonds Levot" 1991 [17].
[85] Ibid.
[86] *Lettre des Commissaires envoyés à Brest . . .*; Brest "Fonds Levot" 1991 [18].

instead with the publication of new regulations governing promotion and the adoption of a new naval ensign incorporating the national tricolour. These measures were only to be implemented, however, when insubordination ceased in the squadron. Just as firm was the condemnation of the Brest municipality for overstepping its authority, particularly in detaining Le Ferme and in demanding to inspect the correspondence of naval commanders.[87] The attached Bill stated that the navy must remain independent of local administrative corps and municipalities, which must stay within the exact limits of their powers. Various deputies had asked for this kind of disciplinary measure since the first news of mutiny at Brest, de Foucault having proclaimed on September 18: "It is time to put a brake on the aristocracy of the municipalities."[88]

Distrust of royal executive power, however, distracted the Assembly from the local defiance of central government. The condemnation of Brest's Commune provoked opposition, but the more contentious part of the joint Committees' proposal denounced the king's ministers. Attributing the mutiny to the fleet's loss of trust in the Minister of Marine, the report blamed public disorder and obstacles to the achievement of the Constitution in general on the inertia and negligence of all ministers. Since this amounted to a motion of non-confidence, the proposal precipitated a major debate on whether the Assembly had the right to call for ministers' dismissal. The heated arguments on this constitutional principle quickly distanced the discussion from the situation at Brest. Deputies from both the "Left" and the "Right" attacked the ministers, but a motion of censure was defeated on October 20 and thus the entire joint proposal was somewhat discredited.[89] Malouet tried unsuccessfully to focus debate on the mutiny, which he attributed to the municipality's assault on central government:

If it proposes to attack the ministers as the root of the problem, I cannot support the decree. If it proposes, on the contrary, to declare that government has ceased to exist, I adhere to this declaration. I have never been more struck with the necessity of establishing a centre of unity than at this moment. It is

[87] "De Menou présente le rapport de l'insubordination de l'escadre et des troubles qui se sont manifestés à Brest, 19 octobre 1790"; AP, vol. 19, pp. 714–715.
[88] AP, vol. 19, p. 48. On September 13, 1790 de Murinais stated that the interference of local civil administration was the cause of insurrection at Brest, AP, vol. 18, p. 729.
[89] For the entire debate on the motion of censure, see AP, vol. 19, pp. 728–737.

necessary to reestablish royal authority without which the legislative body also will be nullified.[90]

The following day Vaudreuil again proposed that the Assembly censure Brest's muncipality for its actions, and Menou responded by laying blame for the mutiny on the malevolence of the ministers.[91] This debate became mixed up with the issue of the tricolour flag for the fleet. Mirabeau thundered that the white ensign was the standard of Counter-Revolution, and that sailors must be given a symbol for their patriotism.[92] Eventually the deputies accepted a proposal which adopted a new flag for the navy and criticized Brest's civil authorities for excessive zeal.[93] The Constituent Assembly did not return to the subject until October 26, when the Marine Committee reported that Borie and Gandon had ended the mutiny with the assistance of the Jacobin Club and the municipality. Nompère de Champagny secured a vote of gratitude for the king's commissioners and the patriotic citizens of Brest, as well as the authorization to amend the Penal Code.[94] The Assembly suppressed the articles containing the hated punishments the following day,[95] and the original tough stance proposed by the joint Committees was completely overturned: the Constituent Assembly yielded to the mutineers' demands and vindicated the municipality's interference in naval affairs.

The entire affair thus represented a major blow to executive power and the navy's autonomy, and the Minister of Marine was one of its major casualties. Denounced earlier in 1790 for supposed misconduct when governor of Saint-Domingue,[96] La Luzerne believed that the new

---

[90] Ibid., p. 729.

[91] Ibid., pp. 742–743.

[92] Ibid., pp. 745–746. Mirabeau also demanded the amendment of the sailors' traditional cheer of *"Vive le roi,"* to *"Vive la Nation, la loi et le roi."*

[93] AP, vol. 19, pp. 748–749. It should be noted that the new naval ensign was not a full tricolour, but a white flag with a tricolour in the upper quarter next to the staff; see Guérin, V, pp. 271–272; Rouvier, p. 11.

[94] AP, vol. 20, p. 44; see also pp. 41–44.

[95] Ibid., pp. 49–50. Introducing these amendments, Nompère de Champagny further validated the justice and patriotism of the mutineers' demands: "Le comité de la marine a vu, dans les événements qui ont eu lieu dans le rade de Brest, moins un esprit de licence et d'insubordination que des inquiétudes sur la délicatesse et l'honneur . . ."; p. 49.

[96] For his justification of his conduct as colonial governor, see: *Mémoire envoyé le 18 juin 1790, au Comité des rapports de l'Assemblée Nationale, par M. de La Luzerne, Ministre & Secrétaire d'Etat* (Paris: Imprimerie Nationale, 1790) [BN 8 Le29 718A].

animosity aroused by the motion of non-confidence gave him no choice but to resign. He stepped down on October 23 and was replaced by the comte de Fleurieu.[97] In his final *Mémoire*, La Luzerne described the paralysis of the French navy at a time when foreign powers were preparing for war: "The fleets of other nations cover the seas and our naval forces remain in chains . . . condemned to inaction and inertia by the indiscipline of the sailors."[98] While neither popular nor dynamic, La Luzerne was an honest administrator and a sincere proponent of opening the service to talent and diminishing the role of privilege. His resignation marks the end of the movement to reform and modernize the French navy under the leadership of strong royal government.

The supposed resolution of the situation at Brest freed the Marine Committee to proceed with its primary task: naval reorganization. Historians of the French navy claimed that the proposals and the debates on this subject were driven by ideological concerns, and that the organization which resulted was disastrous for the fleet.[99] Yet as Hampson pointed out, the opinions of professional officers had a strong influence on the Assembly's decisions.[100] Nevertheless reform of the aristocratic *Grand Corps* was a sensitive political issue and produced heated debate. This parliamentary conflict demonstrated the continuity of eighteenth-century controversies over the status of auxiliary officers. Outside interest groups continued to pressure the Marine Committee. On October 30, 1790 a deputation from the merchant marine had been admitted to the bar of the Assembly and had demanded the direct admission of merchant captains into the navy as lieutenants.[101] The idea of assimilating the merchant marine with the fighting navy, at least in regard to the

[97] Charles-Pierre Claret, comte de Fleurieu was born at Lyons in 1738 and joined the navy as a *garde de la marine* in 1755. Following service in the Seven Years' War, he became interested in scientific endeavours. He was named director of ports and arsenals in 1776, and helped to plan the campaigns of the American War and to prepare instructions for the voyages of Lapérouse and Entrecasteaux. Fleurieu was Minister of Marine from October 1790 to May 1791; Taillemite, *Dictionnaire*, p. 120. See also Ulane Bonnel (ed.), *Fleurieu et la Marine de son temps* (Paris: Economica, 1992).
[98] AN Colonies F 3/138, ff. 522–549; cited in Dupont p. 118. See also Taillemite, *L'Histoire ignorée*, p. 281.
[99] For example, Guérin, V, p. 278 suggests the belief that naval training and experience were unimportant was embodied in the reforms of the Constituent Assembly which subsequently ruined the French navy. Mahan, *Influence of Sea Power upon the French Revolution*, I, p. 53 states that the Assembly's reorganization of the officer corps was "radically vicious."
[100] Hampson, "Comité de Marine," p. 148.
[101] AP, vol. 20, p. 141.

training and appointment of officers, certainly had support within the Committee. Yet the Committee also included staunch advocates of the complete separation of the services, deputies who insisted on the need to maintain a distinct, professional officer corps. According to Hampson, the issue had profound ideological implications: "The alternative of a full-time navy or of service in wartime only, so far as junior officers were concerned, was regarded by both sides as a political choice between hierarchical and equalitarian principles."[102]

Given this context, the Marine Committee's first proposal to the Assembly on January 13, 1791 was a compromise. Presented by Nompère de Champagny, this report stated that the French navy consisted of all citizens submitting to maritime conscription, and it paid tribute to commercial shipping which formed the seamen employed in the fleet during war. Regarding the fundamental question of whether a permanent officer corps should be dispensed with, Nompère de Champagny argued that the navy's special function required particular skills and, therefore, a full-time officer corps, trained in the science of naval warfare.[103] There was to be a close link between the two services, however, with the constant recruitment of merchant officers into the fleet. Merchant captains were to be given the automatic rank of *enseigne*, the lowest grade in the reformed officer corps, or could be made *lieutenant surnuméraire* if they exceeded the age of forty. This would be one route to become a naval officer. The other was to be through the ranks of the *aspirants*, which were to replace the *élèves* of 1786. Young men, without distinction of birth, would be admitted as *aspirants* by competitive examination and undergo two and a half years training at sea before becoming *enseignes (entretenus)*, distinct from those commanding commercial ships.[104] *Aspirants* would be roughly the equivalent of midshipmen in the British navy. The same men would serve both services, according to Nompère de Champagny, sailing as *aspirants* on warships or mates on merchantmen according to their interest, and would provide the navy with officers during war.

The proposal also included a fixed age limit for every rank which was intended to help alleviate the problem of too many aged and infirm flag officers.[105] Promotion to the rank of captain was to be an award

[102] Hampson, "Comité de Marine," p. 141.
[103] Nompère de Champagny, *Rapport fait à l'Assemblée Nationale, au nom du Comité de marine; sur l'organisation de la Marine Militaire* (Paris: Imprimerie Nationale, 1791), pp. 2–4 [BN 8 Le29 1229]. See also AP, vol. 22, pp. 193–202.
[104] Nompère de Champagny, *Rapport*, pp. 5–11, 15–16.
[105] Ibid., pp. 13–14.

for merit but, like the command of ships or squadrons, would be left to the king's discretion in order to prevent the "dangerous privilege" of promotion by senior officers or the "abusive right" of selection by inferiors: the idea of elected officers was repudiated.[106] General-grade officers would include *amiral*, *vice-amiral*, and the new rank of *contre-amiral*.[107] The Committee's report also proclaimed that there were no longer obstacles to a sailor's promotion to officer rank, but this could happen only after he had advanced through all levels of petty-officer.[108]

Deputies on both sides of the issue criticized this proposal. Some argued that it had not gone far enough to end the privileged position of the *Grand Corps* or to improve the standing of merchant officers. The marquis de Sillery expressed this opinion on January 14, and proposed the amendment of the articles on *aspirants*. Instead of recruiting these midshipmen exclusively in the three great naval ports, where they would come from the same rich families who previously dominated the navy, he proposed the establishment of state-funded maritime colleges in all French ports where boys could learn the elements of navigation necessary for the competitive examination.[109] The most vocal opposition to the Committee's proposal, however, came from deputies who believed any amalgamation would weaken the fleet disastrously. Vaudreuil and La Coudraye both argued that the commercial spirit would undermine honour which was essential to the officer corps, a sentiment put even more bluntly by La Galissonnière: "If you accept the Committee's plan, you will not have a navy, you will have only merchant warriors. The commercial spirit does not inspire courage and the man who calculates does not fight."[110] Malouet also criticized the reorganization, but without social prejudice. He admitted that the *Grand Corps* had been privileged and that auxiliary officers during the American War had often received humiliating treatment. Yet the benefits of equality of opportunity should not end the distinction between the two services which was necessary, he claimed, due to the military training required in the fleet.[111]

---

[106] Ibid., pp. 18–19.
[107] Ibid., p. 20.
[108] Ibid., pp. 22–23.
[109] Sillery, *Opinion de M. de Sillery et projet de décret, sur l'admission des aspirans dans le corps de la marine militaire, 14 janvier 1791* (Paris: Imprimerie Nationale, 1791) [BN 8 Le29 1232]. See also AP, vol. 22, pp. 220–223.
[110] AP, vol. 22, pp. 249–250.
[111] Malouet, *Opinion de M. Malouet, sur l'organisation de la marine militaire, prononcée dans la séance du 14 janvier 1791* (Paris: Imprimerie Nationale, 1791) [BN 8 Le29 1233]. See also AP, vol. 22, pp. 223–227.

The Assembly returned the proposal to the Marine Committee, which itself underwent upheaval with several new deputies being added and others resigning. The new members had naval experience, but Hampson argued that the "Right" still represented a minority on the Committee.[112] Perhaps more importantly, professional opinion remained influential in the Assembly. On April 12, 1791 Sillery presented the Committee's new proposal on naval reorganization which, he insisted, respected Constitutional principles without compromising the good of the service. The new plan modified the admission and training of an unlimited number of *aspirants*, obliging them to serve for a period aboard merchantmen, and making provision for *enseignes* to undertake a competitive examination to return to the fleet as lieutenants.[113] Once again an attempted compromise drew fire from both sides. Ricard de Séalt attacked the proposal for excluding most merchant captains from the fighting service due to the age limit of thirty for lieutenants, and for promoting too few former *sous-lieutenants*.[114] Gualbert, on the other hand, condemned the proposal and presented his own plan which reasserted the need to keep separate the navy and merchant marine.[115] The Committee responded to these criticisms with the first of a series of conciliatory counter-proposals. This awarded merchant captains the honorary rank of *enseigne (non-entretenu)*, which they would hold when serving aboard warships. The proposal indicated, however, that those wishing a permanent naval career should begin as full-time *enseignes (entretenus)*.[116]

---

[112] Hampson, "Comité de Marine," p. 143. Among those nominated to the Committee were de Sillery, Gaulthier de Biauzat, La Gallissonière, and de Menonville, although this last member would soon resign as Vaudreuil and La Coudraye already had done.
[113] Sillery, *Développement du projet du Comité de la Marine sur l'organisation de la Marine française, par M. de Sillery* (Paris: Imprimerie Nationale, 1791) [BN 8 Le29 1417]. See also AP, vol. 24, 723–727, and Hampson, "Comité de Marine," pp. 143–144.
[114] Ricard de Séalt, *Opinion sur un projet de décret du Comité de la Marine, et nouveau projet de décret sur l'admission & l'advancement dans le corps de la marine; par M. Ricard, Député de Toulon* (Paris: Imprimerie Nationale, 1791) [BN 8 Le29 1421]. See also AP, vol. 25, pp. 15–20.
[115] Gualbert, *Projet de décret sur l'organisation d'une Marine militaire. Proposé par M. de Gualbert, Major de vaisseau, Député à l'Assemblée Nationale* (Paris: Imprimerie Nationale, 1791) [BN 8 Le29 1422]. See also AP, vol. 25, pp. 20–23.
[116] *Projet de Décret sur l'organisation de la Marine militaire, et sur le mode d'admission et d'avancement, présenté par le Comité de la Marine* (Paris: Imprimerie Nationale, 1791) [BN 8 Le29 1426]. See also AP, vol. 25, pp. 60–63. Article 24 of the *project de décret* stated: "Sur la totalité des enseignes, il en sera pris un nombre déteminé, pour les

Debate on naval reorganization dragged on for more than two weeks, with opponents of the Marine Committee's proposal continuing to press for a separate professional officer corps,[117] and others advocating a single service.[118] The Assembly adopted some non-controversial articles of the Bill and Moreau de Saint-Méry attempted to break the exhausting stalemate, convincing deputies to concentrate on the issues of whether the number of *aspirants* should be limited and if all merchant captains should be given the rank of *enseigne*.[119] The Marine Committee made concessions on these points: it fixed the number of *aspirants* at three hundred; it required *aspirants* to serve one year in merchantmen before becoming eligible for promotion; it established a competitive examination for the rank of *enseigne (entretenu)*; it made the rank of *enseigne (non-entretenu)* a non-permanent honorific post.[120] These changes cleared the way for adoption of all remaining articles. Finally on April 28, the Assembly approved the naval reorganization Bill in its final form.[121]

The naval officer corps which emerged from these debates remained distinct and separate from the merchant service: despite the opinion of some contemporaries and the interpretation of naval historians, the Constituent Assembly paid great heed to the advice of specialists in its midst. Naval reorganization in 1791 ended aristocratic privilege as a means of promotion in the fleet: the path from cabin boy to admiral was cleared of any obstacles of birth. The navy could now recruit merchant officers directly through the rank of *enseigne (non-entretenu)*, and these men could aspire to the rank of lieutenant in the reformed

destiner uniquement au service public. Ils seront payés constamment, et tenus à résider dans leur département."

[117] See: La Coudraye, *Opinion de M. La Coudraye, ancien lieutenant de vaisseau, de l'Ordre Royal & Militaire de Saint-Louis, Député du Poitou; sur le nouveau projet d'organisation de la Marine militaire, proposé par le Comité de la Marine* (Paris: Imprimerie Nationale, 1791) [BN 8 Le29 1420]; La Gallissonnière, *Nouvelle opinion de M. de La Gallissonnière, sur le nouveau projet d'organisation de la Marine militaire, proposé par le Comité de la Marine; prononcée le 14 avril 1791* (Paris: Imprimerie Nationale, 1791) [BN 8 Le29 1419]; Malouet, *Deuxième opinion de M. Malouet, sur le nouveau projet de Décret du Comité de la Marine, relativement à l'organisation militaire* (Paris: Imprimerie Nationale, 1791) [BN 8 Le29 1427]. For the entire debate of April 14, 1791, including these three speeches, see AP, vol. 25, pp. 70–90.

[118] On April 15, 1791 several deputies defended the Committee's proposal, including Lanjuinais and Defermon; see AP, vol. 25, pp. 107–110.

[119] AP, vol. 25, p. 148; for the entire debate of April 16, 1791, see pp. 145–152. See also Hampson, "Comité de Marine," pp. 145–146.

[120] AP, vol. 25, pp. 192–199; 214–218.

[121] Ibid., pp. 397–401. See also Guérin, V, pp. 289–291.

fleet. The new regulations indicate clearly, however, that young men seeking a permanent naval career should begin as *aspirants* and opt for the fighting service as quickly as possible. The *enseignes (non-entretenus)* serving aboard merchantmen constituted an officer-reserve for wartime, but the navy would continue to rely on a core of full-time professionals. The method by which the reorganization was implemented is even more revealing.[122] There was no purge of the *Grand Corps*. The Marine Committee fixed the number of officers for every rank based upon the fleet's permanent strength. The government formally dismissed the whole of the existing officer corps on May 1, 1791, but on May 15 reappointed its members to grades in the new organization.[123] This list excluded some aged or medically unfit senior officers, but retained most of the officers from the old navy. Ironically the new organization appointed only one quarter of the non-noble *sous-lieutenants* as lieutenants or *enseignes (entretenus)*, excluding most on account of their age: "The immediate outcome of the long series of debates had therefore been to leave the navy with a higher proportion of aristocratic officers than it had had in 1789!"[124]

Given the result of the Marine Committee's work, Hampson argued that the navy was left virtually unchanged by the Constituent Assembly.[125] The above examination of debate and legislation substantiates this conclusion in regard to naval reorganization, but suggests that the Assembly's stance on naval affairs had a more fundamental effect. Hampson's analysis of political conflict in terms of a division between "Right" and "Left" placed great emphasis on the issue of privilege,[126] but very little on the significance of the Brest mutiny.

---

[122] "Sillery présente le rapport du comité de la marine sur les moyens d'appliquer au corps actuel de la marine les décrets relatifs à l'organisation de ce corps, 22 avril 1791"; AP, vol. 25, pp. 241–245. See also Troude, II, pp. 253–256.

[123] The naval officer corps created on May 15, 1791 is often called "*la liste Thévenard*," referring to the Commandant at Lorient who succeeded Fleurieu as Minister of Marine on that date. For an analysis of this reorganized officer corps, see Lévy-Schneider, I, pp. 300–305. See also Rouvier, pp. 13–14 and Chevalier, p. 27.

[124] Hampson, "Comité de Marine," p. 147.

[125] Ibid., p. 148.

[126] The idea that privilege was the basis of political conflict in 1789–1791 is qualified by Patrice Higonnet, *Class, Ideology and the Rights of Nobles During the French Revolution* (Oxford: Clarendon Press, 1981), pp. 66–71, who suggests a fundamental distinction between the Constituent Assembly's anti-corporatism, which opposed nobility as an institution, and its acceptance of individual nobles as citizens with rights. In this context it is understandable, not ironic, that the *Grand Corps* was destroyed while its aristocratic members were retained.

Despite the heated debates, the reform of officer recruitment and promotion had far less impact on the fleet than the Assembly's reluctance
to support the authority of naval commanders as agents of the nation.
Professional officers of all backgrounds expected the support of central
government which was necessary to enforce discipline and to maintain
the navy's autonomy. Bougainville's tenure as commander of the Brest
fleet illustrates that this attitude was not unique to unpopular members
of the *Grand Corps*, and it demonstrates that the Assembly's response
to the events at Brest solved nothing.

Despite the Constituent Assembly's congratulations to Borie and
Gandon, and expressions of gratitude to Brest's municipality and Jacobin
Club, a state of mutiny continued to exist in the Atlantic port long
after October 1790. Amendment of the Penal Code had not ended
insubordination. One of the commissioners' proposals to help restore
discipline was to appoint a popular admiral to succeed Albert de
Rioms.[127] It is unclear whether this expressed sailors' demands, or
simply the wishes of Brest's municipality. The new Minister of Marine
appointed Louis-Antoine, comte de Bougainville to command the fleet.[128]
Like d'Estaing, Bougainville was both a naval hero and an outsider to
the *Grand Corps*, and thus seemed a likely candidate to become a
Lafayette-like figure in the navy. His arrival at Brest in November 1790
coincided with signs that discipline might be reestablished. The crews
of *Le Superbe* (74) and *L'America* (74) presented addresses to the Jacobin
Club in which they swore to return to obedience and to renounce all
those who continued to advocate mutiny.[129] While the sailors heaped

[127] See the communication of dispatches from the commissioners by Guignard,
Minister of the Interior, 20 Octobre 1790; AP, vol. 19, p. 732.
[128] Louis-Antoine, comte de Bougainville was born in Paris in 1729. He studied
mathematics at the Sorbonne and published a *Traité de calcul intégral* in 1754–1756. As
an army officer, he served with distinction in Canada under Montcalm from 1756 to
1761. Bougainville joined the navy in 1763 and commanded a voyage of scientific
discovery around the world in 1766–1769. During the American War he served
admirably under d'Estaing and de Grasse; yet as an *intru*, he was made a scapegoat
and reprimanded by a Court Martial in 1784 for his conduct at the Battle of the
Saints. This did not diminish his standing with Castries, who employed him in
projects of naval and scientific interest: Martin Nicolai, "Bougainville, Louis-Antoine
de Bougainville, Comte de," in Allan Gallay (ed.), *Encyclopedia of the Colonial Wars of
America* (New York: Garland, Publication pending); Taillemite, *Dictionnaire*, pp. 42–
43.
[129] *Adresse de l'Equipage du vaisseau le Superbe, en rade de Brest, à la Société des Amis
de la Constitution. Séance du 4 novembre 1790* (Paris: Imprimerie Nationale [no date])
and *Pétition de l'Equipage du vaisseau l'America, à la Société des Amis de la Constitution.*

praise on the patriotism of the "Friends of the Constitution," they made no mention of their officers which perhaps indicates their attitude towards naval authority.

Bougainville's command at Brest was fraught with difficulty from the beginning. He reported a serious insurrection aboard *Le Duguay-Trouin* (74) on November 10, which required that he put ashore the worst mutineers to be imprisoned.[130] The following day he was called upon to suppress a similar uprising aboard *Le Téméraire* (74), whose crew Bougainville referred to as "one of the best in the roadstead." Bougainville had his own quarrels with the *Grand Corps*, but his reaction to mutiny was little different. Indeed, he seemed even more determined to take a hard line against mutineers: "I will leave no insurrection unpunished, and, if one of those detestable subjects, of which we have too many, can be put before a Court Martial, I will seize the occasion to make an example."[131] Subsequent rebellions aboard the frigate *La Surveillante* and *L'America* presented the opportunity to implement this tough policy. On November 19 Bougainville ordered seventeen crewmen from *L'America*, whom he claimed had been inciting insurrection for three months, to be put ashore and taken to the *Bureau des Classes*. There they were stripped of their status as seamen, thus denying them livelihood in commercial shipping, and publicly conducted out of the city's gates as an example of the price of insubordination.[132]

Bougainville's campaign to restore order in the fleet also involved the distribution of propaganda among the crews. An address from the Society of Seamen at Saint-Malo, aimed specifically at the *malouins* in the warships, exhorted sailors to return to their duty while reminding them of the benefits they had already received from the National Assembly, including reform of the Penal Code.[133] This address and Bougainville's own General Orders insisted that subordination to commanders was merely obedience to the nation, the law, and the king:

Séance du 4 novembre 1790 (Paris: Baudouin [no date]); Brest "Fonds Levot" 1988 [13] and [14].
[130] Marine BB 4/1, ff. 52–53.
[131] Ibid., f. 54.
[132] Ibid., ff. 57–58, 62.
[133] *Adresse de la Société des Marins de St Malo aux citoyens du département de Saint-Malo embarqués sur l'Armée actuellement à Brest* (St Malo: Valais, 1790); Marine BB 4/1, f. 58. See also *Adresse des Capitaines & officiers de la Marine Nationale de Dieppe, aux marins Dieppois employés sur la Flotte de Brest, pour le service de la Patrie* (Dieppe, 1790); BB 3/1, f. 99.

Plate 3. Louis-Antoine, comte de Bougainville.
(Phot. Bibl. Nat. Paris)

naval authority was equivalent to national authority.[134] These pamphlets also contained paternalist sentiment typical of Old Regime leadership,[135] but Bougainville's demands for submission appealed to Revolutionary principle. It was not so easy to convince the politicized sailors at Brest

[134] Marine BB 4/1, ff. 59, 58.
[135] See for example Marine BB 4/1, f. 59: "J'espère que, convaincus de ces principes simples, nos Equipages ne mettrent plus leurs officiers que dans le cas d'en rendre de bons témoignages. Ils savent qu'en même temps qu'ils ont toujours reçu de ces officiers des exemples glorieux à la guerre, ils ont trouvé en eux de véritables amis et des pères intéressés à leur bien-être et à leur procurer tous les avantages qui ont pu dépendre d'eux."

that an admiral's orders represented the Will of the Sovereign People. Bougainville also warned that he would make severe examples, by ending hope of future maritime employment or even by capital punishment, of "perverse men for whom the voice of reason is powerless."[136]

Bougainville believed that the distribution of these pamphlets and the threat of harsh punishment had produced good effect and, despite a riot on November 26 aboard *Le Jupiter* (74), he hoped that order was returning to the fleet.[137] At the end of November the Nootka Sound controversy was resolved, thus ending the threat of war and the need for extraordinary mobilization, and copies of the amended Penal Code finally arrived in Brest. The situation remained critical, however, because the navy was still expected to send a squadron to the West Indies. Continued insubordination hindered these preparations tremendously.[138] Both Bougainville and Commandant Hector felt that the only ships which should be sent to the islands were those whose crews could be trusted to obey orders, while the remainder of the fleet should be decommissioned to purify it of the "naval epidemic."[139] A severe shortage of supplies, particularly of wine, furnished another pretext for mutiny. Bougainville observed that only the appearance of order existed in the fleet, and that the sailors were still "infected with the venom of their first insurrection." Eight hundred casks of wine had to be transferred from other ships in the roadstead to the squadron destined for the West Indies, and Bougainville informed the minister that "it is strongly to be feared that this cannot be done without violence."[140] Insubordination and strife continued in Brest until the squadron sailed for the West Indies on February 5, 1791. Bougainville resigned from his command shortly afterwards, and he would not serve in the Revolutionary navy again.[141]

The continuation of mutiny at Brest during the winter of 1790–1791 reflects the larger connection between the French navy and the advancing Revolution. The Constituent Assembly broke the corporatism of the

---

[136] Marine BB 4/1, f. 59; see also ff. 62, 63.
[137] Ibid., ff. 63, 65.
[138] Ibid., ff. 66, 70, 73.
[139] Ibid., ff. 71–72.
[140] Ibid., ff. 74–77.
[141] See: Havard, II, pp. 160–162; Guérin, V, p. 273; Rouvier, p. 29; Chevalier, p. 19. Bougainville would not accept his promotion to *vice-amiral* in 1792 and resigned from the navy, retiring to his home in Normandy.

old navy, and organized a more egalitarian officer corps. The impact of this reorganization has been exaggerated. It did not assimilate the fleet with the merchant marine, and professional naval officers remained distinct from those in commerce. The Assembly's distrust of executive power, however, had a profound impact on the navy. Deputies did not support the authority of naval officers, agents of the royal executive, against the defiance of mutineers or the interference of Brest's popular authority. This reaction by representatives of the nation, combined with the rhetoric of local Jacobins and colonial rebels, denied even a popular commander like Bougainville legitimacy in the eyes of many sailors. Thus the distrust of noble officers was less crucial than the conflict between executive authority and Popular Sovereignty. Despite Malouet's warnings that the survival of central government was at stake, it is even more significant that the Assembly refused to condemn the arrogation of naval authority by the municipality. Some parallels might be drawn between the Brest mutiny of 1790 and the great mutinies at Spithead and the Nore which paralyzed the British navy in 1797. In both cases a combination of grievances against the conditions of service and radical politics lay behind revolt, although the importance of the latter was much more important at Brest.[142] The key difference, however, was the situation facing naval commanders in the ports. Unlike Hector and Albert de Rioms, the British admirals could count on the support of parliament and the armed forces of the realm.[143] What happened at Brest was not mutiny; it was revolution.

---

[142] For discussions of the causes of the 1797 mutinies, see: G. E. Manwaring and Bonamy Dobrée, *The Floating Republic* (London, 1935; repr. London: The Cresset Library, 1985), pp. 245–251; Conrad Gill, *The Naval Mutinies of 1797* (Manchester: Manchester University Press, 1913), pp. 261–358; James Dugan, *The Great Mutiny* (London: Andre Deutsch, 1966), pp. 53–64.

[143] Acerra and Meyer, p. 102. See also Gill, pp. 192–208, and Manwaring and Dobrée, pp. 191–201.

5

BERTRAND DE MOLEVILLE AND THE DISSOLUTION OF THE OFFICER CORPS, 1791–1792

The French navy's officer corps fell apart following the Brest mutiny of 1790. The majority of the old *Grand Corps* abandoned the service. Many of these aristocratic officers left France altogether during 1791 in what has been called "the year of the military emigration."[1] The Constituent Assembly published a table of all officers needed to command the reorganized fleet on May 15, 1791, but according to Norman Hampson this roster had hardly been established before emigration rendered it invalid.[2] The flight of so many officers should not be dismissed, however, as merely a reaction against naval reorganization or the increasingly egalitarian Revolution. Rather it was related to increasing insubordination and the rising incidence of mutiny during 1791. The desertion of naval officers was primarily a response to the collapse of their authority, a collapse owing principally to the ascendancy of Revolutionary municipalities in the ports.

The mutiny of the fleet at Brest in 1790 demonstrated the danger of the conflict between local popular authority and naval authority. When the Constituent Assembly vindicated the mutineers and also failed to support naval commanders against Brest's municipality, increasing numbers of officers saw future service as untenable. Emigration, however, was not simply a result of this conflict of authority. It was a cause as well as a consequence. Officer absenteeism increased Revolutionary suspicions and heightened tension between the navy and local civil

---

[1] Donald Greer, *The Incidence of the Emigration During the French Revolution* (Cambridge, Mass.: Harvard University Press, 1951), p. 25. Greer refers specifically to the army and states that by the end of 1791, 6,000 officers had emigrated; p. 26. In his table on "The Military Emigration," p. 112, Greer has obviously included *émigrés* from the navy (one column is for "Soldiers and Sailors") yet he does not differentiate the numbers for each service.

[2] Hampson, *La Marine de l'an II*, p. 44.

administrations. Although played out in the naval ports, the essentially political nature of the conflict is best illustrated in Paris where the Minister of Marine, Bertrand de Moleville, was accused of encouraging the emigration and of trying to conceal its extent. From November 1791 to February 1792 his enemies in the Legislative Assembly waged a fierce campaign to impeach him. Bertrand de Moleville's loyalty to the king and his contempt for the Constitution are evident in his *Memoirs*, and were suspected by his opponents. Yet these sentiments are not the key to the debates over officer emigration. The Minister may have been sympathetic to noble officers, but fundamentally he represented the view that national executive authority must predominate over local interests. This ideal of governance, crucial to the navy, was in direct opposition to the Revolutionary concept of Popular Sovereignty in which the "People's Will," embodied ambiguously in both the Legislative Assembly and the port municipalities, must be the ultimate arbiter of every issue.

Many naval officers feared that the Constituent Assembly's failure to punish those who had attacked Albert de Rioms in 1789 would lead to general insubordination in the navy. These predictions were premature by one year. It was the mutiny at Brest in the fall of 1790 which signalled the beginning of a wave of indiscipline throughout the French fleet. The continuation of rebellion at Brest in 1790–1791 during the tenure of Bougainville's command has already been discussed, but mutiny was not confined to the principal naval ports. In November 1790 the crew of *L'Uranie*, fitting out at Lorient, submitted a petition demanding an advance on their pay. The naval Intendant had refused a request for advance pay to this frigate in October on the grounds that if the navy favored this crew, many others in the same position would use it elsewhere as a pretext for revolt.[3] Not all mutinies, however, took such mild form. On December 23, 1790 sailors on *La Capricieuse* locked up their commanding officer when he attempted to go ashore at the Ile d'Aix. They viewed the captain, de Boubée, as a Counter-Revolutionary and the incident concluded a period of tension between the frigate's officers and crew.[4] The mutiny of the *flûte Le*

---

[3] Marine BB 3/3, f. 195; BB 3/2, f. 209.
[4] Cabantous, *La Vergue et les fers*, p. 161, emphasizes the geographic solidarity between local civilians and the sailors, most of whom had been recruited in the Rochefort *quartier*. See also Havard, II, pp. 479–502.

Dromadaire at Rochefort in June 1791 illustrated sailors' increasing confidence in defying their superiors. In this case the mutineers declared that if naval authorities attempted to punish the ringleaders, the crew would desert *en masse*.[5] Warships on station in the colonies also experienced upheaval and, as in French ports, sailors were often influenced by political conflict ashore.[6] This was particularly true in the West Indies where the popular forces in rebellion against the colonial governments sought to win over the crews of ships sent to support metropolitan authority.[7] The affair of *Le Léopard* (74) was not unique: one of the most notable mutinies in 1791 also occurred in the Caribbean.

L'Embuscade was sent to Martinique late in 1790 as part of the small division intended to support government forces against rebels in the Windward Islands. The colonial governor praised the frigate for helping to restore order, but other elements at Fort Royal infused the crew with doubts about the patriotism of their mission and suspicions against their officers.[8] In September 1791 *L'Embuscade*'s commanding officer, the vicomte d'Orléans, received orders to transport civil commissioners to the island of Sainte-Lucie. Shortly after weighing anchor, the crew demanded that he sail instead for France and, when he refused, the sailors took over the ship.[9] The frigate arrived eventually at the Ile d'Aix where the mutineers delivered the following declaration, which they had signed at the time of the mutiny, to the naval authorities there:

[5] See the letter of June 23, 1791 from Commandant Vaudreuil to the Minister; cited in Havard, II, pp. 451–452.

[6] Sailors refused to obey orders on two French frigates at the port of Mahé, India, in January 1792. Although the mutiny occurred in an isolated location, the evidence suggests that the crews had become politicized before they left Brest in 1791 and had been influenced by the Revolutionary administration at the Ile de France. See: Norman Hampson, "Une mutinerie anti-belliciste aux Indes en 1792," *Annales historiques de la Révolution française*, 22 (1950), 156–159; A. Lajuan, "La mutinerie de la Cybèle en 1792," *Annales historiques de la Révolution française*, 26 (1954), 74–75.

[7] For a classic discussion of the interaction between the navy and Revolution in the islands, see: Guérin, V, pp. 300–301, 331–332, 347–348, 359–362.

[8] "Il va sans dire que quiconque obtenait l'approbation d'une partie des colonies, avait mérité par cela même tous les blâmes de l'autre"; Guérin, V, p. 305. See Marine BB 4/5, ff. 68–71, 121–122. *L'Embuscade* was outfitting at Brest when *Le Léopard* arrived, thus it is likely that some of the crew were exposed to colonial propaganda even before the frigate reached Martinique.

[9] "Lettre de M. Bertrand, ministre de la marine," and "Copie d'une lettre de M. d'Orléans, capitaine de la frégate *l'Embuscade*, en rade de l'île de Ré"; AP, vol. 35, pp. 316, 316–318. See also Havard, II, pp. 503–524.

This day, 30 September 1791, we, being united and having asked for the Captain, have communicated to him with a unanimous voice our will to sail to France rather than to Basse-Terre, Guadeloupe, seeing that we are uncertain of our mission, relative to the troubles which reign currently, such as those in Pointe-à-Pitre on the island of Sainte-Lucie, and that we do not want to commit the same hostilities against our brothers as those they have reproached in our past conduct and for which we are denounced in all the clubs of the kingdom as treasonous criminals, that we are determined to set course for France.[10]

This declaration demonstrates that patriots at Martinique had influenced the crew.[11] It also suggests a more general phenomenon, that sailors in the navy were much concerned with their image in the eyes of the nation and did not wish to be perceived as accomplices of despotic repression. This had certainly been a factor at the beginning of the mutiny at Brest in 1790 and in the symbolic violence against *major-général* Marigny. Alain Cabantous has argued that the mutiny of the *L'Embuscade* showed that French sailors had become so highly politicized that, seeing themselves as defenders of the Revolution, they might interpret any order as Counter-Revolution.[12] In Cabantous' view, the explosion of Revolutionary mutinies resulted partly from traditional maritime causes such as insufficient pay, bad provisions and poorly planned operations, as well as from political causes. He refered to a "new political sociability" among sailors developing as early as 1790.[13] In practice this meant a profound suspicion of the officer corps resulting in fierce surveillance of aristocratic commanders and a willingness to denounce them. The implications of this for discipline are obvious. Norman Hampson placed a similar emphasis on the heightened political consciouness of naval crews to explain the rise of insubordination during the early period of the Revolution.[14]

---

[10] "Extrait du procès-verbal des déliberations de l'équipage de *l'Embuscade*"; AP, vol. 35, p. 318. See also Havard, II, p. 516.

[11] Captain Orléans believed that wintering at Fort Royal had destroyed his crew's subordination: "L'inaction, l'oisiveté, une communication libre et quotidienne avec la terre, tout a favorisé les projets de séduction et de corruption des malintentionnés principalement attachés aux équipages de *la Ferme* et de *l'Embuscade* qui s'étaient montrés fidèles à leur devoir et paraissaient inébranlables"; AP, vol. 35, p. 317. See also Marine BB 4/5, f. 86.

[12] Cabantous, *La Vergue et les fers*, pp. 172–173.

[13] Ibid., pp. 163–164, 171–177. See also Alain Cabantous, *Le ciel dans la mer: Christianisme et civilisation maritime, XVIe–XIXe siècle* (Paris: Fayard, 1990), pp. 310–313 for a discussion of sailors' participation in the Revolutionary sociability of port Jacobin Clubs.

[14] Hampson, *La Marine de l'an II*, pp. 46–48.

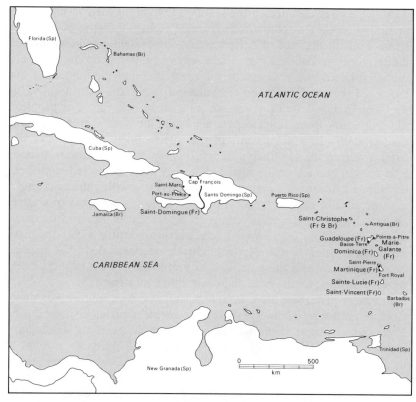

Map 4. The French West Indies, c. 1789. *After* "Caribbean Sea" in William B. Cohen, *The French Encounter with Africans* (Bloomington and London: Indiana University Press, 1980), p. xxi.

These interpretations suggest that political conflict developed independently within the fleet, born of traditional grievances and the different reactions of officers and men toward the Revolution. Granting the importance of material conditions in the navy, Revolutionary politics did not simply give expression to internal tensions. The importance of outside forces should not be minimized. Hampson acknowledged that the position of officers had become particularly difficult when the Penal Code could not exact obedience from crewmen who were frequently protected by Jacobin Clubs or municipalities.[15] Whether these groups

[15] Ibid., p. 47.

outside the navy encouraged the sailors' agitation for their own purposes or simply supported spontaneous action is perhaps a matter of interpretation. Even in the case of *L'Embuscade*, the evidence suggests that the influence of the political atmosphere ashore provoked the mutiny. The captain praised the conduct of his crew in other circumstances and requested that he be allowed to command them on a return voyage to the West Indies.[16] Orléans was not unusual in believing that problems did not stem from fundamental alienation between lower deck and quarter deck. It is significant, in the aftermath of this episode, that royal government was unable to try *L'Embuscade*'s mutineers because Rochefort's municipality insisted that they were protected under the Constituent Assembly's amnesty for those charged with political crimes.[17] This defence of mutiny by local popular authority was part of a larger pattern. Following the insurrections aboard *La Capricieuse* and *Le Dromadaire*, as well as on several other warships during 1791, the navy established juries as the Marine Penal Code demanded. Yet in each case the jury cleared those accused of mutiny of any culpability. There were no investigations at all following other incidents.[18]

Far more disturbing than insubordination or even mutiny was direct violence against naval officers. Several incidents occurred at Brest during 1791 and the most notorious, an attack on the marquis de Lajaille, took place on November 27. Naval Commandant Marigny's account of the event, which the Minister of Marine reiterated, is similar in detail to the municipality's account, but the two versions are very different in their interpretations of the attack's significance. Lajaille came to Brest to take command of a ship of the line, *Le Duguay-Trouin* (74), designated to sail for Saint-Domingue. As in 1790, turmoil in the West Indies influenced events in Brest: the port's Jacobin Club protested Lajaille's appointment, claiming that he had helped to oppress colonial patriots in 1790.[19] On the same evening that he arrived, a group of armed

[16] AP, vol. 35, p. 318.
[17] Bertrand de Moleville, "Faits relatifs à l'Insurrection de l'équipage de la frégate l'Embuscade, 20 décembre 1791"; AP, vol. 36, p. 272. Regarding the amnesty declared on 13 September 1791, see Stewart (ed.), p. 272.
[18] Bertrand de Moleville, "Note sur quelques insurrections qui se sont manifestées à bord des bâtiments de l'Etat, et des jurys qui ont été tenus à cette occasion" [Part of Supplement to his *Compte Rendu* of March 27, 1792]; AP, vol. 40, pp. 551–552.
[19] Letter of Marigny to Minister of Marine, November 28, 1791; Brest 1 A 127. Brest's civil administration claimed that Lajaille was clearly suspect for having failed to respond to his public accusation in the Constituent Assembly: "Lettre des administrateurs du district et de la municipalité de Brest qui rendent compte à

men entered his lodgings, accused him of *incivisme*, and demanded that he leave Brest immediately.[20] At one of the city gates, the Porte de Landernau, a large crowd attacked Lajaille. It remains unclear whether this crowd included sailors or arsenal workers, but only the intervention of the National Guard prevented the officer's murder. Civil authorities eventually imprisoned Lajaille in the Château as the only way of ensuring his protection.[21] The municipality also reported that the crowd, when ordered to disperse, declared that Lajaille was a villain who had tried to kill patriots in Saint-Domingue and would bring about Counter-Revolution in the colonies if not punished.[22]

More important than any connection between this incident and events in the West Indies, however, was the fact that the accusations against Lajaille turned into an attack against the Minister of Marine. The administrators of Brest's municipality and District placed blame for the riot squarely on Bertrand de Moleville for giving command to an officer who was suspect in popular opinion. Moreover, they linked this denunciation to the Minister's claim that no naval officers had abandoned their posts except for those few who had suffered threats or outrages. No officer had been insulted, according to Brest's popular authorities, since the last review of the Port's officer complement had shown 403 of 600 officers absent, most of them without leave: the real issue was the emigration of naval officers which the Minister was trying to conceal.[23] Deputies in the Legislative Assembly seized upon this interpretation

l'Assemblée d'un soulèvement arrivée dans leur ville et occasionné par la nomination de M. Lajaille, suspect d'incivisme, au commandement d'un des vaisseaux destinés à Saint-Domingue"; AP, vol. 35, p. 527.
[20] Marigny, in his letter of November 28, 1791 to the Minister, was unsure whether these men were "citoyens ou militaires," but he stated that most of them wore uniform and carried swords; Brest 1 A 127.
[21] See the letters of congratulations from the Department of Finistère to the District, municipality, and National Guard of Brest for saving Lajaille and restoring order on November 27, 1791, in *Procès-verbal des séances des administrateurs du Départment du Finistère, assemblés à Quimper, pour tenir la session annuelle prescrite par le Décret du 22 décembre 1789* [15 novembre–16 décembre 1791] (Quimper: J. L. Derrien, 1792), p. 67; AD Finistère 100 J 324. See also "Lettre écrite au ministre de la marine, par M. Lajaille, capitaine de vaisseau, au cachot du château de Brest, le 29 novembre 1791"; *Moniteur*, vol. 10, p. 554 (7 décembre 1791).
[22] "Procès-verbal de l'émotion populaire qui a eu lieu à Brest, le 27 novembre 1791, relativement à M. Lajaille, capitaine de vaisseau"; AP, vol. 35, p. 528. Havard, II, pp. 198–248 claims that the municipality falsified this account in several respects, including its lack of responsibility for encouraging the riot and its efforts to save Lajaille.
[23] "Lettre des administrateurs . . . de Brest . . ."; AP, vol. 35, p. 527.

when the correspondence concerning the Lajaille incident was read on December 3, 1791. One member declared that the executive power should be accused as the source of the riot, and he demanded the replacement of all officers who had abandoned their posts.[24] Bréard elaborated on this, asking that they be replaced with officers of the merchant service.[25] The Assembly debated whether the Minister of Marine should be made to submit a list of all officers of the fleet who had emigrated, but decided to await a statement on replacements promised for December 15: there was no discussion of Lajaille's fate or of the implications of the attack for naval authority.

Bertrand de Moleville defended Lajaille's appointment and accused Brest's Jacobin Club of responsibility for the attack.[26] For the Minister, the significance of the incident was clear. Disorder was paralyzing naval operations, as the government's difficulty in sending forces to the colonies demonstrated, and it was destroying the fleet. Officers who had accepted commands were now refusing to assume them and many had submitted their resignations. The Minister expected this trend to escalate:

I congratulated myself, a few days ago, to be able to say that no naval officer had left his post, because effectively none of those who were in service, whether at sea, or in the ports, had abandoned his duty; but I fear that, soon, this will no longer be true; that, in a very short time, these officers will abandon posts where they are exposed to such great dangers, and will not risk taking commands.[27]

There seems little doubt that the attack on Lajaille was symptomatic of an atmosphere of dark suspicion and of a fierce conflict of authority at Brest, as in other naval bases. The Minister was correct that such

[24] AP, vol. 35, p. 528.
[25] Ibid., p. 529. Bréard reminded the Assembly that he had previously brought its attention to the fact that the port of Rochefort was missing 200 naval officers.
[26] "Lettre de M. Bertrand, ministre de la marine, pour rendre compte à l'Assemblée des troubles arrivés à Brest dans la journée du 27 novembre, à l'occasion de la nomination de M. Lajaille au commandement d'un des vaisseaux destinés à Saint-Domingue"; AP, vol. 35, p. 526. Bertrand de Moleville stated that another officer, Kerlérec, designated to command a ship in the Saint-Domingue expedition had been denounced by the Brest Jacobins on November 26 and "exposed to some danger."
[27] "Lettre de M. Bertrand . . ."; AP, vol. 35, p. 527.

violence would cause many officers to abandon the navy. Yet part of the Brestois interpretation rings true: Bertrand de Moleville was being deliberately misleading if he sought to imply that this incident began the wave of desertion. The dissolution of the officer corps was well under way before November 1791.

Indeed, the navy's loss of officers began as early as the summer of 1789. A rumour that officers were plotting to deliver the port of Brest to the English aroused sufficient popular hostility to convince several to flee for their own safety.[28] The number who abandoned the service did not become significant, however, until 1790 and it was in 1791 that the deficit escalated dramatically. Yet it is difficult to determine the exact extent of desertion or emigration among naval officers. Those not on active duty were relatively free to leave their bases, and thus Revolutionary authorities could not be sure whether an officer had abandoned his post or was absent legitimately.[29] Eric Joret, who has written a thesis on this issue as it affected Brest, avoided the imprecise term of emigration and referred to the entire phenomenon as absenteeism. Most officers sought to leave the navy by legal means, according to Joret, and it was only when these became too difficult that large numbers resorted to outright desertion.[30] Legal departure was preferable because it prevented pursuit and, moreover, left options open for a possible return. The common pattern was for officers to request a leave of absence, or *congé*, from their Commandant. Commandants gave such leaves usually to those who had returned from extended service at sea, but they could be awarded for other reasons. The lists of leaves granted at Brest in 1790 and 1791 indicate that 449 officers received leave and that 231 of these failed to return to duty when their leave had expired. The rate of this delinquency rose markedly in 1791: in 1790, 86 of 212 officers given leave, or 40.5 percent, returned; while in 1791 only 44

---

[28] Eric Joret, *Absentéisme des officiers de la marine à Brest pendant le Révolution, 1789–1793.* 2 vols. (Mémoire de maîtrise, Université de Bretagne Occidentale, 1985), I, pp. 8–10. See also Bertrand de Moleville, "Extrait sommaire des comptes successivement rendus de plusieurs insurrections qui se sont manifestées dans les ports" [Part of Supplement to his *Compte Rendu* of 27 March 1792]; AP, vol. 40, p. 552, who states that popular emotion forced Lelarge, *directeur du port*, to leave Brest in August 1789. Havard, II, pp. 52–56, lays the blame for this rumour on "English conspiracy" in general and the machinations of Lord Dorset in particular.

[29] This problem was acknowledged by Le Tourneur, "Rapport et projet de décret relatif à la revue général de formation, 6 février 1792"; AP, vol. 38, pp. 232–233.

[30] Joret, I, pp. 16, 19.

of 237, or 18.5 percent, reported back to Brest.[31] These officers, although departing by legal means, had become indistinguishable from those who simply deserted their posts.

Absenteeism produced a critical shortage of officers in France's naval ports for the commissioning of warships as well as for duties ashore. The navy felt such effects in 1790, but the situation worsened in the following year.[32] The results of three extraordinary reviews of the officer corps at Brest, carried out during 1791, illustrated the increasing rate of absenteeism. Aware of the shortage of officers in the port, local popular authorities demanded the first of these roll calls, held on March 6, and Intendant Redon de Beaupréau authorized it despite the Commandant's protests. There were 806 officers in the contingent assigned to Brest and its respective squadrons, and 367 were not present for the review, a figure representing 43.9 percent absenteeism.[33] The extraordinary review of October 1 indicated that absenteeism had risen to 47 percent, or 378 of 804 officers. The number absent without leave had also escalated to 271, representing 33.7 percent of the total, and added to these were 31 officers who had requested retirement.[34] These figures show an alarming trend. The extraordinary reviews were carried out because of pressure from Brest's municipality and Jacobin Club, and so the exact results might be disputed: the Minister of Marine did so, with fateful consequences. Yet there seems little doubt that the officer corps was collapsing as its members fled the port or failed to return from furloughs. The extent of this dissolution was even more apparent after the third roll call, held on November 20, reported 338 officers absent without leave.[35] It is probable that

[31] Ibid., pp. 25–27. See also: "Listes des officiers ayant bénéficié de congé en 1790 et 1791 (excepté les aumôniers et les officiers du Corps Royal des canonniers)," Brest Registres I L 4 I et 3 E/2, 16–25; in Joret, II, Anexe 2.

[32] See Joret, I, pp. 33–36 for the situation at Brest, where he claims replacements were beginning to change the social composition of the officer corps. See also: Hampson, *La Marine de l'an II*, pp. 43–45; Mahan, *Influence of Sea Power upon the French Revolution*, I, pp. 49–50.

[33] Joret, I, pp. 40–50. If the number of officers listed as being on leave is excluded the percentage of absenteeism drops to 26.8 percent, still a significant level; Joret, I, p. 51.

[34] See: "Etat de situation des officiers de la marine, en activité à la revue du 1er octobre 1791," attached to "Pétition des citoyens actifs de la Ville de Brest à l'Assemblée nationale demandant le remplacement des officiers de marine absents, 26 octobre 1791"; AP, vol. 35, p. 666.

[35] Joret, I, p. 88. See also the following documents, given as *pièces justificatifs* following Cavellier's "Rapport à l'Assemblée nationale, au nom du comité de marine, le 13 janvier 1792"; AP, vol. 37, pp. 362–363: "Liste des officiers de la marine qui se sont trouvés absents à la revue extraordinaire du 20 novembre dernier, émargée des

some of these men were still in France, but many had taken the drastic step of emigrating.

Historians of the Revolution have focused on the exodus of the aristocratic cadres of the French army, rather than the navy, and it is useful at this point to examine recent interpretations of that phenomenon. Samuel Scott and John Lynn provide similar explanations for officer emigration. Scott contended that, while few noble officers emigrated in 1789, most military aristocrats were reluctant to accept the equality implicit in Revolutionary reforms. He explained the growing insubordination in the army and the soldiers' mutinies of 1790–1791, the most dramatic of which was the revolt of the Châteauvieux regiment at Nancy, in terms of fundamental alienation between officers and men.[36] The Revolution defined social and professional differences between commanders and their troops in political terms and this, combined with their frustration at the collapse of discipline, made officers more susceptible to the encouragement and threats from their comrades who had already joined Condé's *émigré* army.[37] Yet, according to Scott, most noble officers might have sworn the new oath of loyalty in June 1791 had it not been for the king's attempted flight. Varennes was a decisive turning point: "Until mid-1791 the major drain on military personnel had been the desertion of soldiers; afterwards, it became the emigration of officers."[38] Lynn also emphasized the Flight to Varennes as the major factor which prompted the mass resignations and emigration of noble army officers in 1791.[39] Attachment to the monarchy was a motivation for those aristocrats who departed, but they were also resentful of the democratization of the army. Lynn argued that the relationships between officers and men had changed to a degree that few nobles could accept: "The Revolution precipitated a conflict between habits of deference and ideals of equality, between discipline based on authority and discipline based on voluntary compliance."[40]

---

notes demandées par le ministre, conformement à sa dépêche du 10 décembre 1791," AP, vol. 37, pp. 379–385; "Revue extraordinaire des officiers et autres entretenus de la marine, faite le 20 novembre 1791, par ordre de M. l'Intendant [*by squadron and rank*]," AP, vol. 37, pp. 390–401; "Résultat de la revue du 20 novembre 1791 par ordre de M. l'Intendant [*Table*]," AP, vol. 37, p. 402.

[36] S. F. Scott, pp. 82–97.

[37] Ibid., p. 102.

[38] Ibid., p. 106.

[39] Lynn, p. 69.

[40] Ibid., p. 92. For a discussion of the changing relationships between officers and men from 1789–1794 as one aspect of leadership in the army, see pp. 87–96. See also Chapter 5, "Discipline in an Army of Citizen-Soldiers," pp. 97–118.

Thus these modern historians explained the emigration of army officers as a reaction against the equality of the Revolution: equality in the general sense of undermining the social and political hierarchy, and in its specific application to military subordination. The question is whether this same explanation should be applied to the French navy. Joret refered to the *Grand Corps* as a "bastion of Counter-Revolution,"[41] but it is unclear whether this charge is based on anything beyond the Revolutionary logic that the tendency to emigrate is Counter-Revolutionary by definition. Moreover, Joret argued that officers' desire to leave Brest coincided with an explosion of hatred against them,[42] which implies that the Revolution had rejected them rather than the other way around. Contemporary evidence suggests that naval officers in general did not abandon their posts because of opposition to the Revolution in principle, but because they found it impossible in practice to carry out their duty.

It is, of course, difficult to assess the individual motivations of most naval officers who resigned, deserted, or otherwise abandoned their profession in 1790–1792. Many *émigrés* may have been worried by the democratic implications of naval reorganization, or may have opposed all Revolutionary incursions into their traditional privileges. Yet these are not among the reasons given by naval officers for their resignations and refusals to accept rank in the reorganized officer corps. A sample of the motives which officers expressed is contained in the extracts of letters to the Minister of Marine which Bertrand de Moleville included in an account of his administration, submitted after his resignation in March 1792.[43] All of these officers cited the collapse of discipline in the navy as the major reason they found further service intolerable,

---

[41] Joret, I, pp. 9, 3.
[42] Ibid., pp. 6, 11–12.
[43] "Compte Rendu à l'Assemblée nationale par M. Bertrand de Moleville, ci-devant ministre de la marine, 27 mars 1792"; AP, vol. 40 pp. 549–551. The extracts from, or copies of, sixteen letters are part of a supplement which follows the *Compte Rendu*, AP, vol. 40, pp. 555–558. This evidence might be challenged because the letters are *pièces justificatifs*, which might be considered biased by definition, and because the names of the officers are not given: Bertrand de Moleville claimed that he wished to protect the officers from possible persecution. It should be noted, however, that the ex-minister insisted on the validity of these extracts long after the fact; see Bertrand de Moleville, *Private Memoirs of A. F. Bertrand de Moleville, Minister of State, 1790–1791, Relative to the Last Year of the Reign of Louis the Sixteenth*, 2 vols., trans. R. C. Dalls (London, 1797; repr. Boston: J. B. Millet Company, 1909), II, p. 12. Most importantly, the extracts follow the spirit of all other officer correspondence.

and most emphasized the fatal consequences of the failure to punish insubordination, mutiny, and even attacks against officers. One captain warned the Minister that:

a frightful fate awaits those who will command ships in the future, because they will be disobeyed and scorned with impunity. That which has occurred aboard various vessels proves that the juries can palliate faults of any kind: the most complete revolt becomes the crime least punishable. These offenses are recent, and no order of things permits the hope of a happier future. . .[44]

Samuel Scott argued that the essential cause for insubordination in the army lay within the service itself, and that civilian suppport for the soldiers was only of secondary importance.[45] This, however, does not appear to be true for the navy. In all of the cases of mutiny which have been discussed in the preceding pages the powerful influence of outside forces was apparent. These forces were generally local civil administrations, sometimes in alliance with Jacobin Clubs, and they sought to undermine the authority of the naval officer corps. Such authority was based on national executive power and not on a notion of Popular Sovereignty liable to local manipulation.[46] This was particularly evident in the greatest manifestation of insubordination, the mutiny of the fleet at Brest in 1790. The nature of the navy, an institution tied to its great arsenals, left its officers particularly vulnerable to conflict with local popular authority, and made its personnel particularly susceptible to being used in such a conflict. Naval commanders certainly claimed that the rash of mutinies was not due to fundamental alienation between themselves and their crews: "they are due to the efforts of those who, behind the mask of patriotism, deceive and abuse the people to whom they render all authority suspect."[47] The nullification

---

[44] "Extrait de la lettre écrite à M. de Bertrand, par M. — — capitaine de vaisseau, à Paris, le 27 février 1792"; AP, vol. 40, p. 556.
[45] S. F. Scott, p. 100. On the other hand, Bertaud, pp. 31–34 places much more emphasis on the importance of Jacobin Clubs in politicizing soldiers; the influence of the Club at Nancy helped to incite the mutiny of the Châteauvieux regiment.
[46] Naval officers recognized the existence of conflict between competing definitions of authority. See for example the letter of 10 May 1792 from Captain Beaurepaire to the Minister of Marine: "Une révolution totale et subite a surpris les esprits; la méfiance s'est emparée des coeurs. Dans cette agitation générale les citoyens devenus libres suspectaient les agens du pouvoir exécutif, et ceux-ci à leur tour craignaient en eux des sujets rebelles à la loi"; Marine BB 3/13, f. 79.
[47] "Extrait de la lettre de M. — — capitaine de vaisseau, à M. de Bertrand, ministre de la marine, en date du 24 janvier 1792, à Brest"; AP, vol. 40, p. 555.

of officers' authority and credibility due to the efforts of local Revolutionary bodies must not be underestimated as a motive for resignation or
emigration:

the influence of the clubs, the supervision of purely military operations which
has been arrogated by administrative corps, their authority often in opposition
to that of the King; all these considerations, sir, have determined me not to
accept a position in which I would have no real authority and which, consequently, would be for me a continual source of grief, perhaps of disgrace and
humiliation.[48]

It is clear that, whatever the motivations, absenteeism exacerbated
the situation of those officers who remained at their posts. Sea-officers
had come to recognize the danger of hostile public opinion,[49] yet the
disappearance of fellow officers undermined any efforts to demonstrate
their patriotism. Resignations, desertion and emigration cast suspicion
on the entire officer corps. This was particularly true of the attitude
of local popular assemblies which saw in absenteeism the vindication
of their suspicions regarding all aristocratic commanders. It has been
suggested that the flight of officers was as much a result of civil–military
conflict in the ports as it was a cause, and there can be little doubt
that Revolutionary administrators used the accusation of emigration as
a weapon against their naval rivals.

Thus naval commanders in Toulon were under pressure in June 1791
to have the port's entire officer contingent present for an extraordinary
review.[50] Commandant Glandevès used the commissioning of two frig-

---

[48] "Extrait d'une lettre écrite au ministre de la marine par M. — — capitaine de
vaisseau. De Saints-Pons, département de l'Hérault, en date du 12 mars, 1792"; AP,
vol. 40, p. 558.
[49] A Declaration by naval officers at Rochefort, dated 26 April 1791, condemned the
actions of a Lieutenant de Negrier who had made a profit by selling his crew shoddy
provisions, *fait de pacotille*. Such abuses had occurred throughout the eighteenth
century, but the Revolution could give the crime great political significance. Officers
recognized this and the Declaration, copies of which were to be sent to several
newspapers, began: "Dans un moment où tous les Corps militaires, et surtout les
officiers, sont en batte aux plus odieuses inculpations, le corps de la Marine, jaloux de
conserver l'honorable opinion qu'il a meritée dans tous les temps, et particulièrement
dans les circonstances critiques où se trouve aujourd'hui le Royaume, croit devoir
prévenir tous les citoyens honnêtes contre lui au sujet de la conduite honteuse d'un de
sa membres"; "Déclaration des officiers de la marine sur le compte de M. de Negrier,
lieutenant de vaisseau"; Toulon 4 A 1/364.
[50] "Lettre de M. de Castelan écrite aux officiers de la marine ci-après [List], Toulon,
20 juin 1791"; Toulon 4 A 1/364.

ates, and therefore the chance of a command, as an incentive for delinquents to return, and he also reminded officers that they would not be required to swear the new oath of loyalty until after the formation of the new officer corps.[51] Despite the fact that it was not mandatory, Glandevès' successor seized the opportunity provided by the June 22 oath to demonstrate the patriotism of naval officers. The Commandant informed the Minister in July that he and his subordinates would follow the example of their brothers in Brest, Rochefort, and Lorient, and swear the oath as new proof of their good citizenship.[52] It seems that this did little to counteract the suspicions caused by absenteeism. There is a sense of growing desperation in the correspondence of senior officers who tried to recall all officers for a general review to be held in Toulon at the end of December: Captain Rochemore stated clearly that those who missed the review would be beyond help from the Commandant.[53] The navy's lack of success, both in recalling the absentees or in dispelling the resulting political distrust, is demonstrated by the Department of the Var's demand for information: "The rumour has spread for some time, gentlemen, that a great number of naval officers have emigrated . . . Charged with surveillance, and with public tranquility, we believe it is our duty to demand from you information on this subject . . ."[54] This included lists of all officers not present and of all leaves awarded, a statement of payments made in the last six months, and the current residence of all officers.

A struggle of authority is even more evident in the pressure put on the naval establishment at Brest. The extraordinary review of March 1791, as noted above, was held at the demand of Brest's municipality and Jacobin Club and it represented a victory over Commandant Marigny.[55] The loyalty oath of June 1791 was also an issue of authority

[51] "Lettre de M. de Castelan écrite aux officers de la marine ci-après [List], Toulon, 26 juin 1791"; Toulon 4 A 1/364.
[52] "Lettre de M. Dufort à M. Thévenard, 31 juillet 1791"; Toulon 4 A 1/364.
[53] "Lettre de M. de Rochemore aux officiers ci-après [List], Toulon, 22 décembre 1791"; see also "Lettre de M. Castellan . . . 13 août 1791," "Lettre de M. Castellan . . . 23 aôut 1791"; Toulon 4 A 1/364.
[54] "Copie de la lettre des administrateurs composant le Directoire du Département du Var, à M. de Ruyter, commandant par interim la marine et Possel, Commissaire-général ordonnateur. Toulon, 27 décembre 1791"; Toulon 4 A 1/364.
[55] Joret, I, pp. 38–39. Charles-René-Louis Bernard, vicomte de Marigny was born at Séez in 1740 and entered the navy as a *garde de la marine* in 1754. He served with distinction during the American Revolutionary War, and captured *HMS Ardent* (64) while commanding a frigate in 1779. He was promoted *chef de division* in 1786, was named *major-général* at Brest in 1790, and replaced Hector as Commandant in 1791;

because, according to local administration, the oath represented the submission of naval to civil power. The decree of June 22 horrified naval officers at Brest because it made no mention of the king or of maintenance of the existing constitution. Although they did swear an oath on June 25, it included the words, "nation, law *and king*."[56] Following the extraordinary review in October, citizens of Brest sent petitions to the Legislative Assembly which demanded the replacement of all absent naval officers and the suspension of their pay.[57] Commandant Marigny defended the dedication of the officer corps. He informed the Minister that those officers who remained on duty in Brest faced constant threats, and that their heroism only increased the efforts of those who wished to shake their zeal.[58] Marigny insisted that order could only be reestablished in the port if the different authorities knew the proper extent of their duties,[59] and he protested bitterly against the extraordinary review of November as a flagrant usurpation of the naval sphere by local power. Marigny was appalled at the Intendant's authorization of the review,[60] and he identified the imposition of the roll-call with the defiance of legal authority:

The extraordinary review will take place, and the multitude will continue to give us orders; when I say multitude I should say with more truth the Club ... If all this could contribute to a better order of things, to a more perfect

Taillemite, *Dictionnaire*, p. 228. Henwood and Monage, p. 102 state that Marigny was a sincere liberal who tried to reconcile naval authority with Revolutionary principle.
[56] Joret, I, pp. 58–63.
[57] "Pétition des citoyens actifs de la Ville de Brest à l'Assemblée nationale demandant le remplacement des officiers de marine absents, 26 octobre 1791"; "Pétition des citoyens de Brest tendant à demander la suppression des traitements et appointements des officiers de la marine, absents sans congé, que l'on continue de payer, même à ceux actuellement émigés, 6 novembre 1791"; AP, vol. 35, pp. 666–667.
[58] Marigny to Minister of Marine, 23 November 1791; Brest 1 A 127.
[59] Marigny to Minister of Marine, 14 November 1791; Brest 1 A 127.
[60] Bertrand de Moleville claims that although Redon de Beaupréau was associated with Brest's Jacobin Club, the Intendant was also intimidated. The Minister rejected the name of Bellanger, President of the Brest Club, from a list of possible candidates submitted by the Intendant for service as civil commissioners to Saint-Domingue. Bertrand de Moleville wrote that he reversed this decision due to a letter from the Commandant: "M. de Marigni informed me, that the life of Beaupréau was in my hands, as Bellanger would cause him to be assassinated, as soon as he was informed of my motive for refusing to appoint him [Redon de Beaupréau had denounced Bellanger six months before]. And although M. de Marigni had been the object of the Intendant's persecution from the commencement of the Revolution, he had the generosity to intercede for his enemy, and solicit me to replace the name of Bellanger in the list"; Bertrand de Moleville, *Private Memoirs*, I, p. 264.

tranquility, to the advantage of the public good, the number of criticisms would not have surprised me, but the law must be respected by all.[61]

The District of Brest had already accused Marigny of granting too many requests for leave, and he would resign his command at the end of 1791.[62] The ultimate target of the local reaction against emigration, however, was not the Commandant. Revolutionaries in Finistère aimed their allegations of abetting officer emigration, and the consequent implication of Counter-Revolutionary sentiment, at the Minister of Marine, Bertrand de Moleville. This was true even of the petitions from Brest which had called for the removal of absent officers and the cancellation of their pay. The petition of October 26 condemned the Minister for failing to implement the new organization of the navy decreed by the Constituent Assembly: "This delay, which nothing can justify, discourages the true patriots who remain in the service, while encouraging the traitors who have left to race to the frontiers to increase the numbers of the *émigré* army."[63] The subsequent petition went further and accused him of: "the depredation of public funds in favour of his cherished caste, the former nobles, serving in the navy; to whom he pays salaries that they deserve to lose because of emigration and illegitimate absence."[64] Both submissions insisted that deputies must enforce the accountability of ministers.

The culmination of such protests was the Department of Finistère's outright denunciation of Bertrand de Moleville on November 30. In an address which was sent to both the Legislative Assembly and the king, the Departmental administrators condemned the Minister of Marine for deceiving the nation by his claim that no naval officer had left his post. The results of the November 20 review in Brest demonstrated the perfidiousness of such a claim, but the denunciation went far beyond charges of concealing or encouraging emigration. It accused Bertrand de Moleville of entrusting naval forces for the colonies to "men tainted in public opinion and who inspire only distrust and contempt."[65] This

---

[61] Marigny to Minister of Marine, 18 November 1791; Brest 1 A 127.
[62] Joret, I, pp. 53, 75. In a letter of December 26, 1791 to the Minister, Marigny said of his successor that: "le choix du Roi puisse porter sur quelqu'un dont la naissance ou la profession de foi sur les bases de la Révolution ne puisse donner lieu à aucunes préventions . . ."; Brest 1 A 127.
[63] "Pétition des citoyens actifs . . ."; AP, vol. 35, p. 666.
[64] "Pétition des citoyens . . . tendant à demander . . ."; AP, vol. 35, p. 667.
[65] "Adresse de dénonciation du Ministre du Marine," in *Procès-verbal . . . du Département du Finistère*, p. 65; AD Finistère 100 J 324.

referred specifically to Captain La Jaille who was "denounced by all of France" as an instigator of troubles in the colonies and for "shedding French blood" while commanding *L'Engageante* in 1790.[66] The administrators also warned of dire consequences if France's military was not commanded by men of known principles and recognized patriotism. They blamed Bertrand de Moleville for all of these evils but the Finistère address went even further, denouncing the Counter-Revolutionary action of all ministers:

It is of the utmost importance to prevent these corrupt ministers from plotting openly the loss of our liberty. Never, no never will we be at peace as long as you trust in them. Without tact, without principles, they have deceived your predecessors, they have deceived you, and they will deceive you again. They will lure all of France into the frightful trap that they have prepared beneath its feet.[67]

This amounted to an attack on the principle of national executive power. The authority of the king's ministers, like naval officers in the ports, was not subject to the direct supervision of elected assemblies. The Revolutionary principle of the absolute separation of powers made it very difficult to coordinate government policy, set by the ministers, with legislative control embodied in the Legislative Assembly. Nevertheless, the two branches of government shared national authority under the Constitution of 1791.[68] By equating executive power with conspiracy, either actual or potential, the Administration of Finistère suggested that the Sovereignty of the Nation did not reside exclusively with central government. Thus it is significant that a denunciation from local popular authority apparently initiated the campaign against Bertrand de Moleville in the Legislative Assembly.

Antoine-François Bertrand de Moleville had been the Intendant of Brittany before the Revolution, and he claimed to enjoy the respect

[66] Ibid., pp. 65–66.
[67] Ibid., p. 66.
[68] Title III of the Constitution of 1791, "Of Public Powers," states that sovereignty is indivisible and belongs only to the nation, which exercises its powers by delegation: "The French Constitution is representative; the representatives are the legislative body and the king. The legislative power is delegated to a National Assembly, . . . The government is monarchical; the executive power is delegated to the king, to be exercised, under his authority, by ministers and other responsible agents . . ."; in Stewart (ed.), p. 234.

and confidence of Breton deputies to the Estates General.[69] Several of these men tried to have Bertrand de Moleville named Minister of Marine following the resignation of Fleurieu in May 1791. The former Intendant refused the king's offer because he disapproved of the limitations imposed on Louis XVI in choosing ministers, and he congratulated himself at not having been in the Royal Council during the uncertain period between the Flight to Varennes and the implementation of the new Constitution.[70] Thévenard, who had been naval Commandant at Lorient, held the Marine portfolio from May to September of 1791,[71] but upon his resignation the king again offered the Ministry to Bertrand de Moleville. Despite continued misgivings, he accepted the post but requested a personal audience with the king on October 1 at which he asked for the king's sentiments on the Constitution. Louis' response, as recorded in Bertrand de Moleville's *Memoirs*, reveals not only royal strategy but the attitude which governed the future conduct of the Minister of Marine:

"That is but just," said the king. "This, then is what I think. I am far from regarding the Constitution as a *chef d'oeuvre*. I believe there are great faults in it; and if I had been allowed to state my observations upon it, some advantageous alterations might have been adopted. But of this there is no question at present;

[69] Bertrand de Moleville, *Private Memoirs*, I, pp. 157–159. The pre-Revolutionary struggle in Britanny was particularly bitter, thus the Breton Patriots were among the most radical in 1789. Bertrand de Moleville had been forced to flee Rennes in June 1788 because of riots in support of the Parlement, and it is very likely that he was seen as an ally by deputies of the third estate from Brittany; see Jean Egret, "The Origins of the Revolution in Brittany (1788–1789)," in Jeffry Kaplow (ed.), *New Perspectives on the French Revolution* (New York: John Riley and Sons, 1965), pp. 136–152. For a discussion of Bertrand de Moleville's background, see G. K. Fortescue's "Introduction" to the *Private Memoirs*, pp. 1–5.

[70] *Ibid.*, pp. 202–204. He referred to the continuation of government during this time as the "revolting and absurd spectacle of a monarchy without a king."

[71] Antoine-Jean-Marie Thévenard was born in 1733, the son of a merchant captain in Saint-Malo. A skilled naval engineer as well as a sailor, he entered the navy from the *Compagnie des Indes* in 1769 as a *capitaine de port*. Promoted into the *Grand Corps* as *capitaine de vaisseau* in 1773, he was named Commandant at Lorient in 1779. Following his brief tenure as Minister, Thévenard was appointed Commandant at Brest and promoted to *vice-amiral* in June 1792. See: Taillemite, *Dictionnaire*, p. 319; Six, *Dictionnaire biographique*, II, pp. 491–492. Regarding Thévenard as Minister of Marine, Guérin, V, p. 294 states: "Il ne trouva rien de mieux que de se mettre sous la tutelle absolue de ses bureaux." He also suggests, however, that Thévenard believed sincerely that he could reconcile his loyalty to the king with his support for the new Constitution.

I have sworn to maintain it, such as it is, and I am determined, as I ought, to be strictly faithful to my oath; for it is my opinion, that an exact execution of the constitution is the best means of making it thoroughly known to the nation, who will then perceive the changes proper to be made. I have not, and I cannot have another plan than this. I certainly shall not recede from it; and I wish my ministers to conform to the same."[72]

It is unclear whether or not this reply was sincere,[73] but such an attitude, even if sincere, posed extreme difficulty for a minister and made conflict with the legislature virtually inevitable.

Bertrand de Moleville demonstrated his adherence to this plan, his determination to follow the Constitution to the letter but not in spirit, by refusing to correspond with the Committees of the Assembly. This was not a duty mentioned specifically in the Constitution and he claimed that by communicating only with the President of the Assembly ministers could best protect themselves. He recognized, no doubt, that this would antagonize many people, and his refusal led to a conflict with the comte de Narbonne, the Minister of War, who believed that the Constitutional Monarchy would be served best by its ministers cooperating fully with the Assembly.[74] Narbonne contended that the proof of Bertrand de Moleville's intention to undermine the Constitution lay in his failure to implement the navy's new organization,[75] a charge echoed by port municipalities as well as by deputies in Paris. Certainly the Minister of Marine's initial account of the state of his department, read to the Legislative Assembly on October 31, indicated a policy of inertia:

My first care, upon entering the Ministry, was to occupy myself with the means to hasten the execution of the new laws which concern the department which has been entrusted to me; but I have soon perceived the mistakes and dangers into which an unconsidered precipitation would lead me; and the more that I have reflected, the more I am convinced of the necessity to implement all the parts which must compose the new organization of the navy all at once.[76]

[72] Bertrand de Moleville, *Private Memoirs*, I, pp. 207–208.
[73] See for example "Counter-Revolutionary Letter from Louis XVI to the King of Prussia, 3 December 1791"; in Stewart (ed.), pp. 279–280. See also J. M. Thompson, p. 276, and Marcel Reinhard, *La Chute de la Royauté* (Paris: Gallimard, 1969), pp. 209–222, esp. p. 220.
[74] Bertrand de Moleville, *Private Memoirs*, I, pp. 212–214, 222–226, 330–340. See also Reinhard, pp. 251–252.
[75] Bertrand de Moleville, *Private Memoirs*, I, p. 337.
[76] Bertrand de Moleville, *Compte Rendu à l'Assemblée nationale par le ministre de la marine, sur les loix de détail qu'exige l'establissement de la nouvelle organisation de ce*

The Minister's insistence that the Assembly pass all laws pertaining to each particular aspect of naval service before the general plan could be executed meant, by his calculation, that reorganization could not be completed until at least January 1792.[77] It is hardly surprising that his relationship with the Marine Committee was one of "continual warfare."[78]

Yet equally important as the Minister's seeming reluctance to move quickly to form the new navy was his resolution that the fleet and its arsenals belonged to the entire nation and were not to be subject to private or local interests. This interpretation of how the navy was to be controlled, and to what end, was a major factor creating the antagonism toward Bertrand de Moleville. Work in the arsenals, he stated, had to be regulated more carefully and with greater economy. Public assistance for the needs of port workers was just, but such acts of generosity should not be "masked as salaries for work which was not being done."[79] The new Minister of Marine maintained further that laws were needed to clarify the exact powers of the naval Commandants and the new *ordonnateurs civils*, and to regulate all relations between military service and civil administration.[80] He referred to the critical need to reestablish discipline in the fleet and, while proclaiming confidence that the Assembly would welcome his efforts, he asserted that local popular authority must respect the jurisdiction of central government:

I hope also that the administrative corps and the municipalities of the ports will be eager to second the measures which will be necessary to take; the patriotism of those who compose these corps will doubtless carry them to concur with what will be demanded by the nation's general interest, when it would not appear entirely in accord with local and private interests.[81]

The greatest problem that Bertrand de Moleville inherited as Minister of Marine was that of officer emigration. The king's letter to the port Commandants of October 13 showed that the new Minister was well aware of the seriousness of the situation. He co-signed the document

département. 31 octobre 1791 (Paris: Imprimerie Nationale, 1791), p. 1 [BN 8 Le33 3T{2}]. See also AP, vol. 34 pp. 543–547.
[77] Bertrand de Moleville, *Compte Rendu . . . sur les loix de détail*, pp. 5, 20.
[78] Bertrand de Moleville, *Private Memoirs*, I, p. 263.
[79] Bertrand de Moleville, *Compte Rendu . . . sur les loix de détail*, pp. 13–15.
[80] Ibid., p. 8.
[81] Ibid., p. 16.

and may well have drafted it in the first place. The letter, which was to be distributed by the Commandants to all their officers including those on leave, attempted to recall absentees through a combination of paternal reassurance and an appeal to honour: "today, now that the major and the most sane part of the nation wants the return of order and the submission to laws, could it be possible that generous and faithful sea-officers dream of separating themselves from their king?"[82] The letter told naval officers that their duty to the king lay, above all, in remaining at their posts and in assuring the execution of the nation's laws: this would be true proof of their loyalty and their love of *la patrie*.[83] The king's proclamation on emigration echoed this definition of the loyal subject's responsibility. Those who believed that they showed their attachment to the king by emigrating had been misled or seduced by a harmful "party spirit."[84]

These declarations indicated that royal government, and the Minister of Marine in particular, hoped to stem the tide of emigration and possibly recall some of those who had left by treating officers as loyal individuals whose sense of honour and duty could be reached. Such an attitude was foreign to many deputies in the Legislative Assembly who were determined to respond to the situation with harsh repression. Regarding the threat of Counter-Revolution led by the princes and the *émigrés*, Isnard stated: "We must amputate the gangrened limb to save the rest of the body."[85] The Assembly voted a decree on November 9, 1791 which proclaimed that all *émigrés* assembled beyond the frontiers were suspected of conspiracy, and that all those who did not return by January 1, 1792 would suffer

---

[82] "Lettre du roi aux commandants des ports. Paris, le 13 octobre 1791"; AP, vol. 34, p. 323.
[83] Ibid. The stated duty of naval officers towards the new Constitution was remarkably similar to that the king had expressed to Bertrand de Moleville: "On ne peut plus dissimuler que l'exécution exacte et paisible de la Constitution, est aujourd'hui le moyen le plus sûr d'apprécier ses avantages, et de connaître ce qui peut manquer à sa perfection."
[84] "Proclamation du roi concernant les émigrations. Du 14 octobre 1791"; AP, vol. 34, pp. 323–324. This public criticism of the *émigrés* was repeated in Louis XVI's "Secret Memorandum to his brothers concerning his acceptance of the constitution, 25 September 1791," where he stated that France's troubles could only be worsened by the *émigrés* who "are capable only of exercising a suicidal revenge – and this means recourse to war," Feuillet de Conches, *Louis XVI*, II, pp. 365–375; cited in Hardman (ed.), pp. 136–138. For a discussion of the king's distrust of the self-exiled nobility, see Higonnet, pp. 296–298.
[85] Cited in Sydenham, *French Revolution*, p. 90.

the death penalty.[86] The king vetoed this legislation, and there was considerable confusion when his ministers appeared at the bar of the Assembly to deliver this response. Deputies protested that the Constitution prohibited ministers from initiating business, to which Bertrand de Moleville replied that they were there only to inform the Assembly of the measures taken by the king against emigration.[87] This statement was misquoted in the *Moniteur* as stopping the emigration of naval officers.[88] The Minister of Marine wrote to the editor of the newspaper to correct the error that his only purpose had been to describe actions taken relative to his department. Yet Bertrand de Moleville felt compelled to add that:

there has not been a single naval officer who has left his post; that within the number of those who are absent, several have been forced, by attacks more or less serious against their persons or property, to leave their ordinary place of residence, and will doubtless return as soon as order, peace and submission to laws will be reestablished in the kingdom; the others have indicated to me, on departure, the means by which I could relay to them the king's orders, and assured me of their readiness to make their way anywhere His Majesty would judge appropriate to employ them for the service of *la patrie*.[89]

This claim, that no naval officer had abandoned his post, had a sensational effect. It was the justification for Finistère's denunciation and it helped to provoke the virulent campaign to impeach the Minister of Marine.

Bertrand de Moleville first responded to the outcry in a speech on December 5. The speech made specific reference only to the accusations from Brest,[90] but it was a reply to all criticism resulting from his letter

---

[86] Death was also to be inflicted on those found encouraging military desertion. See "Decree Ordering *Emigrés* to Return to France, 9 November 1791"; in Stewart (ed.), pp. 272–274. Higonnet, pp. 73–78, explains the contrast between the Legislative Assembly's proposals for harsh anti-*émigré* legislation and its reluctance to definitively deny *émigré* nobles their civil rights in terms of ideological extremes in the Assembly; an élitist or Feuillant compromise disintegrated between these extremes.
[87] "Séance du 12 novembre 1791"; AP, vol. 35, pp. 27–29.
[88] *Moniteur*, vol. 10, p. 364 (14 novembre 1791). See also Bertrand de Moleville, *Private Memoirs*, I, pp. 230–232.
[89] "Lettre de M. de Bertrand, ministre de la marine, au rédacteur du Moniteur universal, 14 novembre 1791"; AP, vol. 35, pp. 667–668. See also *Moniteur*, vol. 10, p. 390 (17 novembre 1791).
[90] The petitions from the naval port had not only charged the Minister with wilful negligence in regard to emigration, but also with refusing to implement the new naval organization and with appointing known suspects like Lajaille.

131

to the *Moniteur* including the condemnation by the Department of Finistère. He provided an account of the measures taken by the Marine department to suspend the pay of officers who were absent without legal sanction, to dismiss those who had not taken the oath, and to demonstrate that he and his commanders had kept strictly to the letter of the decrees of the National Assembly.[91] Regarding his letter to the *Moniteur*, he emphasized a distinction between officers known to have emigrated and desertion from active duty:

> I certainly do not ignore that at this moment, many naval officers are outside the kingdom; but it is also true that among these officers, there is not one who has abandoned his service; that is to say, none of those who were employed, whether at sea, or in the ports, deserted his post. They have reproached me for having publicly announced this fact; but it was certain then, and I have reason to believe it still is. I could therefore say it, and it was my duty to publish it.[92]

The Minister would reiterate this distinction several times in the weeks ahead and, just as often, his detractors would label it treacherous equivocation.

There can be little doubt that the Minister of Marine was juggling definitions of "service" to justify his position, but this did not mean that he sought to conceal the facts for the purpose of conspiracy. While his *Memoirs* reveal his strong sympathy for the naval officer corps, this is not the same as admitting that he supported, encouraged, or abetted emigration. He believed it was his duty to protect and reassure officers at a time when the navy was in a virtual state of mutiny. Since the attendance of all officers at the ports was not an absolute necessity, he claimed that a rigorous insistence on this point would only drive more of them to resign their commissions.[93] The Minister acknowledged the existence of naval *émigrés*, but he defended the need to contrast these men, in the public eye, with the officers serving faithfully in the ports. His argument, which rings true, was that if the officers who remained were treated as potential *émigrés*, the attitude would become a self-fulfilling prophecy.[94] Most importantly, Bertrand de Moleville perceived

[91] Bertrand de Moleville, *Discours du Ministre de la Marine, prononcé à la séance du 5 décembre 1791* (Paris: Imprimerie Nationale, 1791), pp. 2–6 [BN 8 Le33 3T{8}]. See also AP, vol. 35, pp. 587–590.
[92] Bertrand de Moleville, *Discours . . . 5 décembre 1791*, pp. 6–7.
[93] Bertrand de Moleville, *Private Memoirs*, I, p. 279.
[94] Bertrand de Moleville, *Discours . . . 5 décembre 1791*, pp. 8–9.

the situation of naval officers in the context of a general attack on executive power. As he said on December 5, the attack against himself was only part of a larger assault:

I have waited with impatience until a formal accusation against myself should furnish me with an opportunity of submitting to the wisdom and to the justice of the National Assembly some reflections, to induce them to receive with circumspection the perpetual accusations, so often unfoundedly renewed, against the principal agents of the executive power.[95]

Bertrand de Moleville thus phrased his speech as a reply to injustices against all ministers, and not simply as a personal defence. Very shortly afterwards, however, the Minister of Marine found himself the sole target of a concerted campaign in the Legislative Assembly. "The storm which had been so long preparing against me at length broke out," he wrote in his *Memoirs*, "and Cavellier, clerk of the office of marine at Brest came forward as my accuser."[96] He claimed that the origins of the conflict between himself and this deputy from Finistère, whom he deemed "as great a knave as the Revolution produced," were personal: Cavellier was motivated not only by opposition to the Minister's proposed reforms to stop pillaging and fraud in the ports, from which he and his friends benefitted, but by Bertrand de Moleville's refusal to award him a higher position in the department.[97] This is impossible to verify, but it was true that Blaise Cavellier, acting as spokesman for the Marine Committee, presented the formal denunciations of the Minister of Marine and argued fiercely for his removal. The duel in the Assembly developed through Cavellier's successive reports and Bertrand de Moleville's ripostes.

Cavellier struck the first blow on December 8 with a report on the Marine Committee's examination of the petitions from Brest, along with

---

[95] Ibid., p. 1. See also Bertrand de Moleville, *Private Memoirs*, I, pp. 241–242.

[96] Bertrand de Moleville, *Private Memoirs*, p. 239. There is some confusion in the *Memoirs* about the sequence of events since he claims that the December 5 speech was in direct response to Cavellier's accusation. Cavellier, however, did not present the first of his reports against the Minister until December 8.

[97] Ibid., pp. 239–241. Blaise Cavellier had been a *commis de marine* at Brest and was elected municipal *procureur* in March 1790, with the protest of Commandant Hector who saw this function as incompatible with Cavellier's administrative duty to the navy. Henwood and Monage, pp. 75, 108 describe Cavellier as an influential Jacobin and interpret his election to the Legislative Assembly as evidence of anti-monarchical sentiment in Brest.

the result of the October extraordinary review and lists of absent officers still on the navy's payroll. The report was, however, as much a thrust against Bertrand de Moleville's letter to the *Moniteur* as it was an analysis of the documents from Brest. The Committee was shocked, according to Cavellier, that the Minister could state that no naval officer had left his post given the Brest roll-call or the notorious cases of naval emigration such as the comte d'Hector's known presence at Coblenz.[98] The Minister's attempt to justify the departure of some officers from the ports on the grounds of supposed attacks against them was even worse: such an apology for emigration marked an ordinary citizen as a coward, but it constituted treason from a member of the military. "Could the Minister of Marine have authorized such guilty conduct?" asked Cavellier rhetorically, "could he have accepted such wretched excuses? could he have developed them himself? and by wanting to palliate the crime, is not this in some ways to share it?"[99] The Minister's justifications for officer absenteeism were nothing more than poorly disguised pretexts, and, combined with his efforts to reconcile ficticious existence in the ports with real existence outside the kingdom, revealed his desire to conserve naval rank and salaries for *émigrés*. Having thus established Bertrand de Moleville's guilty responsibility, Cavellier proclaimed that all officer deserters must be replaced, preferably from the skilled but non-noble elements within the navy whose patriotism would more than compensate for their lack of "theory."[100] The report, and the Bill which accompanied it, concluded with a demand for an end to the abuses of Commandants and the Minister in granting leaves: "the Minister of Marine should not and must not accord or prolong leaves at his pleasure, and it is fitting to limit, by a precise disposition, his authority in this regard."[101] The problem of officer emigration was thus blamed specifically on the excessive and treacherous power of executive authority.

Bertrand de Moleville responded by refuting specific charges. He declared that he could account legitimately for every leave of absence

---

[98] Cavellier, *Rapport fait à l'Assemblée nationale au nom du comité de la marine, sur la nécessité de mettre à exécution la loi du 15 mai, concernant l'organisation de la marine; de remplacer les officiers émigrés, ou qui ont déserté leur poste; et de réformer quelques abus relatifs au congés* (Paris: Imprimerie Nationale, 1791), pp. 5–6 [BN 8 Le33 3T{9}]. See also AP, vol. 35, pp. 662–665.

[99] Ibid., p. 7.

[100] Ibid., pp. 8–9.

[101] Ibid., p. 11.

awarded during his ministry and he insisted that if any *émigrés* had received payments it was because treasury officials had broken the law requiring certificates of residence. He disputed the results of the reviews at Brest, which he said had neglected numerous legitimate absences, and he reiterated his distinction between officers deserting from active duty, which had not occurred, and the abuse of leaves by many to flee the country. He pointed again to his efforts to dissuade naval officers from leaving and lashed out at his accusers, blaming them for favouring emigration by their continued refutation of his assertion to the *Moniteur*.[102]

The Minister of Marine was clearly unperturbed by the denunciations. This failure to shake him, or weaken his political position, helped focus the general assault against the executive into a personal attack. Cavellier's report of December 29 was concerned not with emigration, but with Bertrand de Moleville. The Marine Committee's spokesman challenged the Minister's claim that officers were free to return home when not on active duty on the basis of existing regulations. The results of Brest's November review showed, even more than previous roll-calls, that he had lied and had sought to mislead the nation. The report's proposed decree had, therefore, a single objective:

The National Assembly, having listened to the report of its Marine Committee, considering that the Minister of Marine wanted, . . . to deceive the king, to abuse the confidence vested in him by the legislative corps, and to impose on the French people; considering that he has rendered himself guilty to some extent of crimes which he has tried to palliate; considering its importance to public security and to the maintenance of the Constitution, that an offense so serious should not remain unpunished; decrees to declare to the king that his Minister of Marine has lost the confidence of the nation.[103]

A motion of non-confidence in the Legislative Assembly would not lead automatically to a minister's loss of office, as it would in the British parliament. Because of the Revolutionary insistence on the separation of powers, ministers were neither appointed by nor responsible to the Assembly. Failing their cooperation, which Bertrand de Moleville

---

[102] "Lettre du ministre de la marine. Paris, le 13 décembre 1791"; AP, vol. 36, pp. 200–203.
[103] "M. Cavellier, au nom du comité de marine, fait un Rapport sur les dénunciations portées contre le ministre de ce département, 29 décembre 1791"; AP, vol. 36, p. 638.

specifically withheld, the only means to remove ministers from office, or to control royal policy, was to attack them as individuals. Thus Cavellier's motion was equivalent to a call for the minister's impeachment, which meant placing him on trial for treason.

Cavellier repeated his denunciation two weeks later in an even stronger report. There remained two primary issues, Cavellier said, despite the Minister's efforts to divert the Assembly: the clearly false claims that no officer had abandoned his post, and the Minister's prolongation of leaves for officers who were absent illegally or whose furloughs had long expired.[104] Cavellier supported these charges by reiterating past arguments, with minor variations, and attached extensive documentation particularly of the November 20 extraordinary review at Brest.[105] It was the Assembly's duty, he declared, to denounce agents of the executive power who prevaricated. The deputies were charged with surveillance of the ministers and they could not tolerate or excuse any misdeed in their administrations. Therefore, Cavellier insisted, it must be declared to the king that the Minister of Marine had lost the nation's confidence.[106]

Meanwhile, Bertrand de Moleville submitted an extensive memoir of justification of his own to the Assembly, complete with copious supporting documentation, in which he again responded to the specific accusations directed against him from the ports.[107] Indeed, he expressed surprise that the Marine Committee had neglected these and had concentrated instead on his letter to the *Moniteur*.[108] Why, asked the Minister, was this contentious claim not rebuked as inexact or the product of

---

[104] Cavellier, *Rapport fait à l'Assemblée nationale, au nom du comité de marine, le 13 janvier 1792* (Paris: Imprimerie Nationale, 1792), p. 4 [BN 8 Le33 3T{14}]. See also AP, vol. 37, pp. 362–363.

[105] Cavellier, *Rapport . . . 13 janvier 1792*, pp. 9–27. See also AP, vol. 37, pp. 376–393.

[106] Cavellier, *Rapport . . . 13 janvier 1792*, p. 8.

[107] Along with the petitions from Brest, Bertrand de Moleville included a "Pétition des citoyens de la ville de Rochefort, à l'Assemblée nationale, 8 novembre 1791"; AP, vol. 37, pp. 21–22. See: "Pièces Justificatifs du mémoire du ministre de la marine sur les inculpations dirigées contre lui par des citoyens de Rochefort et de Brest et sur lesquelles il a été fait un rapport par le comité de marine"; AP, vol. 37, pp. 20–25. For further justification of the *congés* which he had awarded, see: Bertrand de Moleville, *Lettre du Ministre de la marine, à M. le Président de l'Assemblée nationale. Paris, 20 janvier 1792* (Paris: Imprimerie Nationale, 1792) [BN 8 Lb39 10399].

[108] "M. Bertrand, ministre de la marine, fait lecture d'un mémoire justificatif des inculpations dirigées contre lui par des citoyens de Rochefort et de Brest et sur lesquelles il a été fait un rapport par le comité de marine, 2 janvier 1792"; AP, vol. 37, p. 11.

simple misinformation instead of condemned as a criminal deceit? It was, he replied, supplying his own answer, because his accusers were concerned with demonstrating and interpreting secret intentions rather than facts.[109] He pursued this analysis of the logic of Revolutionary denunciation further in his speech to the Assembly on January 19, 1792. Bertrand de Moleville argued that as a minister and public figure, he should be held accountable for the acts of his administration, but not for the expression of private opinion such as his letter to the newspaper.[110] The real issue was whether, by sentiment, he was an "enemy of the People and of the Constitution." It was all the more difficult to defend himself from such vague, but damning imputations because many of them came from within his own department. Many clerks of the naval administration at Brest, fearing the loss of their positions through his measures of economy, had supported the petitions against the Minister.[111] The parallel with the situation facing all naval authority is clear. According to Bertrand de Moleville, government would become untenable if his attackers were successful:

What would this bring, Gentlemen, and what economic operation, what act of administration would be possible, if all subordinates can ceaselessly join their resentments, their interests to accusations against their superiors? If these accusations, always welcomed, leave them with the certainty of impunity, even when they are calumnious, what Constitution would be able to resist this combination of attacks and protection? Disadvantages just as serious will strike you, separate from my own grievances, and you will perceive, Gentlemen, that the responsibility with which ministers are charged can only be exercised when they themselves will be, as citizens and public functionaries, under the safeguard of the law.[112]

The Minister of Marine asked that a decision be reached on the denunciations against him as soon as possible,[113] but it was not until

---

[109] Ibid., AP, vol. 37, pp. 12–13.

[110] "M. Bertrand, ministre de la marine, demande et obtient la parole pour répondre aux divers rapports du comité de marine sur les dénonciations portées contre lui, 19 janvier 1792"; AP, vol. 37, p. 509.

[111] AP, vol. 37 p. 510. Aside from the animosity of Cavellier, Bertrand de Moleville gives other examples of naval *commis* who agitated against ministerial authority in his *Private Memoirs*, I, pp. 201, 210–211, 245, 248.

[112] "M. Bertrand, . . . répondre aux divers rapports . . . 19 janvier 1792"; AP, vol. 37, p. 510.

[113] "Lettre de M. Bertrand, ministre de la marine, par laquelle il prie l'Assemblée de porter, sans délai une déceision sur les dénonciations dont il a été l'objet et qui ont déjà éprouvé de très long rétards, 21 janvier 1792"; AP, vol. 37, pp. 559–560.

February 1, 1792 that the Legislative Assembly considered its Marine Committee's proposal of non-confidence. The vote on such a question had great significance and therefore the debate which preceded it was charged with emotion.[114] At one point the session dissolved into complete chaos, individuals threatening the President and demanding to speak, and deputies screamed mutual recriminations from all parts of the hall. The actual debate displayed a wide range of political positions and ideological rhetoric. Accusations of plots featured prominently. All of the Minister's actions, according to Ducos, could be explained by a sinister conspiracy to place the fleet in the hands of enemies of the People. Quatremère-Quincy suggested that the denunciations against the Minister were themselves the product of secret motivations, and that dark forces sought to transform the Assembly into an instrument of intrigue.[115] His admonition, with reference to the British parliament, that a motion of non-confidence should not be used lightly was in opposition to Grangeneuve's insistence that such a proposal was not strong enough: Grangeneuve demanded a decree of accusation, the equivalent of impeachment.[116] Lagrévol, who spoke in the Minister's defence, also recognized that there were no consti-tutional grounds for a decree of non-confidence. He gave the debate's final speech and dismissed each of the specific charges against Bertrand de Moleville on the grounds that judgment must be based on positive fact and not on interpretation. After warning the Assembly of the danger in seeking public confidence through condemnation of innocents, Lagrévol asked the deputies if they were prepared to face the real constitutional issue: what if the king, having been told that the Minister of Marine had lost the confidence of the Assembly, replied that the Minister continued to hold his confidence?[117]

The hour was already late when the Assembly decided not to deliberate on a decree of accusation. Many of the deputies most hostile to the Minister of Marine called for an *Appel nominal* to decide on the Marine Committee's motion of non-confidence.[118] This was the first of these roll-calls, in which

---

[114] "Discussion du projet de décret du comité de marine sur la dénonciation portée contre M. Bertrand, ministre de ce département, 1er février 1792"; AP, vol. 38, pp. 80–92.
[115] AP, vol. 38, p. 89.
[116] "Le décret d'accusation est une arme remise en vos mains par la nation, pour le salut du peuple, c'est un droit qui vous est délégué"; AP, vol. 38, p. 84.
[117] AP, vol. 38, p. 92.
[118] In point of fact, the vote was on the *question préalable*, the necessary preliminary question before the *projet de décret* could be voted into law. Therefore the actual votes

each deputy was called upon in turn to declare his opinion, to be held in the Legislative Assembly and it indicated the importance of the issue.[119] It was almost midnight when the deputies cast the final vote and the result was very close: 196 for the proposal and 208 against.[120] Despite the denunciations and the passions aroused, a slim majority of deputies rejected a demand for the impeachment of the Minister of Marine.

Thus the Assembly shied away from a direct questioning of the Constitution, and reaffirmed the legitimacy of executive power as part of national government. But this majority decision was not accepted. The Legislative Assembly was bitterly divided. Whether this is seen in terms of a "Right"–"Left" split, or in terms of division between more specific factions such as "Feuillants" and "Brissotins," it is clear that great ideological differences separated the deputies.[121] Some of them espoused an interpretation of Popular Sovereignty which did not confine the "People's Will" to the Assembly's legislation, and did not accept the legitimacy of executive authority.[122] Those deputies who rejected

were given in response to the question: "Y a-t-il lieu à délibérer sur le projet du comité, oui ou non?"

[119] C. J. Mitchell, "Political Divisions within the Legislative Assembly of 1791," *French Historical Studies*, 13 (1984), 358 states the importance of the *appels nominaux*: "The significance of such occasions in the Legislative Assembly was that opinions on the motion before the Assembly were strongly held, either rendering the opposing sides irreconcilable or ensuring that at least one side considered the motion important enough to warrant its stand and its opponent's stand being fully recorded."

[120] AP, vol. 38, p. 92. For a list of the deputies who were present for the *appel nominal*, and their votes, see: "Liste des membres qui, dans la séance du mercredi, 1er février 1792, au soir, ont pris part au vote par appel nominal sur cette question: 'Y a-t-il lieu à délibérer sur le projet du comité de marine tendant à déclarer au roi que le ministre de la marine a perdu la confiance de la nation? Oui ou non"; AP, vol. 39, p. 493. Bertrand de Moleville, *Private Memoirs*, I, p. 243 claims that the *appel nominal* was so close because many who supported him were overconfident that a majority would reject the motion and so had gone home before the vote.

[121] C. J. Mitchell, pp. 356–389 uses the seven *appels nominaux* during the life of the Legislative Assembly to develop a new terminology by which to designate deputies as either "*non*-voters," broadly designating conservatives, or "*oui*-voters," the radicals. Whether or not this is a convincing method of identifying the division, Mitchell illustrates the polarization of debate in the Assembly. For a discussion specifically of the leading radical deputies associated loosely with Jean-Pierre Brissot, see M. J. Sydenham, *The Girondins* (London, 1961; repr. Westport, Conn.: Greenwood Press, 1976), pp. 99–122. For discussions of the different factions or divisions in the Legislative Assembly, see: J. M. Thompson, pp. 248–257; Reinhard, pp. 197–208; Doyle, *Oxford History*, pp. 174–176.

[122] It should be noted that some deputies used rhetoric which suggested a more radical vision of Popular Sovereignty than they actually held. Brissot and his associates denounced the "Austrian Committee" and the existing ministry, but their goal was the establishment of the "Patriot Ministry" in the spring of 1792; it could be argued that

the results of the *appel nominal* presented further criticisms of the Minister of Marine to the king in March.[123] Bertrand de Moleville remained in office for only another month and a half, but he resigned because of a political crisis within the Royal Council rather than because of the continuing campaign against him.

The crisis involved Narbonne, with whom Bertrand de Moleville had quarreled over the appropriate behavior of the executive towards the Assembly. In March, Narbonne published letters from Generals Rochambeau, Luckner, and Lafayette which claimed that they would retire if the Minister of War left office.[124] This flagrant appeal to popular support, without consultation of king or cabinet colleagues, alienated all the ministers. They wanted nothing more to do with Narbonne, but were concerned with the effect that his dismissal might have. According to Bertrand de Moleville, they decided that he must also resign to appease public opinion. The Minister of Marine protested that such an act would appear as an acknowledgment of the claims made against him in the Assembly. He wished instead to continue in his administration until March 15, the day fixed for the general review of the new naval officer corps, which was the symbolic date he had decided upon for his own resignation. Cahier de Gerville, Minister of the Interior, insisted that the Council could not wait. Bertrand de Moleville agreed finally to step down, provided his resignation was not made public until the king answered the new criticisms from the Assembly.[125] The Council accepted this proposal. The king dismissed Narbonne on March 9, and expressed his satisfaction with the conduct of his Minister of Marine the following day.[126] Jean de

they wished to control and not to dispense with executive authority. See Sydenham, *Girondins*, pp. 103–107. This explains, in part, the break between Brissot and Robespierre. Furet, pp. 65–68 stresses the difference in their use of Revolutionary Discourse: "The Girondins were, as has so often been said, 'light-weight' not so much in their failure to implement their policies (for revolutionary politics were not concerned with means) as in their half-hearted use of the language of the Revolution. Robespierre, who identified completely with that language, could dispatch them in advance to a guillotine of their own making"; p. 68.

[123] AP, vol. 39, pp. 30–31, 391–392, 482–493.

[124] See "Lettre du maréchal Luckner à M. Narbonne," *Moniteur*, vol. 11, p. 582 (10 mars 1792). See also Bertrand de Moleville, *Private Memoirs*, I, pp. 339–341, and Reinhard, pp. 252–253.

[125] Bertrand de Moleville, *Private Memoirs*, I, pp. 241–242. Regarding the king's response, see pp. 347–352.

[126] King's Response, 10 March 1792; AP, vol. 39, p. 531. Regarding Narbonne's dismissal, see *Moniteur*, vol. 11, pp. 588, 590 (10, 11 mars 1792); for a letter which

Lacoste formally replaced Bertrand de Moleville on March 15, 1792.[127] Bertrand de Moleville's description of the last Council meeting he attended gives a pathetic picture of the helplessness of the king and, by extension, of royal government in general.[128] It might be concluded that his own resignation as Minister represented the collapse of national executive power in regard to the navy. It has been argued in the preceding pages that the attempt to impeach Bertrand de Moleville reflected an offensive against the authority of naval officers being waged in France's naval bases. Local popular assemblies, particularly port municipalities, perceived the authority of Commandants and their subordinates as a threat because it was derived from the distant and distrusted royal executive and was not dependent on local approval. Thus naval officers seemed to be responsible only indirectly to the "Will of the Sovereign People," of which local assemblies saw themselves as the embodiment. The fact that officers were predominantly aristocratic helps to explain Revolutionary suspicion and animosity toward them, but equality was certainly not the only issue behind the conflict.

Port municipalities, often in alliance with Jacobin clubs, sought to undermine the governance of naval officers in keeping with the principle of Popular Sovereignty. They subverted the navy's efforts to enforce discipline over its sailors and workers, and they defended, even encouraged, the rising tide of mutiny. In response to this dissolution of its authority, a large portion of the fleet's officer corps abandoned the

ascribes the Minister's dismissal explicitly to Counter-Revolutionary machinations, see *Moniteur*, vol. 11, p. 662 (19 mars 1792).

[127] Letter from the king announcing nomination of Lacoste to replace Bertrand as Minister of Marine, 16 March 1792; AP, vol. 40, p. 56. Lacoste's appointment was included in the formation of Dumouriez's "Patriot Ministry," but the new Minister of Marine is usually seen as a nonentity in comparison to some of his colleagues or to his predecessor. He had been *chef au bureau des colonies* and then served as civil commissioner to the Windward Islands before being named to the Royal Council. Although Lacoste's correspondence shows his high opinion of his own merits, Guérin, V, pp. 352–353, 530 states bluntly that "comme ministre de la marine, il fut un paperassier et rien de plus." Bertrand de Moleville is more generous: "This man, so violent in his temper, and coarse in his manners, ought never to have been raised from the sphere in which he had before passed his life, . . . but, with all that was faulty or ridiculous in his manners, Lacoste was, at bottom, an honest man: he detested the cruelties of the Revolution; he always behaved respectfully to the King, and gave his Majesty some proofs of attachment which required courage"; *Private Memoirs*, I, pp. 357–358. Lacoste would resign from the Ministry on July 10, 1792, stating that the powers of the executive had become inadequate to carry on government.

[128] Bertrand de Moleville, *Private Memoirs*, I, p. 354.

service or found ways to avoid duty in the ports. This absenteeism, often only a step towards emigration, was both the result of local Revolutionary activity and its vindication. Bertrand de Moleville was denounced when he appeared to minimize the extent of officer emigration, and even to protect naval suspects, as a logical extension of the attack by the muncipality of Brest and the Department of Finistère on the authority of local naval commanders. This did not represent merely a power struggle in the ports, but an integral element of Revolutionary ideology. The campaign against the Minister of Marine in the Legislative Assembly was part of a larger conflict over the equation of the Sovereignty of the Nation with the authority of royal government.

Yet Bertrand de Moleville resigned, he was not impeached. Despite the powerful influence of Revolutionaries from Brest, Rochefort, and elsewhere, the Legislative Assembly retreated from a direct assault on the principle of executive authority in this case.[129] The rigid and practically immutable Constitution, which the Minister of Marine had enforced to the limit in order to undermine it, remained in operation and continued to give legal justification to ministerial government. Its collapse awaited a second revolution, directed in part against the Assembly,[130] and the violent overthrow of the monarchy by the armed force of the Paris Sections and provincial *fédérés*, the Brestois prominent among them.[131] Though shaken severely by the emigration of so many subordinates and by the opposition of local popular assemblies, the authority of naval commanders also remained intact. The actual support from central government waned, but naval officers who remained at their posts were still responsible, in theory, only to Paris. Further local domination of the navy was achieved only through violence. Yet such violence did not occur at Brest, the focus of hostility against Bertrand de Moleville, but at Toulon.

---

[129] Outrage in the Assembly over the dismissal of Narbonne led to the impeachment of Delessart, Minister of Foreign Affairs, on March 10, 1792. His removal preceded the king's dismissal of the entire Council and appointment of the "Patriot Ministry," including Dumouriez, Roland, and Clavière. See: Doyle, *Oxford History*, p. 180; Reinhard, pp. 256–257; J. M. Thompson, pp. 281–282.

[130] See Sydenham, *Girondins*, p. 113, and *French Revolution*, pp. 109–113.

[131] For a detailed discussion of the August 10, 1792 attack on the Tuileries Palace, see Reinhard, pp. 389–410, 581–589. Regarding the participation of the *fédérés* from Brest, see Henwood and Monage, pp. 120–125.

6

NAVAL OFFICERS AND THE JACOBIN REGIME, 1792–1793: THE COURT MARTIAL OF CAPTAIN BASTEROT

The fall of the monarchy signalled a new phase in the French navy's relationship to the Revolution. The majority of the old officer corps had left the service by 1792 principally owing to the interference of popular assemblies in the ports. Municipalities viewed naval commanders as rivals for local power and did not hesitate to undermine their authority with sailors and arsenal workers. Put in terms of Revolutionary ideology, the officers' authority appeared to be an obstacle to the exercise of Popular Sovereignty because it was derived from suspect national executive power and not directly from the "People." The overthrow of this distrusted executive on August 10, 1792 heralded not only the collapse of a weak central government, but the installation of local radical, or Jacobin, regimes. In the naval port of Toulon this involved a bloody coup against moderate opponents followed by terrible acts of popular violence which ensured, at least temporarily, local Jacobin control over the naval establishment.

Yet naval officers, both the newcomers promoted into the corps as well as the important minority who remained from the old service, generally welcomed the inauguration of the Republic. Those serving in French ports hoped that the new government in Paris would not only restore order, but establish strong national authority vital to the fleet. This became critical in 1793 when the Convention escalated the war against Austria and Prussia to include hostilities with Spain, Holland, and Great Britain. War with Britain meant a major maritime struggle and the navy suddenly became vital to the survival of the Republic. The need for rapid mobilization and central control of naval operations brought into the open the fundamental tension between national interests and the control over France's naval bases by local Revolutionary administrations.

This tension created the difficult situation faced by naval officers during the early period of the Republic. Their authority as agents of a government ruling in the name of the Sovereign People should have been upheld by local Jacobins. Events showed, however, no such automatic shift in attitude. Despite the patriotic enthusiasm for the war effort, radical suspicion of the officer corps became more intense and interference became more flagrant. This was particularly true in Toulon. A steady deterioration of the relations between local Revolutionaries and the navy in that port led to an incident in the spring of 1793 which illustrates the larger dilemma facing French naval officers. The incident was the Court Martial of Captain Basterot.

Two days after the declaration of the French Republic on September 21, 1792, Gaspard Monge delivered his *Compte Rendu* on the state of the navy to the National Convention. The celebrated mathematician, who had been named as Minister of Marine on August 10,[1] admitted that the Republic had inherited a service in disarray, but insisted that future prospects were bright. Port administration had been reorganized and the naval arsenals were well supplied.[2] The fleet was strong and, Monge claimed, manned by enthusiastic patriots: "Union and fraternity reign in all crews of these ships. Officers, sailors and soldiers, all have

[1] AP, vol. 47, p. 660. A student of the *Ecole du Génie de Mézières*, Monge was appointed professor there in 1772 and elected to the Academy of Sciences. In 1788 he published a *Traité élémentaire de statique à l'usage des collèges de marine*; see Taillemite, *Dictionnaire*, p. 238. Monge replaced the vicomte Dubouchage, who had acted as Minister for less than three weeks. Monge was a friend of the Rolands, according to Sydenham, *Girondins*, p. 114, but was also well known to Condorcet. Assessments of his performance as Minister of Marine vary. Guérin, V, p. 357 stated that, despite the best of intentions, Monge's incapacity as an administrator "fut si flagrante que, dans le temps, les plus grands admirateurs de son génie scientifique en avaient honte pour eux-mêmes et pour lui." A similarly harsh judgement is given by Lévy-Schneider, I, p. 309 who characterizes Monge as a "Girondin" nominee and states that, although a great mathematician, he was no sailor and that "il se montra très au-dessous de sa tâche." Thus despite the great difference in their political orientations, both of these classic historians of the French navy are highly critical of Monge's administration. A more positive, and perhaps less ideologically driven, assessment is given by Joret, I, pp. 130–148. Joret argues that Monge was the first Minister to acknowledge the true situation of the officer corps and that his action was decisive in beginning the creation of a Republican navy.

[2] Monge, *Compte Rendu à la Convention Nationale par le Ministre de la Marine, de l'état de situation de la Marine de la République, le 23 septembre de l'an premier; imprimé & envoyé aux 83 Départements et à l'Armée, par ordre de la Convention Nationale* (Paris: Imprimerie Nationale, 1792) pp. 2, 6–10 [BN 8 Le37 2H].

sworn with enthusiasm to maintain liberty and equality; they are full of confidence in their commanders."[3] Even more striking was Monge's assessment of the state of the officer corps: "Today, the Minister assures the Convention that it will find in the national navy a nursery of fine navigators, capable of defending the Republic's flag, and devoted to the maintenance of its liberty."[4]

After three years of Revolution, this optimistic picture of the French navy is misleading. The ships, whether commissioned or in the dockyards, were in poor condition[5] and naval authorities had long complained of the lack of sailors.[6] Moreover, the alleged enthusiasm of seamen masked much insubordination and a high incidence of outright mutiny. Even worse, the shortage of officers seems to have reached its most critical level in mid-1792.[7] This collapse had prompted the Legislative Assembly, as one of its last measures, to introduce emergency legislation on September 17 to fill gaping holes in the officer corps. Retired officers were recalled to duty, and the promotion of lieutenants was accelerated; *enseignes entretenus* would fill half the vacancies for lieutenant and

---

[3] Ibid., p. 3.

[4] Ibid., p. 2.

[5] Although Monge admits that the navy was not prepared for any major programs of construction, his generally optimistic tone regarding the state of the arsenals is in marked contrast with Hampson, *La Marine de l'an II*, pp. 18–43. Hampson's research reveals that the fleet was in poor repair and that the ports were desperately short of material needed for ordinary maintenance. Monge, *Compte Rendu*, p. 5 states that twenty-one ships of the line were at sea and that thirty-four were outfitting. The Minister issued a circular to all naval ports in November asking for information on all warships which could be commissioned by January, February, and March of 1793. Based on the replies to this, Hampson, *La Marine de l'an II*, pp. 34–39 estimates that fewer than thirty-four ships of the line could be commissioned by the spring of 1793. Even accepting Monge's figures, the French fleet was in poor shape to begin a naval war with Great Britain.

[6] Marine BB 3/13, ff. 61, 75, 109. See also Hampson, *La Marine de l'an II*, pp. 45–46.

[7] The results of the March 15, 1792 general review of the officer corps are cited in Lévy-Schneider, I, p. 306. The number of officers remaining at their posts compared to the table drawn up for the reorganized corps in May 1791 were: 2 of 9 *vice-amirals*; 3 of 18 *contre-amirals*; 42 of 170 *capitaines de vaisseaux*; 356 of 530 *lieutenants de vaisseaux*. Guérin, V, p. 354 cites the same figures except for the rank of lieutenant in which case he states that 390 of 750 remained, of which 180 were former *sous-lieutenants*. For the situation in Brest, the figures given by Joret, I, p. 118 indicate that 304 of 540 officers were absent; only 19 captains were present for the five squadrons based in Brest. The situation had become so bad in Toulon by June 1792 that Commandant Flotte reported to the Minister that only two lieutenants remained in the port and that all details rested on himself and *major-général* Castellan; Marine BB 3/13, f. 109. See also: Marine BB 3/13, ff. 58, 75, 95.

Plate 4. Gaspard Monge.
Engraving by Jacob (Phot. Bibl. Nat. Paris)

merchant officers could compete for places as ensigns.[8] Perhaps the Minister referred to these measures when he claimed that the navy contained a "nursery of fine navigators," yet he certainly implied that the morale and dedication of all naval officers was high.

[8] "M. Le Tourneur, au nom du comité de marine, donné lecture d'un projet de décret sur les retraites et sur le mode d'avancement et de remplacement des officiers de la marine, 17 septembre 1792"; AP, vol. 50 pp. 75–76. A Bill was also adopted which eliminated the old ranks of *élève* and *volontaire* and created *aspirants* – roughly

Monge's picture of the navy in September 1792 raises an important question: what was the reaction of the naval officer corps to the advent of the Republic? In some cases officers rejected the new regime totally. Many in the West Indies responded to the news of August 10 by striking the tricolour and raising the white flag of the Bourbons. Chief among these rebels was the chevalier de Rivière, Captain of *Le Ferme* (74) and commander of the Windward Islands station, who had been involved in the early stages of the mutiny at Brest in 1790. Rivière united with colonists on Guadeloupe and Martinique who had declared for Counter-Revolution, and the commanders of at least three other warships followed him in this drastic course. This rebel squadron prevented the arrival of a troop convoy carrying the new Governor-General for the Windward Islands, and Rivière eventually turned his ship over to the Spanish in 1793.[9] Yet at least one officer in the Windward Islands, Lieutenant Duval commanding *La Perdrix*, continued to fly the National flag in defiance of his comrades' action.[10]

Significantly, the fall of the monarchy provoked no outcries of indignation in the naval bases of France. The officers continuing to serve at Brest and Toulon quickly demonstrated their loyalty to the nation. A *fête* held in Brest's harbour on August 23 celebrated the swearing of the new civic oath which no longer mentioned the king. The festivities included gun salutes, a double ration of wine for all hands, and the dedication of large Phrygian bonnets aboard the ships of the line.[11] The

the equivalent of midshipmen in the British Navy – which would be immediately junior to *enseignes*. There was to be an unlimited number of *aspirants* and the grade was to be open to all; AP, vol. 50, pp. 77–80.

[9] Marquis de Valous (ed.), *Avec les Rouges aux Iles du Vent: Souvenirs du chevalier de Valous (1790–1793) pendant la Révolution française* (Paris, 1930; repr. Paris: Editions Caribéennes, 1989), esp. 137–173. See also: Louis Dermigny and Gabriel Debien (eds.), "La Révolution au Antilles: Journal maritime du commandeur de Villevielle, commandant de la frégate La Didon (septembre 1790 – septembre 1792)," *Revue d'histoire de l'Amérique française*, 9 (1955), 55–73, 250–271; H. J. K. Jenkins, "The Leeward Islands Command, French Royalism and the *Bienvenue*; 1792–93," *Mariner's Mirror*, 71 (1985), 477–478; Guérin V, pp. 359–362, 392–394.

[10] AP, vol. 53, pp. 314–315. Guérin V, p. 360; significantly, Guérin subtitles this discussion "Guerres civiles de la marine française."

[11] Maurice Loir, "La Marine et la proclamation de la première République," *Revue maritime et coloniale*, vol. 127 (1895), pp. 258–260. Loir describes these bonnets, painted and shaped to resemble the headgear of the *sans-culottes*, as approximately 80 cm in diameter and made of either tin or wood; those of tin were mounted on the poop deck while the wooden bonnets were raised to the mizzen masthead. Phrygian bonnets were also inaugurated aboard warships in Toulon with pomp and ceremony

comte de Latouche-Tréville, *chef de division* and Captain of *Le Languedoc* (80), wrote to inform Monge that:

The crew, the officers and myself have sworn the new oath decreed by the Assembly. It is with the greatest pleasure that I have the honour to assure you that all officers and crews of the battleships are in the best dispositions, and I would wish that all military corps would be as well disposed as we are here to fulfill the oath to live free or to die.[12]

Toulon staged a similar celebration on September 2–3 and Monge praised the zeal and patriotism of the officers and men of the Mediterranean fleet in glowing terms.[13] The Minister singled out for special mention the exemplary conduct of the commanding officer, *contre-amiral* Truguet, who had reported on the devotion of his subordinates: "Never has a commander begun under happier auspices. All have sworn to me their friendship, confidence and submission, and my principles must demonstrate to you that I have neglected nothing to justify the general sentiment which it is believed I warrant."[14]

The acceptance of the fall of the monarchy, revealed in these declarations of loyalty to the new regime by Truguet and Latouche-Tréville, was not merely a demonstration of the naval officer corps' changing social composition. Latouche-Tréville was a count from a distinguished naval family and Truguet had also begun his career as a *garde de la marine*.[15] Both men could be considered liberals politically but, more

which included the participation of local civil authorities. See "Extrait du procès-verbal de ce qui s'est passé dans les journées des 2 et 3 septembre en rade de Toulon"; AP, vol. 50, pp. 53–55.

[12] Cited in Loir, "La Marine et la proclamation," p. 259.

[13] "Lettre de M. Monge, ministre de la marine, au Président de l'Assemblée nationale, 15 septembre 1792"; AP, vol. 50, p. 53. See also Marine BB 4/9, f. 17.

[14] "Lettre de M. Truguet, contre-amiral, commandant les forces navales de la Méditerranée, à M. Monge, ministre de la marine, 4 septembre 1792"; AP, vol. 50, p. 53.

[15] Louis-René Levassor, comte de Latouche-Tréville was born in 1745 into a naval family at Rochefort, and became a *garde de la marine* in 1758. He saw active duty in the Seven Years' War, but transferred into the army in 1768. He returned to the navy in 1772 as a *capitaine de brûlot* and, following promotion back into the *Grand Corps*, distinguished himself as a frigate captain during the American War. Elected as a deputy of the nobility in 1789, Latouche-Tréville was one of the early liberals to join the National Assembly. Promoted to *contre-amiral* in January 1793, he participated in the campaigns against Nice and Sardinia. Laurent-Jean-François Truguet was born at Toulon in 1752 and entered the navy as a *garde de la marine* in 1765. As an ensign and then lieutenant, he served in the American Revolutionary War. He was promoted to *capitaine de vaisseau* in January 1792, to *contre-amiral* in July, and given command

148

importantly, they were professional naval officers and their actions were not unique. The course of emigration taken by the majority of the *Grand Corps* entailed a definite personal choice. It is equally true that those officers who continued to serve in the navy by September of 1792 had also made a conscious choice. The decision to remain at their posts under difficult circumstances indicates the professional commitment of these men to their careers and, perhaps, to their country's service.[16] Their displays of apparent enthusiasm for the Republic should not be dismissed as insincere or as pragmatic trimming to the prevailing political wind. Monge's circular of February 15, 1793 to sailors, gunners, and soldiers illustrates the hopes that the French navy's commanders placed in the new regime. The Convention had declared war against Great Britain and Holland on February 1, and the Minister of Marine sought to recall the crews to necessary discipline:

But if on one side the Republic assures you a happy fate; if it anticipates your needs and desires; if the brave and patriotic captains under whom you have long served, are today aboard our ships and frigates; if our navy, purged of traitors and entirely regenerated, offers to the Republic only sure defenders on whom it can count, you will want, doubtless, to show your gratitude: Well! Citizens, do not abuse the softening of your duties given by the laws of liberty.

Consider that to command a ship properly it is necessary to be assured of the crew's obedience. . . . consider, dear fellow citizens, that in giving you patriotic and experienced captains, the Republic has the right to demand from you that you obey their orders without murmurs or reflection. It is essential to disappoint your enemies; they count on indiscipline and the spirit of fermentation: know therefore, citizens, that the most cruel enemies of your glory will be those who search to destroy your confidence in your captains. These are no longer aristocrats who command you, they are soldiers of *la Patrie* like you; it is therefore necessary to obey them, to take confidence in them, and to regard them as your friends and agents.[17]

of the Mediterranean fleet in August. See Taillemite, *Dictionnaire*, pp. 199–200, 327–328, and Six, *Dictionnaire biographique*, II, pp. 66–68, 515.

[16] Some officers of the old navy may have remained primarily because of financial dependence on their pay, but the number is difficult to determine. While some naval families had substantial holdings in Provence or Brittany, officers before the Revolution were renowned for their indebtedness. See Loir, "La Marine et la proclamation," p. 259, and Vergé-Franceschi, *Les officiers . . . Provençale*, pp. 214–235.

[17] Monge, *Circulaire aux Matelots, Canonniers et soldats de la Marine Française. Paris, le 15 février 1793* (Paris: C. F. Patris, no date); [BN Fol Lb41 4791].

Officers of the navy shared with other segments of the French population the hope that the founding of the Republic would bring a return of order and stability. This aspiration is perhaps too often neglected amidst historical assessments of widespread enthusiasm for a new era of equality and liberty. The Constitutional Monarchy had been a shaky edifice from its inception and its authority had always been tenuous. By 1792 naval authorities, like other agents of the executive power, wanted desperately to see the establishment of recognized and effective national government. Naval officers, whether "rouges" from the *Grand Corps* or newly promoted "bleus," could support the Republic wholeheartedly when the new regime's Minister of Marine was prepared to restore discipline in the fleet and arsenals. Moreover, they hoped that because the democratically elected National Convention – surely the embodiment of Popular Sovereignty – supported the Minister's authority, and that of his commanders, Revolutionaries in the ports would now support naval officers as arms of the Republic.

The overthrow of the monarchy was not, however, merely an act of political will. The assault on the Tuileries was a bitter and extremely bloody affair and heralded the beginning of a protracted period of violence, even anarchy, in Paris. The triumphant Revolutionary Commune and the Legislative Assembly were deeply suspicious of one another. The location of legitimate authority was far from clear, and the inauguration of the Jacobin Republic neither ended radical suspicion of executive power nor easily provided a national focus for Popular Sovereignty. Indeed, divisions between committed republicans appeared early and hardened as attitudes favouring compromise were gradually discarded. While the parliamentary history of 1792–1793 can be interpreted as the struggle by various factions to appropriate the legitimacy of Popular Will,[18] this picture of political and ideological conflict should not be confined to the benches of the National Convention. The phenomenon was national and was reflected in the experience of the navy as well as in Paris. Naval officers were particularly exposed to the trauma and violence of the Republic's birth in Toulon where events which gave control of the port to local extremists prefigured August 10.

The position of naval commanders in Toulon remained difficult following the "Affair" of December 1789. Continuing unrest among arsenal workers resulted from the failure of the economic situation to improve

---

[18] See for example Sydenham, *French Revolution*, esp. pp. 129–140, 155–161, 236–238, and Furet, esp. pp. 46–69.

during 1790. Workers continued to protest against the new system of contract payment which had replaced the old day wages in the dockyards.[19] The Constituent Assembly did not act to remedy conditions in Toulon, despite support for the workers' grievances submitted by the Commandant and the Intendant, and the navy's shortage of funds forced new lay-offs in the arsenal.[20] These measures provoked a riot on May 3, 1790 which was directed against the Commandant. A threatening crowd outside naval headquarters surrounded Glandevès, who had been formally appointed to replace Albert de Rioms, and dragged him to city hall, where he was forced to explain his position concerning several worker demands.[21] Although the effect of naval economies on the arsenal's labour force was the principal cause of the riot, the insurrection also had important political dimensions. The demands presented to Glandevès included, along with the recall of workers who had been dismissed, the release of several naval personnel imprisoned following the events of December 1 and the delivery of arms and ammunition from the arsenal to the National Guard. According to D. M. J. Henry, the prominent radical Jean-Sébastien Barthélemy interrogated Glandevès at city hall. Barthélemy also helped write the report on the riot which represented the municipality as the steadfast supporter of the workers in opposition to the navy.[22] Social unrest, therefore, was not isolated from the conflict of authorities in Toulon. Further evidence of the continuity of hostility against naval commanders came in August 1790. On August 11 *chef d'escadre* Castellet, one of those imprisoned with Albert de Rioms in December 1789, returned to Toulon from Nice to swear the new civic oath. A crowd demanded that he leave the city. Castellet was attacked on the highway while trying to flee Toulon, an incident remarkably similar to that involving Lajaille a year later, and only the arrival of a detachment of National Guardsmen led by Mayor Richard prevented his murder.[23]

---

[19] Hampson, "Ouvriers," pp. 294–295. See also Brun, II, pp. 162–164.
[20] Henry, I, pp. 116–118. See also letter of January 15, 1790 from the Minister of Marine to Glandevès denying his request to end payment *à l'entreprise*; Henry, I, pp. 350–351.
[21] Bertrand de Moleville, "Affaire de M. le commandeur de Glandevès. Mai 1790," [Part of the Supplement to his *Compte Rendu* of 27 March 1792]; AP, vol. 40, p. 554. See also Crook, *Toulon*, p. 95 and Brun, II, pp. 165–166.
[22] Henry, I, pp. 118–123.
[23] Brun, II, pp. 168–169. There is some dispute as to who actually saved the officer from his attackers. Bertrand de Moleville, "Affaire de M. de Castellet. Août 1790," [Part of Supplement to his *Compte Rendu* of 27 March 1792]; AP, vol. 40, pp. 554–555 and Henry, I, pp. 140–141 claim that the mayor was ineffectual and that only the

The struggle between naval and Revolutionary authority in Toulon should not obscure the fact that the port's inhabitants were themselves divided. A dialectic of naval establishment versus homogenous civil population is far too simplistic. Recent historical studies, principally those of Malcolm Crook, illustrate the complexity of the situation in Toulon. Crook suggested that a bitter conflict for control of the city developed following the Revolution of 1789 and that the opposing factions were based on deep social divisions.[24] The first year of Revolution had merely given power to the wealthy élite of lawyers, wholesale merchants, and property owners who had dominated Toulon before 1789. Yet the emergence of a popular movement soon challenged these notables. Crook referred to the opposing factions as "Radicals" and "Conservatives." The radicals were drawn from the fringes of Toulon's élite: minor legal figures, clerks, retailers, surgeons; and their powerbase was the city's Jacobin club – the Club Saint-Jean. The conservative notables, on the other hand, relied on dominating the higher local administrations: the District and Departmental Directories, the Criminal Tribunal.[25] The key factor, however, was the support the radicals received not merely from the *sans-culottes* of Toulon, but from the mass of workers and sailors in the arsenal.[26]

Just as Toulon's Revolutionary municipality used economic discontent in the dockyards to undermine and challenge naval authority, so could the port's radicals turn it against their civic rivals. Such discontent mobilized workers against Commandant Glandevès in May 1790 and the situation in the arsenal did not improve in subsequent months. The Constituent Assembly's decree of October 1790 which granted the return of day wages for repair work made little difference.[27] Conditions worsened during 1791 as more unemployed were allowed within the arsenal gates and the financially strapped navy began to use *assignats* for a portion of its workers' wages.[28] Their introduction in Toulon caused

chance arrival of some troops from the Barrois regiment prevented Castellet's death. See also Havard, I, pp. 70–71.

[24] Crook, *Toulon*, esp. pp. 36–47, 64–65, 83–87. See also M. H. Crook, "Federalism and the French Revolution: The Revolt of Toulon in 1793," *History*, 65: 215 (1980), pp. 383–397, and Vovelle, pp. 165–210.

[25] Crook, *Toulon*, pp. 89–93, 100–103; "Federalism and the French Revolution," pp. 384–385.

[26] Vovelle, pp. 173–175.

[27] Hampson, "Ouvriers," p. 294.

[28] Ibid., pp. 299–301. See also Brun, II, pp. 172–174.

great resentment. Given that acceptance of the paper money meant a loss of 20 percent value at a time of rising prices, naval *ordonnateur* Possel informed the Minister that payment in *assignats* should be accompanied by a raise in wages to alleviate worker suffering.[29] The distribution of bread from the arsenal's bakery in February 1792 indicates the continued misery of the workers.[30] It was in this context of a growing social and economic crisis in the dockyards that the internecine conflict in Toulon reached a violent climax.[31]

The arsenal was obviously the key to the unstable environment in the Mediterranean port, yet the strictly "social" nature of the municipal struggle should not be overemphasized. Suggestions that the concentration of labour and enterprise in the dockyards produced a modern variety of "class struggle" should be heavily qualified. The organization of operations, the paternalism of naval administrators, and the traditional behaviour of the artisans themselves all belong more to the eighteenth century than to the nineteenth.[32] The arsenal workers constituted a third force outside the membership of either opposing faction and, while their support could be critical, they always remained uncertain allies. Crook has shown the importance of antagonism between the élite and those on its fringes. An appreciation of this social division, as well as the presence of the arsenal's volatile workforce, is crucial to an

[29] Marine BB 3/14, ff. 04–06; BB 3/13, ff. 07–09. See also the demand of sailors for payment in specie, raised in the Legislative Assembly on May 21, 1792; AP, vol. 43, p. 657.
[30] Marine BB 3/14, ff. 18–30. In April 1792 Possel asked the Minister for authorization to extend bread distribution to workers' families; Marine BB 3/14, f. 35. Hampson, "Ouvriers," pp. 297–298 states that bread had been distributed in Toulon as early as October 27, 1791, but became regular following the Legislative Assembly's decree of January 1792. See "M. Granet présente un rapport sur une pétition des marins et des ouvriers de l'arsenal de Toulon, relative à la distribution du pain aux ouvriers des ports et arsenaux, 2 janvier 1792"; AP, vol. 37, pp. 4–6. See also "M. Granet, au nom du comité de marine, fait un rapport et présente un projet de décret sur les secours à accorder aux enfants des ouvriers des ports, . . . 6 février 1792"; AP, vol. 38, pp. 231–232.
[31] See for example the petitions from Toulon arsenal workers read in the Legislative Assembly on June 24, 1792; AP, vol. 45, p. 529.
[32] Vovelle, p. 173 states that: "à Toulon, la modernité des structures et des rapports de classe dans l'arsenal rend la situation explosive. Contre les licenciements, contre les retards de paiements, . . . contre le système de l'entreprise, des mouvements de grève de type moderne se multiplient, . . ." On the other hand Hampson, "Ouvriers," pp. 309–313 shows, despite his own suggestion of the importance of a "Revolutionary sense of community," that worker relations in Toulon's arsenal were determined more by regional loyalties and antagonisms than any sense of class consciousness.

understanding of the situation. Yet these factors do not tell the full story. A fundamental division in Toulon was the political or ideological one which Crook acknowledged when he characterized the radicals as espousing "democratic, even participatory sovereignty," while the conservatives "regarded the Constitution of 1791 as a final revolutionary settlement."[33] Both sides claimed to represent the ideals of 1789; therefore the Jacobins and their opponents might be referred to as Revolutionary extremists and political moderates. The conflict between these factions had profound implications for the situation of the officers and men of the navy.

The political division of Toulon was apparent in the city's rival popular societies. The Club Saint-Jean was established in June 1790 and affiliated with the Paris Jacobins. A second popular society, the Club Saint-Pierre, was founded the following year in direct opposition to the first. The hostility between the "blancs," as the clubists of Saint-Jean called themselves, and the "noirs," as they referred to their enemies, was immediate and bitter.[34] Moderates, concerned with the growing power of local extremists, appear to have formed the Club Saint-Pierre. Although the Club Saint-Jean's candidates were relatively unsuccessful in the municipal elections of November 1790, Hyacinthe Paul, whom Henry described as "Barthélemy's creature," succeeded Richard as Toulon's mayor in March 1791.[35] The "blancs" had gained effective control over the municipality. The "noirs" would throw their support behind the Departmental Directory which, in June 1791, sought to prevent the supposedly fraudulent election of Jacobins as justices of the peace.[36] This struggle to control Toulon also involved the efforts of both clubs to win over the National Guard companies with the result that, by the summer of 1791, the militia was itself divided into hostile factions.[37] The tension in the city exploded on August 23 when rival

[33] Crook, "Federalism and the French Revolution," p. 385; see also *Toulon*, pp. 103–104.
[34] H. Labroue, *Le Club Jacobin de Toulon, 1790–1796* (Paris, 1907), pp. 1–37. Henry, I, pp. 129, 159–161 dates the foundation of the Club Saint-Pierre from January 31, 1791 when a deputation made a formal application to the municipality to establish a second popular society; the Club did not hold its first session until July 26. Crook, *Toulon*, p. 108 points out that this coincided with the nation-wide Feuillant secession from the Jacobin Club. For a contemporary description of the passionate rivalry between the two Clubs, see Richaud, pp. 11–12.
[35] Henry, I, pp. 162–163. See also Crook, *Toulon*, pp. 101, 106.
[36] Crook, *Toulon*, pp. 106–107. See also Richaud, p. 14.
[37] Henry, I, pp. 179–180; see also pp. 146–147 where Henry suggests that as early as November 1790 National Guard companies were divided over whether the Club should be allowed involvement in the affairs of the militia.

groups of guardsmen exchanged fire on the Place d'Armes leaving six people dead.[38] The factions blamed each other for this bloodshed, and continued their political struggle in the local elections during the fall of 1791. If Toulon experienced relative calm in the winter of 1791–92,[39] the profound conflict of principle between the Jacobins and their opponents remained. This was evident in the different responses by the two factions to national events. The Departmental and District administrations, in opposition to Toulon's municipality, expressed marked relief in July 1791 when the National Assembly confirmed the maintenance of a Monarchical Constitution, which to them implied the continuation of order and legality.[40] Distrust of the constitutional settlement and the king, on the other hand, motivated the Club Saint-Jean to petition the Department in May 1792 to dispatch five hundred armed men to join the army of *fédérés* converging on Paris.[41] It was no coincidence that the most heated quarrel over national developments came in July 1792 when the municipality publicly denounced the Department's earlier condemnation of the June 20 invasion of the Tuileries.[42]

Toulon's internal struggle culminated shortly afterwards in an appalling massacre. On July 28 a group of the Club Saint-Jean's affiliates from la Valette, along with militia companies from several neighbouring villages, entered the city and besieged the *Hôtel du Département*. Armed men murdered at least four administrators in the streets that morning

[38] Vovelle, p. 175 puts the number killed as seven. See also Crook, *Toulon*, pp. 109–110, Richaud, p. 15, and Havard, I, pp. 74–78, esp. his citation of the report by interim Commandant Dufort to Minister of Marine Thévenard, p. 78. Henry, I, pp. 186–191 cites the mutual recriminations after August 23 between the municipality and the Department, but he lays the blame for the violence squarely on the former.

[39] Crook, *Toulon*, pp. 110–113 suggests that both factions called for reconciliation after the inauguration of the new constitution, and that they cooperated to contain popular anger over rising prices.

[40] Henry, I, pp. 169–176; see esp. his citation of the Address sent to Paris, pp. 175–176.

[41] Michael L. Kennedy, *The Jacobin Clubs in the French Revolution: The Middle Years* (Princeton: Princeton University Press, 1988), pp. 254–255. Kennedy also quotes a letter of May 27, 1792 from the Jacobin Club of Marseilles: "Here and at Toulon we have debated the possibility of forming a column of 100,000 men to sweep away our enemies." The Club Saint-Jean persuaded the municipality to send fifteen National Guards to Paris who participated, along with perhaps sixty-five *fédérés* from the Var, in the attack on the Tuileries on August 10; Edmond Poupé, "Les fédérés varois du 10 août," *Révolution française* (1904), pp. 305–325.

[42] Henry, I, pp. 219–220. Crook, *Toulon*, p. 108 states that the celebration of July 14, 1791 showed there was no trace of republicanism in Toulon; but he acknowledges that divergent attitudes towards the monarchy had developed by June 1792, pp. 113–114.

and by dawn of July 31, twelve prominent Toulonnais, including members of the Departmental Directory, the District Council, and the Criminal Tribunal, were dead.[43] Whether the Club Saint-Jean encouraged, even orchestrated, the killings, or whether they were acts of uncontrolled popular violence remains debatable.[44] What is clear is the outcome; Jacobins controlled Toulon's three Administrative Corps and, thus, all civil authority.[45]

Naval officers did not remain isolated from the effects of the municipal power struggle in Toulon. The experience of Joseph, marquis de Flotte leaves this in no doubt. Flotte appeared in the "Toulon Affair" of 1789

[43] Report by extraordinary deputies from Toulon, delivered at the bar of the Legislative Assembly on August 7, 1792; AP, vol. 47, p. 549. See also: Vovelle, p. 176; Brun, II, p. 185. For a particularly chilling account of the events, see Richaud, pp. 19–22.
[44] All sources agree that at the Club's session of July 27, 1792, Jean-Victor Sylvestre called for a march through Toulon by clubists carrying hangman's nooses as symbols, and some add that he boasted of inviting emissaries from la Valette: Vovelle, p. 176; Henry, I, p. 227; Richaud, p. 19 (editor's footnote). M. Kennedy, *Jacobin Clubs . . . Middle Years*, p. 20 documents the formation at Toulon of a Jacobin Central Committee for Clubs in the Department of the Var on July 18–19, 1792. One can speculate that, since this committee was disbanded in November, its essential purpose was to coordinate the coup that gave the Club Saint-Jean control of Toulon. Crook, *Toulon*, p. 115 argues that although the radicals "rhetorically fanned the conflagration," the outbreak of popular violence took them by surprise. According to Antoine Tramoni, of the *Service éducatif des archives*, the Club Saint-Jean was divided internally, with extremists like Sylvestre far to the Left of Jacobins like Barthélemy; the massacre in July 1792 occurred because the Club had temporarily lost control of the extremist elements (based on a conversation with M. Tramoni, Toulon, August 29, 1988). The account of the massacre in Henry, I, pp. 230–245 implies that the initiative may have come from the Club, but that the municipality was to blame for not preventing the murders.
[45] Hérault de Séchelles, "Rapport, au nom de la commission extraordinaire des Douze, et un projet de décret tendant à ratifier la nomination d'un nouveau directoire de département et d'un conseil de district faite par les citoyens de Toulon, . . . 30 août 1792"; AP, vol. 47, p. 110 declares that a provisional Departmental Directory and District Council had been established from those members who "n'ont point abandonné la chose publique," (or as Henry, I, p. 245 puts it, "c'est-à-dire non massacrés") and had united themselves with the General Council of the Commune. In asking the Legislative Assembly to ratify these provisional commissions, Hérault was vindicating the conduct of Toulon's municipality and sanctioning its domination of the other administrations. He presented a second bill for the election of a new District Tribunal for Toulon. The Assembly did not adopt this on August 30, but the new Minister of Justice, Danton, supported the proposal in a letter to the Assembly of September 13, 1792; AP, vol. 49, p. 614. Regarding the results of the events of July and August in Toulon, see also M. Z. Pons, *Mémoires pour servir à l'histoire de la ville de Toulon en 1793* (Paris: C. J. Trouvé, 1825), pp. 9–10, and Crook, *Toulon*, pp. 117–118.

as the officer who took on the duties of Commandant following Albert de Rioms' imprisonment. The subsequent correspondence between the two men reveals a profound disagreement over how the navy should respond to the Revolution. Flotte's refusal to endorse the condemnations of Toulon voiced by sea-officers from Brest and Rochefort demonstrates that he acknowledged the legitimacy of popular authority. His actions won him considerable patriot sympathy,[46] and when he succeeded Glandevès as Commandant at Toulon he expected to enjoy a good relationship with local Revolutionary administration. Yet Flotte was unsuccessful in his attempts to balance acceptance of Popular Sovereignty with the maintenance of executive authority required by his position as Commandant. The political conflict in Toulon involved a struggle for Revolutionary legitimacy and the Jacobins viewed naval authority as an obstacle to popular will, as well as a support for their moderate rivals.

Flotte may have adopted Revolutionary principles,[47] but he expressed the same concerns as other naval commanders regarding the decline of discipline. The Commandant made appropriate comments on the "true patriotism" of the workers and sailors at Toulon,[48] but he also stated that "liberty must always be accompanied by order and respect for the law."[49] The continuing problem of insubordination was compounded by the atmosphere of escalating suspicion in Toulon. Popular opinion limited the Commandant's freedom to assign officers to command, and even his acts of cooperation with civil authorities were distrusted.[50] By June of 1792 Flotte viewed his position as hopeless and asked to be replaced: "I have . . . done all that was possible for me to do to

---

[46] Henry, I, p. 255.

[47] Brun, II, pp. 183–184, and Havard, I, pp. 126–136 make much of Flotte's participation in the *fêtes civiques* and fraternal banquets of 1792.

[48] See for example Marine BB 3/13, ff. 28, 38.

[49] Marine BB 3/13, f. 96. In a letter to the Minister of June 27, 1792, Flotte wrote that it was urgent to revitalize subordination to prevent "an atrocity parallel to that committed against M. Dillon," a reference to the French general murdered by his own troops in April; Marine BB 3/30, f. 146.

[50] The mutiny of *L'Alceste* in May 1792 created sufficient popular suspicion of all its officers that Flotte was unable to appoint the frigate's first officer, Ramatuelle, to command another warship; Marine BB 3/13, f. 77. On May 30, 1792 Flotte's delivery of naval artillery to Toulon's *commandant de la place*, for defence of the city, at the request of the Department caused the agitation of arsenal workers by the Club; Marine BB 3/13, f. 98. According to Henry, I, p. 255 and Crook, *Toulon*, p. 112, Revolutionaries searched Flotte's headquarters in March 1792 looking for Counter-Revolutionary correspondence.

preserve harmony and subordination here; but different interests prevail and destroy good intentions. I desire strongly to be exempted from this struggle in which it is impossible not to succumb, if the laws are without force . . ."[51] The precarious nature of naval authority in Toulon was evident on June 15 when an armed sailor burst into a meeting of the port's *Conseil de Marine* and threatened the assembled officers. Flotte was obliged to do nothing beyond protesting to the municipality because the offender was a member of the National Guard, and he eventually had to be satisfied with an assurance of the man's repentance.[52] The Commandant's helplessness was all the more apparent following the Jacobin coup[53] and by September Flotte, who had been promoted to *contre-amiral* in July, reported that Revolutionary activity was overriding arsenal work and that he was powerless to stop it. He blamed Toulon's Administrative Corps for weakening the navy, but he expressed the hope that the confidence inspired by the appointment of Monge would enable the new Minister to restore order.[54]

Flotte's anticipation that the authority of the Republic could save the navy was qualified by grim resignation regarding his own fate. He foresaw, with chilling irony, that his letter to the Minister of September 9 would be his last as Commandant. The commissioners of the Assembly who had arrived in the port intended to replace him due to complaints from naval personnel.[55] Flotte swore that he had done nothing to lose the esteem of

[51] Marine BB 3/30, f. 134.
[52] Marine BB 3/13, ff. 122, 140. Flotte's complaint to the Minister and his plea that naval personnel be exempt from service in the militia echo the words of Albert de Rioms three years earlier.
[53] Although Havard, I, p. 128 claims that Flotte distributed arms to the guardsmen from outside Toulon who were involved in the massacre, Flotte's letter to the Minister of July 31, 1792 indicates helplessness rather than complicity: "J'ai eu nombre de pétitions avec les égards qu'on devait à ma place; J'ai accordé les demandes qui m'ont été faites: j'ai rempli tous les devoirs d'un chef"; Marine BB 3/13, f. 161. On August 23, 1792 the Commandant and the *Ordonnateur* were unable to prevent the release of the port's chain-gang of convict labourers which rampaged through Toulon causing terror and chaos. The official report of the *Commissaire de chiourmes* implied that the release had been arranged by National Guards, perhaps with the sanction of the Administrative Corps; Marine BB 3/13, ff. 173–175. Moreover Possel, in his letter of August 30, 1792, stated that it would be best if those arrested following the incident were pardoned: a trial, in which 900 people could be implicated, would be explosive; Marine BB 3/14, f. 80.
[54] Marine BB 3/13, f. 183.
[55] "MM. les Commissaires . . . ont promis avant leur départ de me faire remplacer à la demande de quelques cannoniers matelôts, meneurs, aidés par d'autres intérêts particuliers qui n'ont pas permis à la vérité de se montrer"; Marine BB 3/13, f. 186.

his fellow citizens or of the corps he commanded, and that he had sought above all to be useful to the nation. "Command at this moment is a burden which is difficult to bear," he wrote, adding that if Lacoste had replaced him earlier, "it would have spared me many vicissitudes, great dangers and the unpleasantness which tests me today."[56] On the morning of September 10 a group of armed men dragged Commandant Flotte from his residence. They took him to the gate of the arsenal, hacked him to death and hanged his corpse from a lamppost.[57] Others murdered his *major-général*, Captain Rochemore, in the same ghastly fashion.[58] The naval *ordonnateur* Possel escaped this fate only because an arsenal worker intervened at the last moment to proclaim his *civisme*.[59]

Michel Vovelle, who made no specific reference to the murder of Commandant Flotte in his essay on Toulon during the Revolution, argued that the killings during 1792 should be interpreted neither as the result of the supposedly "bestial nature of the popular classes" nor as proof of a Jacobin conspiracy. Rather, he suggested they be placed in the context of recent studies of prison massacres in Paris and explained in terms of a matrix of politicization, social conditions, and *mentalités*.[60] Such an approach has validity, but the meaning of the violence against naval officers is lost in Vovelle's assertion that the Jacobins "restored order when the storm had passed." Proving the direct responsibility of the Club Saint-Jean and its political machine for the murders of Flotte and Rochemore is not the point: what is important, as with the massacre of July, is to assess the results of the violence.

Responsibility for the naval base following September 10 fell largely on Possel's senior subordinate, Thivend. Thivend formed a permanent

[56] Marine BB 3/13, f. 186.
[57] See: Henry, I, p. 256; Richaud, p. 26; Havard, I, pp. 136–138; Brun, II, p. 186; Guérin, V, p. 355.
[58] According to Henry, I, pp. 253–255 Rochemore had been imprisoned earlier in September on the accusations of peasants from la Garde who claimed he had insulted the People. The *capitaine de vaisseau* was dragged from his cell and murdered on a signal from the balcony of the *Hôtel de Ville*. Havard, I, p. 126 adds the gruesome detail that one of Rochemore's killers, Barry, washed his hands in the victim's blood.
[59] Jacques Ferrier, "Les singuliers successeurs de Malouet à Toulon (1792–1797)," *Bulletin de l'Académie du Var* (1979), pp. 132–134. Despite his rescue, Possel was so distraught by the experience that he took to his bed and could not continue with his duties. See also Henry, I, pp. 261–262, and Havard, I, p. 138. Further violence may have included the murder of *capitaine de vaisseau* Saqui-des-Tourrets, a possible founder of the Club Saint-Pierre; see Guérin, V, p. 355, and Crook, *Toulon*, p. 116.
[60] Vovelle, p. 177. The explanation of violence in the inherent brutality of the popular classes is attributed to Henry's *Histoire de Toulon*.

Marine Council to share his dangerous burden,[61] and his letter to the Minister of September 23 indicated how desperate was the situation facing the navy:

You must be told with horror and truth, that it is impossible that the administration can be sustained much longer in the pitiful state in which it finds itself. Most commanders, the principal subordinates are either sick or with the fleet, the others are in despair or fear for their lives. Nevertheless operations multiply, circumstances are more difficult every day, and our arsenal has become the resource of the army, the fleet, and of neighbouring Departments.[62]

Four men acted as *ordonnateur* before the end of October and when Vincent, a naval administrator summoned from Bordeaux, arrived to replace Mayor Paul, who had been filling the post, a petition of protest was sent to the Minister.[63] The Toulonnais, or at least the Jacobins, had no desire for an outsider appointed by the Minister to oversee the dockyards. Vincent reported in November that he had been warned not to make any inquiries and that only the personal popularity of Commandant Chaussegros, the naval captain who had replaced Flotte, maintained a semblance of naval authority.[64] Hostility towards Vincent in Toulon seems to have worsened and by January 1793 the *ordonnateur* had decided to get out of the port. He told the Minister it was imperative that he report in person, but the three Administrative Corps withheld his passport, demanding that he reveal the orders which required him to travel to Paris.[65] Vincent's outraged reply showed that, beyond the denial of his personal freedom of movement, he viewed the move as a clear abrogation of national authority: "No law has pronounced that the Administrative Corps can impede the *ordonnateur* from leaving his assigned post, above all when this is to go before the Minister of the

---

[61] Marine BB 3/14, f. 190.
[62] Ibid., f. 197.
[63] Ferrier, p. 136. Monge replaced Possel with Jean-Nicolas Pache, a member of the Paris Commune and protegé of the Rolands. This appointment was presumably to appease local Jacobins, but Pache only spent from October 1 to 8, 1792 in Toulon before returning to Paris to become Minister of War. Pache turned over administration of the arsenal to Paul when he left, but Monge needed an experienced naval administrator to deal with the mobilization of the Mediterranean fleet: it may be suggested that he also wanted a subordinate with national, rather than local priorities.
[64] Marine BB 3/14, ff. 86–88. Martin-Benoît de Chaussegros was born in Toulon and entered the navy via the coast guard and the marine infantry. He was promoted to *contre-amiral* in January 1793; see Havard, I, pp. 141–142.
[65] Marine BB 3/31, ff. 17–21.

Republic. . . . The administration of the navy is entirely under the orders of the executive power, . . ."[66] Yet the violence at Toulon had effectively wrested control of the navy from central government. The local Jacobin regime took full advantage of the intimidation of commanders. If "order was restored" after the killings, naval authority was treated thereafter as subordinate to Toulon's popular authority.

Local Revolutionary domination of the navy carried with it the patriotic responsibility of advancing the war effort. The port of Toulon had great strategic importance. The first major naval operations of the war took place in the Mediterranean where Admiral Truguet's squadron supported the French army's conquest of Nice and Villefranche in September and October of 1792.[67] Truguet received subsequent orders to carry out an invasion of the island of Sardinia using troops from the Army of Italy and National Guard volunteers from Corsica and Marseilles.[68] Although this expedition ended in failure and the return of the demoralized Mediterrranean fleet in March 1793,[69] Toulon's Club and Administrative Corps appear to have done much to support Truguet's efforts. In September they attempted to prevent desertion from the squadron before it sailed,[70] and in November they made efforts to assist the *ordonnateur* to restore calm in the arsenal by persuading workers to accept a portion of their wages in *assignats*.[71] Malcolm Crook emphasized that the radicals, once firmly in power, were dedicated to restoring order in the dockyards and promoting the vital work of naval mobilization.[72] The war at sea in 1793 also included attacks on merchant

---

[66] Ibid., f. 22; see also ff. 24–25.

[67] See Marine BB 4/9, ff. 14–15 for the Minister's instructions to Truguet of September 15, 1792. For an account of the operations see Chevalier, pp. 37–38, and Guérin, V, pp. 366–367.

[68] Marine BB 4/9, f. 20; BB 4/21, f. 05.

[69] The armada assembled off Cagliari in January 1793 and began to put its troops ashore on February 14. The Marseillais, however, panicked under fire and retreated to the beach in disorder. Truguet held his warships close inshore to provide support, and rough seas caused at least two battleships to run aground; *Le Léopard* (74) could not be salvaged and so was burned. Substantial numbers of French soldiers and sailors were killed or captured and the invasion ended in disaster. For Truguet's account, see Marine BB 4/21, ff. 39–43. See also: Marine BB 4/21, ff. 189–193; BB 4/22, ff. 149–153, 192–204, 214; Chevalier, pp. 41–46; Guérin, V, pp. 371–385.

[70] Marine BB 4/9, f. 52.

[71] Marine BB 3/14, f. 96; see also BB 3/31, f. 31.

[72] Crook, *Toulon*, pp. 127–128, "Federalism and the French Revolution," pp. 386–387. See the reports of February 8 and 10, 1793 by *représantants-en-mission* Rouyer, Brunel, and Le Tourneur which praise the Club and Administrative Corps for seeking to enforce discipline in the arsenal and accelerate naval mobilization; in F. V. A.

shipping and the three Administrative Corps, blaming the lack of protection for commerce on the negligence of the executive power, demanded that the *ordonnateur* buy small vessels to be armed for use against enemy privateers. Toulon's Revolutionary authorities also nominated suitable candidates, "*sans-culottes* of recognized patriotism," to command the vessels.[73]

Patriotic support for the war effort clearly did not mean relaxing local control of the navy. Beyond requisitioned smallcraft, civil power in Toulon also influenced the Commandant's appointment of commanding officers for frigates and line-of-battle ships.[74] The Administrative Corps requisitioned warships for special missions and dominated administration of the arsenal.[75] Propaganda was not neglected and Toulon's Jacobins expended much effort on the politicization of sailors and workers.[76] Thus the atmosphere in Toulon by spring 1793 was paradoxical. The Club and the civil authorities were enthusiastic supporters of the war against the Republic's enemies and were, therefore, committed to ensuring that the Mediterranean fleet was an effective fighting force. On the other hand, naval authority as an extension of executive power was not allowed to impinge on the direct sovereignty of the "People," which in practice meant increasing interference in naval operations and continued encouragement of Revolutionary "surveillance" of commanders by sailors and workers. The mutiny aboard the frigates *La Melpomène* and *La Minerve* in April 1793, and the events which followed, demonstrate the position of naval officers in Toulon and their response to these circumstances.

Aulard (ed.), *Recueil des Actes du Comité de Salut Public* (Paris: Imprimerie Nationale, 1893–1911), II, pp. 77–80, 102–107.
[73] Marine BB 3/31, ff. 125–127. M. Kennedy, *Jacobin Clubs . . . Middle Years*, p. 158 states that Toulon's Club outfitted a corsair at its own expense, but in this case the *ordonnateur* Huon complained to the Minister that the navy was expected to fund the Club's suggested acquisitions.
[74] Toulon's three Administrative Corps pressured the Commandant into appointing their candidates to command the frigate *L'Iphigenie* on October 8, 1792, *Le Duqesne* (74) on April 18, 1793, the frigate *La Minerve* on April 23, 1793, as well as various other vessels; Toulon 4 A 1/259. See also Cottin, pp. 26–27, and Guérin, V, p. 532.
[75] Marine BB 3/13, ff. 220, 223; BB 3/14, f. 164.
[76] See Marine BB 4/21, f. 35 for the foundation of a club aboard Truguet's flagship, *Le Tonnant* (80), in January 1793. See also the letter of February 28, 1793 from the Club Saint-Jean to the Minister which refers to sailors as members and praises them for swearing to burn before surrendering; Marine BB 3/43, f. 213. For a description of how Revolutionary activity was nullifying work in the arsenal, see the letter of May 31, 1793 from Doinet, *Chef des Travaux*; Marine BB 3/30, ff. 171–173. See also Hampson, "Ouvriers," pp. 309–313 who cites Doinet's Reports; BB 3/44, ff. 158–174.

The navy ordered the two frigates to sail from Toulon on April 17 and escort two Algerian xebecs to Africa.[77] *La Melpomène* and *La Minerve* were at anchor in the harbour's *Lazaret*, still in quarantine since returning from a six-week voyage,[78] when the orders arrived and touched off the mutiny. The sailors refused to put to sea again before receiving shore leave within the city, and the ships' captains were unable to quell this defiance.[79] A deputation from the Club Saint-Jean and the three Administrative Corps accompanied *contre-amiral* Trogoff de Kerlessy, who had replaced Truguet as commander of the Mediterranean fleet, to the *Lazaret* to persuade the crews to return to duty. Speeches had no effect on the seamen who shouted down the commissioners and threatened them by brandishing nooses and by hanging corpse-like manikins from the yard-arm. Toulon's Revolutionary authorities called for the use of force against the defiant mutineers, but were soon diverted by the idea that an investigation of the crews' insurrection would expose the machinations of enemies and traitors.[80] Even when it was reported that the crews had submitted,[81] the civil authorities persisted with plans for an inquiry and ordered all officers and men from the two frigates disembarked for interrogation.[82]

Jerome Laurent, a sailor on *La Melpomène* identified as the mutiny's ringleader, was the first object of suspicion.[83] He was politically suspect because he had been formerly employed as cook by the comtesse de

---

[77] Marine BB 3/30, f. 98. The xebecs had been sunk on the French coast in May 1792 by a Sardinian warship. The navy salvaged the vessels and planned to return them to the Dey of Algiers; Edmond Poupé, "L'Affaire de la Minerve et de la Melpomène, avril–mai 1793," *La Revue historique de Provence* (juin–août 1902), pp. 6–16.

[78] Marine BB 3/31, f. 120.

[79] See: Captain Basterot's letter to Admiral Trogoff, April 20, 1793, in Henry, II, pp. 10–11; "Adresse au contre-amiral Trogoff, de capitaine de vaisseau Féraud, 20 avril 1793," Toulon 4 0 1.

[80] "En exécution de l'arrêté des Trois Corps administrative réunis pris le jour d'hier séance de relevée, 30 avril 1793"; Toulon 4 0 1.

[81] "Lettre de capitaine de vaisseau Basterot aux citoyens membres de la société Républicaine de Toulon et du corps administratif de cette ville, 22 avril 1793"; Toulon 4 0 1.

[82] See the Address of April 23, 1793, "Les membres des trois corps administratifs, ceux de la société populaire, des comités de sûreté générale, du bureau central, et autres, réunis à leurs frères des équipages des frégates la Minerve et la Melpomène," in Henry, II, pp. 12–13.

[83] See for example "Résumé des dépositions faites par les officiers de la frégate de la Minerve sur les troubles qui ont agité cette frégate, dans l'époque commence au mois de février et finir le 24 avril 1793"; Toulon 4 0 1.

Choiseul-Gouffier, wife of the former French ambassador to Constantinople and, since October 1792, an accused traitor to the Republic.[84] It was not long, however, before the Captain of *La Melpomène*, François-Gabriel de Basterot, became the prime target of the investigation.[85] Mutinous sailors criticized Basterot when they sent ashore their signed petition,[86] but the more damning accusation came from Pierre-Jacques Féraud, Captain of *La Minerve*.[87] Denounced by his own crew, Féraud may have hoped to shift suspicion away from himself. His charges, however, were based upon the account in his log of the recent cruise made by the two frigates, and his journal remains the principal source of evidence on the events which preceded the mutiny.[88]

La Melpomène and *La Minerve*, under Basterot's command, had sailed from Hyères on March 6, 1793 with orders to patrol the Straits of Gibraltar to warn French shipping entering the Mediterranean of the outbreak of war with Britain.[89] The frigates never reached the straits and arrived instead at the Algerian port of Bone on March 12. Although the Dey of Algiers was an important French ally, Basterot ordered the warships to enter the harbour flying English colours and with their decks cleared for action. Several vessels were anchored within the harbour including an Algerian corvette and a *flûte* of Dutch construction. Basterot gave the order for *La Melpomène* to fire twice on the Dutch ship, an act which constituted serious aggression against Algerian sovereignty.[90] Féraud claimed in his journal that he had stopped this attack only by persuading his commander that the *flûte* was clearly a prize

[84] Poupé, "L'Affaire," pp. 24–25. Regarding the replacement of Choiseul-Gouffier as ambassador, see Guérin, V, p. 368.
[85] François-Gabriel de Basterot de la Barrière was born in 1762 at Rochefort and entered the navy as *aspirant garde de la marine* in 1777. After serving in the American War under Orvilliers and De Grasse, he was promoted to *lieutenant de vaisseau* in 1786 and *capitaine de vaisseau* in 1793; Poupé, "L'Affaire," pp. 41–43.
[86] Address from the crew of *La Minerve* to Toulon's Jacobin Club, April 18, 1793; Toulon 4 0 1.
[87] Pierre-Jacques Féraud was born in 1744 at la Seyne (Var) and entered the navy as a cabin boy in 1756. He was promoted from the lower deck to the intermediate grade of *capitaine de flûte* in 1784 and was made a *sous-lieutenant de vaisseau* in 1787. Féraud's advancement during the Revolution was rapid: he was appointed lieutenant in 1791 and captain in 1793; Poupé, "L'Affaire," pp. 44–47.
[88] "Extrait du Journal de la frégate la Minerve, commandée par le citoyen Féraud, pour servir de procès-verbal"; Toulon 4 0 1.
[89] Marine BB 4/21, ff. 189, 196.
[90] The notice regarding Basterot's trial in the *Moniteur*, vol. 16, p. 549 (5 juin 1793) indicates Revolutionary concern to maintain good relations with Algeria, a major supplier of grain to the Republic.

captured by the Algerians. This was confirmed three days later when the frigates, having left the port, encountered the same vessel at sea. The Algerian crew abandoned the ship in panic and the French towed it back to Bone. Basterot then went ashore to repair some of the diplomatic havoc he had caused. This direct contact with the African coast made quarantine necessary when the frigates returned to Toulon.[91] Yet before this strange voyage ended, the two ships sailed to Leghorn in Italy to meet a French convoy. The convoy was not ready to depart immediately and Basterot again went ashore: an incident which would later be given sinister connotations.

Barthélemy, the prominent Jacobin who had become Toulon's *commissaire-auditeur* attached to the naval Courts Martial as well as President of the Criminal Tribunal, questioned the crews of *La Melpomène* and *La Minerve* regarding the mutiny, and afterwards imprisoned the sailors in the fortress of la Grosse Tour. On April 26 the city's Committee of Surveillance and General Security recommended Captain Basterot be tried before a Court Martial for treason.[92] The Administrative Corps ordered Barthélemy to prepare the indictment,[93] and he pursued this task with relentless determination. His interrogations of Basterot and Laurent on May 1, as well as his statements of Accusation, are terrifying examples of the Jacobin obsession with plots and hidden enemies.

Barthélemy began questioning Laurent by establishing the sailor's past association with the aristocrat Mme Choiseul-Gouffier. He then asked Laurent about the events at Bone, thus leading up to accusing Basterot, at which point Barthélemy demanded to know why he had not denounced the captain when the frigates had returned to Toulon? This was a trap from which the sailor could not escape because, in Barthélemy's words, "his indifference, or his negligence to make this denunciation is a proof that he was in connivance with his captain to betray the French nation."[94]

---

[91] Marine BB 3/31, ff. 107, 120.
[92] "Copie du Rapport des membres composant le Comité de Surveillance et de Sûreté général de Toulon, 26 avril 1793"; Toulon 4 0 1.
[93] "Extrait des registres des délibérations des Trois Corps administratifs de Toulon. Séance du 27 avril 1793"; Toulon 4 0 1.
[94] Barthélemy's Interrogation of Laurent, May 1, 1793. This document is part of a file entitled: "Jerome Laurent, François-Victor Gaudier, dit 'la France'; matelots de la Melpomène accusés le premier d'avoir secondé le Capitaine Basterot, le second d'avoir concerté le projet de l'opposer à l'exécution de l'ordre de départ pour Algers et d'avoir menacé le Capitaine"; Toulon 4 0 1. The shadowy figure of "la France" emerged during Barthélemy's interrogation of the crews as one of the violent instigators of the mutiny at the *Lazaret*. According to several witnesses including Laurent, Gaudier, or

All strands of the supposed conspiracy were drawn together when he accused Laurent of inciting mutiny among his shipmates in accordance with a diabolical plot hatched by Basterot and Mme Choiseul-Gouffier to destroy Toulon's Administrative Corps. This charge, vague as it was, constituted the major plank of Barthélemy's Statement of Accusation against Laurent which he submitted to the Court Martial.[95]

The pattern of Barthélemy's interrogation of Captain Basterot was somewhat different.[96] He did not pose questions regarding a vast conspiracy, but concentrated on the captain's actions at Bone. Basterot's responses indicate that he not only admitted his errors, but conceded that they merited the punishment of death. Basterot also accepted full blame for the mutiny, though he was led to implicate Laurent. The most suspect part of the entire testimony was a note tacked on the end which claimed to be an additional statement made by the captain following the interrogation. It declared that in 1792 Basterot had been persuaded by Mme Choiseul-Gouffier and her daughter to betray the Republic. In consequence, he had gone ashore at Leghorn to communicate with French *émigrés*, particularly those from the navy, and had later burned most of his papers.

The authenticity of this final declaration is highly dubious as it differed completely from all of Captain Basterot's earlier testimony;[97] Barthélemy could have inserted it after the interrogation.[98] Basterot's actions during the voyage are certainly difficult to explain. He had complained of ill-health since March and, when he was imprisoned, his wife requested that he be given a medical examination. Although the physicians declared him sane,[99] it would seem possible that he had

"la France," had threatened, with a hangman's noose, any sailors who tried to obey orders to sail.

[95] "Seconde Plainte contre Laurent et 1er Plainte contre Victor Gaudier (dit la France) de Marseilles, également matelot, 7 mai 1793"; Toulon 4 0 1.

[96] "Interrogats et Réponses du Capitaine Basterot devant le Commissaire auditeur, 1 mai 1793"; Toulon 4 0 1.

[97] The declaration differs not only from the rest of Basterot's testimony of May 1, 1793, but from that of April 25 when he was the first witness questioned by Barthélemy: "Interrogats et Réponses de l'état major et équipage de la frégate la Melpomène"; Toulon 4 0 1.

[98] This charge was made by the Sections' Popular Tribunal which tried Barthélemy in August 1793. See "Extrait du jugement de Jean-Sébastien Barthélemy"; in Henry, II, pp. 276–277.

[99] "Note aux citoyens composant les trois corps administratifs réunis de Rose-Geneviève Lagrange Basterot, 2 mai 1793"; and "Rapport des Chirurgiens-major d'artillerie et d'infanterie de la marine, 3 mai 1793"; Toulon 4 0 1.

Map 5. The voyage of *La Melpomène* and *La Minerve*, March–April 1793. *After* "Europe about 1560" and "Europe about 1740" in William R. Shepherd, *Historical Atlas* (New York: Henry Holt and Co., 1929), pp. 118–119, 130–131.

suffered a nervous breakdown.[100] What remains highly doubtful is that this officer confessed suddenly to involvement in a conspiracy when he had previously admitted only to errors of judgement. Although the only evidence of Basterot's involvement with *émigrés* or Counter-Revolutionary plots, the final statement constituted the basis for the major charges in Barthélemy's indictment submitted to the naval Court Martial.[101]

On the demand of the *commissaire-auditeur*, Admiral Trogoff assembled a military jury aboard his flagship, *Le Tonnant* (80), to determine Basterot's guilt.[102] Given the involvement of Mme Choiseul-Gouffier in the accusations, the jury's officers wished to delay proceedings until the lady could be arrested and brought to testify. She was not apprehended and the jury, under considerable pressure, found the prisoner guilty.[103] The Court Martial convened on May 28 and condemned Captain Basterot to death. He was guillotined the same day on the shore of the roadstead before the eyes of the assembled fleet.[104]

This episode illustrates, in several ways, the larger situation facing the French navy in 1793. The investigation of the mutiny aboard *La Melpomène* and *La Minerve* revealed that sailors had become highly politicized. The revolt in April was merely the culmination of continuous insubordination aboard the two frigates. Disobedience and desertion were serious enough at the beginning of March for the Representatives on Mission Brunel, Rouyer, and Le Tourneur to be asked to address the crews in the hope of returning them to duty.[105] Two of *La Melpomène*'s officers, *enseigne entretenu* Jean-François Gohier and *enseigne non-entretenu* Jean-François Ollivier, told Barthélemy that indiscipline had been constant since they had embarked, and Féraud reported similar

---

[100] Basterot's will, written before the voyage, suggests not only declining health, but a mood of despair: "Mon testament. A bord de la Melpomène, le 1er avril 1793, Basterot, capitaine de vaisseau, commandant"; Toulon 4 0 1. Poupé, "L'Affaire," p. 38 argues that ill health, which was the beginning of *"aliénation mentale,"* diminished Basterot's responsibility for his actions at Bone; this is echoed by Henry, II, p. 9.
[101] "Plainte du Commissaire auditeur contre François-Gabriel Basterot, Capitaine de vaisseau ci-devant commandant la division des forces navales de la République la Melpomène et la Minerve, et contre Jerome Laurent, matelot, 1 mai 1793"; see also "Further Accusations, 3 May 1793," and "Addition to Act of Accusation, 5 May 1793"; Toulon 4 0 1.
[102] Marine BB 4/21, f. 94.
[103] Poupé, "L'Affaire," pp. 33–34; Marine BB 4/21, f. 95.
[104] Marine BB 4/21, f. 110. See also *Moniteur*, vol. 16, p. 591 (10 juin 1793), and Rouvier, p. 91.
[105] Poupé, "L'Affaire," pp. 13–15.

conditions among his seamen.[106] What is particularly significant is that this insubordination took the form of Revolutionary political practice. Popular societies had been established aboard ship and throughout the voyage the sailors on both frigates had used these clubs to question their orders and to debate whether they should be carried out.[107]

Politicization did not mean that unanimity prevailed among the crews. All accounts of the mutiny aboard *La Melpomène* and *La Minerve*, from both officers and men, indicate that a number of violent sailors intimidated others who might have obeyed their commanders. Of course, given the circumstances of the investigation, many crewmen may have hoped to mitigate their own guilt by claiming that threats from others compelled them to acts of mutiny. Barthélemy, moreover, was seeking specific individuals who could be punished and this too may have coloured the testimony.[108] Yet the evidence strongly suggests that the seamen were divided. One witness, carpenter's mate Jean-Pierre Cabry, stated explicitly that when Captain Basterot announced the orders to sail: "two parties emerged, one for the departure, the other against. . ."[109] The nature of this division is not clear,[110] but it is suggested here that it paralleled the division among the civilian population of Toulon ashore and would have dramatic results in August.

[106] "Interrogats et Réponses de l'état major et équipage de la frégate la Melpomène"; "Lettre de Capitaine Féraud aux citoyens composant la société de la liberté et de l'égalité séante à St Jean à Toulon, A bord la Minerve, 20 avril 1793"; Toulon 4 0 1. Flotte had reported insubordination aboard *La Minerve* as early as May 1792; Marine BB 3/13, ff. 68–71.

[107] "Address from the crew of the *La Minerve* to Toulon's Jacobin Club, 18 April 1793"; "Interrogats et Réponses de l'état-major et équipage de la frégate la Melpomène," see esp. Basterot's testimony: Toulon 4 0 1.

[108] The pattern of testimony given by the crew of *La Melpomène* suggests that Barthélemy was exerting considerable influence as interrogator and/or the sailors were aware of each other's responses. Initially, the hands who could name any of the instigators of the mutiny all gave "la France" as the one who intimidated the faint-hearted with a noose. Once Laurent was named, virtually every subsequent witness accused him of leading the revolt in the *Lazaret* and, when one sailor added the detail that Laurent had served a noble, testimony which followed escalated this to complicity with *émigrés*; "Interrogats et Réponses . . . la Melpomène"; Toulon 4 0 1.

[109] Testimony of "Jean-Pierre Cabry, de Toulon, second-maître charpentier," in "Interrogats et Réponses . . . la Melpomène"; Toulon 4 0 1.

[110] The testimony of some sailors indicates regional antagonisms by attaching regional labels to the instigators of the mutiny. Some identify the mysterious "la France" as "the sailor from Marseilles". Félix Beaussier, *lieutenant d'infanterie de la marine* from Marseilles, identifies the mutineers as *Ponantais*. There is not, however, enough consistency to establish clearly that the fundamental division was between Bretons and Provençaux. "Interrogats et Réponses . . . la Melpomène"; Toulon 4 0 1.

More significant than the mere continuity of insubordination is the sailors' acknowledgement of Toulon's Revolutionary authorities over their own commanders, as *La Minerve*'s submission of an address denouncing Féraud to the Club Saint-Jean illustrated.[111] Féraud also acknowledged this authority, trying to justify his conduct before the Club and addressing the condemnation of Basterot not to Admiral Trogoff but to Toulon's municipal officers.[112] Thus the incident is further evidence of the domination of the naval establishment by Revolutionary authority at Toulon. There can be little question that Barthélemy's prosecution demonstrated the strong antipathy among fervent Jacobins for officers of the old corps.[113] It would appear, therefore, that Captain Basterot was the victim of Revolutionary fervour, an argument supported by Edmond Poupé in the only detailed study written on the affair.[114]

Such a conclusion certainly has validity, yet neglects a crucial aspect of the events. Basterot was not tried by a Revolutionary Tribunal, but by a duly constituted naval Court Martial. The military jury found him guilty of specific crimes: failing to carry out his orders to patrol the Straits of Gibraltar; failing to keep an exact journal; leaving his ship at Leghorn in the presence of enemy forces; failing to suppress the mutiny on the two frigates with firmness and rigour. Significantly, no mention was made of inciting the mutiny nor of communication with *émigrés* nor of any conspiracy. The Court Martial of eight captains and one admiral which condemned Basterot to die did so with specific reference to two Articles of the 1790 Penal Code which demanded the death penalty.[115] Therefore, according to the Court Martial, the captain

[111] "Address from the crew of *La Minerve* to Toulon's Jacobin Club, 18 April 1793"; Toulon 4 0 1.
[112] "Lettre de Captain Féraud aux citoyens composant la société . . . 20 avril 1793"; Féraud's Statement of Accusation against Basterot, dated April 25, 1793, appears at the beginning of the extract from his log: "Extrait du Journal de la Frégate la Minerve . . ."; Toulon 4 0 1. It is also significant that Féraud reported to the Minister on Basterot's actions on May 31, 1793, two days after the Court Martial; Marine BB 4/22, f. 254.
[113] The judgement against Barthélemy at his own trial reports that, at the time of the Court Martial, he told the crew of *Le Tonnant*: "Méfiez-vous de vos chefs; lorsqu'ils vous mènent avec douceur et bonté, c'est pour vous séduire et faire de vous autres ce qu'ils voudront"; Henry, II, p. 277.
[114] Poupé, "L'Affaire," pp. 34–40. Poupé, however, argues that the Court Martial was legally competent to try Basterot. This differs from the interpretation in Henry, II, pp. 9–10.
[115] "Jugement de la Cour Martiale maritime qui condamne à mort le Capitaine Basterot, 28 mai 1793"; Toulon 4 0 1. See Section 2, Articles 35 and 38 of the Penal Code of 22 August 1790; AP, vol. 18, pp. 207–212, esp. p. 211. It should be noted

was executed for professional misconduct and not for treason. Similarly, the other jury baulked at convicting Jerome Laurent for Counter-Revolutionary plotting and the sailor was eventually condemned to be keel-hauled in keeping with the Penal Code's punishment for direct disobedience accompanied by insults and threats.[116] These judgements represented the attempt by Toulon's naval officers to retain a semblance of legality and order in their operations despite tremendous local pressure. Thus the Court Martial of Captain Basterot fits into a larger context. For the navy the collapse of the monarchy in August 1792 meant the end of a national government which had been unable to enforce its will against the growing power of Revolutionary authorities in the ports. Those naval officers who remained at their posts, facing interference by local civil administrations and the virtual collapse of discipline in the fleet, looked to the Republic to restore order and executive authority based on a new democratic legitimacy. If naval commanders were willing to accept some Revolutionary principles, they also continued to assert the need for the authority of a strong central government which lay beyond local power. The advent of the Republic did not, however, ensure the acceptance of such a position, and in Toulon Commandant Flotte's claim to represent national authority proved fatal. His murder was the culmination of a violent coup which gave local Jacobins control of Toulon over their more moderate rivals.

Flotte was thus a victim of a conflict between Revolutionary factions. Yet the commanders who followed him also tried to maintain the navy's integrity and to remain aloof from the local situation. The atmosphere in Toulon did not improve during 1793 as the local Jacobin regime continued to view naval officers, particularly those remaining from the old corps, as potential traitors. Barthélemy's efforts to link Basterot to a vast and sinister conspiracy testified to this obsession.[117] The verdict

that *contre-amiral* Léandre-François Martel, not Admiral Trogoff, presided over the Court Martial.

[116] See: "Verdict of Military jury assembled aboard *Le Tonnant* for affair of Jerome Laurent and François-Victor Gaudier, 8 May 1793"; and "Jugement du Conseil de Justice qui condamne Victor Gaudier à passer par la Cour Martiale et Jerome Laurent à la calle pour fait de complicité à un projet de trahison à la patrie, 9 mai 1793"; Toulon 4 0 1. See also Penal Code, Section 2, Article 15; AP, vol. 18, p. 210. Gaudier was condemned to three years in the galleys; Marine BB 4/21, f. 110.

[117] Basterot's case was not unique. Captain Prévost-Lacroix of *l'Apollon* (74) was arrested in Toulon on April 18, 1793 for crimes against the Revolution committed in the West Indies in 1790. Although acquitted by the Tribunal of Digne, Prévost-Lacroix was sent before the Revolutionary Tribunal in Paris which condemned him to death on January 5, 1794; Marine BB 4/21,. f. 101; BB 4/22, ff. 06–23. See also Chevalier, p. 63, Guérin, V, p. 429. Chaussegros wrote to the Minister on May

of the Court Martial, however, demonstrates that officers of the French navy still endeavored to operate as agents of a national institution governed by the rule of law despite very difficult circumstances. Although men like Admiral Trogoff tried desperately to keep the fleet and arsenal above local Revolutionary politics, the culmination of Toulon's internal struggle in the summer of 1793 drew the navy away from its position of local neutrality and into its greatest crisis.

25, 1793 to inform him of the arrest of Captain Poulain of *Le Pompée* (74) and stated: "Il me reste à vous prier, citoyen Ministre, de me donner vos ordres pour le remplacement des capitaines et commandants qui, avec le plus grand désir de servir la patrie, ne sont plus dans le cas de pouvoir espérer de leurs subordonnés toute la confiance qu'ils avaient droit attendre"; Marine BB 3/30, f. 117.

THE GREAT TREASON: THE SURRENDER
OF THE MEDITERRANEAN FLEET IN 1793

The defection of Toulon in 1793 was one of the greatest disasters to befall France in the whole course of the Revolutionary War. The summer of 1793 was a time of crisis. The tide of the war, which had seen French armies conquer Belgium in 1792, turned against the Republic. The threat from foreign invasion became more dangerous with the growing menace of internal rebellion and civil war. The potential link between the political divisions within France and the deteriorating military situation was realized in August when the city of Toulon, in revolt against the National Convention, declared its allegiance to Louis XVII, an imprisoned child, and opened its port to a British fleet under Admiral Hood. This defeat for the Revolution was also a terrible blow to the French navy. Far worse than the loss of strength represented by the seventeen battleships stationed at Toulon was the stigma of dishonour and treason: the Mediterranean fleet surrendered to its traditional enemy without firing a shot.

The notion of conspiracy dominates historical treatments of Toulon's revolt and surrender. Jeanbon Saint-André, the Montagnard naval expert, claimed in his report on the treason of Toulon that the entry of the British was the outcome of a vast plot against the Republic contrived by "Girondin" deputies, provincial rebels, and the foreign enemy.[1] Thus Toulon's declaration for the monarchy was proof of the true nature of its machinations. Republican historiography has tended to support Jeanbon's thesis by emphasizing the importance of a royalist conspiracy.[2] Ironically, this interpretation was also held by ultra-royalist

[1] "Rapport sur la trahison de Toulon, par Jeanbon Saint-André, au nom du Comité de Salut public, 9 septembre 1793"; AP, vol. 73, pp. 575–582. The Report is followed by a decree and extensive documentation, pp. 583–598.

[2] The classic account of Toulon's surrender, which claims that a Royalist conspiracy usurped a "Federalist" rising, is Cottin, *Toulon et les Anglais en 1793*. Although much of Cottin's study is devoted to denouncing "Perfidious Albion," he is adamant on the

historians who drew enthusiastically on works of self-justification which appeared during the Restoration.[3] While rejecting conspiracy as an explanation for Toulon's revolt and pointing instead to the primary importance of internal conflict, modern studies have continued to assume that when Counter-Revolution did emerge it found willing allies among commanders of the fleet.[4] Historians of the navy, while generally sympathetic to officers and antipathetic to the Jacobins, have seized upon individual betrayal as a way of salvaging the honour of the service. Admiral Trogoff has most frequently been singled out as the Royalist arch-traitor, but some naval historians have accused his second-in-command, Admiral Saint-Julien, of being the true author of the fleet's shameful capitulation.[5]

This search for scapegoats has obscured rather than clarified the situation in Toulon in 1793. Neither conspiracy nor isolated treasons explain the navy's surrender. Even Jeanbon Saint-André, who condemned the Toulonnais for arrogating control of naval forces which belonged to the entire Republic, conceded that the fate of the squadron was inextricably linked to Revolutionary politics in the port.[6] Yet Jeanbon's interpretation did not acknowledge the confusion and agonizing dilemma which faced naval officers, a context that is crucial to understanding the course of events. Admiral Trogoff and the other commanders at Toulon attempted to maintain the navy's autonomy during 1793, despite Jacobin hostility and a lack of support or direction from the government in Paris. Such a position was very difficult when local domination could be justified by the principle of Popular Sover-

treachery of royalist naval officers; esp. pp. 95–116. Lévy-Schneider, I, pp. 444–449 defends the interpretation of Jeanbon's Report, delivered to the Convention on September 9, 1793, from what he sees as excessive criticism.
[3] Havard, I, pp. 152–210 insists that, from the beginning, Toulon's only cause was restoration of the monarchy. Havard's interpretation of Toulon's revolt echoes the accounts of royalist memorialists. See Lebret d'Imbert, *Précis Historique sur les événemens de Toulon en 1793* (Paris: Chez Poulet, 1814) [BN 8 Lb41 938], Gauthier de Brécy, *La Révolution royaliste de Toulon* (Paris, 1795) [BN 8 Lb41 939], and J. L. Panisse, *Histoire des événemens de Toulon, en 1793, pour le rétablissement de la monarchie* [manuscript] (Toulon, 1815); Archives Municipales de Toulon L 2 XIX – 17.
[4] Vovelle, esp. pp. 179–185. See also Crook, *Toulon*, pp. 126–152.
[5] Maurice Loir, "La livraison de Toulon aux Anglais (1793)," in *Etudes d'histoire maritime*, pp. 140–144 does not damn Trogoff as utterly as Cottin, but he places full blame on the Admiral for the surrender. Trogoff is defended, and Saint-Julien condemned, by Guérin, V, pp. 440–451. For a recent example of such an interpretation, see Ferrier, "L'événement de Toulon," pp. 129–176.
[6] AP, vol. 73, pp. 575–582.

eignty, and when opposing factions sought to recruit allies among naval personnel. Commanders were unable to keep the squadron and the dockyards aloof from the city's political strife and their control and independence slipped away. The navy was drawn inexorably towards a crisis as Toulon's internal struggle escalated to become a revolt against the Convention. When the officers and men faced their terrible decision they were not united by common loyalty, but bitterly divided and uncertain of what authority should be recognized as legitimate. Using the language of Popular Sovereignty, both Jacobins and "Federalists" claimed to represent the nation and thus deprived the navy of any clear focus for its loyalty. It was this moral dilemma, resulting from the nature of Revolutionary conflict, which accounts for the surrender of the Mediterranean fleet.

The dramatic events in Toulon fit into a national context as well as a local one. The advent of the Republic, far from ending political strife, ushered in a new stage of bitter conflict between Revolutionaries. This was most clearly apparent in the National Convention where the trial of Louis XVI revealed a fundamental division between those deputies who saw ruthlessness toward the king as both virtuous and expedient, and other more moderate men who feared the implications of such an act. The king's execution on January 21, 1793 marked not only victory for the Montagnards, led by the core of deputies affiliated with the Paris Jacobin Club, but the ascendancy of a more radical vision of the Republic. The appointment of a new Minister of Marine in April 1793 symbolized this shift for the navy: the new Committee of Public Safety replaced the intellectual Gaspard Monge with the former privateer Jean Dalbarade.[7]

The struggle in the Convention intensified during the spring of 1793 while other factors pushed France towards a crisis. In March, religious

---

[7] Jean Dalbarade was born at Biarritz, near Bayonne, in 1743 and served as an officer aboard privateers during the Seven Years' War. He commanded a privateer during the American War, and entered the navy as *capitaine de vaisseau* in 1792; Taillemite, *Dictionnaire*, p. 79. Guérin, V, pp. 415–416 acknowledges Dalbarade's exploits as a corsair, but is contemptuous of his appointment as Minister: "Il fallait un administrateur, on nomma un pirate." Lévy-Schneider, I, pp. 327–328 agrees with Guérin that Dalbarade was devoted to the *Montagne*, but argues that this political commitment improved the situation for the navy: "Quand on parcourt la correspondance du successeur de Monge et qu'on examine ses actes, on voit en lui un ardent démocrate, décidé à ne placer que des républicains dans la marine, et aussi un esprit prudent, pratique, très lucide, un grand travailleur."

and social tensions in the west exploded in a savage civil war with the "Catholic and Royal Army of the Vendée" routing republican forces sent against it. Counter-Revolution thus created a second front just as French Armies were recoiling from the advance of the Allied Coalition. Meanwhile scarcity and rising prices were causing popular militants in the cities to demand the government assure supplies and take harsh measures against hoarders and other hidden enemies. The Montagnard-dominated Convention decreed a wave of emergency legislation, including the first *maximum* and the institution of the Revolutionary Tribunal, but the continuation of parliamentary opposition was unacceptable to radicals in Paris. Hence the Sections purged the outspoken opponents of the Montagnards, the "Girondins," from the Convention in the Revolution of May 31–June 2.[8]

The expulsion of the "Girondins," however, coincided with a wave of anger throughout France against Montagnard extremism. Since the beginning of 1793 many administrative councils and popular societies in the provinces had complained that national representation was hostage to the Paris mob, incited by demagogues like Marat within the Convention, and had supported calls for measures such as a Departmental Guard to ensure its independence. These sentiments were often accompanied by great uneasiness about the radical policies associated with the *Montagne*. The Revolution of May 31–June 2 appeared to confirm all these fears. Alongside a storm of protest against the purge, many provincial centres proclaimed themselves to be in rebellion and refused to recognize the legitimacy of a government which no longer represented the nation. The scale of action taken and the intensity of feeling varied greatly. Some local administrations levied troops for military action against the Convention while others only drafted proclamations, but the entire movement has come to be known as the "Federalist Revolt."

This phenomenon has been the subject of considerable historical revision in recent years. The term "Federalism" was used first by the

---

[8] Historical interpretations of May 31–June 2 vary according to the view of the groups in the Convention. Alison Patrick, *The Men of the First French Republic* (Baltimore and London: Johns Hopkins University Press, 1972), esp. pp. 132–136 claims that the purge broke the obstruction of the minority party, the Girondins, to the wise national policy pursued by the majority Montagnards. However, Sydenham, *Girondins*, esp. pp. 194, 205, 207–212 argues convincingly that the "Girondin party" was a creation of Montagnard propaganda. Those termed "Girondins" were merely the outstanding, or most eloquent, of the *Montagne*'s opponents and represented the view of the amorphous majority in the Convention. In this context, the Revolution of May

Montagnards who saw in the rebellion of provincial cities a vast conspiracy by the "Girondins" against Revolutionary authority and national unity.[9] Historians of the nineteenth and early twentieth centuries continued this direct association between the provincial revolts and the struggle in the Convention, their interpretations indicating with which deputies they sympathized.[10] The arguments of studies favourable to the Montagnards, characterizing "Federalism" as particularist and anti-Parisian, were incorporated into the Marxist interpretation of the Revolution which explained the revolts as the work of rich provincial bourgeoisie concerned for their property and threatened by Revolutionary democracy.[11] Recent studies, however, have shown that provincial events were not the direct result of May 31–June 2. The purge of the Convention was not the cause of resistance, rather it provided further justification for existing opposition to Revolutionary measures. The recognition that revolts against central authority in great cities like Marseilles and Lyons grew out of internal struggles to control local government, struggles which culminated before June 2, undermined the interpretation of a parliamentary conflict spreading to the provinces. Anti-Jacobins who controlled Lyons' electoral assemblies, the Sections, overthrew the Jacobin municipality led by Joseph Chalier on May 29. The situation was similar in Marseilles where the Sections arrested radical activists on May 18–19 and went on to shut down the Jacobin Club. Primarily because the Jacobins in both cities had received support from

31–June 2 signalled an end to Parliamentary democracy and the beginning of the Terror; see Sydenham, *The French Revolution*, pp. 159–162.
[9] See J. Julien (de Toulouse), *Rapport fait au nom du Comité de Surveillance et de Sûreté Générale, sur les administrations rebelles, 15 octobre 1793* (Paris: Imprimerie Nationale, 1793).
[10] H. A. Wallon, *La Révolution du 31 mai et le fédéralisme en 1793*, 2 vols. (Paris, 1886) shows great sympathy for the "Girondins" and, as the title implies, sees the Revolt in the provinces as a direct response to the assault on national representation. This interpretation is in contrast to that of F. V. A. Aulard, *The French Revolution: A Political History, 1789–1804*, 4 vols., trans. B. Miall (London: T. Fisher Unwin, 1910), II, pp. 136–138 who argues that the provincial risings were motivated by fears of a Parisian dictatorship and opposed the wise Montagnard view that Paris must act as the ruling capital of a united Republic.
[11] Albert Mathiez, *The French Revolution*, trans. C. A. Phillips (London, 1928; repr. New York: Russell and Russell Inc., 1962), pp. 319, 333, 340 views the Revolt as a "Girondin" conspiracy and, as such, the expression of bourgeois selfishness. The increasing emphasis on class struggle is evident in the work of his successors: Lefebvre, *French Revolution: From 1793 to 1799*, pp. 56–57; Soboul, *French Revolution*, p. 310; Marc Bouloiseau, *The Jacobin Republic, 1792–1794*, trans. J. Mandelbaum (Paris, 1972; repr. Cambridge: Cambridge University Press, 1983), pp. 64–72.

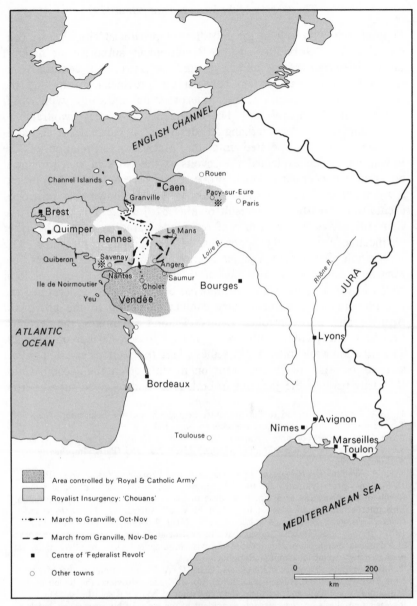

Map 6. Resistances to the Revolution in 1793. *After* "Resistance to the Revolution, 1793–9" in William Doyle, *Oxford History of the French Revolution* (Oxford: Clarendon Press, 1989), p. 225.

Representatives on mission, the coups against the local radical administrations soon developed into defiance of the Montagnard Convention.[12] Toulon also experienced a municipal revolution in 1793. Revolutionary extremists, mostly from the fringes of the urban élite and based in the Club Saint-Jean, had dominated Toulon since the violence of 1792. The local struggle was related to social tensions in the city, but is also explicable in political terms. The events of August 10 in Paris, and the subsequent establishment of the Republic, had appeared to legitimize the Jacobin coup in Toulon. Yet developments in the Convention during the spring of 1793 confused local radicals and rendered Jacobin rule vulnerable. This vulnerability was revealed in June 1793 when Toulon's Administrative Corps released seventy notables, imprisoned as suspects, owing to pressure from the new Sectionary regime in Marseilles. The fate of their comrades in Marseilles shocked the Toulonnais Jacobins but provided their opponents, strengthened by the release of the notables, with an example of how they might achieve power.[13] The Administrative Corps were determined to deny them such an opportunity and proclaimed death as the punishment for anyone demanding that Toulon's Sections, which had not assembled since the fall of 1792, be reopened. On July 12 the Club Saint-Jean staged an armed procession, led by Montagnard Representatives on mission Baille and Beauvais, through the city's streets to give substance to this threat.[14] Yet this march of intimidation proved to be the catalyst for the coup which overturned Toulon's Jacobin regime. That evening the Jacobins' opponents gathered at the church of Minimes to draft a petition demanding that the Sections be opened, and two hundred National Guards signed it. Thus with the protection of the

---

[12] Regarding Lyons, see W. D. Edmonds, *Jacobinism and the Revolt of Lyon, 1789–1793* (Oxford: Clarendon Press, 1990), pp. 167–185. For Marseilles, see John B. Cameron, *The Revolution of the Sections of Marseilles: Federalism in the Department of the Bouches-du-Rhône in 1793* (Ph.D. Thesis, University of North Carolina, 1971). Recent surveys suggest this pattern of national alignment being secondary to local conflict was common throughout France: W. D. Edmonds, " 'Federalism' and Urban Revolt in France in 1793," *Journal of Modern History*, 55 (March 1983), 22–53; Sutherland, *France 1789–1815*, pp. 177–181; Doyle, *Oxford History*, pp. 230–232.
[13] See Richaud, pp. 33–34 and Cottin, p. 24. Crook, *Toulon*, pp. 128–129, 136 explains that Jacobins in Toulon were critical of developments in Paris, but could not break with the Convention.
[14] See Pons, p. 13, and Richaud, p. 34. See also Henry, II, p. 29, and Vovelle, p. 181.

militia, the Sections assembled during the night without waiting for municipal approval.[15]

The support of the guardsmen for the opening of the Sections, and the surprising ease with which the municipal revolution was accomplished, illustrate a dramatic loss of popular support for the Jacobin regime in Toulon. Malcolm Crook argued that the radical administration became isolated principally because of its efforts to subdue popular effervescence and to reestablish order in the dockyards once in power.[16] This alienation of support from the arsenal coincided with a declining standard of living for workers which was little alleviated by the distribution of bread from naval bakeries.[17] Crook also suggested that the shift in popular opinion during 1793 was related to the influx of conscript workers into Toulon, these outsiders being critical of the radical atmosphere in the arsenal.[18] Thus the case of Toulon supports the argument, made in recent studies of other provincial cities, that "Federalism" often had substantial popular support.[19]

The Jacobins in Toulon may have lost their grip on power by forfeiting their appeal in the arsenal, but a major reason for the Sections' support was emotional rather than material: there was widespread fear of a new round of massacres. The murders of 1792 had terrified political moderation at all levels of society into silence, thus allowing Revolutionary extremists to dominate local government. A repetition of such atrocities seemed imminent in July 1793 and this prompted many Toulonnais to act. The Montagnards, and many historians subsequently, claimed that Toulon's revolt was fundamentally the work of royalist conspirators.[20] The retention of republican forms in July and August

[15] For various accounts of the opening of Toulon's Sections, see: Pons, pp. 18–20; Richaud, pp. 35–36; Henry, II, pp. 30–31, 278–279; Vovelle, p. 181; Crook, *Toulon*, p. 130.
[16] Crook, *Toulon*, pp. 126–128. Crook points out that the radicals, as part of their efforts to facilitate work in the arsenal, had persuaded workers and sailors to withdraw from duty in the militia. Thus by July, the National Guard was composed principally of artisans and shopkeepers.
[17] Crook, *Toulon*, pp. 127–128. See also Hampson, "Ouvriers," pp. 321–322, 327–328.
[18] Crook, *Toulon*, p. 128. Marine BB 3/30, f. 171; BB 3/31, ff. 173–174. See also Hampson, "Ouvriers," pp. 309–311, and Vovelle, p. 180.
[19] See for example Albert Goodwin, "The Federalist Movement in Caen during the French Revolution," *Bulletin of the John Rylands Library*, 42 (1960), 313–344. See also Sutherland, *France 1789–1815*, pp. 180–182. Edmonds, *Jacobinism and the Revolt of Lyon*, pp. 193–196 suggests that the lower classes did not see their interests at stake in the struggle between Lyon's factions; see also W. D. Edmonds, "A Jacobin Debacle: The Losing of Lyon in Spring 1793," *History*, 69 (1984), 1–14.
[20] See the section of Jeanbon Saint-André's report in the *Moniteur*, vol. 17, pp. 615–620 (11 septembre 1793). See also Havard, I, pp. 156, 162, 188–189.

thus appears as either ruse or hypocrisy. Yet such an interpretation cannot be supported. Rather than a conspiracy, a coalition of moderates, both royalist and republican, gained control of Toulon through the Sections.[21]

The new regime moved quickly to consolidate its own power and to crush that of its enemies. The Sections, having declared themselves permanent, entrusted executive authority to a General Committee of thirty-two members on July 14.[22] This General Committee closed the Club Saint-Jean and arrested many of its prominent activists. The Sections dissolved Toulon's municipality, replacing it with a new elected body on July 18, and purged the District and Departmental Councils at the end of the month. More importantly, the new regime reorganized the National Guard and created a Popular Tribunal which eventually tried and executed over thirty Jacobins, mostly on charges relating to the violence of the previous year.[23] The Sections were not, however, concerned only with the situation in Toulon. The local Jacobins had received support from Montagnard Representatives on mission, and it is not surprising that the General Committee arrested Baille and Beauvais on July 15.[24] This was an act of defiance, but Toulon's irreparable break with central government resulted from its union with rebel Marseilles.

On July 16 the Sectionary regimes in Toulon and Marseilles exchanged deputations carrying messages of fraternity and offers of support.[25] This unity was put to the test two days later when a letter from the Minister

[21] Cottin, p. 24 suggests this interpretation, and Pons, p. 12 states it explicitly: "Les partisans de la monarchie, ceux que quatre années de malheurs n'avoient pas désabusés, et ceux qui croyoient encore à la possibilité d'établir une république, oubliant leurs divisions passées, se réunissent pour conjurer le danger qui les menace."

[22] Eugène Coulet, *Le Comité général des sections de Toulon (13 juillet–17 décembre 1793)* (Toulon: Gallinari, 1960), pp. 8–9.

[23] Regarding the purge of the administrations, see: Richaud, pp. 36–40; Pons, pp. 21–25; Henry, II, pp. 38–39; Coulet, pp. 13–14, 19; Vovelle, p. 181. For the persecution of the Sections' Jacobin enemies, see: A. J. Parès, "Le tribunal populaire martial de Toulon, juillet–décembre 1793," *Bulletin du comité des travaux historiques et scientifiques* (1925), 75–130; Henry, II, pp. 40–43; Crook, "Federalism and the French Revolution," pp. 392–393.

[24] The two Montagnards may have been forced to take part in a parade and Mass, after which Jacobin emblems were burned in the public square. Regarding their arrest see: Henry, II, pp. 37–39; Cottin, p. 41; Coulet, pp. 10–12; Crook, *Toulon*, p. 135. Pierre Baille committed suicide while imprisoned in Toulon.

[25] See: Richaud p. 40; Pons, pp. 35–36; Coulet, p. 12; Vovelle, p. 183. See also Georges Guibal, *Le Mouvement fédéraliste en Provence en 1793* (Paris: Plon-Nourrit, 1908), pp. 226–227.

of Marine arrived in Toulon which required its naval commanders to place an embargo on all ships sailing for Marseilles by virtue of a decree from the Committee of Public Safety.[26] Toulon's General Committee decided to defy such a decree, stating: "these orders have arrived at the moment when the city of Marseilles and that of Toulon are to unite in sentiments, principles and resolution, to contribute effectively and in concert to saving the *patrie* from the attacks of the anarchists; . . ."[27] The Sections elaborated the principles of Toulon's revolt in a printed letter of August 12 to the Minister and the Provisional Executive Council,[28] and in an "Address to all citizens of the French Republic" of August 13.[29] Both documents justified the events of July in Toulon by virtue of the violence and arbitrary measures of local Jacobins, and both went on to repudiate the Revolutionary government in Paris as illegitimate due to the violation of national representation on June 2. The Sections did not propose any measures to federalize France, or to weaken national unity, but declared their devotion to the ideal of a Republican Constitution which would protect property and promote law and order:

We want a Republic one and indivisible, and they have never wanted to organize it. We want a constitution, fruit of wisdom and of reflection, and they propose to us only a phantom of government which must propagate factions and anarchy, and leave the ship of state tossed ceaselessly by the stormy waves of popular insurrections.[30]

The principles which prompted Toulon to burn the Constitution of 1793 in the public square and to dispatch troops to Marseilles' "Depart-

---

[26] *Vigilance et Fermeté. Copie de la lettre écrite le 9 juillet 1793, par le Ministre de la Marine au citoyen Trogoff, contre-amiral, commandant les Forces navales en rade à Toulon* (Toulon: Imprimerie de Rochebrun & Mazet, no date) [BN 8 Lb41 3149]. This pamphlet also includes the deliberation of Toulon's General Committee on the letter, and the reaction of the General Committee of the Sections of Marseilles.

[27] "Extrait du procès-verbal de la séance du comité général des sections en permanence, en date du 19 juillet 1793, l'an II de la république française"; in Pons, p. 215.

[28] "Le Comité général des Sections de Toulon en permanence, au Conseil exécutif provisoire, et au citoyen d'Albarade, ministre de la marine. Toulon, 12 août 1793, l'an second de la république française, une et indivisible"; Marine BB 3/30, ff. 190–193. Also in Pons, pp. 234–244.

[29] "Addresse, au nom des sections de Toulon, à tous les Citoyens de la République française"; in Pons, pp. 219–233.

[30] Ibid., pp. 224–225.

mental Army" were the same as those used to defend the opening of the Sections. The city's moderates did not repudiate the Revolution, rather they opposed the violence and radical policies of the Jacobins. This ideological basis for resistance to the Convention was very similar to that expressed by rebels in Marseilles and throughout France.[31] Thus the "Federalist Revolt," despite unique circumstances in Toulon and elsewhere, reflected a nationwide division of Republicans.[32]

The studies of Toulon's revolt considered above suggest that the loss of support among arsenal workers and, to a less certain extent, sailors led to the demise of the local Jacobin regime. No historian has argued that naval commanders numbered among the Jacobins' strong supporters in Toulon, yet those officers who still served in the port in 1793 appeared willing to acknowledge local Revolutionary authority. Had such an attitude changed by July? Naval officers did not figure in the political manoeuvres which brought the Sections to power, but they did nothing to defend the existing civil administration.[33] Whether or not such inaction demonstrated tacit approval for the coup,[34] it was certainly in keeping with the navy's constant position of non-

---

[31] See for example the discussion of the political objectives of "federalists" in Normandy and Brittany, as indicated in the printed "Projet d'Arrêté. L'Assemblée extraordinaire des députés des Départements, etc. séante à Rennes (19–22 June 1793)," in Goodwin, "The Federalist Movement," pp. 339–340. See also: the oath sworn on June 9, 1793 by the rebel "Commission Populaire de Salut Publique" in Bordeaux, cited in Alan Forrest, *Society and Politics in Revolutionary Bordeaux* (Oxford: Oxford University Press, 1975), p. 109; the speech of François de Nantes to the Assembly of delegates of the primary assemblies of the Department of Isère on June 25, 1793, cited in A. Prudhomme, *Fédéralisme dans l'Isère et François de Nantes* (Grenoble, 1907), p. 107; the discussion of the revolt in the Department of the Jura, in Michael J. Sydenham, "The Republican Revolt of 1793 in Widening Perspective," *The Consortium on Revolutionary Europe, 1750–1850. Proceedings*, XIII (1984), pp. 116–123.

[32] See M. J. Sydenham, "The Republican Revolt of 1793: A Plea for Less Localized Local Studies," *French Historical Studies*, 12 (1981), 120–138.

[33] Henry, II, p. 33 quotes a requisition addressed by the municipality to Admiral Trogoff at 3:00 a.m. on July 13, 1793 which required him to prevent crews from coming ashore for the maintenance of public order. Henry uses this as an illustration of the municipality's efforts to prevent Jacobin-inspired violence and thus its support for the campaign to open the Sections. Confirmation that Trogoff forbade the squadron from communicating with the city on July 13 is given in Edmond Poupé (ed.), "Journal d'un Ponantais de l'Apollon," *Revue historique de la Révolution française* (jan–mars 1911), p. 37. The security measures taken by him, and by *ordonnateur* Puissant, that night, however, appear as precautions against popular violence affecting the arsenal and not as positive support for a coup; Marine BB 3/31, f. 215.

[34] Chevalier, p. 68.

intervention. Joseph-Maurice Puissant de Molimont, who arrived in Toulon in May to assume the duties of *ordonnateur civil*, stated years later that he had no legal right to oppose the opening of the Sections.[35] The initial attitude of Toulon's naval officers towards the Sections was restrained, but conditioned by their unhappy relationship with local Jacobins during 1793.

Despite the argument that the Club Saint-Jean and the Administrative Corps sought to restore stability in the dockyards after the coup of 1792, Revolutionary fervour continued to create chaos in the naval base during 1793.[36] Puissant reported in June that disorganization and inefficiency severely impaired the construction and outfitting of warships. There were too many conscript workers in the port for the facilities, but layoffs would be dangerous for arsenal security and for the *ordonnateur* personally unless they were given unanimous consent by the Workers' Central Committee and the three Administrative Corps. "Order, subordination, emulation," wrote Puissant, "are the only means to advance the work."[37] Insubordination, of course, was not confined to the dockyards and the Basterot affair demonstrated that mutiny continued to be an expression of sailors' politicization. In July the crew of *La Topaze* refused to obey orders to sail from Marseilles where the frigate, along with *L'Artheuse*, had been forced to take refuge from enemy warships. The report of the incident by the Captain of *L'Artheuse*, Duchesne-Gohët, reveals the frustration of naval officers faced with mutinous patriots:

Behold the reptiles who call themselves *sans-culottes* at the tavern's door, and who at sea one could qualify with the just title of *sans-armes* and cowards. When will examples be made, when will the Republic be purged of the villains which infect it or, better say, when will we have wise laws. . .[38]

[35] Puissant, *Précis de la conduite de Puissant, ordonnateur de la marine à Toulon, pendant les événemens de 1793* (Paris: Gallettie, An V), p. 3; Archives Municipales de Toulon L 2 XIX – 4. For Puissant's background and his appointment to Toulon, see: Ferrier, "Les singuliers successeurs de Malouet," pp. 131–154; Guérin, V, pp. 427–428; Havard, I, p. 154.
[36] See the report made by Doinet, *Chef des Travaux*, to Minister Dalbarade, May 31, 1793: Marine BB 3/30, f. 171. See also Hampson, "Ouvriers," pp. 309–311.
[37] Marine BB 3/31, ff. 173–174.
[38] Marine BB 4/21, f. 166; see also ff. 163, 165, 307. For other examples of mutiny at Toulon in 1793, and complaints by officers that the Penal Code was insufficient, see: Marine BB 4/22, ff. 229–231, 251; BB 4/21, ff. 90, 92. In a letter to the Convention of June 28, 1793 Admiral Truguet stated: "La discipline est la première des armes:

Sailors' misconduct and insubordination could not be blamed entirely on Toulon's popular authority. There were, however, other legitimate causes for officers of the navy to dislike, and to fear, the local Jacobin regime. Admiral Truguet left for Paris in April to explain the failure of the Sardinian expedition, and command of the Mediterranean fleet passed to the comte de Trogoff de Kerlessy. *Contre-amiral* Trogoff, a professional officer from an old but poor Breton family, had served in the West Indies during the early phase of the Revolution and, in January 1793, had sailed with a division from Brest to support Truguet's squadron against Sardinia.[39] From the beginning of his tenure as commanding officer, Admiral Trogoff realized that his authority was severely limited by the power of Toulon's Club and civil administration. By withholding his passport, the three Administrative Corps forced him to remain at his post despite an executive order to report to Paris, and Trogoff advised the Minister to enclose future correspondence in the regular pouch for Commandant Chaussegros.[40] Local popular authority declared its confidence in the Admiral but, at the time of Basterot's Court Martial, Trogoff believed that his noble birth might be held against him.[41]

The fates of Basterot and of Captain Prévost-Lacroix, arrested for Counter-Revolutionary crimes in April,[42] indicated Jacobin suspicion

l'armée navale et Toulon l'attend, et son chef vous déclare qu'il peut rien sans elle"; *Moniteur*, vol. 17, pp. 34–35 (5 juillet 1793).

[39] Jean-Honoré, comte de Trogoff de Kerlessy was born at Lanmeur (Finistère) in 1751 and served for three years as a volunteer before becoming a *garde de la marine* in 1767. Promoted *lieutenant de vaisseau* in 1779, he served aboard *Le Glorieux* (74) during the War of American Independence; at the Battle of the Saints, he took command of the ship when his captain was killed and only surrendered when much of the crew was dead or wounded. He was promoted *capitaine de vaisseau* in 1784, commanded *Le Duguay-Trouin* (74) in the West Indies during 1790–1791, and was made *contre-amiral* in January 1793. See Taillemite, *Dictionnaire*, pp. 326–327, and Six, *Dictionnaire biographique*, II, pp. 512–513. For details of Trogoff's participation in the attack on Cagliari in February 1793, where he was wounded, and his appointment as interim-commander of the Toulon fleet, see: Guérin, V, pp. 365–385, 423–425.

[40] Marine BB 4/21, f. 90. See also "Extrait des registres des trois corps administratifs. Séance du 5 avril 1793"; Ibid., f. 91. The issuing of passports was not the only means for local popular authority to control naval officers. *Certificats de civisme* were first issued in Toulon in February 1793 and allowed the municipality to place considerable pressure on suspect *fonctionnaires*; Cottin, pp. 22–23.

[41] "Je puis même dire que je jouis à Toulon de toute la faveur qu'un ci-devant peut avoir, dans un moment où la trahison d'un Bourgeois à fait crier contre les ci-devants"; Marine BB 4/21, f. 99.

[42] Marine BB 4/22, ff. 06–35. See also Chevalier, p. 63.

and hostility. The dangerous position of naval officers in Toulon was made clear in May when the Administrative Corps imprisoned several captains, as well as Rear-Admirals Léandre-François Martel and Edouard-Thomas de Burgues, comte de Missiessy, along with the other suspect notables.[43] The Representatives on mission in Toulon informed Trogoff of the arrests, and the Admiral felt very unsure of how to respond.[44] Commandant Chaussegros echoed this uncertainty: "It remains to beg of you, citizen Minister, to give me your orders for the replacement of captains and commanders who, with the greatest desire to serve *la patrie*, are not in a position to hope from their subordinates all the confidence they have a right to expect."[45]

A final example of the domination of the navy's commanders can be seen in the pressure exerted on Admiral Trogoff to take his ships of the line to sea to engage the enemy. The appearance of Spanish warships in June led the French Consul in Genoa, backed by Representatives on mission to the Army of Italy, to demand a sortie by the Toulon squadron.[46] Trogoff favoured, in principle, a fleet action before the Spanish could link up with their British allies. He feared that a British fleet might already be in the Mediterranean, however, and he knew the profound weakness of the forces under his command: a sortie, therefore, could have only disastrous results.[47] Pressure for a battle also came from inside Toulon where Jacobins, led by Barthélemy, encouraged sailors to sally forth to meet the enemy.[48] Local authority forced Trogoff

[43] Guérin, V, p. 429; Cottin, p. 24. Henry, II, pp. 284–285 lists some of the prisoners released from Fort Lamalgue on May 31, 1793, on the order of Representatives Baille and Beauvais, including *contre-amiral* Saint-Julien and sixteen *capitaines de vaisseaux*. Given the demands for the release of naval officers during June, either the date of May 31 is incorrect and/or this list does not contain all those who were imprisoned.
[44] Marine BB 4/21, f. 109.
[45] Marine BB 3/30, f. 117.
[46] Marine BB 4/21, f. 154; see also BB 3/31, f. 193.
[47] Marine BB 4/21, ff. 126, 152, 131. Trogoff's caution was eventually sanctioned by the Minister of Marine who, in a letter of June 29, 1793, ordered him not to take the fleet to sea unless he judged it to be equal to the strength of enemy forces: Marine BB 4/21, ff. 81, 84; see also copies of Dalbarade's orders to this effect, June 29 and July 6, 1793, in Guérin, V, p. 536.
[48] Poupé (ed.), "Journal d'un Ponantais," pp. 35–36. The anonymous memorialist aboard *L'Apollon* also suggests that the Jacobins' harangues supported rumours that they were plotting to deliver the French fleet to its enemies, rumours which help explain the sailors' relative support for the Sectional coup of July 13, pp. 37–38. See also Brun, II, pp. 206–207. Cottin, pp. 49–50 claims that, although Clubists did try to force the squadron to sortie, the plot was created by royalists to discredit their enemies.

to justify his professional judgement,[49] and thus he saw his position, if such pressure continued, to be terribly insecure: "all these writings will produce only a very bad effect if the Administrative Corps of Toulon doubts for an instant my patriotism and my attachment to the public good."[50]

All of these difficulties were related to, or exacerbated by, a pointed lack of direction or support from the central government.[51] Just as Admiral Trogoff asked the Minister to uphold his decision to keep the fleet in port, so did he request repeatedly that national executive authority assert itself regarding the officers imprisoned in Toulon. These men, whom Trogoff vouched for as loyal servants of their country, were held without formal charges and their release was vital if the navy was to be capable of giving battle.[52] Moreover, the Admiral could hardly be expected to take responsibility for such a battle, with or without orders from Paris, when he had never received formal appointment to command of the Mediterranean fleet. Trogoff told the *chargé d'affairs* at Genoa that he assumed Truguet would return to resume his command but he had no idea of his predecessor's plan of campaign, and he reiterated this frustration to the Minister.[53] Trogoff claimed that his authority as mere interim-commander was insufficient for the trying situation he faced in Toulon. Indeed his correspondence prior to the opening of the Sections contains no less than six requests that his post be fixed or that he be transferred elsewhere.[54]

Naval commanders in Toulon probably welcomed the collapse of Jacobin power, but they did not contribute to it. Puissant's account of the Sectional coup suggests that the events came as a complete surprise to senior officers. His letter of July 12, written on the eve of municipal

---

[49] Marine BB 4/21, f. 156.

[50] Ibid., f. 162.

[51] Puissant complained on July 17, 1793 that he had received no orders for thirteen days; Marine BB 3/31, f. 221.

[52] Marine BB 4/21, ff. 120, 126, 152. Guérin, V, p. 431 claims that although the officers were released on June 30, 1793, the clubists opposed their return to duty.

[53] Marine BB 4/21, ff. 119, 152.

[54] In his letter to the Minister of May 29, 1793, Trogoff wrote: "Malgré que je vous ai reitéré plusieurs fois de décider où et comment je servirai, vous ne m'avez jamais repondu. Je vous avouerai que cela m'affecte infiniment, cette incertitude me met dans l'impossibilité de faire tout ce que je voudrais pour le plus grand bien de la République. D'ailleurs ma position depuis deux mois est si épineuse qu'elle ne peut plus exister comme cela, je vous prierai donc de prononcer tant pour moi, que pour le bien du service"; Marine BB 4/21, f. 110; see also ff. 92, 99, 116, 120, 152.

revolution, evoked an atmosphere of tension as Toulon swarmed with Jacobins seeking refuge from the mounting "Federalist" wave in the Var and the Bouches-du-Rhône. The port was thus isolated and the *ordonnateur*'s correspondence had been intercepted at Aix and Marseilles. Puissant knew there was an assembly at the Minimes and that it called for the opening of the Sections, but he clearly had no idea the campaign would succeed.[55] His subsequent reports, which described the evolution of the Sectionary regime, were favourable to the new state of things.[56] When Puissant informed Paris of the Sections' arrest of several individuals, however, he felt compelled to add that "we are always directed by true principles."

It is unclear whether Puissant sought to reassure the government in Paris or to distance himself from the course of events in the port. He later stated that, while he applauded the initial wisdom of the Sections, he had warned the Toulonnais of the danger of declaring their permanence and had spoken against the extension of their authority.[57] His concern is at odds with the notion that the navy was in full support of the new regime in Toulon. Admittedly, at least a dozen officers or administrators sat on the General Committee of the Sections, which included the *ordonnateur* along with Chaussegros and Trogoff from its creation.[58] Yet with their refusal to allow the blockade of Marseilles, the Sectionaries showed they had as little regard for the independence of naval authority as had their Jacobin opponents. This flagrant interference in naval affairs has been condemned as the beginning of Toulon's treason.[59] Such defiance was less a "Federalist" innovation, however, than it was the continuation of the pattern of Revolutionary politics in the port. Since 1789 those who controlled local government in Toulon showed little reluctance to override naval authority. What changed in July 1793 was that the local manifestation of Popular Sovereignty had become diametrically opposed to the radical direction of the Revolution in Paris. The commanders of the navy at Toulon faced increasing pressure as the municipal coup became a revolt against central government.

[55] Marine BB 3/31, ff. 214–215.
[56] Ibid., ff. 216–221.
[57] Puissant, *Précis de la conduite de Puissant*, p. 3.
[58] Guérin, V, p. 433; see the list of naval members on the *Comité général*, p. 537. See also the comprehensive list of all known original members in Coulet, pp. 8–9, which includes some naval administrators not on Guérin's list.
[59] See for example Lévy-Schneider, I, p. 430.

Despite the General Committee's claim that the decision to defy government orders to blockade Marseilles was reached in accordance with the port's senior military officers,[60] it is unclear whether naval commanders could have opposed the Sections.[61] The Sections controlled communication between the naval base and Paris, and they scrutinized officers' correspondence. Some historians suggest that Puissant and others employed double meanings to alert the government to their fears.[62] Admiral Trogoff, who warned the Minister that no orders could be considered secret from the General Committee,[63] stated explicitly that he was forced to conform to public opinion "to maintain order and tranquility between the men I command and the inhabitants which surround them."[64] Trogoff's correspondence reveals not only this pressure on the navy, but the continued lack of support or direction from the government in Paris. The Admiral stated on August 14 that he had received nothing from the Minister of Marine since July 22, and he vented his frustration:

I asked you to name a commander for this fleet. . . . if you no longer intend on corresponding with me, you must ask the Executive Council to name another. It is frightful that after all that I have suffered, after working as I have, after finding myself in the most dreadful circumstances for four months, they do not have the regard for me which is due an officer who occupies himself day and night only with his station, with the responsibility to procure all that is within his power and to attain supplies for two land armies and one of the sea, and to protect the commerce of the Republic despite the superior forces of the enemy in these waters.[65]

Thus, despite his mounting frustration, Trogoff's fundamental position had not changed under the Sections. He opposed calls in the General

---

[60] "Extrait du procès-verbal . . . 19 juillet 1793 . . ."; in Pons, p. 215.
[61] See the enigmatic summary of a letter of July 21, 1793 from Chaussegros, Puissant, and Trogoff to the Minister relating the defiance of the executive order; Marine BB 4/21, f. 200. See also the summary of a letter of July 23 which reports the arrest of Peyron, an agent of the Minister of Marine and former associate of Barthélemy; Marine BB 4/21, f. 200. The originals of these letters do not appear in BB 4/21 or BB 3/30 or 31. Guérin, V, p. 435 claims that Trogoff, Chaussegros, and Puissant were forced to comply with the defiance of the orders to blockade Marseilles.
[62] Ferrier, "L'événement de Toulon," p. 132. See also: Cottin, pp. 104–105; Lévy-Schneider, I, pp. 428, 430; Chevalier, p. 69.
[63] Marine BB 4/21, f. 173.
[64] Ibid., f. 179.
[65] Ibid., f. 177.

189

Committee to disarm part of the fleet, stating that the force under his command "does not belong to the cities and neighbouring territories but to the entire Republic," and declared that he would resign if such measures were taken. This threat was successful initially, but he warned that the Executive Council must take responsibility to end such danger.[66] Admiral Trogoff strove to maintain the navy's integrity from local political strife just as he and other officers had done during the period of Basterot's Court Martial. The fleet's survival, however, depended on the central government recognizing the non-partisan loyalty of its commanders and not allowing Toulon's revolt to isolate them: "I say also with the same frankness, that the same Executive Council must occupy itself essentially with the supplies and the money which the fleet needs and consider that a quarrel of opinion must not be a reason to abandon forces which belong to the entire Republic."[67]

Admiral Trogoff had every reason to fear that the fleet would soon be cut off from all financial and logistical support as the vengeful forces of the Convention advanced to crush the rebel cities. The Marseillais Departmental Army, repulsed from Avignon at the end of July, retreated in disorder before troops commanded by General Carteaux.[68] A detachment from the Army of Italy was marching westward towards Toulon, and the Representatives on mission with both armies proclaimed harsh measures to isolate the revolt.[69] The imminent siege would make it impossible to retain any independence for the fleet. Marine troops had been enrolled in the Departmental Army in July,[70] and the proposals to disarm warships in August showed that the Sections had no qualms

---

[66] Ibid., f. 179.
[67] Ibid. Trogoff suggested in the same letter of August 15, 1793 that the squadron might be removed from the turmoil of Toulon to Brest so that it could be "usefully employed in the colonies during the winter," and he ended with a desperate appeal, "ne me laissez pas, citoyen Ministre, sans réponse: car vous me mettriez dans l'embarras le plus affreux."
[68] Guibal, pp. 228–234.
[69] See the letter of July 26, 1793 from Barras and Fréron, in Nice, to the Committee of Public Safety; in Aulard (ed.), *Actes*, IV, pp. 383–392. See also William Scott, *Terror and Repression in Revolutionary Marseilles* (London: Macmillan, 1973), pp. 119–124.
[70] Marine BB 4/21, f. 263. Puissant, *Précis de la conduite de Puissant*, p. 2 states that detachments from the fleet were sent on August 7. See also Ferrier, "L'événement de Toulon," p. 134. Marine troops were disembarked from *L'Orion* on July 27 and 30, 1793, presumably to join the Departmental Force. See "Précis en rade de Toulon 1793: Journal de l'enseigne Absolut du vaisseau Orion"; Archives Municipales de Toulon L 2 XIX – 18.

about subordinating naval concerns to their defense against the Convention. Trogoff's anxiety does not mean, however, that he anticipated surrender to the British.[71] The character of the Sectionary regime in Toulon might appear increasingly reactionary because of its revival of traditional Catholicism, exemplified by the public *Te Deum* to celebrate the fall of the Jacobins and the *fête* held on July 28 for the coronation of the Virgin,[72] and due to its ruthless treatment of prominent extremists.[73] Political moderation may have given way to vengeance and social conservatism, but the evidence does not substantiate an inevitable slide towards Counter-Revolution. Toulon's alliance with Admiral Hood resulted from the force of circumstances, not premeditated strategy.

The British fleet was sighted off Toulon as early as July 17 and on July 19 Hood sent one of his officers, Lieutenant Cook, into the port to negotiate a prisoner exchange.[74] The ulterior motive for the parley was to gain information on French naval strength and not to seek an opening for political intervention.[75] Hood had no orders regarding such a project and he saw the occupation of Toulon as a tremendous but unforeseen opportunity.[76] British involvement began on August 23 when a delegation from Marseilles presented itself to Hood, ostensibly to procure free passage of food supplies but in fact to negotiate a military

[71] Guérin, V, pp. 438, 537–538 suggests that Trogoff foresaw the Sections' treasonous negotiations with Hood, which he claims are anticipated in the General Committee's printed letter to Dalbarade of August 12, 1793: "Songez enfin que deux escadres formidables d'Angleterre et d'Espagne embrassent toute l'étendu de nos côtes, et que dans leurs calculs, peut-être, elles se flattent d'obtenir de notre détresse et de nos besoins ce que la trahison (des clubistes) devait leur livrer."

[72] See Marine BB 3/31, f. 218. See also: Coulet, pp. 10, 20; Pons, pp. 38–40; Henry, II, pp. 43–44; Guérin, V, p. 436.

[73] Henry, II, pp. 42–43 claims that the Sections' Popular Tribunal ordered twenty-four executions, beginning with Sylvestre on July 27, before they were stopped by the English governor in November. Parès, "Le tribunal populaire," pp. 75–130 suggests that over thirty death sentences may have been pronounced. For interpretations which stress the growing reaction in Toulon, see Vovelle, pp. 181–184, and Ferrier, "L'événement de Toulon," pp. 134, 141–142.

[74] Marine BB 3/30, f. 161. For the text of Hood's letter of July 19 to Toulon's Governor and *Commandant de la place*, and the reply of Doumet see BB 4/21, f. 210.

[75] Suspicion was aroused because Cook's boat flew the white flag of the Bourbons, rather than a Tricolour, as a sign of parley; Poupé (ed.), "Journal d'un Ponantais," p. 38. There is, however, no basis for the claims of Henry, II, p. 46 that Hood arrived off the coast of Provence with plans to exploit the political situation ashore, or of Brun, II, p. 214 that the English were aware of the changes in Toulon since July 12.

[76] J. Holland Rose, *Lord Hood and the Defence of Toulon* (Cambridge: Cambridge University Press, 1922), esp. pp. 8, 12; "Admiralty Instructions to V.-Adm. Lord Hood," pp. 95–101.

alliance.[77] The Marseillais expressed surprise at the absence of delegates from Toulon aboard Hood's *Victory*, and they composed a letter which encouraged that city to open negotiations with the British fleet.[78]

It was this initiative from Marseilles that prompted the return of Lieutenant Cook to Toulon on the night of August 23 with a package for the General Committee which contained the letter from the Marseillais delegation, along with a Proclamation and a Preliminary Declaration from Admiral Hood.[79] The Proclamation described the wretched condition of France, suggesting that the only remedy was the re-establishment of the monarchy, and it offered Hood's support to crush factions, restore regular government and to spare further bloodshed.[80] The conditional nature of Hood's offer of military alliance was made clear in his Preliminary Declaration:

If a candid and explicit declaration in favour of monarchy is made at Toulon and Marseilles, and the standard of royalty hoisted, the ships in the harbour dismantled, and the port, and forts provisionally at my disposition, so as to allow of the egress and regress with safety, the people of Provence shall have all the assistance and support his Britannic Majesty's fleet under my command can give; . . .[81]

The Declaration guaranteed private property and promised that the port, the forts, and the warships would be held in trust and restored to France upon the arrival of peace. It was clear that if the Toulonnais decided to enter an alliance with Hood's fleet they must declare for a restoration of the monarchy.[82]

---

[77] Rose, pp. 19–20. It is unclear whether an alliance, rather than simply passage of supplies, had been agreed to in the Sections of Marseilles or was initiated by the members of the delegation. See: Pons, pp. 60–63; W. Scott, pp. 123–126; Henry, II, pp. 50–51; Guibal, pp. 267–271.

[78] "Les Commissaires du Comité de sûreté générale du département des Bouches-du-Rhône, aux membres composant le Comité général des Sections de Toulon. A bord du vaisseau la Victoire, commandant de l'escadre anglaise aux ordres de l'amiral Hood, le 23 août 1793, l'an second de la république française"; in Pons, pp. 259–261. See also Cottin, pp. 80–84.

[79] Rose, pp. 20–21; Cottin, p. 85; Pons, pp. 63–65.

[80] "Proclamation, by the right honourable Samuel Lord Hood, vice-admiral of the red, and commander in chief of his Britannic Majesty's squadron in the Mediterranean, To the inhabitants of the towns and provinces in the south of France"; in Pons, pp. 262–265.

[81] "Preliminary Declaration"; in Pons, p. 266.

[82] It is probable that Hood could not conceive the option of moderate republicanism. He did not, however, seek to impose the restoration of the *Ancien Régime* as shown by his approval of Toulon continuing to fly the Tricolour: "Nouvelles conditions

The General Committee convened an extraordinary session of Toulon's Sections on the night of August 24 to decide on the propositions of Admiral Hood. The leaders of the new regime needed this democratic sanction, but the violence of the ensuing debate demonstrated the great reluctance of many Toulonnais to embark on such a drastic course of action.[83] Resistance to the alliance resulted as much from national distrust and antipathy as from uneasiness with the reimposition of the monarchy.[84] A number of factors, however, outweighed these sentiments and persuaded the Sections to entrust themselves to the traditional enemy. The city was becoming dangerously low on food supplies and would be unable to sustain a long siege.[85] Refugees from Marseilles, which fell to Carteaux the following day, streamed into Toulon and told of terrible reprisals carried out by forces of the Convention.[86] The expectation of Montagnard vengeance was the strongest argument for an alliance with Hood, but this was made more urgent by the resurgence of Jacobinism within Toulon. The execution of two radicals, Lambert and Barry, provoked a dangerous riot among arsenal workers on August 20.[87] Although suppressed, this insurrection demonstrated the threat

présentées par l'amiral Hood"; in Pons, pp. 274–275. Harvey Mitchell, *The Underground War against Revolutionary France* (Oxford: Clarendon Press, 1965), pp. 33–35 argues that although the British Government gradually came to see the restoration of some sort of reformed monarchy as essential to securing a peace settlement, it always wished to avoid imposing any form of government on the French people. See also Hutt, pp. 107–114. This argument is substantiated in the case of Toulon by a "Déclaration du Roi de la Grande Bretagne . . .," presented to the Sections on November 20, 1793 by Sir Gilbert Elliot, which stated: "Sa Majesté desire ardemment le bonheur de la France, mais elle ne prétend pas, à ce titre, lui prescrire la forme de son Gouvernement, et elle ne réclame le droit de s'y intéresser, qu'autant que l'Anarchie qui désole ce pays, peut troubler la tranquillité de ses propres sujets, et celle des autres Puissances de l'Europe, dont la sûreté dépendent essentiellement du rétablissement de l'ordre en France, et d'un systeme régulier, qui puisse leur offrir une base assurée de Négociation et d'amitié"; Toulon 1 L 139 (4).

[83] Panisse, pp. 55–62; Archives Municipales de Toulon L 2 XIX – 17. See also: Coulet, pp. 29–31; Crook, *Toulon*, p. 140; Vovelle, pp. 184–185.

[84] Pons, p. 65; Richaud, p. 46.

[85] Naval commanders noted the threat to Toulon's food supplies from both the actions of Representatives on mission and the British blockade; Marine BB 3/30, f. 167; BB 3/31, f. 222. Cottin, pp. 52–56 argues that the Toulonnais were deliberately misled regarding the shortage, but Crook, *Toulon*, p. 139 estimates that no more than eight weeks' worth of food remained.

[86] See Richaud, pp. 45–47, and Guibal, pp. 301–303.

[87] The Workers' Committee in the arsenal had denounced the sentences against Lambert and Barry, convicted by the *Tribunal Populaire martiale* of murder and extortion during 1792, and its agitation led to an uprising by workers and sailors aimed at preventing the executions. A firm stand by National Guards and marine

from internal enemies as the Sections prepared for an assault from armies of the Convention and overcame reservations to seeking Allied support.[88] The Sections accepted Hood's terms but, significantly, their declaration to the British Admiral referred specifically to the Constitution of 1791, which is further evidence of the continuation of a coalition between moderates.[89] Toulon's alliance with the British and its declaration of the monarchy was less a royalist coup than an act of desperation.

There were individuals in Toulon, however, who rejoiced at the irrevocable rejection of the Republic. The most notorious was Thomas Lebret, baron d'Imbert, a captain in the Mediterranean fleet. In his account of events at Toulon, Lebret d'Imbert stated that he had been a dedicated royalist since 1790 and he had returned to active duty in the navy after the fall of the monarchy as a secret agent.[90] He was assigned to Toulon,[91] where he replaced the arrested Prévost-Lacroix as interim-commander of *L'Apollon* (74) in May 1793.[92] Involved in shadowy intrigue and sedition as a member of the General Committee, Lebret d'Imbert claimed that he had sounded out Allied support through

troops frustrated the attempt, and the strong personal authority of Commandant Chaussegros dispersed the workers. See Panisse, pp. 32–35; Archives Municipales de Toulon L 2 XIX – 17. See also: Pons, pp. 51–60; Henry, II, pp. 46–47; Coulet, pp. 27–28; Ferrier, "L'événement de Toulon," pp. 147–148. Following these events, the General Committee named a six-member *Comité de sûreté générale*. Crook, *Toulon*, p. 138 suggests that while moderates despaired, the influence of reactionary elements increased after this episode.

[88] Panisse, pp. 59–60, indicates that it was the fear of the internal Jacobin enemy which finally overcame objections to the alliance with Hood; Archives Municipales de Toulon L 2 XIX – 17. See also Richaud, p. 45.

[89] "Déclaration de la ville de Toulon"; in Pons, pp. 268–271; see also p. 69: "Les républicains eux-mêmes, qui depuis quelque temps, s'étaient unis aux royalistes, et pénétrés, en quelque sort, de leurs sentiments, répètent le cri cher aux Français. La monarchie constitutionelle, telle que l'Assemblée constituante l'avait décrétée en 1791, et que Louis XVI l'avait approuvée, en conciliant toutes les opinions, réunit tous les suffrages."

[90] Lebret d'Imbert, pp. 12–13. See also Cottin, pp. 111–114.

[91] Lebret d'Imbert, p. 13 states: "on me nomma au commandement d'une des escadres de la Méditerranée; je m'étais chargé d'une grande et importante mission dans le but d'en faire manquer les effets, ainsi que le portaient mes ordres secrets et les seuls légitimes." In fact, Lebret d'Imbert was given command of the frigate *L'Impérieuse* for a minor diplomatic voyage to Algeria; see Guérin, V, p. 535 who criticizes Lebret d'Imbert as much for his pretentions to undeserved rank as for his treason.

[92] Marine BB 4/21, f. 101. Trogoff cannot be accused of intriguing to place this officer in command of *L'Apollon*. The Admiral opposed the arrest of Prévost-Lacroix, and Lebret d'Imbert arrived in Toulon with government recommendation; see Guérin, V, p. 430.

an agent in Genoa and that he proposed Toulon proclaim for Louis XVII as early as August 19.[93]

While his influence on events is dubious, Lebret d'Imbert's professed sentiments and description of his activities have contributed to the view that the navy in Toulon was a bulwark of royalist treachery. Yet Lebret d'Imbert himself acknowledged that the greatest obstacle to the conclusion of the foreign alliance was resistance from the anchored squadron.[94] The Sectionary regime's relationship with the naval commanders was strained, and the General Committee's control over the officers and men aboard the warships was even more tenuous. The Sections knew that Hood would not come to their rescue if he had to fight his way in past the guns of a determined French fleet. It was vital, therefore, to prevent such opposition and to make sailors accept the surrender of Toulon. The General Committee dispatched an address to the squadron, which Lebret d'Imbert claimed to have drafted, on the morning of August 25.[95] The address stated that the crews would be read the propositions of the English Admiral and, having examined them, would see the necessity for having a king. It went on to assure those favouring royalty that they could count on the assistance of a generous friend, but promised those who opposed that they would be paid and returned to their homes.

Despite such reassurances, sailors received the news that the Sections had agreed to disarm the fleet and surrender it to the English with shock. Lebret d'Imbert alleged that he was successful in winning over his own ship,[96] but the journal of an anonymous member of *L'Apollon*'s company stated: "This proposition aroused the crew and the commander was unable to impede the murmurs which it excited."[97] The sailors

[93] Lebret d'Imbert, p. 19; see also the *Pièce justificatif*, "Extrait des régistres des Sections et du Comité générale de Toulon, 27 août 1793," pp. 33–34. It is significant that all of Lebret d'Imbert's *pièces*, including testimonials from Hood and Gilbert Elliot, are included to prove his royalist credentials.

[94] Lebret d'Imbert, p. 19.

[95] "Adresse des trois corps administratifs réunis au Comité général des Sections de Toulon à l'escadre française, le 23 août 1793"; in Poupé (ed.), "Journal d'un Ponantais," p. 53. There is some confusion regarding dates because several sources suggest that the General Committee delivered this Address on August 24. Yet it was the meeting of the Sections during the night of August 24–25 which committed Toulon to the surrender, and thus it is most likely that the fleet received this Address, and began its resistance, on the morning of August 25; see Coulet, p. 31 and Crook, *Toulon*, pp. 140–141.

[96] Lebret d'Imbert, p. 19.

[97] Poupé (ed.), "Journal d'un Ponantais," p. 41.

drafted a petition demanding defiance of Toulon and defense of the port against the enemy, and this was sent to the rest of the squadron. According to Ensign Romeiron, the reaction of *L'Apollon*'s quarter deck was similar. The ship's officers were horrified but initially subdued by Lebret d'Imbert's report that the Convention was dissolved and most of France had proclaimed Louis XVII, so that peace with the English was in accord with the National Will. When the captain returned ashore, however, the officers realized they had been deceived and rallied in opposition to the "black treason of the Toulonnais."[98] This pattern of disbelief changing to anger and defiance was not unique.[99] The crew of Trogoff's flagship, *Le Commerce-de-Marseilles* (118), expressed its outrage immediately. A placard at the foot of the mainmast which declared, *"La Constitution ou la Mort!"*, greeted Flag-Captain Pasquier upon returning to his command at the head of a delegation from the General Committee. Sailors' indignation at the proposal to surrender was so great that Pasquier disembarked the Sectionaries to save their lives.[100] Banners, petitions, and oaths by officers and men swearing to die rather than allow entry to the English, demonstrated resistance throughout the fleet. Crews raised halters to yard-arms and threatened to hang captains suspected of supporting Toulon's treason.[101]

The fleet directed its hostility, above all, at Admiral Trogoff. He had not been aboard his flagship for nine days, and his association with Toulon's General Committee discredited him. Leadership of the defiant fleet passed to Trogoff's second-in-command, *contre-amiral* Saint-Julien de Chambon.[102] On the evening of August 25, Saint-Julien intercepted

---

[98] "Précis de Journal du citoyen Romeiron de Marseilles, Enseigne non-entretenu, faisant fonction de Lieutenant à bord du vaisseau L'Apollon à l'époque que les Toulonnais ont livré leur pays aux Ennemis"; Marine BB 4/22, ff. 30–31.

[99] See "Journal de l'enseigne Absolut"; Archives Municipales de Toulon L 2 XIX – 18.

[100] Cottin, pp. 118–119.

[101] Puissant, *Pétition au Conseil des Cinq-Cents, concernant l'événement de Toulon en 1793* (Paris: Galletti, An 5), "Faits exposés au Corps Législatif," p. 1; Marine BB 3/30, ff. 218–223. See also: Poupé (ed.), "Journal d'un Ponantais," p. 42; Cottin, p. 119; Guérin, V, p. 443.

[102] Jean-René-César Saint-Julien de Chambon was born at Brest in 1752, and entered the navy as a volunteer in 1763 before becoming a *garde de la marine* in 1764. *Lieutenant de vaisseau* in 1778, he was named *major de vaisseau* in 1786. Injured during the riot of December 1, 1789 at Toulon, he was promoted *capitaine de vaisseau* in 1792 and commanded *Le Commerce-de-Bordeaux* (74) during the Sardinian campaign. Like Trogoff and Chaussegros, he was made *contre-amiral* in January 1793. See: Six, *Dictionnaire biographique*, II, p. 415; Guérin, V, pp. 425–426; Cottin, pp. 110–111.

a brig leaving the inner roadstead carrying messages to Hood from the General Committee. He signalled all warships to clear for action and gave orders for armed longboats to guard the harbour entrance against further attempts to contact the enemy.[103] The fleet recognized the authority of the new admiral enthusiastically and, on the morning of August 26, Saint-Julien summoned all captains or commanding officers to a council of war aboard his flagship, *Le Commerce-de-Bordeaux* (74). He gave orders to seize the harbour forts of l'Eguillette and Balaguier, which gave the navy control of all batteries on the south shore, but sailors failed to capture Fort Lamalgue on the opposite side of the roadstead.[104]

Alarmed at the escalation of the navy's resistance, the General Committee responded with more proclamations. One, addressed to the entire squadron, combined idealism with the appeal of desperation. Toulon, it stated, would always remain attached to France, but part of the nation had abandoned Toulon and was threatening it with armies which could only return the city to the yoke of factions and assassins. The English had not come to threaten French freedom, but to destroy the party which tore the heart from *la patrie*: "We will not recognize the English as masters, but as allies who come to aid us in maintaining our liberty, to restore peace to France and among the Toulonnais who want the Constitution of 1789, the nation, the law and the king, to live free and to die French."[105] The General Committee supplemented this attempt to win hearts and minds with a proclamation to Saint-Julien

[103] "Journal de l'enseigne Absolut"; Archives Municipales de Toulon L 2 XIX – 18. Ensign Romeiron was inspired by Saint-Julien's intervention and volunteered for duty in one of the guard-boats, "Journal du citoyen Romeiron"; Marine BB 4/22, f. 31. Cottin, p. 120 says that Lieutenant Cook and two members of the General Committee escaped from the brig, but were forced to reach Hood by travelling overland to Hyères. Lebret d'Imbert, p. 20 states that he was one of the new commissioners sent to the British fleet.

[104] Captain Boubennec reports sending twenty-five men to secure Fort Balaguier: *Mémoire du citoyen Boubennec, capitaine de vaisseau, commandant ci-devant le vaisseau de la République, l'Entreprenant venant de Toulon, à tous mes concitoyens de Brest, Frères et Amis (6 ventôse 1794 an II)* (Landernau: Havard, no date); Brest "Fonds Levot" 1988 [35]. According to the "Journal du citoyen Romeiron," the squadron encountered little resistance from National Guards manning the batteries; Marine BB 4/22, f. 31. Puissant, *Pétition*, "Faits," p. 1 claims that, despite the enthusiasm and devotion of the officers who attended, Saint-Julien's council was "long, tumultuous, and indecisive," and he makes no mention of operations against shore batteries. See also Cottin, p. 120.

[105] "Proclamation des sections de Toulon à l'escadre"; in Poupé (ed.), "Journal d'un Ponantais," p. 55.

which contained a less subtle message. It informed the Admiral that Toulon had made peace with the English for the good of the city and of all France. The Sections invited Saint-Julien, whose projects of resistance were well known, to return the fleet from its error and, while evoking principles of naval honour, they also issued a direct warning: "but if this horrible project, if the obstacles opposed presently to the will of the Sections that the fleet has no right to master, continue, it is proclaimed that Toulon has decided to repel force with force."[106]

This ultimatum from the General Committee outraged Saint-Julien who threatened to hang the Sections' delegates. Moreover, he threatened to bombard the city if it interferred with his preparations to defend the port.[107] During the night of August 26–27, the Admiral ordered the fleet to anchor in line-of-battle, positioned to sweep the entrance of the inner roadstead.[108] The Sections in Toulon made defensive preparations, notably the placement of hulks before the commercial port as a shield against cannon fire, for what appeared an inevitable and deadly confrontation with the navy.[109]

Despite Saint-Julien's words of defiance and his bellicose manoeuvre, the French fleet was deeply divided and not resolved to fight both the British and the Toulonnais. These divisions have been explained, and characterized, in various ways. The anonymous journal from *L'Apollon* stated that, following Saint-Julien's orders, not all warships took up their assigned stations:

the *Provençaux* put themselves beyond range of the forts, using the other ships as shields, all taking the part of the city; several had resolved to favour the English and to fire on the *Ponantais* [those from Atlantic ports] if they opposed their entry, which demonstrated their treason and put the squadron into confusion. Saint-Julien sent his orders to the squadron, above all to the four *Ponantais* ships of the line, *le Héros*, *l'Entreprenant*, *l'Apollon*, *le Généreux*, to fire on the city and on the forts when he gave the signal.[110]

[106] "Copie de la proclamation faite par les sections de Toulon au citoyen Saint-Julien, contre-amiral commandant l'escadre française, ainsi qu'à toute l'escadre"; in Poupé (ed.), "Journal d'un Ponantais," pp. 53–54.
[107] See Lévy-Schneider, I, p. 438, and Guérin, V, p. 446.
[108] Poupé (ed.), "Journal d'un Ponantais," pp. 42–43. "Journal de l'enseigne Absolut" describes defensive manoeuvres, but it is unclear when they were initiated; Archives Municipales de Toulon L 2 XIX – 18.
[109] Panisse, pp. 71–72; Archives Municipales de Toulon L 2 XIX – 17. See also Henry, II, pp. 61–62, and Cottin, p. 121.
[110] Poupé (ed.), "Journal d'un Ponantais," p. 43.

According to this witness, the fleet was divided along clear regional lines. Crews from Atlantic ports, mainly Breton and Norman sailors, were prepared to bombard Toulon to prevent the surrender to the English, whereas those crews from Provence recoiled from the prospect of civil war. Memorialist Louis Richaud reiterated this suggestion, stating that the *Ponantais* had nothing to lose while sailors from Toulon had their families ashore to consider, and at least one report to the Minister of Marine claimed that the regional identity of naval officers determined their loyalty.[111]

This picture of regional division suggests a continuity with the old separation of the French navy into two distinct services, based on traditions and geography. To explain disunity in the fleet completely in terms of antagonisms between two unique maritime cultures, however, ignores both the changes in the navy since the early eighteenth century and the effect of the Revolution. After the Seven Years' War the navy became increasingly national in its composition and its strategic roles. This was reflected by the presence of battleships in Toulon which had been outfitted in Atlantic ports. Conceived as a major arm of the French state, the service intermingled seamen, officers, and warships from both littorals. The Revolution certainly continued this trend and, moreover, it contributed the rhetoric of national political conflict which, by definition, minimized regional differences and emphasized a single struggle.

Ensign Romeiron's account, unlike the journal of the anonymous *Ponantais* on *L'Apollon*, made no mention of a regional split in the fleet and pointed instead to something more ideological.[112] Admiral Hood, in a letter to the Admiralty of August 26, stated: "A captain of one of the ships of the line is now on board and tells me that 11 of the 17

---

[111] Richaud, p. 51. Letter of September 28, 1793 to Dalbarade from P. Adet, Marseilles; Marine BB 3/30, f. 202. The attitude attributed to the *Provençaux* was encapsulated in a speech supposedly made by a Toulonnais captain on the eve of surrender: "Messieurs les Ponantais, vous en parlez fort à votre aise; vous n'avez rien à perdre ici; nous, au contraire, nous avons dans cette ville nos femmes, nos enfants et nos possessions, que nous ne voulons pas livrer aux fureurs et aux vengeances de Carteaux. Je vous préviens, au nom de mon équipage et en général de tous les Provençaux qui sont dans le même cas que moi, que nous sommes décidés à favoriser l'entrée des Anglais, nos amis et nos protecteurs, et que nous ferons feu sur ceux qui voudront s'y opposer"; in Fabre, *Les Bouvet*, I; cited by Loir, "La Livraison de Toulon," pp. 132–133. See also Boubennec, and Cottin, pp. 127–128.

[112] Romeiron stated that, despite the indignation in the fleet at the prospect of surrender, "ils se trouvent toujours des malveillans qui travaillent les équipages en sens contraires de l'intérêt général et contre leur devoirs, . . ."; "Journal du citoyen Romeiron," Marine BB 4/22, f. 34.

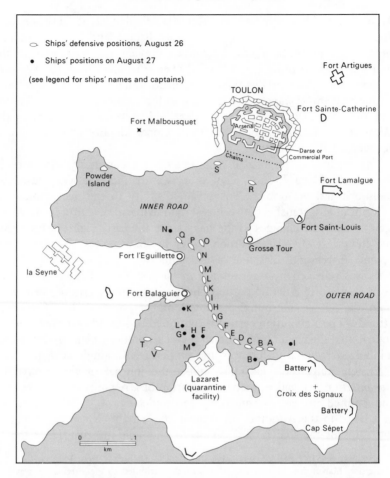

Map 7. Surrender of the Mediterranean fleet, August 1793 [Accompanied by Legend giving names of ships and commanding officers]. *After* "The Defence of Toulon, 1793" in J. Holland Rose, *Lord Hood and the Defence of Toulon* (Cambridge: Cambridge University Press, 1922), Appendix.
"Position de la flotte française le 26 août" and "Position de la flotte française le 27 août" in Paul Cottin, *Toulon et les Anglais en 1793* (Paris: P. Ollendorff, 1898), pp. 123, 125.
"Positions de l'armée navale les 26 et 27 août" in Jacques Ferrier, "L'événement de Toulon du 28 août 1793," *Bulletin de l'Académie du Var* (1985), p. 158.

Ships	Commanding Officers
A Le Duguay-Trouin (74),	Capt. Cosmao-Kerjulien
B Le Tricolore (74),	Capt. Pourquier
C Le Centaure (74),	Capt. Causse
D Le Pompée (74),	Capt. Poulain
E Le Destin (74),	Capt. Eyraud
F Le Commerce-de-Bordeaux (74),	Capt. Barberet;
	Admiral Saint-Julien
G L'Héros (74),	Capt. Haran
H Le Patriote (74),	Capt. Bouvet de Maisonneuve
I Le Commerce-de-Marseille (118),	Capt. Pasquier; Admiral Trogoff
K L'Orion (74),	Capt. Puren-Keraudrin
L Le Tonnant (80),	Capt. Amielh
M L'Heureux (74),	Capt. Gavoty
N Le Scipion (74),	Capt. Goy de Bègues
O L'Apollon (74),	Capt. Lebret d'Imbert
P L'Entreprenant (74),	Capt. Boubennec
Q Le Généreux (74),	Capt. Cazotte
R Le Thémistocle (74),	Capt. Duhamel du Désert
S La Perle (frigate),	Lt. Van Kempen
T L'Aréthuse (frigate),	Capt. Duchesne-Gohët
V La Topaze (frigate),	Lt. Gassin

great ships in the roads are commanded by violent democrats."[113] Hood's informant was probably Lebret d'Imbert, but he was not alone in suggesting that political affiliation divided the squadron with royalists pitted against republicans. An agent of the Revolutionary Government, P. Adet, gave a similar report to Dalbarade. Adet sought to identify the traitors within the navy by describing the character of various ships in the fleet based on intelligence of one of Saint-Julien's councils of war: L'Orion (74), L'Entreprenant (74), and Le Scipion (74) had "demanded a king"; Le Thémistocle (74), L'Apollon (74), Le Duguay-Trouin (74) and Le Commerce-de-Marseilles (118) were ready to "fire on all sides"; Le Patriote (74) and the frigate L'Artheuse wanted "war with the English but peace with Toulon."[114] A declaration circulated to the squadron by the crew of Le Thémistocle further suggested that those most opposed to the surrender were adamant republicans. The Constitution, according to this circular, was crucial:

[113] "Hood to P. Stephens, Victory, August 26"; in Rose, p. 125.
[114] Marine BB 3/30, ff. 188–189.

Friends of Liberty, you have realized like us that the general happiness depends absolutely on the acceptance of a truly republican and popular constitution. Let us hasten therefore to manifest our will; let us not fear the axe of our common executioners. . . .

They have, they say, annihilated the hydra of anarchy. Very well! has not more insolent despotism succeeded it? How can we believe we are free after the arbitrary acts they commit regarding us. Do they not with impunity threaten us with death when we dare to speak for the Constitution? Where is therefore the freedom to express opinions which our representatives have decreed? . . .

My friends, the tyrants more than ever raise their haughty heads . . .[115]

This Jacobin-style denunciation of the Sections not only exhorted crews to stand fast in defiance of Counter-Revolution ashore, but advised them on their conduct towards their officers:

consult your leaders; speak to them with all the deference to which they are due; confide in them your distress and your fears; solicit them to join with you to foil the perfidious projects of our enemies. If they refuse, act without them. If they come to catechize you, scorn their seductive proposals; refuse with horror all propositions which crime will suggest and cry with us: *Vive la République! Vive la Nation, Vive la Constitution!* . . .[116]

This address from *Le Thémistocle* might suggest a scenario of republican sailors versus royalist officers, an interpretation which has had its advocates.[117] Yet more striking than the admonition to defy treacherous leaders was the advice to first confide in commanders. Good relations, and even trust, still existed between sailors and their officers. The journals of Ensigns Absolut and Romeiron bear this out, the evidence of the latter demonstrating that republicanism was not confined to the lower deck. Adet's reports identified as many loyal captains as traitors, and there was no direct correlation between opposition to the Sections and social origin: most of the officers commanding ships of the fleet were non-nobles, but Captain Duhamel du Désert of *Le Thémistocle*, who had been a lieutenant in the *Grand Corps*, was one of those praised

---

[115] "Avis du vaisseau le Thémistocle à toute l'escadre"; in Poupé (ed.), "Journal d'un Ponantais," pp. 56–57.
[116] Ibid., p. 57.
[117] Cottin, p. 115 states that, with some notable exceptions, all captains at Toulon were royalists. See also Vovelle, p. 185.

for his loyalty.[118] The officer corps was just as divided as the crews it commanded.

The lines of these divisions were blurred and their nature was complex. It is clear, however, that they were related to the political conflict ashore and developed from its continual intrusion into the squadron and arsenal. Drafting of petitions, circulation of addresses and delegations, and continual councils and secret meetings aboard the ships of the fleet were all characteristic of the Revolutionary situation. Despite ideological differences, crews wanted desperately to avoid disunity with their mates aboard other ships or with the "General Will" of the nation. Lebret d'Imbert's claim that most of France had proclaimed for Louis XVII subdued Romeiron and the officers of *L'Apollon*. The crews of *L'Entreprenant* and *L'Orion* may have desired a king and asserted their intention to fight the English, but only if this was the majority view.[119] Seen in this context, the issue which was fundamentally unacceptable to the navy was not Toulon's adoption of the monarchy, but its decision to surrender to the foreign enemy. On August 26, a deputation from the fleet went ashore carrying an address to the General Committee.[120] The message assured the Toulonnais of the squadron's goodwill and begged them not to deliver themselves to the English:

We would estimate ourselves happy, brothers whom we cherish like ourselves, if like us, you would take any other part than delivering yourselves to the enemy. Be persuaded that we will always do our duty to keep you loyal to your *patrie* and to protect you from the furor you seem to fear. Our blood, if necessary, will defend you against exterior enemies. Our loyalty and yours

---

[118] Guérin, V, pp. 541–542 lists all ships and frigates at Toulon and gives the professional background for most of the commanding officers. Only five captains of the seventeen ships of the line in commission by August were from the *Grand Corps* and one of them, Pierre-René-Sevran Bouvet de Maisonneuve of *Le Patriote*, had been a *bleu* before promotion to *lieutenant de vaisseau* in 1786. At least seven had entered the regular officer corps as *sous-lieutenants* in the organization of 1786, the others being port officers or *bleus* promoted during the Revolution. The difficulty of pinning down the political affiliation of individual officers is illustrated by Duhamel du Désert, whom Adet praises, Marine BB 3/30, f. 188, and Cottin, p. 115 calls a "sincere republican"; but who is named in a list of "Traitors at Toulon" found in the same dossier as Adet's correspondence, BB 3/30, f. 185. Similarly, Lieutenant Gassin, commanding *La Topaze*, is called a sincere republican by Cottin, a "créature et protégé du club des Adorateurs de l'Egalité" by Guérin, a patriot by Adet, and a traitor by Puissant, *Pétition*, "Faits," pp. 2, 8.
[119] Marine BB 3/30, ff. 188–189.
[120] Lévy-Schneider, I, p. 439.

toward the nation will assure you its cordiality to which you can look forward with the greatest confidence.[121]

This appeal to Toulon to cease its revolt against national authority accompanied a statement of the terrible dilemma in which the city placed the fleet. French sailors desired to remain faithful to their oaths, chief of which was never to bear arms against Frenchmen: "But also we will never consent to dishonor ourselves by allowing our enemies to enter Toulon, as long as we are present. To reconcile our oaths with the honor which is precious to us and which we want to conserve untainted at peril of our lives, this is what we propose to you."[122] The proposed compromise was that, if the Toulonnais had decided irrevocably to open the port, the city should solicit a safe-conduct from the Allies to allow the Mediterranean fleet to sail to another French port. This naive proposal, which would allow the navy to steer between the Scylla of dishonorable surrender and the Charybdis of civil war, demonstrates that the fundamental desire of naval crews was in keeping with the course which Admiral Trogoff had tried to maintain.[123]

The petitions and declarations coming from the fleet reveal the sailors' opposition to the surrender, but they also indicate a need for unity under recognized and trusted leadership. The nature of the city's conflict with the Convention deprived the navy of recognizably legitimate authority outside its own ranks. Therefore the defection of Admiral Trogoff, a respected and capable commander, was disastrous. The question remains why Trogoff accepted Toulon's foreign alliance. Despite the contention that the Admiral did not sign the Sections' acceptance of Hood's proposals or the initial address to the squadron,[124] there is no evidence that he opposed Toulon's decision of August 25 or that he did anything to prevent the entry of the British. According to Paul

[121] "Délibération de l'armée navale adressée aux Toulonnais"; in Poupé (ed.), "Journal d'un Ponantais," pp. 55–56.
[122] Ibid. The same sentiment is expressed by Boubennec: "mais que quant à nous, nous étions décidés à nous opposer de tous nos moyens à l'entrée des Anglais et Espagnols dans la rade de Toulon."
[123] Romeiron states his defiance of the General Committee, when sent ashore by Saint-Julien on August 27, using language strikingly similar to that used by Trogoff to defend the fleet's national ownership: "l'Armée ne souscrivait jamais à des pareilles propositions, et qu'elles ne permettront pas que les Anglais entreraient dans la rade de Toulon, sans être premièrement instruits se c'est toute la République qui a fait la paix avec cette nation, . . . qu'au sur plus l'Armée navale n'appartient pas à Toulon seul, mais à toute la République"; "Journal du citoyen Romeiron," Marine BB 4/22, f. 33.
[124] Guérin, V, pp. 439, 540–541.

Cottin, this treason had been Trogoff's goal all along as part of an insidious conspiracy. Far from being a prisoner of the General Committee,[125] he obeyed secret royalist instructions to ensure the surrender of the fleet.[126] Trogoff, Cottin alleged, opposed a fleet sortie against the Spanish, which would have been possible, in order to await the arrival of the British navy and his resistance to the disarmament of ships of the line in Toulon was feigned, his offer to resign a "comedy."[127] Cottin's only real evidence that the Admiral was a royalist agent, however, was the testimony of Lebret d'Imbert.[128] It has already been suggested that Lebret d'Imbert's account is highly suspect, but a stronger reason for doubting the charges of royalist conspiracy is the evidence of Trogoff's correspondence with the Minister. The Admiral asked repeatedly to be replaced or transferred: if it is assumed that these requests were insincere, how could a conspirator be sure they would be ignored? Cottin dismissed as hypocritical all of Trogoff's pleas to the Executive Council to support him in order to conserve the fleet for the Republic. Such an interpretation is based on his actions after August 24, but it ignores the consistency of Trogoff's efforts since taking command to preserve the navy's integrity as well as the pressure of the rapidly developing situation in Toulon. As Guérin put it: "Circumstances often lead men by a route completely opposite to that which they themselves proposed to take: this was the story for the great majority of Toulonnais."[129]

Guérin explained Trogoff's decision to support the Sections' defiance of the government in Paris by pointing to the culmination of a personal quarrel with Admiral Truguet. Trogoff received a letter from Truguet on August 16 which chastized him for shifting his flag from *Le Tonnant* (80) to the new three-decker *Le Commerce-de-Marseilles* (118). This petty criticism outraged Trogoff. It ignored his freedom under regulations to choose his own flagship and Dalbarade's signature on the document was a further insult.[130] His last letter to the Minister before the surrender expressed great bitterness regarding his treatment and accused Truguet of seeking to retain command of a fleet that he had abandoned:

[125] Ibid., pp. 442, 543.
[126] Cottin, pp. 99–100.
[127] Ibid., pp. 49–52, 99.
[128] Lebret d'Imbert, p. 15.
[129] Guérin, V, p. 436.
[130] In his letter of August 17, 1793, Chaussegros defended Trogoff shifting his flag as perfectly legitimate; Marine BB 3/30, f. 169.

the report he made to you is founded on his fear that the Executive Council, no longer seeing his flag aboard *Le Tonnant*, will suppress the pay which he believes he is due as commander in chief, while he is in Paris, spared all the fatigues and the unpleasantness which he would surely have suffered here, as I have for the past four months. . . Your letter, citizen Minister, reminds me of all I have suffered, all that I suffer, and will certainly continue to suffer in a position which does not belong to me and which must be filled by a man who must make it a point of honour to be at his post. . . . it would be very impolitic for me to remain here under the orders of another, having commanded for so long and during such thorny moments . . . I will tell you, with the frankness you know me for, that never will I serve under Admiral Truguet.[131]

The quarrel between the two officers originated during the Sardinian campaign when Trogoff was wounded and his ship nearly destroyed because of Truguet's incompetence.[132] Trogoff's animosity combined with his frustration at accepting responsibility for the Mediterranean fleet, under particularly trying circumstances, but never receiving formal appointment as its commander. Guérin argued that the General Committee exploited the Admiral's sentiments by presenting him with Truguet's letter at a key moment.[133]

There is little doubt that Trogoff felt despondent and considered himself abandoned by central government: he was a desperate man for whom time was running out. The turning point in his commitment probably occurred, however, on August 19 rather than upon reception of Truguet's letter. *Ordonnateur* Puissant described a critical meeting of the Workers' Central Committee in the arsenal on that date. Rumours ran wild in Toulon regarding the approach of armies of the Convention and the return of marine troops who had been deceived by the Sections, and Puissant wanted the navy to act by negotiation or by force in order to end Toulon's revolt. To this end he invited Admiral Trogoff, along with *major-général* Castelan, Lieutenant Van Kempen, and several other "patriot officers" to the arsenal for an assembly of the workers which Commandant Chaussegros chaired. The *ordonnateur* saw this as a great opportunity to restore unified purpose:

Seeing Trogoff come with Van Kempen, I engaged the workers to welcome him warmly, and I explained to them all its importance. In effect, nothing was

[131] Marine BB 4/21, f. 184.
[132] Guérin, V, pp. 377–385, esp. 383.
[133] Ibid., pp. 438–439.

happier: he knew this was an assembly of patriots, and he came to it. Once in the bosom of patriots, if he was received with due regard, if they had given me time to explain, with or without their goodwill, he and Chaussegros would have transmitted to the fleet all necessary orders, on my requisition supported by the assembly, and, if needed, by force; nothing could prevent or impede the effect of so prompt a measure.[134]

Puissant's hopes were dashed. Despite appeals for calm, the session turned quickly to chaos. Booed and threatened by the workers, Trogoff departed under the protection of Van Kempen.[135] The Admiral would not be seen in public again until after the surrender, and this last meeting of the three commanders marked the end of any real chance for the navy to unite in support of central authority. On August 20 the arsenal workers rose in the streets of Toulon and the attempted insurrection, along with his treatment the day before, probably convinced Trogoff that his only options were to submit to Jacobin anarchy or to resign himself to the rule of the Sections.

There is also no strong evidence to support Montagnard accusations that Chaussegros and Puissant were royalist conspirators. Though called "irresolute" by the *ordonnateur* for not using his authority to halt the progress of Toulon's revolt,[136] and deemed the weakest of the three commanders for his complete submission to the General Committee,[137] Chaussegros was more conscious than his colleagues of the potential violence of Revolutionary extremism in Toulon. He had succeeded the murdered Flotte as Commandant and the burden of recent history, more than weakness of character, probably accounted for his acceptance of the surrender.

Unlike Trogoff or Chaussegros, Puissant was able to defend himself against the accusations of treason. While imprisoned at Coutances in 1797, the former *ordonnateur* petitioned the national legislature protesting his innocence and demanded that the truth of "l'événement de Toulon" be told.[138] In various *mémoires justificatifs*, Puissant detailed his conduct

---

[134] Puissant, *Précis de la conduite de Puissant*, p. 7.
[135] Ibid. See also Ferrier, "L'événement de Toulon," pp. 143–145.
[136] Puissant, *Précis de la conduite de Puissant*, p. 4.
[137] Guérin, V, pp. 445, 543. Guérin does, however, recognize the difficulty of the extraordinary situation which faced the Commandant; p. 427.
[138] Along with the *Pétition au Conseil des Cinq-Cents*, with its accompanying "Faits exposés au corps Législatif," and the *Précis de la conduite de Puissant*, there exists the more extensive *Toute la France a été trompée sur l'événement de Toulon en 1793, voici la vérité* (Coutances: Agnès, An V) [BN 4 Lb42 303]. The publication of these *mémoires*

before and after the entry of the foreigner to show his constant loyalty to the Republic.[139] Following the arrest of the two deputies and the other manoeuvres which indicated Toulon was headed for open defiance of the government in Paris, Puissant attempted to protect the autonomy of his arsenal. The General Committee, however, removed the power of policing the dockyards from the *ordonnateur* and kept him under constant surveillance.[140] Puissant blamed the failure of his efforts to rally "patriots" against the revolt on hidden "agents of the factious," whose agitation had ruined the August 19 meeting and portrayed the workers' protest as a "premeditated massacre."[141] Betrayed, spied upon, and isolated from the crews in the roadsteads, Puissant could do no more than try to delay supplies to the "rebels" in a possible confrontation with the fleet.[142]

There is no reason to doubt the sincerity of Puissant's claims regarding his own loyalty to national authority or even his opposition to the revolt from a very early stage. What remains highly questionable, however, is his clear distinctions between "rebels" and "patriots." Puissant could determine which authority, which faction, truly represented "the nation" only with the benefit of hindsight. In 1793 the situation in Toulon was terribly uncertain. Puissant's failure to make allowances for this uncertainty was particularly true in his denunciation of Admiral Saint-Julien. Puissant did not contribute to the historical judgement against Trogoff, yet his version of the surrender of the fleet was as much a condemnation of Saint-Julien's conduct as a defense of his own.

Saint-Julien committed a major error, according to Puissant, in permitting the General Committee to distribute its propaganda among the fleet, an error which was compounded by his failure to arrest or put ashore all "suspect" officers who aided in the spread of the Sections' sedition.[143] This criticism ignored the nature of the Revolutionary situation: crews circulated petitions and delegations on their own initiative, and it is doubtful that the Admiral could have enforced an order

---

justificatifs provoked controversy and eventually secured Puissant's release in 1798. See Cottin, pp. 103–110, and Ferrier, "L'événement de Toulon," pp. 137–140.
[139] "Je n'y ai parlé qu'en républicain," Puissant, *Précis de la conduite de Puissant*, p. 3.
[140] Ibid., pp. 1–8.
[141] Ibid., p. 7.
[142] Ferrier, "L'événement de Toulon," p. 148.
[143] Puissant, *Pétition*, "Faits," pp. 3–4. Ferrier, "L'événement de Toulon," p. 157 states that, in failing to prevent all communication between Toulon and the squadron, Saint-Julien's "supreme error was political."

forbidding all communication between the ships and Toulon. Puissant's condemnation of Saint-Julien's military preparations was even more damning. There were several key defensive measures Saint-Julien failed to take which lowered the navy's chances of defending itself or denying entry to the enemy: he gave no orders to patriots in the arsenal who awaited his signal; he gave no orders to Captain Duhamel whose battle-ship, *Le Thémistocle*, was anchored in position to gain control of the commercial port; he allowed the rebels to seize vital harbour batteries, or to disarm them, and to supply the forts from the powder magazine situated on a tiny island in the harbour; he failed to seize supply depots with his own forces or to act to cut off all communication between Toulon and the enemy fleet.[144] Puissant claimed that during the critical period of August 25–27 Admiral Saint-Julien did nothing, despite the full support of a fleet resolved to give battle, and that this guilty inaction was made more shameful by continual drunkeness.[145]

Saint-Julien appears in this account as neither resolute, courageous, nor ruthless, but the situation was not so clear-cut as Puissant would have it. The Admiral was engaged in a war of nerves with the General Committee and hoped the Toulonnais would back down before he was forced to fire on the city. This explains his reluctance to take such irreversible steps as seizing supply depots or ordering *Le Thémistocle* into action against the commercial port. Moreover, Puissant dismissed too easily the danger to Saint-Julien from the fortresses controlled by the Sections.[146] The General Committee had threatened to use red-hot shot against the squadron as early as August 26,[147] and even one battery firing these projectiles could destroy the wooden warships. The possibility of such an attack frightened sailors and contributed to their uneasiness about fighting both the British and Toulon. Above all, Puissant's account is inaccurate in its picture of loyal, determined crews united in their desire to keep out the enemy. He acknowledged the existence of divisions in the fleet, particularly in his denunciation of rebel officers, but he did not admit that these limited the Admiral's ability to offer resistance.

[144] Puissant, *Pétition*, "Faits," pp. 3–7. See also Guérin, V, p. 445.
[145] Puissant, *Pétition*, pp. 1–2, "Faits," p. 7.
[146] Puissant, *Pétition*, "Faits," p. 5 claims that most of the troops which manned the forts were marine soldiers whose Republican loyalty had been displayed when they returned, angry and disillusioned, from service in the Departmental Army on August 19, 1793. See also Ferrier, "L'événement de Toulon," p. 146.
[147] Poupé (ed.), "Journal d'un Ponantais," p. 43.

Saint-Julien was all too aware of the disunity and confusion aboard his ships of the line and, on the morning of August 27, he attempted to reopen negotiations with the Toulonnais.[148] The General Committee saw this as a sign of weakness and sought to exploit it by dispatching an address to the fleet which appealed to sailors to unite with their brothers in Toulon, declared that Paris had crowned Louis XVII, and denounced Saint-Julien as a debauched villain.[149] The Admiral countered this by ordering a conference that afternoon aboard *L'Apollon* to which all ships were to send deputations of one officer and two seamen. From *L'Apollon* this assembly went ashore to come to terms with the city, but the Sections stopped it at the chain of the commercial port and allowed only a few delegates to enter. The General Committee rebuffed these sailors, and sent them back to their mates with only the warning that if the squadron did not submit to the will of the Toulonnais it would be "reduced to cinders."[150]

Saint-Julien's position rapidly became impossible.[151] He proposed to his captains, as a final expedient to save the warships, that the fleet declare itself neutral and demand safe-conduct to another French port.[152] Not all captains accepted this proposal,[153] and the Admiral spent the evening circulating throughout the fleet making speeches to inspire the crews to fight to the death rather than allow the enemy to enter. Sailors applauded him and cheered, *"Vive la République!,"* but their will to resist was vanishing. Despite Ensign Absolut's description of *L'Orion's* crew passing the night beside their guns,[154] desertion became general

---

[148] "Journal du citoyen Romeiron"; Marine BB 4/22, f. 33. See also Cottin, p. 121.
[149] "Adresse des sections de Toulon aux états-majors et équipages de l'escadre française"; in Poupé (ed.), "Journal d'un Ponantais," p. 54. For a similar tirade against Saint-Julien, see Panisse, pp. 63, 70, 77.
[150] "Journal du citoyen Romeiron"; Marine BB 4/22, f. 33; Poupé (ed.), "Journal d'un Ponantais," p. 44. See also Cottin, pp. 122, 127 and Loir, "La livraison de Toulon," pp. 129–130.
[151] Richaud, p. 51 states: "des rixes et des voies de fait avaient lieu sur presque tous les vaisseaux et dans ce conflit d'opinions l'autorité du nouvel amiral perdait à chaque instant de son influence."
[152] Poupé (ed.), "Journal d'un Ponantais," p. 44; see also "Dernière ressource que le général a proposée à l'armée pour la sauver"; p. 58.
[153] It was the responses at this council of war which gave Adet his information on the various political dispositions of the ships in the fleet; Marine BB 3/30, ff. 188–189. The anonymous crewman of *L'Apollon* states: "il y avait déjà plusieurs partis dans l'armée et tout le monde était indécis"; Poupé (ed.), "Journal d'un Ponantais," p. 44.
[154] "Journal de l'enseigne Absolut"; Archives Municipales de Toulon, L 2 XIX – 18.

throughout the squadron.[155] Ensign Romeiron tried to stem this tide aboard *L'Apollon*, but most of the crew declared that they would not fight their brothers and expressed a desire for the *congés* to their home departments which Toulon had promised.[156] By dawn, several ships were completely abandoned.

The General Committee, aware of the desertions and the collapse of resistance in the squadron, signalled the waiting British fleet to enter the roadstead. Saint-Julien raised a flag on *Le Commerce-de-Bordeaux* signalling his ships to prepare to engage the enemy. It was at this point that the authority of Admiral Trogoff reasserted itself. Trogoff's command flag was hoisted to the peak of Van Kempen's frigate *La Perle*, anchored before the arsenal, and this was followed by a signal ordering the fleet to rally within the inner road.[157] It is highly unlikely that the crews of any French battleships were still prepared to follow Saint-Julien's orders and dispute Hood's entry with their broadsides. Ensign Absolut and some of his fellow officers aboard *L'Orion*, like die-hards elsewhere in the fleet, pleaded with the sailors to stay at their posts, but the crews raised topsails and inexorably the squadron obeyed *La Perle*'s signal.[158] Soon only a few warships remained in the outer roadstead and these had few hands left aboard.[159] As the British fleet

---

[155] Poupé (ed.), "Journal d'un Ponantais," p. 45. See also Loir, "La livraison de Toulon," p. 133.

[156] "Journal du citoyen Romeiron"; Marine BB 4/22, f. 34.

[157] Controversy exists as to whether Trogoff was aboard *La Perle* or if Van Kempen made the signal alone. Guérin, V, pp. 545–546 insists that it was the General Committee which gave the orders and Van Kempen who carried them out. This exoneration of Trogoff from responsibility for the signal is disputed by Cottin, p. 128, Henry, II, p. 286, and Loir, "La Livraison de Toulon," p. 134. Contemporary witnesses such as Romeiron saw only Trogoff's flag flown from the frigate and drew their own conclusions, "Journal du citoyen Romeiron"; Marine BB 4/22, f. 35.

[158] "Journal de l'enseigne Absolut"; Archives Municipales de Toulon L 2 XIX – 18.

[159] Adet gives two different accounts of which ships remained in the outer road. In his letter of September 3 he states that all except *L'Apollon*, *L'Orion*, and *Le Patriote* rallied to *La Perle*'s signal, but on September 20 he reports that those which did not enter port "to facilitate the entry of the English" were *Le Duguay-Trouin*, *Le Commerce-de-Bordeaux*, *Le Commerce-de-Marseilles*, *L'Artheuse*, *La Topaze*; Marine BB 3/30, ff. 188–189, 202. Boubennec claims that his command, *L'Entreprenant*, was the last of the *Ponantais* ships to accept that resistance was futile and enter the inner road. The anonymous *Ponantais* names *Le Duguay-Trouin*, *Le Commerce-de-Marseilles*, and *Le Commerce-de-Bordeaux* as those which remained because they were abandoned, not heroic; Poupé (ed.), "Journal d'un Ponantais," p. 47. See also Cottin, p. 129, Henry, II, p. 63, and "Journal du citoyen Romeiron"; Marine BB 4/22, f. 35.

appeared in the entrance of Toulon harbour, Saint-Julien abandoned his flagship and encouraged his remaining men to make their way to Carteaux's army. The Admiral went ashore near la Seyne and remained in hiding until, fearful of falling into the hands of the Sections, he surrendered himself to the Allies.[160]

It was for this this final "desertion," above all, that Puissant denounced Saint-Julien as a traitor and a coward who shamed the French navy before the foreign enemy and the eyes of the Toulonnais. Basing himself on Puissant's account, Jacques Ferrier stated that the surrender was not tempered by even a gesture to salvage naval honour as the scuttling of the fleet at Toulon had done in 1942.[161] These condemnations of Saint-Julien suggest that some measure of resistance could have been taken. Yet the mass desertions during the night of August 27–28, the deep divisions in the fleet, and the clear reluctance of crews to fire on Toulon ensured that the squadron would not give battle despite claims to the contrary. Perhaps individuals might have made heroic, if token, acts of defiance, but the reason they did not can hardly be attributed to the Admiral's desertion. Puissant's vitriolic attack on Saint-Julien was motivated not by the Admiral's actions, but by his survival of the events of 1793 to be honourably reintegrated under the Directory while the ex-*ordonnateur* remained a disgraced prisoner.[162]

Beyond the accusations of conspiracy and the attempts to blame individuals for the disaster, the surrender of the Mediterranean fleet points to a fundamental moral dilemma. Resistance to Toulon's alliance with the British would have been possible only with the conviction that the navy's ultimate loyalty was not to local popular authority, but to that of the French state, characterized as the Republic or the nation. Naval commanders such as Flotte, Puissant and, up until the eve of surrender,

---

[160] Puissant, *Précis de la conduite de Puissant*, p. 5 and *Pétition*, "Faits," pp. 2, 7–8 claims that, despite the discouragement of Saint-Julien's desertion, several *Ponantais* officers, particularly Cosmao-Kerjulien and Bouvet, still wished to fight and asked Cazotte, the senior captain, to take command of the fleet. Puissant denounces Cazotte for refusing and he damns Gassin, commanding *La Topaze*, for abandoning ship rather than attempting to sail his frigate out of Toulon.
[161] Ferrier, "L'événement de Toulon," p. 163; see also pp. 136–137. For further condemnation of Saint-Julien, see Guérin, V, pp. 450–451, 547; for a defence of his conduct, see Henry, II, pp. 60, 284–285.
[162] Ferrier, "L'événement de Toulon," p. 155.

Trogoff, had striven to define their duty in this way and to keep the squadron and arsenal aloof from local politics. The Revolution, however, made such a position politically untenable and acceptance of the Republic did not mean that naval officers could resist local interference. Since 1789 the same rhetoric which proclaimed that all citizens owed their supreme loyalty to the nation had also undermined the legitimacy of executive power and made it, and its agents, the focus of suspicion rather than allegiance. It was in this context that Jacobins sought to educate sailors to distrust their commanders. The nature of Popular Sovereignty in Toulon, as elsewhere, meant that "the Nation" was defined by local factions which fought to identify themselves as the true representatives of the "People." It was only in August 1793 that the Administrative Corps could no longer portray their will as identical to national authority. Thus Toulon's decision to accept the alliance with Hood brought about the violent clash of contradictory definitions of national loyalty and confronted the navy with an unprecedented, and agonizing, moral decision. The unity of the Mediterranean fleet as a fighting force foundered on this rock. Both Admirals at Toulon acted from devotion to France: the opposite courses they chose reveal the tragedy of their dilemma.

Although the surrender of Toulon did not prove to be a fatal blow to the Republic – Allied occupation lasted only four months – it had dramatic impact throughout France. News of the disaster led directly to the formal inauguration of the Terror in Paris.[163] Along with calls for an all-out effort to recapture the port came demands that the authors of the treachery be punished, and on September 9 the Revolutionary Government outlawed Trogoff, Chaussegros, and Puissant.[164] These commanders could not absorb all opprobrium and Jacobins saw their suspicions confirmed regarding the entire officer corps: the navy became

---

[163] See for example M. J. Sydenham, *The First French Republic, 1792–1804* (Los Angeles: University of California Press, 1973), p. 16. Regarding the reaction to the news of Toulon's surrender, see the *Moniteur*, vol. 17, pp. 555–558 (4 septembre 1793), 572–574 (6 septembre 1793). See also the petition presented to the Convention on September 9, 1793 from the Panthéon Section of Paris which demanded that the Minister of Marine be kept under house arrest until the traitors who delivered Toulon were known; AP, vol. 73, pp. 572–573.

[164] AP, vol. 73, pp. 573–574, 582–583. The Committee of Public Safety had suspected the three commanders since the end of July and ordered them to be replaced on August 1, 1793, but this decree was suspended. The Committee ordered their recall, and that of Saint-Julien, on August 19; Aulard (ed.), *Actes*, V, pp. 442, 507; VI, p. 24. See also Marine BB 3/30, ff. 177–179.

associated by Revolutionaries with royalism and treason. Moreover, the news from Toulon brought to the surface suspicions and divisions within the navy itself which, aboard the Atlantic fleet in Quiberon Bay, exploded in mutiny.

CHAPTER

8

NAVAL AUTHORITY AND THE NATIONAL
WILL: THE QUIBERON MUTINY OF 1793

The National Convention was still reeling from the impact of Toulon's treason and the loss of the Mediterranean fleet when a naval crisis on the Atlantic suddenly confronted it. On September 13, following the arrival of the news from Toulon, mutiny broke out aboard the ships of the Brest fleet anchored in Quiberon Bay. The sailors demanded to return to port and their commander-in-chief, Vice-Admiral Morard de Galles, failed to prevent their defiance of government orders and his own authority. Nor did the arrival of a Representative on mission prevent the fleet's return, which he could only sanction in order to maintain a veneer of discipline. These events, following the surrender of the Mediterranean fleet to Admiral Hood, appeared to mark the collapse of French naval power and thus to threaten the survival of the embattled Republic.

The Montagnard Revolutionary Government dispatched Jeanbon Saint-André to Brest to deal with the crisis. The Committee of Public Safety's naval expert explained the mutiny as the outcome of a vast and sinister conspiracy to deny the Republic naval protection:

It was necessary to destroy, to annihilate at any price, to deliver to our most cruel enemies this bulwark of our security; to favour the communication with the rebels of the Vendée; to double their means; to furnish to the partisans of Roland and of Brissot the opportunity and the pretext to unite with the rebel fanatics, and to work in concert with them to overturn the Republic.[1]

---

[1] Jeanbon Saint-André, *Rapport sur les mouvemens qui ont eu lieu sur l'escadre de la République, commandée par le vice-amiral Morard-de-Galles, sur sa rentrée à Brest, fait aux Représentans du Peuple auprès de l'armée navale* (Brest: Malassis, 1794), p. 2 [BN 8 Le39 62]. See also AP, vol. 78, pp. 405–431.

Thus the powerful *conventionnel* reported that insurrection in the fleet was linked directly to political rebellion and to the machinations of the Montagnards' opponents. Lévy-Schneider reiterated this interpretation in his biography of Jeanbon, which remains the most authoritative study of political turmoil in the navy. Lévy-Schneider argued that the principal cause of the insurrection at Quiberon was deep and bitter division between loyal republicans and Counter-Revolutionary elements within the fleet, a division which mirrored conflict ashore.[2]

This explanation runs counter to the interpretation prevailing among naval historians. Edouard Chevalier viewed the mutiny as both the result and the culmination of Revolutionary disorder and insubordination which had ruined the French navy:

There was, in Quiberon Bay, neither conspiracy nor Counter-Revolutionary movements. The crews, tired of the cruise, wanted to return to Brest where they expected to find rest and more pleasant conditions. Accustomed, for several years, to impose their will, they mutinied when they were resisted. To claim the contrary was to deny the evidence.[3]

For Chevalier and others, the Quiberon mutiny demonstrated that the Republic was reaping what had been sown since 1789.[4]

Both schools of interpretation, the one concentrating on the collapse of discipline and the other emphasizing political schism, have certain merits. Yet both provide only partial explanations for an incident which reflected a principal characteristic of Revolutionary conflict. The Brest fleet was indeed bitterly divided but, as with the navy at Toulon, not along the clear-cut lines claimed by Jacobin contemporaries or subsequent historians. At the heart of the mutiny was the fundamental issue of Revolutionary authority: was "the Nation" to be identified with executive power and its agents, or was Popular Sovereignty to be found in the decisions of local administrations or even the direct democracy of sailors? The struggle over the location of legitimate authority, more than animosity between officers of the *Grand Corps* and the fleet's extreme republicans, explains the bitter divisions that rendered Morard de Galles and his captains helpless to avert mutiny.

[2] Lévy-Schneider, I, pp. 507–520.
[3] Chevalier, p. 115.
[4] Ibid., pp. 100, 103. See also: Guérin, V, pp. 456–457; Mahan, *Influence of Sea Power upon the French Revolution*, I, pp. 62–63; Tramond, pp. 560–563; Martray, pp. 81–83.

Justin-Bonaventure, comte Morard de Galles had served with distinction under Suffren during the War of American Independence.[5] One of those officers from the *Grand Corps* who chose not to emigrate, he was promoted to *contre-amiral* in January 1792 and given command of a squadron outfitting at Brest in August. The Admiral's original mission to lead a naval expedition to the West Indies was intended to put down rebellion and restore order in the colonies.[6] Promoted *vice-amiral* in January 1793, Morard de Galles was named commander-in-chief of all naval forces at Brest in February. This responsibility had devolved to him due to Vice-Admiral Grimouard's ill health, but according to the Minister of Marine Morard de Galles' nomination was based on his talent, merit, and known *civisme*.[7] Nonetheless, the Admiral accepted his command only with misgivings and trepidation.[8]

Revolutionary France was now at war with Britain and rapid mobilization of the Atlantic fleet became crucial to the Republic's defence.[9] Representatives from the Convention, Rochegude, Defermon, and Prieur de la Côte-d'Or, arrived in Brest to stimulate activity and decided, against the advice of Morard de Galles and Commandant Thévenard, that three ships of the line must sail to patrol the English Channel.[10] Morard de Galles, aboard *Le Républicain* (110), commanded this small division which included *L'Achille* (74) and *Le Tourville* (74) and four frigates. The cruise demonstrated to the Admiral the appalling state of his forces.[11]

Delayed by difficulties in assembling crews,[12] the division finally entered the Channel on March 9. During a violent storm on the night

[5] Justin-Bonaventure, comte Morard de Galles was born at Goncelin (Isère) in 1741. He served as a page for the maréchal de Soubise and a *gendarme de la Garde du roi* before entering the navy as a *garde de la marine* in 1752. Following active duty during the Seven Years' War, he was promoted to *lieutenant de vaisseau* in 1777 and took part in the Battle of Ouessant in 1778. Promoted *capitaine de vaisseau* in 1781, he served under Suffren and was wounded in the attack on the Cape Verdes Islands in 1781 and wounded more seriously at Trincomalee in 1783. See: Taillemite, *Dictionnaire*, p. 241; Six, *Dictionnaire biographique*, II, pp. 225–226; Lévy-Schneider, I, pp. 480–481.
[6] Marine BB 4/8, ff. 40, 44; BB 3/22, f. 38; BB 4/16, ff. 136–138. See also Saintoyant, II, pp. 214–215.
[7] Marine BB 4/16, ff. 8, 140.
[8] Marine BB 4/17, f. 269.
[9] Hampson, *La Marine de l'an II*, esp. pp. 67–73. See also Acerra and Meyer, pp. 150–154.
[10] Chevalier, pp. 50–51.
[11] Ibid., pp. 51–53. See also Georges Bordonove, *Les marins de l'an II* (Paris: Editions Robert Laffont, 1974), pp. 45–46, and Acerra and Meyer, p. 155.
[12] Marine BB 4/16, ff. 146–147.

Plate 5. Justin-Bonaventure, comte Morard de Galles.
Lithograph by Maurin (Phot. Bibl. Nat. Paris)

of March 17, *Le Républicain*'s headsails were blown away and Morard de Galles was unable to wear ship because he could get no more than thirty sailors to come on deck.[13] On board *Le Tourville* Captain Duval's orders also went unexecuted. Sailors refused to secure a sail and a loose block struck and killed the Captain while he was attempting the task himself.[14] The ships eventually limped back into Brest's roadstead, all

[13] Ibid., f. 148.
[14] Ibid., ff. 149, 30–31; BB 4/17, ff. 276–280.

of them damaged and taking on water. Morard de Galles vented his frustration and despair to the Minister:

> The spirit of the sailors is lost entirely, so much that it will not change. One should expect only reverses in encounters which will be made [with the enemy], even being of superior force. This vaunted ardor which is attributed to them consists uniquely in the words of "patriot," and "patriotism" which they repeat ceaselessly, and the acclamations of *"Vive la Nation,"* *"Vive la République"* when they are flattered. Nothing can make them attend to their duties.[15]

His reaction was typical of officers since the early period of the Revolution, but the Admiral believed that the Republican government would agree with his denunciation of the indiscipline of highly politicized sailors. Whether executive power would support his calls for rigorous measures was another matter, and further indications during the spring revealed the degree to which crews were prepared to challenge their commanders.

Following the explosive appearance of Counter-Revolution in western France, the Provisional Executive Council feared that the British navy might land munitions or even troops to support rebels in the Vendée. Thus Morard de Galles received new orders in May to prevent such a landing. He was to take as much of his fleet as was ready for sea to the vicinity of Quiberon Bay to join a small division under Captain Villaret-Joyeuse already operating against the rebels.[16] The Admiral sailed with four ships of the line on May 22, and other units were to follow as soon as they were fitted out. Three ships under Rear-Admiral Lelarge were preparing to get under way on June 13 when the crews of *Le Bretagne* (110) and *Le Terrible* (110), destined to be Morard de Galles' flagship, refused to obey orders to make sail. Failing to end the mutiny through their own efforts, the commanders appealed to the municipality and to Brest's Jacobin Club for help. Order was only restored following the intervention of troops and the arrest of almost

---

[15] Marine BB 4/16, f. 151.
[16] Marine BB 3/22, f. 208; BB 4/16, f. 201. Requisitions for naval support from Brest had been made by the Department of Morbihan as early as March 21: Marine BB 3/22, ff. 137–141; BB 4/16, f. 152. For Villaret-Joyeuse's operations off the Vendéan coast, particularly his division's involvement in the recapture of the Ile de Noirmoutier on April 27–28, see: Marine BB 4/19, ff. 5–10, 54; BB 4/17, ff. 207–209, 220–225; Loïc du Rostu, *Histoire extérieure et maritime des Guerres de Vendée* (Artigues-près-Bordeaux: Le Cercle d'Or, 1987), p. 46.

forty seamen.[17] Interrogation of some of the mutineers convinced Captain Bonnefous in *Le Terrible* that: "there was a plan of insurrection intended to prevent the squadron's departure and imparted to our crews by the perfidious insinuations of malevolent enemies of public affairs hidden in Brest or aboard our ships."[18] Yet though he believed that insubordination in the fleet resulted directly from the intrigues of radicals ashore, it is significant that on this occasion the local civil power upheld the authority of naval officers.

Over the course of the summer, more ships were commissioned and sailed to join Morard de Galles in the vicinity of Quiberon Bay. Despite reinforcements, the state of this fleet became increasingly desperate. The ships were in poor shape and many were damaged in numerous collisions resulting from their crews' inexperience.[19] The problem of supply caused the Admiral even greater concern. Stores taken on at Brest were insufficient and, too often, rations were discovered to be rancid. Facilities for watering at the Ile de Groix, the port assigned by ministerial orders, were inadequate and casks became contaminated with sea water. Sailors suffered from a lack of proper clothing as the weather became cooler, and scurvy reached epidemic proportions.[20] Moreover, the fleet's position courted disaster: Jeanbon was right to describe it as "politically and militarily bad."[21] Morard de Galles' instructions called for him to patrol the area between the Ile de Groix in the north and Belle Ile to the south. Apart from some key centres, royalist insurgents controlled this coast and the countryside, so that sailors could not be

---

[17] Marine BB 4/17, ff. 78, 80; BB 3/22, ff. 249, 252, 323. Flotte-Benzidou, the interim-Commandant, complained that, despite the recent example of Basterot's Court Martial, Brest's *commissaire auditeur* would not prosecute the mutineers; BB 3/22, f. 254. See also Prosper-Jean Levot, *Histoire de la ville et du port de Brest pendant la Terreur* (Brest, 1870; repr. Brionne, Eure: le Portulan, 1972), pp. 90–94, and Lévy-Schneider, I, p. 482.

[18] Marine BB 4/17, f. 231.

[19] Reporting a collision between *Le Jean-Bart* and *Le Suffren* on June 17 to the Minister, Morard de Galles wrote: "J'ai navigué dans des escadres plus nombreuses et dans un an je n'ai pas vu autant d'abordages que j'en ai vu depuis un mois que l'escadre est réunie"; Marine BB 4/16, f. 220.

[20] Marine BB 4/16, ff. 54, 189, 231–232, 240–241, 247, 249–250; BB 4/17, ff. 60–63, 189–191; BB 3/22, f. 398. Over 600 men were hospitalised when the fleet returned to Brest; BB 3/38, f. 381. See also Chevalier, pp. 56–57, 98, and Taillemite, *L'Histoire ignorée*, pp. 283–284. Cabantous, *La Vergue et les fers*, pp. 163–164 suggests that the poor condition of the fleet, and the sailors' suspicion of ineffective commanders, demonstrated the continuity of traditional maritime discontents in the Quiberon Mutiny.

[21] Jeanbon, *Rapport sur les mouvemens*, p. 7.

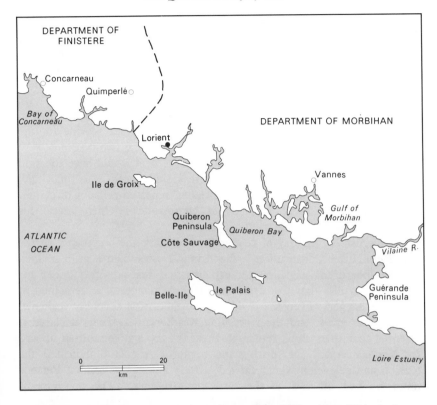

Map 8. The Quiberon mutiny, September 1793. *After* "Principal Sights" in *Michelin Tourist Guide to Brittany* (Harrow: Michelin Tyre Public Limited Company, 1987), pp. 5–8.

allowed ashore.[22] Moreover, the squadron could easily be trapped against a lee shore with no avenue of retreat in the event of attack. Such a possibility appeared all too likely following the sighting of a British fleet on August 1.[23]

[22] *Contre-amiral* Kerguelen stated that this was a major problem and urged the Minister to change the fleet's position to the Bay of Concarneau: Marine BB 4/17, ff. 60–63; Yves-Joseph de Kerguelen-Trémarec, *Relation des combats et des événements de la guerre maritime de 1778, mêlée de réflexions sur les manoeuvres des généraux et terminée par un précis des principaux événements de la guerre présente, des causes de la destruction de la marine française et des moyens de la rétablir* (Paris, 1796), pp. 352–353.
[23] Marine BB 4/16, ff. 235–240.

221

The nature of the Admiral's orders made all of these worries worse. They were contradictory, all inclusive, and imprecise. "I repeat to you, Citizen Minister, the request that I have already made to you for clear and precise instructions which will fix my conduct," wrote Morard de Galles in May, "Those contained in the memorandum of the Executive Council [of May 19] contradict themselves at each paragraph."[24] He was to secure the Vendéan coast, preventing all communications between the foreign enemy and the rebels, but he was also to provide for the safe arrival of a convoy from the West Indies.[25] The two missions were mutually exclusive. To protect the convoy the fleet would have to stand at least forty leagues out to sea, whereas ships needed to guard the coast had to hold inshore. Morard de Galles' repeated calls for direction, and his requests to be replaced as commander-in-chief, reveal his desperation.[26]

On August 10, the day of celebrations to mark the acceptance of the new Republican Constitution,[27] the Admiral assembled a grim council of war aboard his flagship. All captains and rear-admirals under his command agreed that the fleet was in grave danger if it remained at sea much longer. Given the dwindling supplies, the severely weakened state of the crews, and the worsening weather, the officers declared it essential that their ships return to Brest.[28] Sabotage committed aboard *Le Northumberland* (74) during the night of August 6 indicated the tension and suspicion which existed already among the sailors. Persons unknown had cut most of the battleship's rigging.[29] The government, however, remained unyielding. The Minister of Marine informed Morard de Galles that his orders continued in force and that the fleet must

[24] Ibid., f. 190.
[25] Ibid., f. 48.
[26] Ibid., f. 247.
[27] Ibid., f. 89. For a brief report of the celebrations and the swearing of oaths of allegiance in the fleet, see AP, vol. 72, p. 233. Regarding celebrations in Brest, see Marine BB 3/22, f. 316.
[28] Marine BB 4/16, ff. 231–232.
[29] Report on the sabotage aboard *Le Northumberland*, at anchor off Belle-Ile, August 7, 1793; in Jeanbon, *Rapport sur les mouvemens*, pp. 60–65. In their investigation, Captain Thomas and his officers discovered that several seamen were overheard expressing fear at the prospect of battle, discontent with bad rations, and distrust of the captain: "l'un d'eux, nommé Lemerle, avait dit, entre autres choses, 'que le captaine était un bougre; qu'il n'était pas patriote, et que si nous étions sortis sans les ordres du commandant, il aurait refusé l'ouvrage.' " Five sailors were put in irons to await court martial. See also AP, vol. 73, p. 20.

remain on station until at least the end of August. He denounced the council aboard *Le Terrible* and admonished the Admiral: "The safety of the Republic rests on your fleet."[30]

Early in September the Provisional Executive Council heaped another task upon the unhappy squadron, ordering Morard de Galles to intercept a large Dutch convoy known to be sailing for Spain and the Mediterranean.[31] The Admiral acknowledged his new orders reluctantly, stating that the fleet was in no condition for such an operation and that he would have to detach five of his most seaworthy battleships. The dispatch of such a division went directly against concern already expressed in the squadron over any separation of forces given reports of an enemy fleet. Morard de Galles also warned the Minister again that, owing to shortage of water and supplies and the illness of crews, his ships would be unable to keep sea after the autumn equinox.[32] Before the division could sail, however, news of Toulon's treason reached the fleet. The city's defection and the surrender of the Mediterranean fleet had profound repercussions throughout France and, when the offical announcement was given to the ships of Morard de Galles' command in Quiberon Bay, it provided the pretext for mutiny.

Officers read the Convention's address on Toulon's treason to the crews on the evening of September 12.[33] The next morning the fleet was alive with rumour, suspicion and agitation to return to Brest. A deputation from *L'Auguste* (80), led by midshipmen Crevel and Baron, came aboard *Le Terrible* and demanded that the Admiral order the squadron to set sail for Brest which, they claimed, was in danger of the same betrayal as Toulon. "I did all that was possible to reassure the sailors who composed this deputation, and to restore the courage that the circumstances demand," wrote Morard de Galles,

but my intentions were destroyed by the vehement speech of citizen Crevel, midshipman, who spoke in the name of the entire crew. I announced to the deputation that, firm in my duty, I would await the orders of the Executive

---

[30] Marine BB 4/16, ff. 96–97, 101; 70–71, 84, 230.
[31] Ibid., f. 110; for detailed orders, see ff. 118–121.
[32] Ibid., f. 250.
[33] For Morard de Galles' orders to this effect, see marine BB 4/16, ff. 113–114. See also the letter from Bréard and Tréhouart, and their proclamation which was to accompany the Convention's Address; BB 3/38, ff. 276–277. For a summary of the mutiny which ensued, see Bordonove, pp. 51–53.

Council to return the fleet to Brest; I treated this midshipman Crevel as a counter-revolutionary: his manner caused me to believe that he was a leader of the mutiny . . .[34]

Other deputations from the fleet followed the first. They were less menacing, but just as resolute in their desire to return to Brest. Several crews set topsails on September 14 in preparation to get under way. Morard de Galles, accompanied by Rear-Admirals Kerguelen and Landais, responded by going aboard several of the most defiant ships. Despite his efforts to calm the sailors, it was apparent to the Admiral that the only way to prevent many ships from sailing independently, and thus the disintegration of even the semblance of authority, was to promise to convene a council of representatives from every crew.[35] These deputies, together with the officers, assembled aboard the flagship to deliberate upon the fleet's course of action. The majority of the deputies refused to remain in Quiberon Bay until new orders arrived. Following a night of tension and agitation, a compromise was reached on September 15. The council sent two sailors ashore to contact the Convention and its Representatives on mission and to communicate the terrible state of the fleet, its fears regarding Brest, and its desire to return.[36] Yet the council's pledge to await instructions did not end the mutiny. Many crews continued to demand violently that the ships sail immediately. Morard de Galles informed the Minister that if the winds became favourable for leaving Quiberon Bay, he would be forced to take his fleet to Brest even without government authorization: "The sailors have forgotten their duty to such a point, that if I persist to hold at sea, supposing that the crew of *Le Terrible* does not force me to return, most ships would abandon me, obedience currently being only a word in sailors' mouths."[37]

---

[34] "Morard de Galles au ministre, le 15 septembre 1793 [#1]"; in Jeanbon, *Rapport sur les mouvemens*, p. 70.

[35] Ibid., pp. 72–75. For Kerguelen's account of this tour of the fleet, see Marine BB 4/17, ff. 67–68. See also BB 3/38, f. 283. Along with the dispositions of his ships, Morard de Galles reported a rumor that a mysterious woman had told a sailor ashore that crews had only to cut their cables in order to receive gold: this would form the basis of the idea that sailors had been seduced by "Pitt's gold"; see "Tréhouart à la Comité de salut public, 22 septembre 1793"; AD Finistère 8 L 88.

[36] Verneuil, a soldier of the *1er régiment d'infanterie de la marine* serving aboard *Le Juste*, was to take the fleet's address to the Convention and Executive Council; Conor, *chef de timonnerie* aboard *Le Côte-d'Or*, was to seek out Representatives on mission at either Brest or Lorient; Marine BB 3/38, f. 287. See also the petition they carried; BB 3/38, f. 284.

[37] "Morard de Galles au ministre, 19 septembre 1793"; in Jeanbon, *Rapport sur les mouvemens*, p. 82.

On September 20 the ships did get under way, but were not long at sea before a frigate appeared carrying the Representative on mission Tréhouart. He ordered Morard de Galles to bring the fleet to anchor at Belle Ile. "I will not hide with what satisfaction I saw the arrival of this dignified Representative of the French People," wrote the Admiral, "so assured that his presence alone could reestablish order and discipline in the fleet."[38] Tréhouart ordered all captains to assemble aboard *Le Terrible* and to inform him of the state of their commands. The record of their responses at the council of September 21 demonstrates the disarray of many ships, their inability to keep sea any longer and, with some exceptions, the captains' general lack of confidence in having their orders obeyed.[39] Tréhouart saw that he had no option, particularly given renewed agitation aboard *Le Côte-d'Or*, but to authorize the fleet to return to port.

During the voyage from Belle Ile, Tréhouart outlined the measures which he and his fellow Representative on mission, Bréard, should take upon the fleet's return to Brest.[40] All ships in the squadron would be isolated from shore and from each other to prevent the escape of the guilty. Tréhouart divided the fleet into three groups, twelve of the most mutinous vessels: *Le Superbe* (74), *L'Indomptable* (80), *Le Côte-d'Or* (118), *Le Terrible* (110), *Le Révolution* (74), *Le Convention* (74), *L'Auguste* (80), *Le Northumberland* (74), *Le Tourville* (74), *Le Suffren* (74), *Le Bretagne* (110), and *L'Achille* (74); four which had demonstrated obedience at Quiberon but had poor records of subordination: *Le Tigre* (74), *L'Audacieux* (74), *L'Aquilon* (74), *Le Juste* (80), and the frigate *La Carmagnole*; and five ships whose crews deserved praise: *Le Jean-Bart* (74), *Le Témeraire* (74), *Le Trajan* (74), *Le Neptune* (74), and *L'Impétueux* (74), and five frigates. He prepared three different addresses, one for each group, which were to be proclaimed aboard the ships in harbour and were intended to encourage sailors to denounce the traitors among them.[41] The Representative believed such denunciations would expose the dark forces behind the mutiny:

---

[38] "Morard de Galles au ministre, 22 septembre 1793"; in Jeanbon, *Rapport sur les mouvemens*, p. 85.

[39] "Copie du procès-verbal du conseil tenu à bord du vaisseau le Terrible le 21 septembre 1793"; AD Finistère 8 L 88.

[40] "Tréhouart à Bréard, 25 septembre 1793"; AD Finistère 8 L 88. See also Marine BB 3/38, f. 345.

[41] See three different addresses from Tréhouart to the captains and crews of the ships of each group, September 29, 1793; AD Finistère 8 L 88. See also "Adresse de la

the malevolent persons, the villains, the counter-revolutionaries have not ceased for very long to do all in their power to destroy the spirit of the crews, they have taken them to such a point that the greatest measures of severity are now necessary if a navy which can be commanded shall continue to exist in France. . .[42]

Commanding officers identified leading agitators, such as Crevel and Baron, and arrested them even before the fleet anchored in Brest's roadstead on September 29.[43] By October 2, Tréhouart and Bréard had imprisoned thirty individuals from the fleet in the dungeons of the Château.[44] The full investigation into the mutiny, involving the interrogation of crews rather than a mere acceptance of captains' depositions, did not get under way, however, until the arrival of Jeanbon Saint-André five days later.[45] This former Huguenot pastor and merchant sea captain was the Montagnards' expert on naval affairs and a member of the Committee of Public Safety; hence he was far more formidable than the Representatives already present. The Convention dispatched Jeanbon to Brest, with his colleague Prieur de la Marne, and gave him unlimited powers to preserve the fleet for the Republic, but also to crush all enemies of the Revolutionary Government.[46] The Montagnards believed a clear connection existed between naval disorder and political rebellion in the ports.[47]

Although rebellion in the Department of Finistère was not as spectacular as that in Toulon, Brest had been involved directly in the "Federalist Revolt." Indeed, the area provides a good example of why the history of the Revolt should not be confined to only those provincial centres where resistance culminated in significant military

Société populaire de Brest aux marins de l'armée navale. Affiche. Septembre 1793"; in Henwood and Monage, p.168.

[42] "Tréhouart au ministre, 22 septembre 1793"; AD Finistère 8 L 88.

[43] See series of letters from Tréhouart to Morard de Galles between September 27 and October 1, 1793; AD Finistère 8 L 88. See also Marine BB 3/22, f. 363; BB 3/38, ff. 318–320.

[44] "Bréard et Tréhouart à la comité de Salut Public, 2 octobre 1793"; AD Finistère 8 L 88. See also Marine BB 3/38, ff. 356, 370, 373, 377, 379.

[45] Bordonove, pp. 55–57.

[46] For the *Arrêtés* of the Committee of Public Safety on September 22 and 30, 1793 which dispatched Jeanbon and Prieur, see Aulard (ed.), *Actes*, VII, pp. 2, 132. For the Convention's Decree of October 4, 1793, see AP vol. 76, p. 45. See also Lévy-Schneider, I, pp. 476, 496.

[47] See Barère's speech in the Convention, August 25, 1793, and the *projet de décret* which sent Bréard and Tréhouart to Brest; AP, vol. 73, p. 20.

action.[48] As in Toulon, the roots of Finistère's opposition to the rule of the Convention in the summer of 1793 went back to the birth of the Republic. *Fédérés* from Brest were prominent in the storming of the Tuileries on August 10, 1792, yet the initial reaction of the Departmental Council at Quimper to events in Paris was one of grave concern.[49] Though certainly accepting the suspension of the king, administrators at Quimper and Brest remained anxious about the nature of the Republic that was to be established. In the fall of 1792 these local authorities, who had shown great distrust of executive power in their own campaign against Bertrand de Moleville, wished to maintain law and order. It has been argued that this reflected growing bourgeois anxiety,[50] but the absence of popular opposition to the administrations in Finistère suggests equally that the evolving conflict was fundamentally about ideas of governance.

Deputies from Finistère, as well as other Breton *conventionnels* such as Lanjuinais, informed their constituents that the demagogy and extremism of the Paris Representatives threatened the Convention. They singled out Marat, Danton, and Robespierre for particular criticism.[51] Motivated by a perception of the growing and dangerous influence of the Paris mob on the course of debates, the General Council of the Department drew up an address to the Sections of Paris on October 19, and sent copies to all Departments. In terms which reflect news of the September Massacres, Finistère warned Parisians against the influence of "agitators":

These men of blood have dared to provoke, in your name, the violation of all laws up to assassination; they have, in the name of your commune of which

---

[48] Edmonds, " 'Federalism' and Urban Revolt in France in 1793," pp. 22–53 separates federalist protest, which he suggests was widespread, from urban revolt which he argues occurred only in settings of deep-seated political violence and instability such as Lyons, Marseilles and Toulon. Sydenham, "The Republican Revolt of 1793 in Widening Perspective," pp. 116–123 suggests that such an approach minimizes the Revolt's significance as a nationwide division of Republicans.

[49] See the letter of August 3, 1792 to Finistère *Fédérés*, and the letter of August 16, 1792 to the Legislative Assembly, which praises the deputies for their courage amidst "horrors"; in "Actes des Administrations départmentales. Correspondance particulière du secrétariat, 4 juillet 1792–25 juin 1793"; AD Finistère 100 J 312. See also Henwood and Monage, p. 127.

[50] Henwood and Monage, pp. 130, 133–136.

[51] Letter of October 2, 1792 to Réné Gomaire; AD Finistère 100 J 312. See also Armand Duchatellier, *Histoire de la Révolution dans les Départements de l'Ancienne Bretagne*, 6 vols. (Nantes: Mellinet, 1836), II, p. 353.

227

they are part, pushed audacity to the extent of threatening the Departments, as if an 83rd of the Republic could inspire a feeling of terror in an entire nation which wants liberty, but abhors anarchy.[52]

Moreover, Finistère informed the Sections that if the Convention could not be assured of security and tranquility in Paris, National Representation could be moved elsewhere:

The National Convention must have calm to work towards the Constitution which it prepares for us. If it can not find it in your midst, there are other cities which we know could provide it.

The danger to *la Patrie*, our interests, yours, all make it our duty to return peace to the heart of the Republic. This desired peace must crown our painful labours.

We unite all our forces against our enemies, and not to serve factions which already have bloodied France many times.[53]

A letter addressed to the eighty-three Departments expressed similar sentiments. The course the Republic might take was in doubt due to the actions of unscrupulous and destructive men:

Citizens our brothers, like us, you have sworn to uphold the Republic. But the free Republic which has its basis in lawfulness. Like us, you want neither dictatorship nor triumvirate; meanwhile there are men who dare to hope to see dictators or triumvirs in France, men who prepare the people for tyrants of a new kind.

Charged at this moment with its confidence, we will betray its interests and our duties if we do not make all efforts to turn away from its head these new scourges.[54]

These condemnations of anarchy and violence and the emphasis on the rule of law show an obvious parallel to the ideals expressed by the Sections of Toulon nine months later.

Proposals for a "Departmental Guard" to protect the Convention had been made in Finistère as early as October and on December 15, 1792

[52] "Adresse aux 48 sections de Paris," October 19, 1792; AD Finistère 100 J 312.
[53] Ibid.
[54] Letter of October 19, 1792 to the eighty-three Departments; see also the letter of October 21, 1792 to the Paris Jacobins, which encourages the Club to purge the "monsters" from its midst; AD Finistère 100 J 312. For a discussion of the various addresses sent by the Administrators of Finistère in October 1792, see Duchatellier, II, pp. 354–361.

The Quiberon mutiny of 1793

the Departmental Council decreed, in public session, the levy of its contingent for such an armed force.[55] The newly elected District Council in Brest supported this proposal in January 1793.[56] The number of workers who abandoned the port's arsenal to enlist in the Departmental force suggests significant popular support in Brest for the principle of defending National Representation. The workers' departure from the dockyards certainly alarmed the Minister of Marine and the Committee of General Defence in Paris.[57] The new battalion of *fédérés* left Finistère for Paris on January 29, 1793, but returned before the insurrection it had been intended to thwart.[58]

The Department of Finistère continued to express concern at the direction national politics were taking during the early months of 1793. While declaring its support for the execution of Louis XVI, the Council denounced the influence of Marat and insisted that, if the Convention was not free to deliberate on the new Constitution, new deputies should assemble elsewhere.[59] Even before May 31, reports of imminent insurrection in Paris caused the administrators to believe such a measure was imperative.[60] On May 27 Brest's Jacobin Club demanded that the municipality open the city's Sections so they could pronounce on the levy of a new battalion of *fédérés* to march to Paris to protect National Representation. Municipal officers, led by Mayor Malassis, feared the reaction to such defiance, but pressure from

---

[55] See the letter of October 21, 1792 to the Convention, the letter of December 15, 1792 to the eighty-three Departments, and the letter of December 30, 1792 to the Deputies of Finistère; AD Finistère 100 J 312. See also Henwood and Monage, pp. 142, 144, and Duchatellier, II, p. 361.

[56] Levot, p. 62.

[57] Aulard (ed.), *Actes*, I, pp. 405–406. Henwood and Monage, pp. 144–145 analyze the social composition of this contingent, as compared to the *fédérés* of August, and argue that the workers' motivation for enlistment was economic rather than political. The evidence is inconclusive, yet this argument seems questionable given the workers' traditional pursuit of security within the arsenal.

[58] The battalion arrived in Paris in February, where it helped to prevent an uprising on March 9–10. The *fédérés* left the Capital two days later and fought a campaign against the Vendéans before arriving in Quimper on May 19; see J. Savina, "Les Fédérés du Finistère pour la garde de la Convention (décembre 1792–mai 1793)," *La Révolution française*, 65 (1913), 193–224.

[59] Letter of February 22, 1793 to Representatives of the People; AD Finistère 100 J 312. See also AP, vol. 59, p. 266.

[60] The Convention's "Commission of Twelve" made such a report on May 24, and the letters from Finistère's deputies stated that their freedom of debate and correspondence would soon be over. See Duchatellier, II, pp. 370–372, and Levot, pp. 87–88. See also the letters of June 1, 1793 to forty-eight Sections of Paris, and of June 2, 1793 to eighty-four Departments; AD Finistère 100 J 312.

229

the Departmental Council as well as from the Club overcame their attempts to stall these petitions.[61] The Sections convened in Brest on June 2 and quickly approved the creation of a Departmental force, designating two hundred men to form the Brest contingent.[62]

Thus the decisions to open the Sections and levy troops in Finistère had been made before definite news of the purge of the Convention reached Brest. This was also true of other manifestations of rebellion against the government in Paris. Brest expelled two agents of the Ministry of War, who had arrived to requisition muskets from the arsenal, on May 5 for political activism on behalf of the Montagnards. The municipality considered their successors equally subversive and arrested the two agents on June 3.[63] The Representatives on mission to the port, Sevestre and Cavaignac, attempted to have the prisoners released. Not only were the Representatives unsuccessful, but general hostility forced them to abandon Brest on June 13.[64] Sevestre returned to Paris to report to the Convention on the grave situation developing in Brittany. Local administrations had thwarted the important missions to coastal defence forces, and tried to disguise their treachery behind the mask of moderation. More importantly, Sevestre recognized that the "Federalists" used Popular Sovereignty to justify their defiance of the Convention:

The administrative and municipal corps, persuaded that you no longer have liberty, and that since May 31 you have been under the yoke of the municipality of Paris, have imagined that they will pull you from oppression through measures which, by their violence and illegality, will consummate the ruin of the Republic, if your wisdom does not curb them instantly. These blind corps no longer recognize the law, they have usurped sovereign authority, and their tyrannical power reverses all that you order.[65]

[61] Levot, pp. 88–90.
[62] Levot, p. 89 states that this step was taken after the arrival of Thomas Raby, a secretary of the Brest Club who had witnessed the events of May 31–June 2 in Paris. Raby, who had been a leading revolutionary in Brest since 1789, later denied that he had done anything to incite "Federalist" sentiment: *Thomas Raby aux vétérans de la Révolution* (Brest, 1794); Brest "Fonds Levot" 1991 [1].
[63] For the municipality's justification, see its letters of June 3, 1793 to the Minister of War; cited in Levot, p. 89. See also Levot, pp. 84–85, and Henwood and Monage, p. 146. Several days later, a package for the agents arrived in Brest which contained over 100 copies of the journal *La Montagne* and almost 200 copies of *Le Père Duchesne*: this confirmed the administrators' suspicions. For Julien de Toulouse's report on the incident to the Convention on August 9, 1793, see AP, vol. 70, pp. 542–543.
[64] Levot, pp. 87, 94; Henwood and Monage, p. 146.
[65] *Rapport fait par le citoyen Sevestre, l'un des Représentans du Peuple envoyés près l'armée des côtes de Brest; 23 juin 1793* (Paris: Imprimerie Nationale, 1793); Brest "Fonds Levot" 1991 [13].

Sevestre reported that the rebel administrations were not only levying their own troops, but were spreading the call for resistance: "The Republic is currently covered with their emissaries."[66] Seeking unanimity of action and purpose was a hallmark of the "Federalist Revolt" throughout France, and Finistère's appeals to neighbouring Departments fit the general pattern.[67] Representatives from five Breton Departments gathered initially at Rennes to coordinate their efforts,[68] but commissioners from these Departments, as well as others in Brittany and Normandy, assembled in Caen at the end of June to form the "Central Committee of Resistance to Oppression."[69] This Committee sought to organize the Departmental Army, which was assembling to march on Paris, and it also drafted a declaration outlining the programme of the "Federalist" rebels. The declaration demanded, among other things, that a Departmental Guard be established for any National Assembly, that the deputies proscribed on June 2 be reinstated, that the dictatorship of the Committee of Public Safety be ended, and "That the Convention, having recovered its liberty, its integrity, be invited to give within two months a Constitution worthy of the French Republic."[70] The Central Committee thus claimed to be a more legitimate expression of National Will than the purged Convention, and its principles are in keeping with the ideals expressed by moderates in Toulon. Even Sevestre admitted that "they seem to want really and sincerely the Republic one and indivisible. . ."[71]

However threatening "Federalism" may have appeared initially, the revolt collapsed quickly in north-west France. The Finistère battalion of 450 men left Quimper on June 23, and the Central Committee ordered it to march to Evreux to link up with the Departmental Army under General Wimpffen. Yet before the Finistère contingent arrived,

---

[66] Ibid.
[67] See the letters of June 10, 1793 to the Department of Loire-Inférieure, and of June 12, 1793 to the Departments of Morbihan, Ille-et-Vilaine, Côtes-du-Nord, Loire-Inférieure; AD Finistère 100 J 312. See also Goodwin, p. 325, and P. Nicolle, "Le mouvement fédéraliste dans l'Orne en 1793," *Annales historiques de la Révolution française*, 15 (1938), 13.
[68] Letter of June 19, 1793 to — — and other deputies of Communes and Districts united at Rennes. AD Finistère 100 J 312. See also Duchatellier, II, pp. 379, 391.
[69] Paul R. Hanson, *Provincial Politics in the French Revolution: Caen and Limoges, 1789–1794* (Baton Rouge and London: Louisiana State University Press, 1989), pp. 142–143. See also Goodwin, p. 329.
[70] "Demands of the Central Committee against Oppression"; Appendix I, in Hanson, pp. 249–251; see pp. 143–145 for a discussion of this declaration.
[71] *Rapport par Sevestre.*

Wimpffen's forces retreated in panic following an inconclusive engagement with troops of the Convention at Pacy-sur-Eure on July 13.[72] This demonstration of the rebels' military weakness was followed shortly by the termination of political resistance. The explanation for this collapse is complex, but a recent study of the revolt at Caen has argued that the principal reason for its failure was lack of popular support.[73] This has been a common interpretation of "Federalism" throughout France and, as in the case of Toulon, should receive qualification. A vital factor which sapped the effective commitment of moderate Republicans in Finistère, and throughout north-west France, was the danger posed by the Vendée. Administrators facing the threat of royalist "brigands" had to be more concerned with defending their own Departments from the Vendéans than overturning the Montagnard regime in Paris.[74]

On July 19, the Convention decreed an Act of Accusation against the Departmental Administration of Finistère.[75] Further resistance appeared futile and terribly dangerous, and the administrations at Quimper and Brest made desperate attempts to demonstrate their repentance and new-found loyalty. They recalled the troops on July 24, and invited the primary assemblies in the Department to examine the new Constitution.[76] It was adopted in Brest by a large majority and on July 28 an elaborate *fête* was held to celebrate the acceptance of the Republican Constitution.[77] The Revolutionary Government was unimpressed, how-

[72] See: Henwood and Monage, p. 149; Goodwin, pp. 332–334; Hanson, pp. 150–152.
[73] Hanson, esp. pp. 156–158.
[74] See the letter of June 19, 1793 to — — and other deputies of the Communes and Districts united at Rennes, and the letter of June 21, 1793 to the Central Committee; AD Finistère 100 J 312. The argument that the Vendée diverted western patriots from their struggle with the Convention is made by Duchatellier, II, p. 366. Norman Hampson, *A Social History of the French Revolution* (London, 1963; repr. Toronto: University of Toronto Press, 1979), p. 172 states that municipal politics in Nantes during 1793 were dominated by a universal concern to defend the city against the Vendéans, negating possible involvement in "Federalism." The authorities in Finistère had already proven their opposition to royalist insurgency in March when they suppressed a peasant revolt in the north of the Department; Henwood and Monage, pp. 149–151.
[75] Duchatellier, V, p. 295.
[76] See the decree pronouncing the dissolution of the Finistère Departmental Force, in Duchatellier, V, pp. 296–298.
[77] See: Levot, pp. 99–103; Duchatellier, V, pp. 295–298; Henwood and Monage, pp. 149, 151. See also: a report on Brest's adherence to the *journées* of May 31–June 2 and its acceptance of the Constitution, AP, vol. 70, p. 203; an account of celebrations on August 10 in Brest, AP, vol. 72, p. 338; a letter from the Sections of Brest stating regret at being misled regarding May 31 and agreeing to form an armed force, AP, vol. 73, p. 348. Levot, p. 99 cites a notable exception to this trend, Le Bronsort,

ever, and the mutiny at Quiberon Bay seemed to demonstrate the lingering menace of "Federalism" and the necessity for drastic action. For Jeanbon the parallel between the situations at Brest and at Toulon was clear: "Federalist Revolt" led to naval surrender.[78] The sailors of Morard de Galles' fleet also emphasized this comparison when they claimed that the ships must return to prevent the betrayal of the port.[79] Jeanbon blamed "Federalist" agitation in Brest primarily on the plotting of the outlawed "Girondin" deputies, but believed they were allied to royalists and the foreign enemy. Hence he reported that the destruction of the Republic's fleet had been the object of a conspiracy.[80] The immediate cause of disorder was not merely the news from Toulon. Two ships, *Le Côte-d'Or* (118) and *Le Tigre* (74), joined the fleet at Quiberon on the eve of the mutiny. According to Jeanbon, these carried the "sectionary spirit" from Brest, as well as direct appeals from "Federalists" for the squadron to rescue them from Revolutionary vengeance.[81] Essentially, however, evidence of the conspiracy could be found in the navy's commanders: "The choice of officers, supposing that it was made with reflection, could only be attributed to the most perfidious malevolence."[82] The presence of ex-nobles and officers from the old navy meant that the officer corps, and indeed the entire fleet, was deeply divided between loyal republicans and wicked Counter-Revolutionaries: "Two parties were very pronounced in the squadron's officers; they awaited only the opportunity to explode."[83] For Jeanbon, this division explained the crews' lack of confidence in their leaders and the impossibility of achieving unity. Lévy-Schneider supported these conclusions with some qualification. Although he thought Jeanbon's insistence on a "Federalist" and royalist plot might have distorted the situation, Lévy-Schneider argued that the Montagnard was absolutely right to see the Brest fleet wracked with division. This was particularly

who refused to endorse the new Constitution: "La Fance entière acceptât-elle la nouvelle constitution, seul je la repousserai parce-qu'elle est la fruit du crime."
[78] Jeanbon, *Rapport sur les mouvemens*, p. 1. See also Lévy-Schneider, p. 499.
[79] "Adresse à la Convention nationale par les marins composant la flotte de l'Océan"; in Jeanbon, *Rapport sur les mouvemens*, pp. 87–90.
[80] Jeanbon, *Rapport sur les mouvemens*, pp. 1–6.
[81] Ibid., pp. 14–19. Jeanbon refers to a mysterious letter from a woman in Brest which supposedly inspired the outbreak of mutiny aboard *Le Côte-d'Or*. The letter told sailors that both the Constituted Authorities at Brest and the commanders of the squadron had been dismissed and summoned to appear before the Convention.
[82] Ibid., p. 6.
[83] Ibid., p. 11.

true regarding the animosity between noble officers remaining from the old navy and commoners recruited from the merchant service. An independent examination of the evidence demonstrates that resentment of noble officers did exist. Captain Coëtnempren of *Le Jean-Bart* (74) was sent to the Revolutionary Tribunal in Paris, and eventually to the guillotine, due to the deposition of a subordinate who was convinced that his aristocratic captain had denied him deserved advancement because he came from the merchant service.[84] Both Ensign Prisset, a leading agitator aboard *Le Convention* (74), and Corporal Beaussard, the marine soldier who led *Le Côte-d'Or*'s deputation on September 14 and incited further mutiny on the 21st, insisted that the presence of noble officers was the real cause of the fleet's disorder.[85] An anguished Morard de Galles wrote from Quiberon Bay: "If by chance I had not been born in a class which excites defiance, I flatter myself that the villains would have been unable to find a pretext for me to lose the confidence of crews and some of the ships' officers."[86]

It is misleading, however, to imply that tensions between nobles and commoners were the primary cause of unrest and division in Morard de Galles' fleet. The situation was far more complex. Some ex-nobles whom Jeanbon dismissed for demonstrating a lack of *civisme*, men like Rear-Admiral Kerguelen and Captain Boissauver, were actually sincere opponents of the *Grand Corps* with personal reasons for welcoming Revolutionary reforms.[87] Con-

[84] "Aux citoyens représentants, Brest, 3e jour de l'an II [No name]"; in Jeanbon, *Rapport sur les mouvemens*, pp. 118–124.
[85] "je dis plus, je dis que les mouvemens qui eurent lieu dans l'escadre, étaient prévus depuis longtemps par les chefs et officiers de l'horrible caste nobiliaire, qu'ils ont mis tout en oeuvre pour les faire réussir à leurs projets perfides, . . ."; *Mémoire Justificatif du Républicain Prisset, enseigne du vaisseau, la Convention, détenu depuis deux mois, à cause des mouvemens qui eurent lieu dans l'escadre de la République, alors commandée par le vice-amiral Morard de Galle* (Brest, 1793); Brest "Fonds Levot" 1988 [5]. See also "Relation de la conduite tenue par les chefs du vaisseau la Côte-d'Or, ainsi que celle de l'équipage, depuis son départ de Brest jusqu'à ce jour, par J. B. J. Beaussard"; in Jeanbon, *Rapport sur les mouvemens*, pp. 91–96.
[86] "Morard de Galles au ministre, 15 septembre 1793 [#1]"; in Jeanbon, *Rapport sur les mouvemens*, p. 69.
[87] Jeanbon, *Rapport sur les mouvemens*, pp. 31, 34. Yves-Joseph de Kerguelen de Trémarec was born at Trémarec (Finistère) in 1734 and entered the navy as *garde de la marine* in 1750. He discovered the islands in the South Indian Ocean which bear his name in 1772 while searching for the fabled *Terra Australis*. Upon his return to France in 1774, he was accused of embarking merchandise for illegal commerce, of neglecting his duty, and of secretly keeping a young woman aboard ship. He was court-martialed in 1775, expelled from the navy and imprisoned for six years. He did not return to the navy until 1793, when he was reintegrated as *capitaine de vaisseau* in February and promoted *contre-amiral* in May. See Taillemite, *Dictionnaire*, p. 179, and

versely, one of the captains who best maintained his crew's discipline and trust was Villaret-Joyeuse, by birth a French count.[88] Sailors respected his competence, and strict enforcement of subordination was part of his professionalism. He quelled demands for increased bread rations aboard *Le Trajan* (74) in April 1793 by placing four men in irons, and in July he had only to threaten such action to abort a refusal to obey orders to sail from the Ile de Groix.[89] This record of discipline was the principal reason that Jeanbon later promoted Villaret-Joyeuse to Commander-in-chief.[90]

Nobles were obvious targets in 1793 and "aristocrat" had become a political label as much as a social distinction.[91] A division along the lines of Revolutionary politics, including different attitudes towards Brest's resistance to the Convention in 1793, was more important than tension between nobles and commoners in the squadron. Insisting that the men of the fleet were involved in political conflict ashore, Lévy-Schneider overstated his case in asserting that the navy was torn between partisans of the *Montagne* and of the "Gironde."[92] Examination of the "Federalist Revolt" in Brest reveals the response of moderate provincial Republicans to Revolutionary extremism, rather than a direct reflection

Six, *Dictionnaire biographique*, II, pp. 4–5. For indications of Kerguelen's enthusiasm for the Revolution and his animosity toward the *Grand Corps*, see Marine BB 4/17, ff. 56, 59–60. Boissauver claimed that, as a port officer, he had been unjustly held back from deserved promotions: *Boissauver, ex-capitaine de vaisseau de la République, à la Convention Nationale et à ses concitoyens* (Brest, 1794); Brest "Fonds Levot" 1988 [7].

[88] Louis-Thomas, comte Villaret de Joyeuse was born at Auch (Gers) in 1748 and entered the navy as a volunteer in 1765, having left the *gendarmes du roi* following a duel. Yet from 1767 to 1770 he was employed as an officer in the *Compagnie des Indes*. He returned to naval service as an auxiliary officer in the American Revolutionary War, commanding a frigate under Suffren. In 1784 he was promoted into the *Grand Corps* as *lieutenant de vaisseau*, and was made *capitaine de vaisseau* in January 1792. See Taillemite, *Dictionnaire*, p. 340, Six, *Dictionnaire biographique*, II, pp. 553–554.

[89] Marine BB 4/19, ff. 20, 50, 67. Villaret-Joyeuse reported to the Executive Council in May 1793 that the Penal Code was insufficient to maintain discipline in the navy, but attributed subordination aboard his own ship to his firmness; Marine BB 4/19, f. 61. See also Bordonove, pp. 46–48, 54, and Cabantous, *La Vergue et les fers*, p. 129, who claims that Villaret-Joyeuse's ability to keep order was part of the solution to the general "crisis of confidence" in the fleet.

[90] Jeanbon, *Rapport sur les mouvemens*, p. 43.

[91] See Higonnet, pp. 106–125. See also Furet, pp. 54–55: "The adjective 'aristocratic' brought to the idea of plot a definition of its content, referring no longer to the methods but to the nature of the adversary. In fact, it was a rather vague definition, since it very soon came to encompass not only the aristocracy but also royal authority, all the old society, the inertia of a world confronted with change, and impersonal as well as human resistance."

[92] Lévy-Schneider, I, pp. 477–479.

of the struggle in the Convention. The situation in Brest was very different from that in Toulon but, seen fundamentally as a clash of political principle, there is merit in linking the Revolt to strife in the navy.

In this context, an alliance between moderates accounts for Brest's municipality and Club assisting naval officers to suppress mutiny on June 13, at the height of the city's resistance to the Convention. These local bodies, which had previously undermined naval authority as representing suspect executive power, agreed with Captain Bonnefous that the mutineers of 1793 were tools of political radicalism in the port. Lévy-Schneider suggested that division between the factions existed aboard ships of the fleet, and no truce was observed between them when they left port.[93] If some officers and men gravitated towards political moderation, there is no lack of evidence that Revolutionary extremism was also present in the Atlantic fleet. The rhetoric in Corporal Beaussard's deposition revealed radicalism akin to that of Parisian *sans-culottes*.[94] A clerk aboard *Le Suffren* (74), while informing the Minister that there were "villains in the navy who do not love the Revolution," boasted of his roots in the Paris Sections where he had idolized Collot d'Herbois, perhaps the most radical member of the Committee of Public Safety.[95]

Such Revolutionary enthusiasm was not confined to the lower deck. Rear-Admiral Landais, a commoner and an *officier bleu* in the navy before the Revolution, regarded those from the *Grand Corps* with hatred and suspicion.[96] The Republic's most dangerous enemies, he told the

[93] Ibid., p. 479.
[94] "Nous avons alors manifesté notre opinion pour rentrer à Brest avant même la rentrée de nos députés, voyant tous les dangers de tenir la mer avec une escadre dont les principaux chefs étaient de cette caste qui avait, par ses atroces perfidies, exposé la patrie aux plus éminents dangers: peut-être nous fait-on un crime de nous être communiqué nos opinions, et de nous être assemblés paisiblement; mais n'est-il pas permis à tout citoyen de s'assembler, ainsi qu'il appert ci-après des droits imprescriptibles de l'homme, de l'Acte constitutionnel?"; "Relation de la conduite . . . Beaussard"; in Jeanbon, *Rapport sur les mouvemens*, p. 95. Jeanbon judged Beaussard to be an "energetic patriot," but one who had wilfully incited disobedience; pp. 19–20. Lévy-Schneider, I, pp. 510–511 refers to the marine soldier as a fanatic.
[95] Marine BB 4/17, ff. 190–191.
[96] Pierre Landais was born at Saint-Malo in 1734. He entered the navy as a volunteer in 1745 and served as an *officer bleu* during the Seven Years' War. As a *lieutenant de frégate*, he accompanied Bougainville on his voyage around the world. Landais left the French navy in 1777 and served in the American navy until returning to France in 1792, when he was made *capitaine de vaisseau* and given command of *Le Patriote* (74). He was promoted *contre-amiral* in January 1793; Six, *Dictionnaire biographique*, II, p. 51.

Convention in March 1793, commanded its forces.[97] In October 1792
Landais had sailed from Brest with the division sent to reinforce Admiral
Truguet's fleet in the Mediterranean. Throughout this campaign, he
had engaged in bitter personal quarrels with other captains, particularly
Captain Trogoff, and was convinced that these aristocrats were conspir-
ing against him:

The public good alone animates me, the service of *la patrie* alone occupies me,
my intentions could only be suspected and badly interpreted by envious rivals
whose souls are gangrened with a secret aristocracy. I am persuaded after what
I have seen and heard, that my frank character and my incorruptible patriotism,
being hindrances to their intrigues, above all in the position I occupy, are more
than enough motives for them to employ everything to harm and discard me.[98]

Landais' relationship with sailors, however, was no better. Before the
division had sailed for the Mediterranean, the crew of *Le Patriote* (74)
mutinied against him on September 27, 1792.[99] Morard de Galles criticized Landais, both for losing his men's trust and for pardoning several
mutineers, and animosity between the two may have resulted.[100] In the
aftermath of the Quiberon mutiny, Landais submitted a memorandum
to the Representatives which denounced both Morard de Galles and
Rear-Admiral Lelarge for suspect behavior: he claimed to have observed
mysterious, and therefore sinister, signals being made from Morard de
Galles' flagship; he described as "insidious" Lelarge's motion at the
September 15 council that once the deputy from the fleet found the
Representatives of the People at Lorient, he should continue on to
Brest to give news to sailors' families.[101] Jeanbon praised his patriotism,
but also recognized that Landais' extremism was dangerously
paranoid.[102]

It should be noted that Rear-Admiral Lelarge was not a noble, but
had served in the old navy as an auxiliary officer like Landais. Lelarge

[97] Marine BB 4/22, f. 152.
[98] Ibid., f.148; see also ff. 149–153. For a discussion of the rivalry between Landais
and Trogoff, see Guérin, V, pp. 365–370.
[99] Marine BB 4/8, ff. 38, 55–57. See Levot, pp. 56–59.
[100] In a letter of October 6, 1793, the Minister of Marine stated that Landais claimed
his Admiral had asked him to resign; Marine BB 4/16, f. 129. For Morard de Galles'
version of their relationship, see ibid., f. 286.
[101] "Extrait d'un mémoire remis par le contre-amiral Landais aux représentants du
peuple près les ports de Brest et de Lorient et signé par lui"; in Jeanbon, *Rapport sur
les mouvemens*, pp. 124–129.
[102] Jeanbon, *Rapport sur les mouvemens*, p. 32.

defended his patriotism, following his dismissal on Jeanbon's orders, by referring to his firm conduct as captain of *Le Bretagne* during the insurrection of June 13: "if my citizenship has been questionable, this has been, doubtless, only due to insubordinate men in the service, who are ready always to cast suspicion on a just, but severe, commander who knows that without obedience all is disorder and confusion."[103] This statement points to the fundamental issue which lay behind the mutiny and over which the fleet was divided. Lelarge appears to have been a political moderate and to have sympathized with Brest's resistance to the Montagnard Convention, but he believed in the need for strong government authority. Yet Brest's rebellion demonstrates the difficulty in identifying such authority: "Federalist" assemblies and the Montagnard Convention presented competing claims to represent the Republic. The location of legitimate Revolutionary authority was not universally agreed upon throughout the fleet. Corporal Beaussard defended his actions, and those of other sailors at Quiberon Bay, by referring to republican rights of assembly and expression of opinion. At Belle Ile on September 21, no information was given to crews after the Representative went aboard *Le Terrible*: "new fears manifested themselves; they were the natural effect of the violent uneasiness which our commanders had inspired in us, and we feared that the announcement of a commissioner of the Convention was only a feint to betray us more successfully."[104] Thus a new wave of protest was legitimate and had the crews at Toulon followed such a course, Beaussard added, they would have defeated the projects of their perfidious commanding officers. Ensign Prisset, in his *Mémoire justificatif*, employed similar arguments to justify mutiny. He also criticized the Representative for going only aboard the flagship and not circulating throughout the fleet to speak with the patriotic sailors: "but no, far from fulfilling this sacred duty, Tréhouart limited himself to confer with the nobles and their creatures; it is thus that the

---

[103] *Le Large, ex-contre-amiral de la République, à la Convention nationale, et à ses concitoyens* (Brest, 1795); Brest "Fonds Levot" 1988 [19]. Jean-Baptiste-Amable Le Large was born at Louisbourg in 1738 and entered the navy as a pilot in 1749. Following service in the Seven Years' War as an *officier bleu*, he was promoted to *lieutenant de vaisseau et de port* in 1775. Le Large was named *Directeur de port* at Brest in 1780, but was not classified as a *capitaine de vaisseau* until 1792. He was promoted *contre-amiral* in January 1793. See Taillemite, *Dictionnaire*, p. 206, and Six, *Dictionnaire biographique*, II, pp. 102–103.

[104] "Relation de la conduite . . . Beaussard"; in Jeanbon, *Rapport sur les mouvemens*, p. 95.

uneasiness of the crews continued, and the squadron returned to Brest. . ."[105] Midshipman Crevel demonstrated that he shared this attitude in a letter to the Minister even before the mutiny began. Crevel had proposed that French warships employ red-hot shot against the British, and he was impatient with the Minister's lack of interest: "if I wait a fourth time without response, I shall make my letter public in the newspapers and your silence may be regarded as a refusal, and all of France will then judge if this means should be adopted, or at least if the proposal merited a response. . ."[106]

Crevel's threat to appeal to public opinion, Prisset's denunciation of a Representative for not conferring with all sailors, and Beaussard's justification of mutiny all point towards a higher authority than that of commanders appointed by the state: the Will of the Sovereign People. When Morard de Galles asked if the crew of Le Northumberland (74) was in a state of mutiny, Captain Thomas replied, "It is Revolution, not insurrection."[107] It is important to clarify that this conception of Popular Sovereignty, which justified the disobedience of executive authority, was not shared by all fervent, even radical republicans. The crew of Le Tigre (74), commanded by Captain Vanstabel, was one of the most obedient in the fleet and swore on September 16 to await the orders of the Admiral, who was "the organ of the law." Yet this oath, and a petition drafted on September 29 which called for the heads of all conspirators, showed that Le Tigre was not dominated by moderation in the usual sense of the word. The key was the crew's attitude towards authority, as is clearly demonstrated in its denunciation of the events at Quiberon: "Yes citizens, the laws were violated and true republicans cannot see without sadness this perfidious coalition show itself and put in the place of the National Will, the will of a few individuals. . ."[108] Thus the fleet was divided not merely by a split between radicals and moderates, but, more fundamentally, by disagreement on the nature of Revolutionary authority.

Once the Nation's Will ceased to be equated with the authority of agents of executive power, the commanding officers, mutiny was unavoidable. The conflict between differing notions of authority was

[105] Mémoire justificatif du Prisset.
[106] Marine BB 4/17, f. 71.
[107] "Morard de Galles au ministre, 15 septembre 1793 [#2]"; in Jeanbon, Rapport sur les mouvemens, p. 73.
[108] Marine BB 4/17, f. 245; see also ff. 235–245.

clear when the Admiral toured his fleet and attempted to convince the sailors that they were acting in opposition to the wishes of the Convention, or when he appealed to the council aboard his flagship to obey the National Will and return to their duty. His efforts were in vain. Morard de Galles recognized that neither his paternalistic concern for his men nor his non-partisan loyalty to the French state were sufficient to guarantee that his orders would be carried out:

My fear in this regard is only too well founded, citizen Minister, in that the insurrections which have taken place prove, evidently, that I have had the misfortune to lose their confidence, although I can affirm with truth that, always firm in the principles of a good citizen, I have done nothing to merit this loss. . .

The movements which have occurred prove clearly that if you persist in leaving me in command of this fleet, which has been strongly compromised, you will leave to disorganizers a fleet which they will turn successfully against the good of the country. . .[109]

Jeanbon's investigation of the Quiberon mutiny led him to conclude that, in order to save the navy for the Republic, the existing amalgam of old and new officers could no longer continue. He had expressed the opinion earlier, as a deputy in the Convention, that true patriotism was to be found in the merchant service rather than in the *Grand Corps*.[110] His report on the mutiny made clear that the principal measure to be taken was a purge of the officer corps:

These sailors expressed in this point the general opinion of all of France, which, weary of the eternal plots of a caste which has not wanted to honour itself by liberty, condemns it irrevocably to political non-existence under all relations. The first measure to take must, therefore, be the purification of the navy, and the full, complete, absolute dismissal of all the ex-nobles who serve in the squadron, to be replaced by those officers who join bravery to capacity, love of *la patrie* to that of equality.[111]

---

[109] "Morard de Galles au ministre, 15 septembre 1793 [#1]"; in Jeanbon, *Rapport sur les mouvemens*, pp. 68–69.

[110] See Jeanbon Saint-André, *Opinion et Projet de décret du citoyen Jeanbon Saint-André, député du Lot, sur l'organisation de la marine française* (Paris: Imprimerie Nationale, 1793) [BN 8 Le38 2037]. See also Jeanbon's speech to the Paris Jacobin Club on July 31, 1793; in F. V. A. Aulard (ed.), *La Société des Jacobins*, 6 vols. (Paris: Imprimerie Nationale, 1889–1897), V, p. 323.

[111] Jeanbon, *Rapport sur les mouvemens*, p. 28.

Yet as much as Jeanbon sought to rid the fleet of aristocrats and to suppress all opposition to the Revolutionary Government, he also strove to reverse the trend of four years of political turmoil. He criticized Morard de Galles severely for assembling the Council to deliberate upon the fleet's course of action,[112] indicating that the navy must remain constantly subordinate to government authority. Ironically, such a position was virtually identical to that held by Admiral Trogoff at Toulon, and Jeanbon's insistence that "discipline must reign"[113] echoed the pleas of all naval officers. The Constitutional Monarchy and the early Republic had tried to persuade local authorities and insubordinate sailors that the legitimate expression of Popular Sovereignty, "the Nation," lay in the government of the state. This had been a failure, and the mutiny of the Brest fleet at Quiberon was a microcosm of that failure. To reassert the authority of central government in the navy, as in all of France, Jeanbon Saint-André and the Committee of Public Safety unleashed the Terror.

---

[112] Ibid., p. 21.
[113] Ibid., p. 36.

CHAPTER

9

A NAVY FOR THE REPUBLIC:
JEANBON SAINT-ANDRE'S MISSIONS
TO BREST AND THE PRAIRIAL
CAMPAIGN, 1793–1794

You would have been enchanted by the imposing and touch-
ing spectacle presented by the departure of our squadron.
Joy and impatience to measure themselves against the infamous English were painted on all faces. The most beautiful
order of sailing, the voices of an immense people lining the
shore at the *goulet* [roadstead's entrance], and the thousand-
times-repeated cries of *"Vive la République!"* were the presage
of our success.[1]

The twenty-five ships of the line which sailed from Brest in May 1794,
described so enthusiastically by Prieur de la Marne, represented the
culmination of eight months of tremendous effort. The formation of a
fleet capable of challenging the British navy, after the disaster at Toulon
and the debacle of the Quiberon mutiny, was a triumph for the Revolutionary Government.[2] Jeanbon Saint-André was the Representative of
the Convention most responsible for rebuilding the Republic's navy.
During two extensive missions to Brest between October 1793 and June
1794, he stimulated the construction of new warships and the refitting
of old ones. He organized the requisition of naval stores and the
levy of personnel. Moreover, the Montagnards' naval expert ended
insubordination and sought to infuse the fleet with the spirit of the
new order.

[1] Prieur to Guesnor and Topsent at Rochefort, 29 Floréal an II (May 18, 1794); AD
Finistère 8 L 9.
[2] It was also a surprise to many officers of the British navy, as illustrated by the
reflections of Captain Cuthbert Collingwood: "is it not astonishing that the French,
who we have despised, ruined in their finances, supplied with great difficulty with
stores, and almost all Europe at war with them, should meet us at sea with a fleet
superior to us? . . ."; cited in Oliver Warner, *The Glorious First of June* (London:
Batsford, 1961), p. 92.

Jeanbon and his missions to Brest also provoked controversy. French naval historians have not seen the powerful Representative as the saviour of the fleet.[3] Despite his undisputed energy, they have characterized him as a meddling amateur or a fanatic who sacrificed the good of the service to his Jacobin convictions. Chevalier's criticism of Jeanbon's proclamations is typical:

If all things could be repaired with words, the Brest squadron would have wanted for nothing. But it was not sufficient to indicate to officers their duties, it was necessary that they be prepared to fulfill them by drill and military education. Sadly these conditions did not exist.[4]

Beyond suggestions of incompetence or inadequacy, naval historians were repelled by the Revolutionary Government's use of Terror to restore order in the fleet and, in particular, its application to the officer corps. Thus Guérin denounced Jeanbon as a cruel dictator who was "superb only when sending brave officers to the scaffold. . ."[5] Lévy-Schneider, on the other hand, opposed such interpretations passionately. Jeanbon's biographer argued that the Terror at Brest was relatively moderate and that repression was necessary to save the navy. Jeanbon was dispatched to the Atlantic port to crush all opposition to the Revolutionary Government as well as to preserve the fleet, two objectives, according to Lévy-Schneider, that were inseparable:

It was by the conflict of royalism and federalism with the *Montagne*, of nobles and bourgeoisie with the people, that the squadron and the navy of the port of Brest had been disorganized . . . In this state of things, the only means to prevent the quarrel and the resulting anarchy being prolonged was to achieve the victory of the *Montagne* and democracy. . .[6]

This examination of Jeanbon's missions to Brest focuses on his restoration of order and subordination in the fleet and his attempt to unify the

[3] Taillemite, *L'Histoire ignorée*, pp. 279–291 does not find Jeanbon or his missions worthy of mention in his discussion of the Revolutionary period.
[4] Chevalier, p. 117; see also pp. 114–118, 120–122, 125–127. For a more vehement condemnation of Jeanbon as ignorant of naval realities, as having no "appreciation of the factors conditioning efficiency at sea," particularly regarding gunnery, see Mahan, *Influence of Sea Power upon the French Revolution*, I, p. 37–40, 58.
[5] Guérin, VI, p. 45; see also pp. 19–20. Tramond, pp. 568–70 is more sympathetic to Jeanbon's ruthless measures, but argues that Terror was unable to fill magazines or create naval expertise. For a balanced but favorable judgement of Jeanbon's missions to Brest, see Acerra and Meyer, pp. 171–172.
[6] Lévy-Schneider, I, p. 417.

navy under Montagnard rule, efforts which involved the politicization of all aspects of naval service. The Terror, both in terms of the policy of the Committee of Public Safety and the means employed by Representatives on mission, lay behind the preparation of the French navy for the Prairial campaign of May–June 1794. Naval reorganization required the powerful assertion of Revolutionary Government in Brest. But this was not due to the over-simplified struggle between "democracy" and its opponents which Lévy-Schneider presents. Beyond Jeanbon's call for a purge following the Quiberon mutiny, the powerful *conventionnel* needed to reverse the trend of four years of Revolutionary politics. Unfettered Popular Sovereignty had eroded state control over the arsenal and produced chaos in the squadrons. Jeanbon Saint-André sought to create a navy for the Republic by imposing a new definition of Revolutionary authority.

In at least one essential respect the Terror began on June 2, 1793, when the purge of the Convention put an end to parliamentary democracy. Terror was not made "the order of the day," however, until September 5 when crowds invaded the assembly to demand that the deputies accept the program of the popular movement. The *sans-culottes* of Paris, whose support had enabled the *Montagne* to triumph over its "Girondin" opponents, had pressured the Convention throughout the summer to alleviate the economic crisis, to pursue the war effort more vigorously, and, above all, to identify and punish all internal enemies.[7] Militant agitation culminated in the uprising of September 4–5 which forced the adoption of key radical measures including the General Maximum on prices of essential commodities, the creation of a popular *Armée Révolutionnaire* to intimidate hoarders, and the Law of Suspects which authorized the arrest of all potential enemies and traitors.[8]

The Terror was not forced upon a reluctant Convention "from below." Many Jacobin deputies had already concluded that saving the Revolution

[7] See George Rudé, *The Crowd in the French Revolution* (Oxford: Oxford University Press, 1959; repr. 1967), pp. 125–127, and Doyle, *Oxford History*, pp. 245–246, 249–250. Regarding the *sans-culottes'* economic concerns and advocacy of violence to secure Revolutionary gains, see Soboul, *Sans-Culottes*, esp. pp. 47–52, 158–161. For a discussion of popular pressure and the August 23 decree of the *levée-en-masse*, see Bertaud, pp. 97–110.

[8] See R. R. Palmer, *Twelve Who Ruled* (1941: repr. Princeton: Princeton University Press, 1973), pp. 44–70, and Doyle, *Oxford History*, pp. 251–252. For the texts of the Law of the Maximum and the Law of Suspects, see: Stewart (ed.), pp. 477–479, 498–500.

required ruthless measures. According to Robespierre, who joined the Committee of Public Safety in July, France needed a single will, "*une volonté une.*"[9] The Montagnards differed fundamentally from popular militants in locating the General Will of the Sovereign People not in the Paris Sections, but in the government of the state.[10] What emerged from the *journées* of September was a powerful Revolutionary Government in which the great Committees of Public Safety and General Security functioned as the first effective and unchallenged executive since 1789. The nature of this government's authority was clear even before the Law of 14 Frimaire Year II (December 4, 1793) codified the sweeping extent of central control to be exercised by the Committees.[11] The Convention decreed on October 10 that continued threats to the Republic made implementation of the new Constitution too dangerous and, therefore, the government must remain "Revolutionary until peace." As Saint-Just indicated when introducing the decree, all authority would thus be vested in the government until the Revolution's ultimate goals were achieved and no dissent would be tolerated:

You can hope for no prosperity as long as the last enemy of liberty breathes. You have to punish not only traitors but even those who are neutral; . . . since the French People has declared its will, everyone who is opposed to it is outside the sovereign body; and everyone who is outside the sovereign body is an enemy.[12]

Jeanbon Saint-André was one of those who personified the sentiments and authority of the Revolutionary Government.

André Jeanbon was born in 1749, son of a Huguenot family in Montauban. Following studies with the Jesuits at the Collège de Montauban, he became an officer in the merchant marine. This career was relatively short, lasting less than six years, and in 1771 Jeanbon went

[9] In Courtois, *Papiers trouvés chez Robespierre et ses complices* (Paris, 1795); cited in David Jourdan, *The Revolutionary Career of Maximilien Robespierre* (Chicago: University of Chicago Press, 1985; repr. 1989), p. 143.
[10] See Alfred Cobban, "The Political Ideas of Maximilien Robespierre During the Period of the Convention," in *Aspects*, esp. pp. 159–161. See also Sydenham, *French Revolution*, pp. 170–171, and Furet, p. 60.
[11] For the text of the Law of 14 Frimaire, "The Constitution of the Terror," see Stewart (ed.), pp. 481–490. See also the diagram, "Jacobin Centralization," in J. M. Thompson, p. 412.
[12] "The declaration of *gouvernement révolutionnaire* preceded by extracts from Saint-Just's speech, 19 *vendémiaire* year II (October 10, 1793)"; in Hardman (ed.), pp. 180–181.

to Lausanne to study Protestant theology. He was consecrated as a minister in 1773 and, in the custom of the *pasteurs du désert*, adopted the name Jeanbon Saint-André to avoid persecution in Catholic France.[13] Jeanbon became pastor at Montauban in 1788 and, like most French protestants, embraced the Revolution enthusiastically. Indeed, Revolutionary politics in the south-west tended to coincide with religious divisions. Jeanbon fled to Bordeaux following an episode of factional violence on May 10, 1790, but returned to Montauban to lead the local Jacobins, predominantly Protestant, who dominated the city into the Terror.[14] Jeanbon failed to become a member of the Legislative Assembly, but was elected to the Convention as a deputy for Lot in 1792. He voted as a regicide and became notable as one of the Montagnards. His Revolutionary zeal matched by a belief in the need for strong government, Jeanbon was named to the Committee of Public Safety on June 12, 1793 and remained following the organization of the "Great Committee" in September.[15] Thus when he was dispatched to save the French navy in October, Jeanbon was one of the most powerful Revolutionary leaders and dominated the other Representatives on mission at Brest.

Jeanbon and his Committee colleague Prieur de la Marne arrived in Brest on October 7 and spent their first four days in the port inspecting Morard de Galles' fleet. They began with the most mutinous ships, whose sailors they chastised, and concluded with the better disciplined vessels where fraternal celebrations of Republican faith, including the singing of the *Marseillaise*, were held.[16] Following this symbolic assertion

[13] Lévy-Schneider, I, p. 10; for details of Jeanbon's early life see pp. 1–9. See also Daniel Ligou, *Jeanbon Saint-André, membre du grand Comité de salut public (1749–1813)* (Paris: Messidor/Editions sociales, 1989), pp. 13–28. Jeanbon was a controversial minister of the *culte réformé* who proposed that, once toleration was achieved under the French Crown, Protestant churches should submit to government regulation: see Jeanbon Saint-André, "Considérations sur l'organisation des églises protestantes"; in Michel Nicolas, *Jean-Bon Saint-André. Sa vie et ses écrits* (Paris: Imprimeurs-Unis, 1848), pp. 276–310. See also: Lévy-Schneider, I, pp. 33–41; Ligou, pp. 28–32.
[14] Clarke Garrett, "Religion, Revenge and the Reign of Terror in Montauban," *Proceedings, Western Society for French History*, 15 (1988), 190–197. See also: Lévy-Schneider, I, pp. 46–170; Ligou, pp. 37–55.
[15] See: Lévy-Schneider, I, pp. 175–214, 229–230, 279–292, 383–385, 463–468; Ligou, pp. 59–85; Auguste Kuscinski, *Dictionnaire des conventionnels* (Paris: Société de l'histoire de la Révolution française, 1916), pp. 346–350.
[16] Marine BB 3/22, f. 377; BB 4/16, f. 285. See also Jeanbon Saint-André, *Rapport des représentans du peuple envoyés à Brest et auprès de l'armée navale* (Paris: Imprimerie Nationale, An II), p. 4 [BN 8 Le39 61]; and the descriptions of the tour in Lévy-Schneider, I, p. 500 and in Palmer, pp. 203–204.

Plate 6. André Jeanbon Saint-André.
Portrait by David (in Léon Lévy-Schneider, *Le conventionnel Jeanbon Saint-André*, 2 vols., Paris: Félix Alcan, 1901, I, frontispiece)

of Revolutionary Government, Jeanbon began his investigation into the origins of the mutiny at Quiberon. The preceding chapter discussed his conclusions. What remains to be examined is the action taken on the basis of his Report. The Convention had already approved, on October 7, a plan to ensure the naval officer corps would be composed

247

only of "true friends of the People" by a process of public scrutiny and local nomination.[17] This was a long-term proposition, as was Jeanbon's call for a purge of all aristocrats. The Representative's initial measures regarding the navy were, however, in keeping with this spirit. The *arrêté* of 1 Brumaire (October 22, 1793), which followed from Jeanbon's Report, dismissed Vice-Admiral Morard de Galles as commander of the Brest fleet.[18] The Admiral had repeated his request to be relieved as recently as October 9 on the basis of failing health and, more significantly, because he had lost the squadron's confidence.[19] Jeanbon ordered him sent to Paris to account for his conduct to the Convention, but not to be delivered to the Revolutionary Tribunal. While he saw Morard de Galles as "weak and irresolute," Jeanbon found no evidence to warrant suspicion of treason.[20] Similarly, the Representatives dismissed Rear-Admirals Lelarge and Kerguelen, but did not find them guilty of explicit Counter-Revolution. Jeanbon accused Lelarge of doubtful *civisme* and of making the "insidious" proposal that the sailor dispatched by the fleet's council on September 15 should continue to Brest even if he contacted Representatives on mission at Lorient. Jeanbon saw Kerguelen as "imbued with prejudices incompatible with the principles of the Republic."[21] The Representatives accepted

---

[17] "Rapport et projet de décret sur le mode d'épurement de la marine civile et militaire, présentés, au nom du Comité de marine, à la Convention nationale, par Topsent, député du Département de l'Eure"; AP, vol. 76, pp. 184–185. This bill, which was a respose to Toulon's surrender rather than the Quiberon mutiny, has been criticized or praised as a proposal for an elective officer corps. In fact, even if it had been fully implemented, the plan left the ultimate decision on officer appointments in the hands of the Minister of Marine and the Convention.

[18] Jeanbon, *Rapport sur les mouvemens*, p. 40. See also Chevalier, pp. 109–110.

[19] Marine BB 4/16, f. 283.

[20] Jeanbon, *Rapport sur les mouvemens*, pp. 30–31. Morard de Galles was permitted to retire to his family home at Auxonne. The local Revolutionary Tribunal recalled him to Brest in April 1794, however, and imprisoned him as a witness for its investigation of the Quiberon Affair. He was not released until after Thermidor; Lévy-Schneider, I, pp. 512–513, II, pp. 755, 991, 1020.

[21] Jeanbon, *Rapport sur les mouvemens*, pp. 31, 40. Lelarge protested that his proposal was seen as "insidious" only by Landais, whom even Jeanbon realized was unbalanced; *Le Large, . . . à la Convention*; Brest "Fonds Levot" 1988 [19]. Kerguelen, trimming to the post-Thermidorian wind, blamed his dismissal on the "intrigues of Robespierrist agents"; Kerguelen-Trémarec, pp. 354–355. The *arrêté* ordered both *contre-amiraux* to leave Brest within twenty-four hours and to take up residence in municipalities at least 20 leagues from the coast or frontier where they would be placed under surveillance. Yet both were imprisoned in Brest, like Morard de Galles, by the local Revolutionary Tribunal as witnesses; Lévy-Schneider, II, pp.

the resignation of Rear-Admiral Landais, although stating that he was a true patriot.[22]

Jeanbon also allotted punishment to various captains and junior officers of the Brest fleet. The *arrêté* of 1 Brumaire stripped Captains Boissauver and Thomas of their commands,[23] and ordered the arrests of Captain Bonnefous and *major-de-l'armée* Augier of the flagship,[24] as well as of Captain Larichery of *Le Bretagne* (110).[25] Jeanbon took more drastic action against six officers whom he linked directly to the "conspiracy" at Quiberon, arresting and dispatching them to Paris for trial by the Revolutionary Tribunal:[26] Captain Duplessis-Grénédan of *Le Côte-d'Or* (118), accused of complicity with the Vendéans; Captain Coëtnempren of *Le Jean-Bart* (74), denounced as a Counter-Revolutionary hypocrite;[27] two lieutenants and an ensign from *Le Tourville* (74); Verneuil, pay clerk on *Le Côte-d'Or*. One of these men died

755–756, 991, 1020. Captain Obet, who commanded *Le Suffren* (74) in Morard de Galles' fleet, was also detained as a witness and he described it as "civil and moral death"; *Précis de la vie militaire et politique d'Yves-Louis Obet, capitaine de vaisseau, suspendu de ses fonctions depuis treize mois, sous prétexte de nécessité de son témoignage dans l'affaire de Quiberon, intriguée par le tribunal révolutionnaire* (Brest: Audran [no date]); Brest "Fonds Levot" 1988 [2].

[22] Jeanbon, *Rapport sur les mouvemens*, p. 42.

[23] Ibid., pp. 41, 34–35. Jeanbon doubted the sincerity of Thomas' patriotism and, significantly, damned his attempt to justify his crew's insurrection. He dismissed Boissauver because the Captain held a ball at Quiberon to celebrate Toulon's surrender. Boissauver claimed that he went ashore before the news arrived and merely to dine with Quiberon's *syndic-des-classes*, not to host a party; *Boissauver, . . . à la Convention*; Brest "Fonds Levot" 1988 [7].

[24] Jeanbon, *Rapport sur les mouvemens*, pp. 42, 32. Along with having an unpatriotic influence on Morard de Galles, these two officers were accused of complicity in the mysterious signals observed by *Contre-amiral* Landais; "Extrait d'un mémoire remis par le contre-amiral Landais aux représentants du peuple près les ports de Brest et de Lorient et signé par lui"; pp. 124–129.

[25] Jeanbon, *Rapport sur les mouvemens*, pp. 42, 35. Jeanbon accused Larichery of being an *émigré* and, thus, ordered him detained as a suspect.

[26] Jeanbon, *Rapport sur les mouvemens*, pp. 41, 33–36. Lévy-Schneider, I, p. 515 claims that Jeanbon's decision ran counter to suggestions by Bréard and Tréhouart, who advocated judgement by military tribunal, and by Prieur, who wanted the officers tried by Finistère's Criminal Tribunal and executed on a pontoon in the harbour.

[27] Duplessis-Grénédan, whose brothers were officers in Condé's Army, had been swept up in a peasant rising in March near la Roche-Bernard. See: "Déclaration du citoyen Lebesque," and "Déclaration du citoyen Herbert"; in Jeanbon, *Rapport sur les mouvemens*, pp. 96–99. For the anonymous denunciation of Coëtnempren, see: "Aux citoyens représentants, Brest, 3e jour de l'an II"; pp. 118–124. Coëtnempren was also damned for putting his library and silverware ashore in anticipation of battle with the English.

in prison, another became ill and was never tried, while four appeared before the Revolutionary Tribunal on January 16, 1794. Verneuil and the two ship's captains were pronounced guilty of treason and guillotined.[28]

Yet before Jeanbon issued this arrêté, or even completed his investigation, the Representatives at Brest were reminded dramatically of the larger crisis facing the French navy. On October 13 *Le Patriote* (74) and *L'Entreprenant* (74) entered the roadstead from Toulon. The two battleships had been disarmed and loaded with sailors whom Admiral Hood considered a threat to his occupation.[29] For their resistance or non-cooperation, these men expected to be welcomed as patriots.[30] They were, however, put ashore and imprisoned.[31] Jeanbon saw their arrival as further proof of a Counter-Revolutionary plot to destroy the navy and to spread the disease of royalism to Brest. This had to be checked:

The most severe precautions were taken to prevent the effects of the contagion. The officers who had the villainy to deliver the Toulon fleet, or at least the cowardice not to have defended it, were put under arrest, awaiting the pronouncement of national justice on their fate. Several, whose crimes were notorious, were sent to the Revolutionary Tribunal. They have paid with their heads for the outrage they have committed against liberty.[32]

Although the Representatives at Brest sent two officers and four seamen to Paris and the guillotine,[33] the treatment of those whom Hood dispatched from Toulon was most ruthless at Rochefort. The deputies

---

[28] For the interrogations and the judgement of the Revolutionary Tribunal, see: "Affaire Lebourg, Verneuil, Coëtnempren, Duplessis-Grénédan"; AN W 311, no. 414. For Chevalier, pp. 113–114, the executions were both unjust and predetermined as soon as the officers were sent to Paris. Lévy-Schneider, I, pp. 515–516 is more discriminating: he claims that Verneuil and Coëtnempren did not deserve death, that Lebourg received unexplained indulgence, but that the conduct of Duplessis-Grénédan was similar to the manoeuvres of Lebret d'Imbert at Toulon and, thus, warranted punishment. See also Bordonove, pp. 66–68.
[29] Marine BB 3/22, f. 375. Hood dispatched four of the oldest, and hence least valuable, ships of the line carrying some 5,000–6,000 French sailors with safe-conducts to Atlantic ports: *Le Patriote* and *L'Entreprenant* to Brest, *L'Orion* to Lorient, *L'Apollon* to Rochefort; see Rose, pp. 32–33.
[30] See *Mémoire du citoyen Boubennec*; Brest "Fonds Levot" 1988 [35]. See also the testimony of Republican loyalty sworn by the sailors on *Le Patriote*: "Adresse des citoyens à bord du Patriote, 26 Vendémiaire l'an II"; AP, vol. 77, pp. 684–685.
[31] Marine BB 3/22, f. 391; BB 3/38, ff. 391–393.
[32] Jeanbon, *Rapport des représentans*, p. 9. See also: "Les représentants à Brest au comité de Salut public, Brest, 30 Vendémiaire l'an II"; AP, vol. 77, p. 682.
[33] See: Lévy-Schneider, I, pp. 520–525; Chevalier, pp. 103–105; Guérin, V, pp. 454, 548; Havard, II, pp. 316–323.

there, Laignelot and Lequino, responded to the arrival of *L'Apollon* (74) by establishing a Revolutionary Tribunal in the port which condemned ten officers to death.[34] It was clear that Representatives on mission to the naval ports were resolved to crush any perceived threat to the Republic: severity, according to Jeanbon, "is the only means to make the conspirators tremble and to frighten intriguers."[35]

Severity was not limited to the punishment of suspected traitors and Counter-Revolutionaries. Jeanbon's Report on the mutiny emphasized the need to restore order and subordination in the fleet as much as it demanded a purge of aristocrats. Jeanbon dismissed Morard de Galles because he proved incapable of suppressing insurrection and, as noted above, replaced him as commander-in-chief with another ex-noble, Captain Villaret-Joyeuse, who had enforced strict discipline aboard his ship.[36] The maintenance of order at Quiberon also explained the promotion of Captains Vanstabel of *Le Tigre* (74) and Bouvet of *L'Audacieux* (74) to *contre-amiral*.[37] It is also significant that Jeanbon did not conclude

[34] For the *arrêté* establishing the Revolutionary Tribunal at Rochefort on October 29, 1793, see Marine BB 3/38, f. 96; and for the prosecutor's charges of treason and conspiracy against the passengers and crew of *L'Apollon*, see: Victor Hugues, *Acte d'Accusation contre les complices de la trahison de Toulon. Rochefort, 29 Burmaire an II* (Rochefort: R. D. Jousseront, Imprimeur du Tribunal révolutionnaire [no date]) [BN 8 Lb41 818]. See also: E. J. Fleury and J. T. Viaud, *Histoire de la ville et du port de Rochefort* (Rochefort: Honorine Fleury, 1845), II, pp. 330–338; Lévy-Schneider, I, p. 526; Chevalier, pp. 105–108.

[35] AN AF II, Cart. 294/Reg. 2463, f. 41.

[36] Jeanbon, *Rapport sur les mouvemens*, p. 43. See also: Jeanbon, *Rapport des représentans*, p. 10; Marine BB 4/19, f. 69. Villaret-Joyeuse remained a strict disciplinarian in 1794. See his Instructions to frigate captains, 10 Pluviôse an II, and his letter to Jeanbon recommending punishment of insubordinate sailors aboard *Le Trente-et-un Mai*, 9 Floréal an II; AD Finistère 8 L 84.

[37] See "Copie de procès-verbal du conseil tenu à bord du vaisseau le Terrible le 21 septembre 1793," and "Tréhouart à Bréard, 25 septembre 1793"; AD Finistère 8 L 88. See also: Hampson, *La Marine de l'an II*, pp. 196–197; Bordonove, p. 87; Lévy-Schneider, I, pp. 531–532. Pierre-Jean Vanstabel was born at Dunkirk in 1744 and became an officer in the *Compagnie des Indes*. He distinguished himself during the American War as an *officier auxiliaire*, and entered the navy definitively as an ensign in 1792. Promoted to *capitaine de vaisseau* in January 1793, Vanstabel commanded the frigate *La Thétis*, capturing or sinking forty English merchantmen, before taking command of *Le Tigre* in Morard de Galles' fleet. François-Joseph Bouvet de Précourt [not to be confused with Bouvet de Maisonneuve, arrested upon arrival from Toulon in command of *La Patriote*] was born at Lorient in 1753. He also began his career in the *Compagnie des Indes* but, son of an aristocratic naval captain, transferred to the navy in 1780 and was made lieutenant in 1786. Following active duty in the West Indies from 1790 to 1791, Bouvet was promoted to *capitaine de vaisseau* in April 1793. See Taillemite, *Dictionnaire*, pp. 46, 333–334, and Six, *Dictionnaire biographique*, I, p. 149, II, p. 532.

that guilt was confined to admirals and captains. Ringleaders of the mutiny on the lower deck were also punished:

Several gunners, sailors and [marine] soldiers have also been placed under arrest. This severity was just, it was necessary; because discipline must reign, . . . this was not recognized and the obedience of subordinates to their commanders, which is only the obedience to the nation itself which named them, was trampled on.[38]

Jeanbon's insistence on discipline continued beyond the immediate response to the fleet's return from Quiberon. On November 10, 1793 Jeanbon delivered a major address to all seamen on this theme. The Revolution, he said, had regenerated the navy and removed the aristocratic officers whose treachery lay behind mutiny and defeat. Moreover, the Revolution had bestowed the benefits of liberty and equality upon all sailors; but, from ship's boy to admiral, order must reign. Crews had the duty to resist those among them who preached insurrection, and Jeanbon warned that further mutiny would not be tolerated: "Do not doubt that the blade of the law will strike all conspirators without pity. The Nation wants only faithful servants: it will punish insubordination and cowardice with firmness; as great in its rewards, it will be more severe and inflexible in its punishments."[39] A new Penal Code for the navy, replacing that of 1790, substantiated this warning. It held officers responsible to maintain discipline in their commands, but backed up their authority with explicit and harsh penalties for insubordination. Sailors not obeying orders quickly would suffer four days in irons. Refusal to obey orders, if accompanied by threats, would result in flogging or five years imprisonment. Raising a hand to a superior warranted the lash, while more serious assault was punishable with death. Death was also the penalty for inciting mutiny.[40] Furthermore, Jeanbon put an end to the conditions which had allowed sailors guilty of flouting naval authority to escape punishment.[41]

[38] Jeanbon, *Rapport sur les mouvemens*, p. 36. See also Marine BB 3/22, f. 399.
[39] "Les Représentans du Peuple aux marins, le 20 brumaire l'an II"; Brest "Fonds Levot" 1965.
[40] "Arrêté: Code Pénal de la Marine, le 20 brumaire l'an II"; Brest "Fonds Levot" 1965. See esp. Articles III–VI, X. Jeanbon's Penal Code, provisionally in force from the date of the *arrêté*, was formally adopted by the Convention on January 5, 1794; AP, vol. 83, pp. 17–20.
[41] The new Penal Code abolished the system of Trial by Jury and judgement by an elected *Conseil de Justice* aboard ship which was established under the 1790 Code. The "Council of Discipline" which remained would pronounce only on corporal

Jeanbon informed the Convention that his new Penal Code, unlike that of 1790, was accepted throughout the fleet:

It is just, but severe; and these same sailors, who were seen to revolt under the Constituent Assembly when it required them to submit to a repressive, weak, and imperfect law, docile under the simple voice of two Representatives of the People, adopted without repugnance and without murmur a much more rigorous law. No complaint, legislators, will come to you. Obedience was complete.[42]

Whether or not crews submitted to the new Code "without murmur," Jeanbon was prepared to enforce its articles ruthlessly. He ordered the Criminal Tribunal of Finistère transferred to Brest in January 1794 to try, in "Revolutionary style," seamen who had mutinied aboard *L'America* (74). Four were guillotined on a pontoon in the roadstead before the eyes of the entire fleet.[43]

Implicit in this restoration of discipline and subordination was Jeanbon's assertion of a clear definition of Revolutionary authority, itself a reflection of the growing strength of the Montagnard government in Paris. In his Report Jeanbon denounced Morard de Galles for convoking the council aboard *Le Terrible* to decide on the fleet's course of action, condemning such behavior as contrary to Revolutionary principle. In this remarkable statement he asserted:

Armed force cannot deliberate, this is a fundamental truth, an essential principle, without which there will no longer be liberty. If the government ceases to direct the action of the physical force for one moment, or if this is not constantly subordinated to it, the most frightful despotism, military despotism, will establish itself with all its horrors.[44]

The Penal Code reiterated that sailors did not possess the right to question or debate their orders; it specifically forbade petitions to

punishments, while commanding officers would allot all major penalties for lapses of discipline [*peines de disciplines*]. Those facing the death penalty would be tried by a Departmental Criminal Tribunal; see ibid., Articles XXXVI, XXXVII, XL, XLI, VII, XI.
[42] Jeanbon, *Rapport des représentans*, pp. 8–9.
[43] Lévy-Schneider, I, pp. 649, 652–653; Henwood and Monage, p. 212. Insubordination aboard *L'America*, which had been one of the most rebellious ships at Brest in 1790–1791, may have dated back to a mutiny in July and August 1793 while the ship was serving in the West Indies; Marine BB 3/38, ff. 273–275.
[44] Jeanbon, *Rapport sur les mouvemens*, p. 21.

commanders.[45] Jeanbon delivered the same message to officers. They must set an example by strict obedience to their admiral.[46] Moreover, officers must accept the nominations made by the Representatives of the People and not petition for themselves. Jeanbon and his colleagues at Brest had been swamped with appeals from potential officers or those seeking advancement, some of which were attached to denunciations.[47] In the eyes of the Montagnard such petitions were not only threats to discipline, but challenges to Revolutionary authority: "We declare to you, in the name of the Nation, of which we are the organs . . . that it will only recognize as its servants those who await the call of *la Patrie* . . ."[48]

All of Jeanbon's efforts to restore order, enforce subordination, and limit place-seeking were united by their identification of the locus of irrefutable authority. As in the army of the Year II, the imperative of discipline in the Republic's navy was to be reconciled with Popular Sovereignty through obedience to the law: "It is no longer, as under the Old Regime, the man that you obey: it is the law; it is *la Patrie*, . . ."[49] The orders of the Representatives on mission, or of the naval commanders they appointed, could no longer be disobeyed in the name of the "Sovereign People," or the "National Will." Under the Montagnards, the nation was identical to the Revolutionary Government and its will manifest in the agents of that Government. No room for debate or dissent remained. As Jeanbon declared to Admiral Villaret-Joyeuse in March 1794, to be disciplined and to respect the law was only to comply with the General Will.[50]

It was, of course, not only mutinous sailors who disputed the location and message of the General Will. The "Federalist" rebels, with their vision of a moderate constitutional Republic, had used the logic of

---

[45] See Articles XIII–XV: "Code Pénal . . ."; Brest "Fonds Levot" 1965.
[46] "Les Représentans du Peuple, aux officiers de la marine, le 20 brumaire l'an II"; Brest "Fonds Levot" 1965.
[47] AD Finistère 8 L 92, 8 L 93. The exaggerated suggestion that unscrupulous place-seeking dominated the navy during 1793–1794 is made by Louis Jourdan, "Remplacement des officiers après l'insurrection de l'escadre à Quiberon," *Bulletin de la Société de géographie de Rochefort*, 34 (1912), 137–147.
[48] "Les Représentans . . . aux officiers . . ."; Brest "Fonds Levot" 1965.
[49] "Les Représentans . . . aux marins . . ."; Brest "Fonds Levot" 1965. According to Lynn, p. 97, obedience to the law, not the commander, was intended to reconcile "the obedience of the soldier with the liberty of the citizen," and the government's insistence that soldiers obey their officers with its fear of generals whom it considered politically suspect; see also pp. 98–118. The point is also made by Bertaud, p. 175.
[50] "Arrêté: Le Représentant du Peuple à Villaret-Joyeuse, commandant l'Armée navale de la République, le 1er germinal l'an II"; Brest "Fonds Levot" 1965.

Popular Sovereignty to challenge the rule of the Convention during the spring and summer of 1793. Despite Jeanbon's insistence on conspiracy and Lévy-Schneider's dialectic between democracy and its enemies, the fundamental issue at Brest, as in Morard de Galles' fleet, was the competition between different claims to represent the nation. When the Representatives on mission sought to crush rebellion and stamp out all remnants of "Federalism," they imposed the Montagnard definition of Revolutionary authority. The introduction of the Terror into Brest's civilian society began slowly with measures taken by Bréard and Tréhouart. The two deputies were impressed with the welcome they received in September from authorities in the port, who had been making desperate gestures of penitence and submission since July,[51] and they reported their satisfaction with the spirit of the Brestois to Paris.[52] Nevertheless, they began to arrest suspects on September 18, and one of the first imprisoned was the *ordonnateur civil* Redon de Beaupréau.[53] Repression accelerated following Jeanbon's arrival in October: "Because all here was gangrenous," he and Bréard told the Committee of Public Safety, "all needed the scalpel of patriotism."[54] They referred specifically to Brest's Jacobin Club, which had been a centre of "Federalism" in the port. Jeanbon informed the clubists that their failure to purge themselves, to take the "billhook of Republicanism" and "prune mercilessly all parasitic branches," forced the Representatives to dissolve the Popular Society:

We cannot doubt . . . that the federalists had accomplices in Brest. It was not without advantage that these accomplices were in your midst: we have ordered the arrest of the most guilty . . .

[51] See: Marine BB 3/22, f. 293; *Les Brestois à la Convention Nationale* (Brest: Gauchlet, 1793); Brest "Fonds Levot" 1991 [34]; "Copie de la déposition du citoyen Belval, sous-chef de l'administration de la marine, faite aux représentants du peuple près les côtes de Brest et de Lorient, le 27e jour du 1er mois de l'an II de la République française, une et indivisible," and "Les Brestois à la Convention nationale," in Jeanbon, *Rapport sur les mouvemens*, pp. 49–53, 57–60. See also: Levot, pp. 99–103; Henwood and Monage, pp. 149–151, 171.
[52] Marine BB 3/38, ff. 273, 292. See also: Aulard (ed.) *Actes*, VI, pp. 468, 484; Levot, pp. 105–109; Henwood and Monage, pp. 171, 174.
[53] See Redon's *mémoires justificatifs*, in which he defends his authorization of the shipment of supplies to Toulon during 1792–1793: *Un Administrateur du port de Brest, devenu la malheureuse victime de la tyrannie, à tous les Républicains de la France, justes, honnêtes et sensibles* (Brest: Malassis [no date]) and *Justification du citoyen Redon, ci-devant ordonnateur de la marine, détenu depuis quatorze mois, tant à Carhaix qu'au Fort-la-Loi, ci-devant le Château de Brest* (Brest: Malassis [no date]); Brest "Fonds Levot" 1988 [1] and [8].
[54] AN AF II 294/Registre 2463, f. 44.

It is necessary that patriotism triumph, that all parts of the Republic attach themselves to the centre of government, to this National Convention which gave the example by expelling its impure members, to this Convention purified by the memorable *journées* of May 31 and June 2.[55]

Although Jeanbon left Brest on November 13 for Cherbourg, which was threatened by the march of the Vendéan army across Brittany towards the English Channel,[56] the imposition of Montagnard authority continued under Bréard. On November 21 the Representative dissolved the municipality and replaced it with a provisional commission. The same day he "regenerated" the District Council with another *arrêté*.[57] Civil administration in Brest was thus fully subordinated to agents of the Revolutionary Government. Even after Jeanbon returned in December, he informed the Committee of Public Safety that the authority of the Representatives in the port was still threatened: "intrigue flourished" as Brest was denuded of troops sent to fight the Vendéans. He requested additional armed force in the form of three companies of gunners from the Parisian *Armée Révolutionnaire* serving in Avranches.[58] The arrival of these *sans-culottes* on January 8, 1794 was followed by the establishment of the institutions which characterized the Terror: a Surveillance Committee and a Revolutionary Tribunal.[59]

[55] Jeanbon Saint-André, *Les Représentans du Peuple près les côtes de Brest et de Lorient; aux membres de la Société populaire de Brest. Arrêté du 3 brumaire an II*; [BN Fol Lb41 4680]. The Representatives named twelve core members of a new Popular Society. These named twelve more, with whom they named the remaining twenty-four. See: Lévy-Schneider, I, pp. 547–548; Levot, pp. 143–144. Henwood and Monage, pp. 184–185 analyze the composition of the new Jacobin Club and suggest that it was more egalitarian in membership, but also stress that it had become powerless.

[56] See: Marine BB 3/38, ff. 34, 416–418, 434, 449, 452, 483–485; Jeanbon, *Rapport des représentans*, pp. 14–18. For a brief assessment of the Vendéan strategy in marching to Granville, "*la Virée de Galerne*," see Rostu, pp. 91–96. For a detailed discussion of Jeanbon's mission against the Vendéans, see Lévy-Schneider, I, pp. 582–622. See also: Ligou, pp. 117–126; Bordonove, pp. 113–118.

[57] Marine BB 3/38, ff. 454, 457, 458, 462, 471. See also: Levot, pp. 167–173; Henwood and Monage, pp. 185–186. Bréard sent commissions into the surrounding area to purge all constituted authorities; see Lévy-Schneider, I, pp. 626–631 and Ligou, p. 127.

[58] Marine BB 3/38, ff. 540–541.

[59] Laignelot and Tréhouart created a "Comité central de surveillance" to coordinate Sectional watch committees in Brest on January 29, 1794: Levot, pp. 196–198; Henwood and Monage, pp. 188–189. Bréard had suggested a Revolutionary Tribunal as early as December 10, 1793; Marine BB 3/38, f. 462. Laignelot established it with his *arrêté* of 17 pluviôse (February 5, 1794): see copy of the *arrêté* in Henwood and Monage, p. 190.

Brest's Revolutionary Tribunal held its first trial on February 9, 1794, in which

Thus the evolution of the Terror in Brest reflected the larger theme of centralization: the Revolutionary Government required complete control over the naval base and was determined to quell any local opposition or interference. It was also true that Brest had been in open revolt against the Convention, and therefore the arrests and purges represented Montagnard vengeance against those they believed to be in league with royalist Counter-Revolution and the foreign enemy. Both of these factors form part of the explanation for Terror in Brest. Yet the logic of the Terror should not be limited to the imposition of central control, or to the defeat of political enemies: both of these goals were included in the definition of Revolutionary authority which flowed from an increasingly exclusive definition of the nation. For the same reason that Jeanbon warned naval crews that they must now obey their commanders, he exhorted local Jacobins to accept the purge of Brest's Popular Society: "Do not think therefore that we usurp your rights, when we defend them: to assist you is not to oppress you; to break your chains, this is not to attack your liberty."[60] Liberty was to be defended by silencing all those who resisted the Montagnards, for they alone represented the General Will of the Sovereign People. If, as Robespierre said, Revolution was the war of liberty against its enemies, then the authority of the Revolutionary Government must be accepted without question in order to save the Republic.[61] Jeanbon Saint-André expressed the same rationale for absolute Revolutionary authority even before going on mission to

four young naval officers were accused of complicity with the chevalier de Rivière's Counter-Revolution in the West Indies. Three of them were found guilty and guillotined. See: "Jugement du Tribunal révolutionnaire condamnant à mort les officiers Rougement, Montecler et [Le Dall de] Keréon. 21 pluviôse an II"; copy in Henwood and Monage, p. 193. See also: Levot, pp. 202–210; Lévy-Schneider, I, p. 701; Bordonove, p. 137.

Following this trial, and Jeanbon's return to Brest, the composition of the Tribunal was modified substantially and it was dominated by three former members of the Paris Revolutionary Tribunal: Ragmey, Donzé-Verteuil, Bonnet. Between its creation and its suspension on August 11, 1794, the Brest Tribunal judged 180 people, of whom 70 were condemned to death. The most spectacular trial was that of 30 administrators of the Department of Finistère on May 22, 1794; 26 of them were sent to the guillotine. See: AD Finistère 100 J 470, 605, 606. See also: Levot, pp. 214–220, 268–372; Henwood and Monage, pp. 191–20 (esp. pp. 198–199, "Liste des 70 personnes condamnés à mort par le Tribunal révolutionnaire").

[60] Jeanbon, Les Représentans . . . au membres de la Société Populaire.

[61] "Rapport sur les Principes du Gouvernement Révolutionnaire fait, au nom du Comité de Salut public, par Maximilien Robespierre, 5 Nivôse an II (December 25, 1793)"; AP, vol. 82, pp. 300–303. For discussion of the speech, see Palmer, pp. 264–266, and Sydenham, French Revolution, pp. 206–207.

Brest: "They say we exercise arbitrary power; they accuse us of being despots: despots! us! hah! doubtless, if it is despotism which is necessary for the triumph of liberty, this despotism is political regeneration."[62] "Regeneration" for the Jacobins implied the complete transformation of society, moral as well as political, because democracy required the creation of a common will.[63] Yet the Montagnard dogma of National Authority which curbed direct democracy and restricted local freedom did not end disagreement within the Revolutionary Government. Just as Robespierre wished to limit the activities of extreme dechristianizers, Jeanbon disapproved of the excessive Terrorism of Laignelot, who replaced Bréard at Brest, and felt that his establishment of a Revolutionary Tribunal was premature.[64]

Jeanbon's dispute with other members of the Committee of Public Safety, however, was more serious in its implications for Revolutionary naval policy. Jeanbon returned to Paris on January 25, 1794, and the Jacobin Club welcomed him enthusiastically.[65] Six days later he pre-

[62] AP, vol. 75, p. 133. Jeanbon's speech on September 25, 1793 was one of several by members of the Committee of Public Safety in support of Robespierre's motion that the Convention declare its full confidence in the Committee and renew the tenure of its members. The specific context was Jeanbon's insistence that the Committee must not be required to reveal its reasons for the dismissal of General Houchard in the Convention.

[63] For a discussion of this concept of "regeneration," and the importance the Jacobins placed on propaganda, see James Leith, *Media and Revolution* (Toronto: CBC Publications, 1968; repr. 1974), esp. pp. 5–10.

[64] Jeanbon opposed early suggestions from Bréard for the establishment of a Revolutionary Tribunal and reported that this prudent restraint made him the object of intrigue at Brest: "Dans quelques dénonciations secrètes qui n'ont pas encore paru au grand jour, on nous reproche de n'avoir pas établi à Brest un tribunal révolutionnaire. Si jamais on ose les porter devant vous, nous nous réservons de vous donner des détails sur l'espionnage bas et vil qui environne dans leurs misions les représentans du peuple, et produit ici tant de méfiances et de personnalités"; Jeanbon, *Rapport des représentans*, p. 14.

Laignelot arrived in Brest on January 8, 1794 with orders from the Committee of Public Safety to establish a Revolutionary Tribunal. He had presided over a more violent Terror at Rochefort than that which existed at Brest. Lévy-Schneider, I, pp. 658–661 argues that Jeanbon's departure was due primarily to his opposition to Laignelot's extremism. Jeanbon made this claim after Thermidor and suggested that bitter conflict existed between himself and Laignelot: *Réponse de Jeanbon Saint-André à la dénonciation des citoyens de la commune de Brest, Paris, le 20 prairial an III* (Paris: Imprimerie Nationale, an III), pp. 12–19. See also: Levot, pp. 156, 174, 179, 211; Henwood and Monage, pp. 189–191; Ligou, pp. 127, 129, 135–136.

[65] For Jeanbon's explanation for his departure from Brest, which hints at conflict with the Committee of Public Safety, see: AN AF II 294/Reg. 2463, f. 66. Regarding Jeanbon's arrival in Paris, see: Aulard (ed.), *Jacobins*, V, pp. 620–621; Lévy-Schneider, I, p. 664; Ligou, p. 138.

sented a Report to the Convention on his mission to Brest: "When the Committee of Public Safety sent us, we were told: go, save Brest and the fleet. We have saved both of them. Our task is fulfilled; . . ."[66] Jeanbon described the measures taken to restore order and discipline, to purify the officer corps, and to rebuild the navy. This great effort had begun, but he stressed that it was yet to be accomplished:

I departed Brest, leaving the work in full swing. If the other ports of the Republic had seconded our zeal or followed our example, the fleet would be at this moment on a respectable footing. Such as it is, it portends the most beautiful destiny for France at sea, if the measures already taken are followed and augmented by everything which national energy can add. The sounds of our axes, of our hammers, of our mallets, have reached London. Pitt has heard them. He will make, have no doubt, the greatest efforts to stifle this first surge of our maritime enthusiasm. We must resist him, we must vanquish him.[67]

The reference to other ports not supporting the measures at Brest echoed Jeanbon's complaints regarding the lack of cooperation from Laignelot and Lequino at Rochefort.[68] The regeneration of the navy required coordination, ideally under the complete control of Representatives at Brest.[69] Jeanbon insisted, moreover, that mobilization of the fleet not be seen as a secondary concern and he exhorted the Convention to devote itself to the only means of defeating the Republic's worst enemy:

The sea must become free like the land, and you can free both. Deploy therefore all the force and power which the People, whom you have the honour to represent, can give to exterminate the most miserable of its enemies, the speculators of London, the oppressors of Bengal, the disturbers of public peace in Europe. You have said that Pitt must pay for the crimes he has committed against all of humanity. Your tribune resounded with this war cry: *Carthage must be destroyed.* When the Romans wished to destroy Carthage, they created a more redoubtable navy than their enemy. Frenchmen, can you be less than the Romans? No. . . .

[66] Jeanbon, *Rapport des représentans*, p. 14.
[67] Ibid., p. 21.
[68] Marine BB 3/38, ff. 540–541, 545–547. In a letter to the Minister of 17 nivôse an II (January 6, 1794), Jeanbon complains of the "deadly inertia" at Rochefort, both in terms of construction and the inaction of warships, and asks Dalbarade, "Voulons nous, oui ou non, avoir une marine?"; Marine BB 3/61, ff. 56–57.
[69] Jeanbon would repeat the demand for coordination of activity at all naval ports during his second mission to Brest; Marine BB 3/61, ff. 63, 74–75, 86.

Ships, cannon, sailors; such must be your rallying cry. Like the Athenians, we will transport ourselves from our houses, our cities, on to our squadrons, and I dare to predict, in the name of the genius of liberty, that liberty will triumph, and that an honourable peace will affirm your rights, consolidate your revolution, and prepare the liberation of the world.[70]

Jeanbon concluded by asking the deputies to transform four of his *arrêtés*, dealing with control of naval stores as well as the instruction and condition of sailors, into general laws of the Republic.[71] The Committee of Public Safety agreed completely that naval preparations should be given priority. Toulon had been recaptured on December 19, 1793, but few of the French warships based there were not burnt or taken away by the departing enemy forces.[72] The need to replace the Mediterranean fleet moved the Committee to propose a decree on January 3, 1794 to accelerate the construction and fitting out of warships in all ports of the Republic. Barère, when introducing the decree, called for a naval effort to parallel the *levée en masse*: "Let us build ships, and let us forge arms. To the dockyards, citizens! To the workshops! This is the cry of the Republic."[73]

---

[70] Jeanbon, *Rapport des représentans*, pp. 21–23.

[71] Ibid., p. 23; the four *arrêtés* follow the text of the Report, pp. 24–36.

[72] Three ships of the line: *Le Commerce-de-Marseille* (118), *Le Pompée* (74), *Le Puissant* (74); and perhaps as many as twelve smaller warships sailed with the British and Spanish when they evacuated Toulon. Nine ships and five frigates were burned on the night of December 18–19; *Le Scipion* (74), sent by Hood to Italy, caught fire and sank at Leghorn on November 28, 1793. See: Hampson, *La Marine de l'an II*, p. 218; Rose, pp. 79–81; Chevalier, pp. 89–93; Guérin, V, pp. 485, 489; David Steel, *Steel's Naval Chronologist of the War, From its commencement in Feb. 1793, to its conclusion in 1801* (London, 1802; facsimile repr. London: Cornmarket Press, 1969), pp. 2–3. Acerra and Meyer, pp. 160–161 suggest that the destruction of timber stocks in the arsenal was more devastating than the loss of ships. For a description of the burning of the French warships and arsenal facilities by the British officer who carried it out, see: "Rapport du Commodore Anglais Sidney Smith, incendiaire du port de Toulon en 1793, à l'amiral Hood"; Toulon 5 S 22, liasse 4. See also Hood's account of the evacuation: "Hood to H. Dundas. *Victory*, Hières Bay, December 20"; copy in Rose, pp. 158–160.

[73] "Rapport sur la marine de la république dans la Méditerranée par Barère, au nom du Comité de salut public, dans la séance du 14 Nivôse an II"; AP, vol. 82 pp. 613–616. The Decree which follows, pp. 616–617, includes articles to requisition men and materials, punish all who paralyze the naval war effort, and to mix sailors from the Atlantic and Mediterranean littorals in order to end *"le féderalisme maritime."* For a similar proposal to mingle administrators from different regions, see: Marine BB 3/59, f. 4. The decree conformed to Jeanbon's policy at Brest and his reaction to it reflected his long insistence that the Revolutionary Government give priority to naval

The Committee disagreed with its naval specialist, however, on fundamental naval strategy. Jeanbon believed that, while a powerful fleet was built up, small battle squadrons should put to sea to attack enemy convoys, and frigate patrols should destroy merchant shipping and report on naval activity. This would place the British on the defensive and give desperately needed training to French officers and crews.[74] To Jeanbon's frustration, the Committee of Public Safety forbade all such sorties and ordered warships to be conserved in port.[75] The Committee wanted to strike at "Perfidious Albion" directly and at the opening of 1794 was committed to an invasion of England.[76] At the end of January it indeed adopted an alternate plan to attack the British islands of Jersey and Guernsey, long known to be transit points for spies, *émigrés*, and arms for *chouans*.[77] Yet this was to be only a prelude to the strike against England itself.[78]

mobilization: "Le moment est donc enfin arrivé, où le Peuple français va s'occuper serieusement de sa marine"; Marine BB 3/61, f. 30, also ff. 56–60.
[74] Marine BB 3/38, ff. 545–547; BB 3/61, ff. 56–57. See also: Jeanbon, *Rapport des représentans*, pp. 12, 16–18; Lévy-Schneider, I, pp. 624, 635–639, II, pp. 745–746; Ligou, pp. 133–135, 139. Admiral Villaret-Joyeuse also told the Minister of Marine that frigate patrols were needed; Marine BB 4/37, f. 164.
[75] Marine BB 3/38, f. 543.
[76] The idea of invading England originated in the Old Regime and, during the Revolution, was suggested by Kersaint as early as January 1, 1793: "Les barques de nos pêcheurs sauront toujours transporter 100,000 hommes qui termineront la lutte sur les ruines de la Tour de Londres"; AP, vol. 56, pp. 111–116. Following the outbreak of war with Britain, invasion became a principal element of Revolutionary naval strategy. The Provisional Executive Council considered a formal proposal, that of Admiral Latouche-Tréville, on March 28, 1793, and on September 22 the Committee of Public Safety ordered Dalbarade to prepare to transport an army of 100,000 across the English Channel. See: Edouard Desbrière, *1793–1805: Projets et tentatives de débarquements aux îles britanniques*, 4 vols. (Paris: Librairie Militaire R. Chapelot et cie., 1900–1902), I, pp. 22–24, 32–34; Aulard (ed.), *Actes*, VII, pp. 1–2; Hampson, *La Marine de l'an II*, pp. 72, 81–83. The Quiberon mutiny and civil war within the Republic thwarted the invasion plans in 1793. But by January 1794 the Committee of Public Safety had again embraced the strategy of invasion; Lévy-Schneider, I, pp. 642–648.
[77] Hutt, pp. 73, 75, 103–104, 140–141. See also Alfred Cobban, "The Beginning of the Channel Isles Correspondence, 1789–94," in *Aspects*, pp. 225–238.
[78] The Committee of Public Safety sent Billaud-Varenne to Port-Malo (*ci-devant* St Malo) to supervise preparations for the Channel Islands invasion. The attack, originally scheduled to begin on February 19, 1794, was to be launched simultaneously against Jersey, Guernsey, and Aurigny, with the Brest fleet providing naval support. See: Desbrière, *Projets et tentatives*, I, pp. 37–53; Lévy-Schneider, I, pp. 671–673, 683 698–699, 704; Hampson, *La Marine de l'an II*, pp. 83–87; Ligou, p. 140.

This strategy required the mobilization of unprecedented naval strength,[79] and the Committee of Public Safety believed that Jeanbon Saint-André was the only Representative capable of supervising such an effort. Thus, on February 19, Jeanbon left Paris for his second mission to Brest. His colleagues invested him with unlimited powers over other agents of the Republic and, moreover, with authority over maritime activity in all ports; this conformed to Jeanbon's conviction that central coordination was essential. The other condition that he obtained was the transfer of Laignelot from Brest to the Vendée.[80] Jeanbon could focus all his attention on preparation of the Republic's navy for its coming trial.

Jeanbon's mobilization of the Atlantic fleet began, of course, during his first mission to Brest. Examination of his *arrêtés* from October 1793 to May 1794 reveals the wide range of concerns and activities pertaining to the maritime war effort. Naval mobilization can be divided roughly into four general categories: the construction, fitting out, and repair of warships; the levy of material and manpower; the regulation of the arsenal and its workforce; the formation and training of crews. Jeanbon's *arrêtés* dealt with all these areas, and they demonstrate that the accomplishments of the Revolutionary Government in the arsenal were achieved through the application of energetic and irrefutable National Authority.

One of Jeanbon's first *arrêtés*, that of October 25, had placed Jacques-Noël Sané in complete charge of all arsenal work at Brest.[81] Sané was France's most talented naval architect and his designs for standard warship types, adopted in 1786, gave the French navy ships which were markedly superior to their British equivalents.[82] Jeanbon appointed Sané, however, as much for the energy and efficiency he brought to the dockyards as for his technical skill. The construction of new warships was not to be Brest's primary role in mobilizing the Republic's navy; the port was to maintain the fleet while ships of the line and frigates were built at Rochefort and Lorient.[83] The main tasks for all three

---

[79] Hampson, *La Marine de l'an II*, pp. 92–93.
[80] See: Aulard (ed.), *Actes*, XI, p. 177; Lévy-Schneider, I, pp. 701–704; Ligou, p. 142.
[81] "Arrêté, le 4 brumaire an II"; Brest "Fonds Levot" 1965. See also: Jeanbon, *Rapport des représentans*, p. 13; Henwood and Monage, pp. 216–217; Bordonove, p. 101.
[82] See: Hampson, *La Marine de l'an II*, pp. 24–32; Lévy-Schneider, I, pp. 554–555; Taillemite, *Dictionnaire*, pp. 307–308; Loir, *La Marine royale en 1789*, pp. 201–202.
[83] Hampson, *La Marine de l'an II*, pp. 98–99, 144, 158.

ports during the winter of 1793–1794, however, was to complete vessels already under construction and to repair those which were in port or arrived from elsewhere.[84] Considerable effort at Brest also went into the salvage of old warships which had been rejected as hulks. They could no longer serve in the line of battle, but Sané cut away their upper gun decks to form *vaisseaux rasés*, or super frigates.[85] Just as important as augmenting the fleet's strength was the maintenance and repair of vessels already in commission. Some of the ships which returned from Quiberon with Morard de Galles were in dreadful shape and all needed to be completely replenished with basic stores.[86] Sané supervised all of this work during Jeanbon's missions to Brest.

The construction, fitting out, or repair of eighteenth-century warships required vast amounts of material.[87] Yet in the fall of 1793, Brest and the other Atlantic ports suffered from critical shortages of timber, iron, and hemp.[88] The Convention had requisitioned all materials necessary for naval mobilization at fixed prices,[89] but this was less significant than the ability of Jeanbon and other Representatives on mission to levy timber and other construction materials on location.[90] The lack of

[84] In the fall of 1793 there were five ships of the line under construction at Brest, and in March 1794 the Representatives ordered four frigates built. Lorient had four 74s and several light warships to finish, and in September 1793 Rochefort had completed only three of eight ships and eight of eleven frigates ordered early in the year; Hampson, *La Marine de l'an II*, pp. 130, 145, 150.
   During the winter Brest's arsenal repaired and armed *Le Patriote* and *L'Entreprenant* from Toulon; Marine BB 3/22, f. 398. The port's dockyards also dealt with *L'Éole* and three frigates from the West Indies, as well as *L'Apollon* (rebaptized *Le Gasparin*) and *L'America* which arrived at Rochefort and Lorient respectively, and were sent on to Brest. Lorient's arsenal repaired *L'Orion* from Toulon, as well as two frigates from India and one from the West Indies; Hampson, *La Marine de l'an II*, pp. 129–130, 145.
[85] See: Jeanbon, *Rapport des représentans*, p. 18; Marine BB 3/61, f. 30. Hampson, *La Marine de l'an II*, p. 129 lists eight ships slated for transformation into *vaisseaux rasés* at Brest, work requiring a dry dock and much labour; see also pp. 27–28.
[86] "Copie de procès-verbal du conseil tenu à bord du vaisseau le Terrible le 21 septembre 1793"; AD Finistère 8 L 88.
[87] Hampson, *La Marine de l'an II*, pp. 236–237 estimates that 100,000 cubic feet of wood and 168,000 pounds of hemp went into the construction and rigging of one 74-gun ship, while to sheathe its hull could require 33,750 pounds of copper and 4,800 pounds of nails. See also Boudriot, I, pp. 50–61.
[88] Marine BB 4/19, f. 320; BB 3/38, ff. 299, 403, 465–466. See also Hampson, *La Marine de l'an II*, pp. 130–131, 145, 151–152.
[89] AP, vol. 74, pp. 544–545. This decree of September 20, 1793 was introduced by Jeanbon, in the name of the Committee of Public Safety, to compensate for the loss represented by Toulon's surrender.
[90] Hampson, *La Marine de l'an II*, pp. 130–131, 144, 152, 158–159.

cannon and powder was more serious, and less easily solved. Jeanbon reported on January 6, 1794 that not a single cannon had arrived during his time at Brest and that arming the fleet was in jeopardy.[91] The cannon foundries, such as that at Indret, required the smooth operation of a widespread system and their production could not be accelerated merely with orders or threats from Representatives in the ports.[92] Jeanbon's *arrêtés* to melt down church bells for the casting of carronades, to strip the guns from harbour fortifications, and to encourage the manufacture of saltpetre demonstrate imaginative expediency.[93] The fleet's armament, however, depended principally upon the efforts of the central government.[94] Similarly, supplying Brest with food required more resources than those accessible to the Representatives on mission. The presence of the fleet after September exacerbated the difficulty of feeding the port's workforce during the winter of 1793–1794.[95] The supplies of grain available to all the naval ports had been diminished due to the Vendéan revolt,[96] and the Representatives made a major effort to revitalize Brest by sea, largely through the use of requisitioned coastal craft.[97] Norman Hampson argued that the success of the Revolutionary Government in supplying the ports with provisions and naval materials was due to the Montagnards' adoption of economic controls, and the political and administrative machinery to impose them.[98] Grant-

[91] Marine BB 3/61, ff. 56–57. See also Hampson, *La Marine de l'an II*, p. 133–136.
[92] See for example Jeanbon's frustration with the Indret foundry on April 3, 1794: Marine BB 3/61, f. 86. For a discussion of the cannon foundries during the Revolution, see Acerra and Meyer, pp. 167–169.
[93] "Arrêté, le 17 Nivôse an II"; Brest "Fonds Levot" 1965; Marine BB 3/61, ff. 13, 56–57.
[94] Along with ordering the transport of cannon to Brest, the Revolutionary Government also dispatched Representatives to the foundries where they used their authority in similar ways to those in the ports. See for example the levy of inhabitants to cut wood for charcoal by Romme, on mission to the foundries of the Dordogne: Marine BB 3/59, f. 112.
[95] See: Dalbarade to Representatives at Brest, September 23, 1793; AD Finistère 8 L 83; Marine BB 3/38, ff. 403, 545–547; BB 4/19, f. 320; BB 4/37, ff. 164, 168.
[96] Hampson, *La Marine de l'an II*, pp. 101–102, 131–133, 146, 152–153.
[97] Marine BB 3/23, ff. 44, 47; BB 3/61, ff. 74–75. See also Hampson, *La Marine de l'an II*, pp. 132–133, 230–233. On May 11, 1794 Jeanbon told the Committee of Public Safety that it was only the food in captured British prizes which enabled him and his colleagues to provision the fleet and feed the workers; Marine BB 3/61, f. 43.
[98] Hampson, *La Marine de l'an II*, pp. 128–129, 158–159, 229–230, 238–240. Hampson claims that with the economic controls under the Terror, France was on the verge of creating a navy which was equal or even superior to Britain's. This opportunity passed with the fall of Robespierre: "Cette dictature, en s'écroulant, entraîna avec elle la marine révolutionnaire qu'elle avait commencé à bâtir mais qu'elle n'eut pas le temps d'achever."

ing the importance of central coordination, it should be emphasized that the Montagnards mobilized the navy through Terror, or the absolute and ruthless exercise of Revolutionary authority. The levy of personnel required less central coordination and the authority of individual Representatives on mission was generally effective. As with needed supplies, a September decree requisitioned all seamen and maritime workers for the navy.[99] Jeanbon sought to augment this supply of sailors with two *arrêtés* which insisted that men from coastal regions, conscripted in the military levies, be allowed to opt for naval service.[100] He and his colleagues also clamped down on desertion, a traditional drain on naval crews, with restrictions on sailors' movements, searches of houses suspected of hiding deserters, and bounties for the capture of deserters.[101] For additional manpower required in the arsenals, Jeanbon's *arrêté* of February 25, 1794 conscripted carpenters and coopers from the Districts of fifteen Departments.[102]

Jeanbon was also concerned with the regulation of this workforce once it arrived in the dockyards and workshops, and with the overall organization of arsenal operations. Severely critical of the existing civil administration of the navy, he had abolished as early as September 27, 1793 the post of *ordonnateur civil*.[103] Once in Brest, Jeanbon was appalled

---

[99] AP, vol. 74, pp. 590–591.
[100] "Arrêté le 18 Nivôse an II," and "Arrêté le 19 Ventôse an II"; Brest "Fonds Levot" 1965. See also Marine BB 3/61, f. 63. As a fleet sortie became imminent, Jeanbon and the Committee of Public Safety ordered more army troops to serve aboard ships. This was to free trained seamen from serving cannon, and to compensate for Jeanbon's suppression of the regiments of marine infantry and the *canonniers matelots* on January 28, 1794. For a discussion of Jeanbon's abolition of the marine troops and gunners, see Lévy-Schneider, I, pp. 667–671. However, some companies of sea-gunners were still together and were sent to the fleet. See: Letter of *Adjoint* of 3rd Division to the Representatives at Brest, 15 Ventôse an II; AD Finistère 8 L 83; "Arrêté le 11 Floréal an II", Brest "Fonds Levot" 1965; Hampson, *La Marine de l'an II*, pp. 139–140, 213–214; Moreau de Jonnes, *Adventures in the Revolution and under the Consulate*, trans. Cyril Hammond (Paris, 1858; repr. in trans. London: Peter Davies Ltd., 1929), pp. 53–55.
[101] See: "Arrêté le 5 Ventôse an II", Brest "Fonds Levot" 1965; Arrêté of Laignelot, 3 Ventôse an II, AD Finistère 8 L 16; Hampson, *La Marine de l'an II*, pp. 210–212. These measures were in addition to articles in the navy's new Penal Code which prescribed harsh punishments for desertion.
[102] Arrêté of Jeanbon and Laignelot, 7 Ventôse an II; AD Finistère 8 L 13. See also: Hampson, *La Marine de l'an II*, pp. 136–138.
[103] AP, vol. 75, pp. 253–254. See also Lévy-Schneider, I, pp. 453–454. The *ordonnateur* was repalced with a *Chef Principal des Bureaux civils*, which was also abolished according to the decree of 14 Pluviôse (February 2, 1794). The *chef* of each particular service in the arsenal, while attending joint meetings of a *Conseil de Marine*, was to report directly to the Minister of Marine.

by the incidence of waste, fraud, and even theft of precious naval supplies.[104] He issued *arrêtés* to try to control both the delivery of materials to the arsenal, and their movement from storage parks and general magazines to individual workshops and ships.[105] As with sailors in the fleet, arsenal workers were insubordinate and undisciplined in 1793.[106] The drillers at Brest submitted a petition to Bréard and Tréhouart on October 1 which, while illuminating the harsh conditions facing workers, demonstrates that the doctrine of Popular Sovereignty had penetrated the arsenal.[107] Jeanbon was sympathetic to the workers, but he was also the Representative of the Revolutionary Government. His *arrêté* of 13 Nivôse (January 2, 1794) stated that order and efficiency must prevail in the dockyards and the workers must obey National Authority:

Considering that it is necessary, at all times, to maintain order and regulation in an establishment as important as that formed by the many workshops at the port of Brest, this necessity becomes more urgent and indispensable at a time when the multiplicity of work, and the necessary speed, demands the greatest attention so that the diverse branches of the service march together, none crossing or colliding to the prejudice of the public good; . . .

Considering that the good citizens who people our dockyards, will make for themselves a severe law to conform to the views of the Representatives of the People, because they know that the glory of the Republic is attached to the completion of the work with which they are charged, and they will themselves support our repression of those who, with less pure intentions, or by slothfulness, would neglect to fulfill the task which has been entrusted to them; . . .[108]

The way to achieve this efficiency and subordination was set out in several articles on various subjects: the precise hours for opening and closing the

---

[104] Jeanbon, *Rapport des représentans*, pp. 2, 13. See also Ligou, p. 112.
[105] "Arrêté le 7 Brumaire an II," and "Arrêté le 9 Nivôse an II"; Brest "Fonds Levot" 1965. The second *arrêté* was proposed as a decree in Jeanbon, *Rapport des représentans*, pp. 28–31.
[106] Arsenal workers submitted a petition to the Convention in January 1793, and in June Sevestre and Cavaignac complained at the lack of discipline in Brest's arsenal: Marine BB 3/43, ff. 30–33; BB 3/38, f. 39. For other complaints by Representatives prior to Jeanbon's arrival, see: Marine BB 3/38, ff. 244, 264–267. See also Hampson, "Ouvriers," pp. 314–327.
[107] Marine BB 3/38, ff. 353–354. See also Hampson, "Ouvriers," pp. 289–290.
[108] "Arrêté le 13 Nivôse an II", Brest "Fonds Levot" 1965; see also Marine BB 3/61, f. 9. For a discussion of this *arrêté*, and Jeanbon's assertion of National Authority into the arsenal, see Hampson, "Ouvriers," pp. 445–446, 442–443.

arsenal; roll-calls to be held at each workshop or yard, and harsh punishments for workers who missed them; regulations to prevent the waste or theft of materials. Despite the thoroughness and rigour of this order, Jeanbon supplemented these regulations with an additional *arrêté* on April 25, 1794 which increased surveillance of conscripted workers in the arsenal, but also improved material incentives.[109] Arsenal workers' traditional behaviour was not changed easily, and even for Jeanbon it was one thing to issue an order and quite another to see amazing results.

Lack of sailors continued to be a problem in 1793–1794, but the state of those already in the navy was also of grave concern. The epidemics which ravaged Morard de Galles' squadron caused Jeanbon to take several measures to improve the health conditions for naval crews. On January 4, 1794 he ordered every sailor or novice embarking on a vessel of the Republic to be issued with a standard kit-bag of adequate clothing.[110] The same *arrêté* also provided for regular laundry, rations of *eau-de-vie* (the *matelot*'s equivalent to British grog) for seamen exposed to foul weather, and made commanders responsible for clean and salubrious conditions aboard ship. Diet was as vital as sanitation or clothing, and one of the first *arrêtés* issued during Jeanbon's second mission to Brest ordered that crews receive daily rations of fresh meat, salt-beef, cod, or cheese in rotation.[111]

Jeanbon was equally determined that naval conscripts receive appropriate training. The Representative sought to establish "schools of seamanship" aboard every vessel by encouraging topmen and able seamen to transform novices into sailors.[112] Yet even before proclaiming

---

[109] "Arrêté le 6 Floréal an II", Brest "Fonds Levot" 1965. The *arrêté* included further attempts to regulate the traditional, and all too easily abused, practice of workers carrying off chips from the dockyards. See also Hampson, "Ouvriers," p. 446.

[110] "Arrêté le 15 Nivôse an II", Brest "Fonds Levot" 1965; the *arrêté* is proposed as a decree in Jeanbon, *Rapport des représentans*, pp. 31–34. See also Bordonove, pp. 92–93. Bréard and Tréhouart's report of October 1, 1793 that the crew of *L'Insurgente* needed to be given clothing, as well as the testimony of several captains in September, indicates the extent of the problem: Marine BB 3/38, f. 360; "Copie de procès-verbal du conseil tenu à bord du vaisseau le Terrible le 21 septembre 1793", AD Finistère 8 L 88.

[111] Marine BB 3/61, f. 36. The menu prescribed in the *arrêté* of February 27, 1794 is printed in Bordonove, p. 145.

[112] This *arrêté*, proclaimed on November 3, 1793, is proposed as a decree in Jeanbon, *Rapport des représentans*, pp. 34–36. See also Bordonove, pp. 91–92. Those sailors who trained novices were to receive pay raises. Villaret-Joyeuse reported in November 1793 that he was seeking to train officers and crews in naval tactics: Marine BB 4/19, f. 322; see also Lévy-Schneider, I, pp. 565–566.

this measure, Jeanbon ordered that sailors receive the benefits of basic education. His *arrêté* of 27 Vendémiaire (October 18, 1793) had established the position of "instructor" for all warships of twenty or more guns, this official being required to give lessons in reading, writing, and arithmetic, as well as elementary navigation theory.[113] The preamble of the *arrêté* stated that the Republic was obliged to provide this opportunity to all citizens, especially when education could reveal hidden talents which would enable them to serve the nation better. The instructors were to occupy the position aboard ship held by chaplains in the old navy and, in his Report to the Convention, Jeanbon expressed the Jacobin conviction that ignorance was the source of Counter-Revolution and that education would destroy "fanaticism," thus providing the Republic's navy with loyal crews:

Upon reflecting on the causes which produced the movements in the squadron, we saw easily that the ignorance of sailors had contributed heavily. These men, roving perpetually from one hemisphere to another, could not participate in the benefits of education and thus have been easier to deceive. A residue of fanaticism, fruit of this same ignorance, reigned aboard the fleet. Several men recalled that they formerly had chaplains, and they had the weakness to miss them. We thought it necessary to destroy this prejudice. But, convinced that error resists force and concedes to reason, we dared propose to these simple and good men the choice between chaplains and instructors: they did not hesitate. The sailor recognizes the advantage of having his son in his sight to supervise his education, and to think that equality is no longer a vain word, since *la Patrie* offers to all the means to qualify for all ranks.[114]

The introduction of instructors aboard ship illustrates that the Montagnards saw naval mobilization, like other seemingly pragmatic concerns, in ideological terms.[115] The fifth article of Jeanbon's *arrêté*

[113] "Arrêté le 27 Vendémiaire an II"; Brest "Fonds Levot" 1965. The *arrêté* is proposed as a decree in Jeanbon, *Rapport des représentans*, pp. 24–28, and in a letter of 30 Vendémiaire from Jeanbon and Bréard to the Convention; AP, vol. 77, pp. 683–684. These lessons were to be mandatory for all boys and novices under eighteen, and were to be available for all older sailors during their watches below.

[114] Jeanbon, *Rapport des représentans*, pp. 6–7.

[115] Romme was the Representative on mission to Périgueux, where he was to accelerate the work of the naval cannon foundries of the Dordogne. His report to the Convention of May 7, 1794, after a brief mention of the state of the foundries, described in great detail an elaborate "Fête du travail" celebrated by the workers which paid homage to Republican principles: "Ainsi s'est terminée cette fête touchante et simple qui a servi à honorer le travail, comme le principal bien de l'homme libre; la vertu, comme le flambeau de la révolution et le fondement du gouvernement républicain; la nature, comme la source des plus douces jouissances de l'homme

ordered the use of materials for the teaching of Revolutionary principles to the sailor-students: "A carefully prepared edition of the Declaration of the Rights of Man, and of the Constitutional Act, will be made directly, to which will be added explanatory notes, short and simple, and historical tracts chosen by preference among the actions of the defenders of liberty."[116] The Republic's navy, like the army of the Year II, was intended to be a "school of Jacobinism."[117] This active politicization did not focus entirely on the lower deck. Despite the decree of October 7, 1793, and Jeanbon's own demands for the complete purification of the officer corps, the removal of nobles from the fleet was neither systematic nor absolute.[118]

vertueux; la Patrie comme celle à qui nous nous devons tout, force, talens, vertu, fortune."; Marine BB 3/59, f. 109.

[116] "Arrêté le 27 Vendémiaire an II"; Brest "Fonds Levot" 1965. Other articles in the *arrêté* ensured the careful political scrutiny of all perspective instructors, and the just as careful surveillance of their behavior and teaching once assigned. Rouver, pp. 118–119 cites a proposal to create libraries aboard ships where sailors could read: "L'histoire de la marine, où ils auraient vu quelles lois absurdes avilissaient, sous le despotisme, les marins le plus utiles par des distinctions ridicules, violant leurs droits les plus sacrés, les excluant des places gênant le commerce maritime, donnant les forces navales de la nation en propriété aux familles nobles; ils auraient vu, de même, que les plus illustres marins furent des sans-culottes: Ruyter, Tromp, Jean-Bart, Duguay-Trouin, Duquesne, Cassard; . . ." For the distribution of such material, see: Letter of Prieur de la Marne to Villaret-Joyeuse, 11 Floréal an II; AD Finistère 8 L 9. Regarding the political education of sailors, see also Lévy-Schneider, I, pp. 540–541.

[117] For detailed discussions of the Revolutionary Government's efforts to indoctrinate the army in 1793–1794, see: Bertaud, pp. 191–229; Lynn, pp. 124–162. The politicization of sailors was linked, at times explicitly, to the Montagnards' repression of any dissent. On March 16, 1794 Brest's Revolutionary Tribunal condemned the quartermaster of *L'Impétueux* to death for Counter-Revolutionary speech. He was guillotined on a pontoon in the harbour and the judgement was posted in all ships of the fleet. See: Lévy-Schneider, II, pp. 723–724; Bordonove, p. 146; Henwood and Monage, p. 212.

[118] There were certainly dismissals of officers on no other grounds than their noble origins. See, for example, Dalbarade's letter of 30 Vendémiaire (October 21, 1793) to the Representatives at Brest regarding an officer serving at Le Havre: "je l'ai chargé seulement de surveiller la construction d'une frégate d'après les excellent témoignages qui m'avaient été rendus de son patriotisme et de sa capacité, mais je viens d'apprendre qu'il est de la classe de ci-devant nobles, et je l'ai destitué"; AD Finistère 8 L 83.

Marc Paillé, "Les Destitutions d'officiers nobles dans la marine de l'an II: un arrêté du Comité de Salut public du 10 frimaire (30 novembre 1793)," *Université de Nantes. Centre de recherches sur l'histoire de la France Atlantique. Enquêtes et documents*, 3 (1975), 105–126 argues that, despite the high number of noble officers dismissed, the Convention had issued no law or decree which explicitly ordered the exclusion of all nobles from the navy. Paillé, however, discovered a previously unknown document in the Nantes Archives: a proscription list of 130 aristocratic officers giving the Committee of Public Safety's reasons for their dismissals. Paillé suggests that this *arrêté* of November 30, 1793 was never published because it was never intended for application, but was held in reserve to respond to *enragé* criticism or to use against specific individuals.

The rhetoric of such a purge, however, allowed the Montagnard Representatives to scrutinize all officers for correct political attitudes. Officers of the Republic's navy needed more than talent or courage. As Jeanbon explained, replacements for those dismissed had to have pure patriotism as defined by the agents of the Revolutionary Government:

We demanded from them observations, information, facts which could determine our confidence; otherwise we removed them, along with nobles, tools of the old navy, and intriguers. No enemy of the People, no equivocal or doubtful man, was admitted when we could tear away the mask behind which he was hiding.[119]

Lévy-Schneider argued that the appointments of naval officers by Jeanbon and his colleagues were based as much on talent as on political conviction.[120] This seems to have been the case with the five captains whom Jeanbon promoted to the rank of *contre-amiral* in October 1793. It has already been noted that Bouvet and Vanstabel distinguished themselves by maintaining discipline aboard their ships at Quiberon. Vanstabel quickly demonstrated the merit of his promotion in November when six ships under his command evaded an enemy fleet in the English Channel and returned to Brest with eleven prizes.[121] Cornic-Dumoulin, the eldest of these five new rear-admirals, had been called to Paris in April 1793 to act as deputy to the Minister of Marine, and he served capably in his new rank as Commandant at Port-Malo (formerly Saint-Malo).[122] Nielly, former captain of *La Résolue*, performed admir-

[119] Jeanbon, *Rapport des représentans*, p. 10. For similar statements of the ideological imperative behind officer replacements, see also: Marine BB 3/38, ff. 396, 405; AN AF II 294/reg. 2463, f. 44, ". . . nous n'avons choisi que des sans-culottes . . ."
[120] Lévy-Schneider, I, pp. 527–529, 536–538. This argument is supported by Hampson, *La Marine de l'an II*, pp. 187–204. An example cited by Lévy-Schneider is that of Thévenard whom Jeanbon released, overriding the Military Tribunal at Rennes which arrested him as a suspect, and reinstated as Commandant at Brest: Marine BB 3/23, f. 33; BB 3/38, ff. 547–551.
[121] Vanstabel's division left Brest on November 16, 1793 to intercept a British convoy supposedly en route to support the Vendéan army; the division encountered Howe's battle fleet instead. Jeanbon was delighted with Vanstabel's performance and the results of his mission, which he reported to the Convention, and it reinforced his belief in the benefits of short patrols by small units of the fleet. See: Jeanbon, *Rapport des représentans*, pp. 10–12; Lévy-Schneider, I, pp. 567, 623–624; Guérin, V, pp. 458–459; Rouvier, pp. 137–138.
[122] Pierre-François Cornic-Dumoulin was born in 1731 at Bréhat (Côtes-du-Nord) and first went to sea as a ship's boy. He served in the navy as an *officier bleu* during the Seven Years' War and an *officier auxiliaire* during the American War. Appointed as an

ably as commander of a squadron during the Prairial Campaign.[123] Martin, like Nielly, was only a frigate captain when he was promoted, but early in 1794 Jeanbon sent him to Toulon to reorganize the Mediterranean fleet.[124] His accomplishments at Toulon were praiseworthy, but there is little doubt that Martin's ardent Jacobinism was partly responsible for his promotion.[125]

The best example of Jeanbon placing talent before ideological imperatives would seem to be his promotion of Villaret-Joyeuse and his subsequent appointment as commander-in-chief of the Brest fleet. The Admiral's merit is not in question, but even in his case evidence of Revolutionary purity influenced the Representative's decision. Shortly after his arrival in Brest, Jeanbon received a letter from some junior officers who, portraying themselves as fervent supporters of the Montagnards, suggested Villaret-Joyeuse as an appropriate fleet commander:

Citizen Representatives, time presses; we need a leader to command the fleet and a leader who, above all, is truly imbued with sincere love for the Republic. We are tormented from all sides and our most cruel enemies surround us. Hasten, citizen Representatives, to name him . . . The firmness and the talents of citizen Joyeuse render him worthy of your choice: we will never fear a firm

officier des classes at Morlaix in 1786, Cornic was promoted to *capitaine de vaisseau* in April 1793. He was sent to Port-Malo, to help direct the invasion of Jersey and Guernsey, principally because of his detailed knowledge of the English Channel. His son commanded a frigate in Villaret-Joyeuse's fleet during the Prairial Campaign. See: Taillemite, *Dictionnaire*, p. 70; Six, *Dictionnaire biographique*, I, p. 264; Lévy-Schneider, I, pp. 532–533; AD Finistère 8 L 85.

[123] Joseph-Marie Nielly was born in 1751 at Brest, the son of an *officier bleu*. As a ship's boy, he was wounded at the Battle of Quiberon Bay in 1759. Nielly became a merchant captain 1774 and entered the navy as *lieutenant de frégate* in 1778. He was made a *sous-lieutenant de vaisseau* in 1786 and promoted to *capitaine de vaisseau* in January 1793. See: Taillemite, *Dictionnaire*, p. 249; Six, *Dictionnaire biographique*, II, pp. 256–257; Lévy-Schneider, I, p. 533.

[124] Pierre Martin was born at Louisbourg in 1752 and entered the navy as a pilot. He served in the American War as a petty officer under d'Estaing and an *officier auxiliaire* in Vaudreuil's squadron. Martin was made a *sous-lieutenant de vaisseau* in 1788 and promoted to *capitaine de vaisseau* in February 1793. Prior to being made *contre-amiral*, he commanded *La Tartue* at Rochefort. See: Taillemite, *Dictionnaire*, p. 231; Six, *Dictionnaire biographique*, II, p. 161; Lévy-Schneider, II, pp. 531–532.

[125] Lévy-Schneider, I, p. 532 refers to Martin as a "montagnard exalté." Levot, p. 156 cites a letter of 24 Nivôse (January 13, 1794) which Martin wrote to Jeanbon from Rochefort expressing his enthusiasm for those who promoted Terror in that port: "J'ai appris avec le plus grand plaisir que Laignelot avait été te rejoindre. Deux sans-culottes comme vous détruiront bientôt à Brest les intrigues calotines. Le fameux Hugues est partie (*sic*) aujourd'hui. Les révolutionnaires de Rochefort l'ont vu partir avec chagrin; ceux de Brest, je l'espère, le verront arriver avec plaisir."

Plate 7. Louis-Thomas, comte Villaret de Joyeuse.
Engraving by Maurin (Phot. Bibl. Nat. Paris)

man, this is necessary to command a fleet. We are true *sans-culottes* and
republicans who want [a Republic] one and indivisible.[126]

Jeanbon's disregard of Villaret-Joyeuse's nobility is less important than
his conclusion that the Admiral's untainted reputation would enable

[126] The letter is printed in full in Levot, p. 123, and Chevalier, pp. 120–121.

him to command a highly politicized fleet more effectively. The Montagnard vision of the Republic included both political purity and complete obedience to the nation: Virtue and Terror.[127] Jeanbon promoted two of the officers who wrote the letter in praise of Villaret-Joyeuse, Lieutenants Lucadou and Lefrancq, and gave them command of *Le Patriote* and *L'Entreprenant* respectively.[128] Lucadou also submitted a violent, if confused, denunciation of "royalists" and "conspirators" among the naval commanders and administrators at Brest.[129] Blatant demonstrations of Jacobin sentiment were rewarded.

It is hardly surprising that Representatives of the Revolutionary Government scrutinized officer candidates for any hint of disloyalty to the new regime, especially given the pall of suspicion hanging over the navy since the surrender of the Mediterranean fleet.[130] Loyalty to the regime, as discussed above, implied complete acceptance of the Montagnard vision of the Republic. Jeanbon's political agenda for the navy, however, had more specific objectives. His Report on the Quiberon mutiny demanded a purge in order to end the divisions and factional conflict which had torn the officer corps apart and produced chaos throughout the fleet. Despite the dismissals, arrests, and appointment of "only true Republicans," Jeanbon was still concerned about unity in the navy in May 1794. He attributed French defeats under the Old Regime to the independence of captains who refused to support their leaders, and he informed the Committee of Public Safety that such sentiment had not yet disappeared:

The spirit of isolation is not so entirely banished, that it is no longer necessary to curb it; it is all the more dangerous that it re-emerges under the uniform of liberty. There would no longer be time to put a brake on pride when, not acknowledging unity in manoeuvres, it led to disaster. . . . It is necessary that Admirals of the Republic not be abandoned at any moment of an action, as

[127] The best statement of this is Robespierre's speech on the Principles of Political Morality, delivered to the Convention on February 5, 1794; AP, vol. 84, pp. 330–337.
[128] Marine BB 3/38, f. 396. In this letter of 2 Brumaire (October 23, 1793) to the Minister, Jeanbon and Bréard wrote: "Nous nous occupons des remplacemens et nous faisons bien en sorte de n'avoir que des vrais et courageux Républicains à la tête des vaisseaux français."
[129] Marine BB 4/39, ff. 13–14.
[130] Hampson, *La Marine de l'an II*, pp. 187–190 supports the necessity of such scrutiny: "Soulignons une fois de plus qu'en l'An II le gouvernement révolutionnaire tenait plus à éloigner des traîtres possibles, qu'à profiter des connaissances et de l'expérience des hommes suspects."

Conflans, d'Estaing and all the others were. The Admiral answers to you with his head for the execution of your orders, this is the rule. But his responsibility disappears if the law does not guarantee the obedience of the instruments which you place in his hands.[131]

Jeanbon had expressed the same concern for potential disobedience bred by disunity to Villaret-Joyeuse in March: "All movements [of the fleet] must be uniform, simultaneous, executed with as much precision as speed; and the divisions, which in the navy of despotism, dishonoured the French flag, must be known no longer in the regenerated navy of the Republic."[132] Thus his *arrêté* of 1 Germinal (March 21, 1794) proclaimed that National Representation, in the person of Jeanbon himself, would accompany the fleet to uphold the Admiral's authority: "There, impassive as the law, severe as justice, indulgent to the weak, but inexorable against the presumptuous, it will distribute acts of authority with which it is entrusted."[133] The same *arrêté* ordered new signals prepared to indicate the instant dismissal and replacement of any ship's captain. Jeanbon also broadened the law he had introduced on February 2, 1794, which promised the guillotine for captains who surrendered their ships,[134] to include those who failed to execute an order signalled by the Admiral or to repeat his signals.[135] This was less than a week before the fleet sailed for its confrontation with the British. Jeanbon had mobilized the navy, but did not intend it to function independently of direct Revolutionary control. He believed that the coercion of punitive regulations, and his presence to enforce them,

---

[131] Marine BB 3/61, f. 43.
[132] "Arrêté, le 1er Germinal an II"; Brest "Fonds Levot" 1965.
[133] Ibid.
[134] "Le capitaine et les officiers des vaisseaux de ligne de la République qui auront amené le pavillon national devant les vaisseaux ennemis, quel qu'en soit le nombre, à moins que le vaisseau ne fût maltraité au point qu'il courût risque de couler bas et qu'il ne restât que le temps nécessaire pour sauver l'équipage, seront déclarés traîtres à la patrie et punis de mort"; AP, vol. 84, pp. 211–213. See also: Lévy-Schneider, I, pp. 690–691; Guérin, VI, pp. 19–20; Chevalier, p. 128; Tramond, p. 569; Bordonove, p. 167.
[135] "Arrêté, le 21 Floréal an II"; Brest "Fonds Levot" 1965. The *arrêté*'s preamble stated: "Que la loi doit, par sa juste sévérité, garantir à la Nation que les scandales et les crimes de l'ancienne marine, où l'on a vu plus d'une fois les commandans généraux et particuliers abandonner indignement leurs chefs, ne se reproduiront pas dans la marine régénerée de la République; . . ." See also Lévy-Schneider, II, pp. 787–788.

would assure Admiral Villaret-Joyeuse of his subordinates' obedience in battle. An examination of the Prairial Campaign will reveal whether or not the purges and politicization of the navy under the Montagnards created an officer corps which was loyal to its commander.

Despite the Revolutionary Government's plans to invade British territory, the navy's strategic priority in the spring of 1794 was defensive. On December 24, 1793 a small squadron under the command of Admiral Vanstabel sailed from Brest bound for the United States. On board was the new French Minister plenipotentiary, Jean-Antoine-Joseph Fauchet, and five million *livres* in gold with which he was to purchase American grain and flour.[136] The Committee of Public Safety anticipated serious food shortages in the spring and Fauchet expressed the importance the government placed in his mission: "to save our *patrie* from the horrors of famine and to rid it of intriguers who would sell it to despotism."[137] Vanstabel arrived in Chesapeake Bay on February 12, 1794 and began to assemble a convoy of French ships, many of which had fled Saint-Domingue following the slave revolt, civil war, and foreign invasion of the colony,[138] and American vessels chartered to carry food and naval supplies.[139] Vanstabel left the United States with 127 merchantmen on April 10, and both the Admiral and the

---

[136] Marine BB 3/38, ff. 528–529, 540–541; BB 3/23, f. 55. For Fauchet's instructions from the Committee of Public Safety, see: "Mémoire pour servir d'instructions aux commissionaires du Conseil-exécutif provisoire près les Etats-Unis, 25 Brumaire an II"; Frederick J. Turner (ed.), *Correspondence of the French Ministers to the United States, 1791–1797*, Vol. II: *Annual Report of the American Historical Association, 1903* (Washington: United States Government Printing Office, 1904), pp. 288–294. See also: Lévy-Schneider, I, pp. 634–635; Bordonove, pp. 120–121.

[137] Fauchet to the Minister of Foreign Affairs, 2 Nivôse an II (December 22, 1793); Turner (ed.), p. 300. The Revolutionary Government also required Fauchet to repair the diplomatic damage caused by his predecessor, Edmond-Charles Genêt, who had abused American neutrality to promote French privateering and an expedition against Spanish Florida; Melvin H. Jackson, *Privateers in Charleston, 1793–1796; an account of a French Palatinate in South Carolina* (Washington: Smithsonian Institution Press, 1969), pp. 3–14, 21–36.

[138] Genêt to the Minister of Foreign Affairs, October 5 and December 9, 1793; Turner (ed.), pp. 263–264, 275–276. See also: Saintoyant, II, p. 130; Jouan, p. 181. Regarding the situation in Saint-Domingue, see David Geggus, *Slavery, War, and Revolution: The British Occupation of Saint Domingue, 1793–1798* (Oxford: Clarendon Press, 1982), pp. 33–78.

[139] French Commissioners to the Minister of Marine, 24 Ventôse and 1 Germinal an II (March 14 and 21, 1794), Commissioners to the Minister of Foreign Affairs, 28 Ventôse and 1 Germinal an II (March 18 and 21, 1794); Turner (ed.), pp. 302–320.

Committee of Public Safety knew that the convoy needed more protection than his small escort force could provide.[140]

The invasion of Jersey and Guernsey, already much delayed, was aborted in March[141] and the Revolutionary Government dispatched a battle squadron to rendezvous with Vanstabel's convoy in the Atlantic. Admiral Nielly sailed from Brest with five ships of the line, along with smaller warships, on April 10.[142] This force would certainly stiffen the convoy's escort, but the government was prepared to send the entire Brest fleet to sea if the American convoy was in jeopardy and it sent Jeanbon and Villaret-Joyeuse orders to this effect.[143] A large British fleet commanded by Admiral Howe was sighted off Ouessant on May 5 and, given expectations of Vanstabel's imminent arrival, Jeanbon ordered the Admiral to prepare to sail.[144] Jeanbon was already established aboard *Le Montagne* (120), Villaret-Joyeuse's flagship, when Prieur de la Marne arrived to replace him as Representative at Brest while he was at sea.[145] Contrary winds, which had kept the fleet inside the

[140] See Vanstabel's letter to the Committee of Public Safety of April 5, 1794; cited by Bordonove, p. 152. See also Lévy-Schneider, II, pp. 744–745.

[141] The Committee of Public Safety ordered the army assembled near Port-Malo to break up on March 21, 1794, however it denied Jeanbon's repeated requests to recall the naval forces stationed at Cherbourg and in Cancale Bay under the command of *Contre-amiral* Cornic. The Committee hoped these would still escort an army of invasion and this denied Villaret-Joyeuse eight ships of the line and several frigates at the Battle of 13 Prairial. For Jeanbon's correspondence to Cornic regarding the junction of his forces with the Brest fleet in May, see: Marine BB 3/61, ff. 44, 49–50. See also Lévy-Schneider, II, pp. 735–743, 762–765, 787.

[142] Lévy-Schneider, II, pp. 745, 762; Bordonove, p. 153. Nielly's squadron included *Le Sans-Pareil* (80), *Le Patriote* (74), *Le Trajan* (74), *Le Téméraire* (74), and *L'Audacieux* (74), as well as three frigates, one corvette, and two dispatch vessels.

[143] "L'intention du Comité de Salut public est que l'armée soit prête à appareiller pour se réunir à Nielly et Vanstabel avec la division de Cancale, dans le cas où l'armée ennemie sortirait elle-méme. Mais dans ce cas le salut du convoi qui est attendu sous la protection de Vanstabel et Nielly, devra être ton seul but, ta seul règle de conduite," Dalbarade à Villaret-Joyeuse, 7 Floréal an II (April 26, 1794); cited in Lévy-Schneider, II, p. 762. Jeanbon echoes this imperative in his letter to Cornic of May 11; Marine BB 3/61, f. 44.

Hampson, *La Marine de l'an II*, pp. 234–236 argues that the decision by the Committee of Public Safety to risk a fleet sortie proves that it was not resolved to preserve the Republic's navy and enable it to equal or surpass the British navy in strength and efficiency. In contrast, Lévy-Schneider, II, pp. 781–785 argues that although the sortie was premature, in that the potentially formidable fleet was still unready for battle, it was absolutely necessary to ensure the convoy's arrival.

[144] Lévy-Schneider, II, p. 766; Henwood and Monage, pp. 225–226. See also Villaret to Jeanbon, 18 Floréal an II (May 7, 1794); AD Finistère 8 L 84.

[145] Prieur to Guesnor and Topsent at Rochefort, 29 Floréal an II (May 18, 1794); AD Finistère 8 L 9.

roadstead, shifted on May 16 and Villaret-Joyeuse's twenty-five ships of the line weighed anchor and began the Prairial campaign.[146] Villaret-Joyeuse set a westerly course into the Atlantic, hoping to make contact with Vanstabel or Nielly before the enemy found the convoy. During the first eleven days at sea, the Admiral and Jeanbon received further intelligence regarding the convoy's departure and anticipated landfall; they also learned that Nielly had not joined the escort.[147] But on May 19, the fleet came upon one of Nielly's ships, Le Patriote (74), which had become separated from its squadron.[148] Along with his concern over the location of friendly and hostile forces, Jeanbon was disappointed with the seamanship of some of the French captains: "There is much enthusiasm in the fleet, and several captains are well trained; but there are three or four whose ignorance is beyond anything one could say."[149] The Representative's response, characteristically, was to inform all captains that they were under his surveillance.[150] At dawn on 9 Prairial (May 28, 1794) the frigates signalled a large number of sails to the north: the British fleet.[151] Villaret-Joyeuse formed his line of battle and steered to maintain the

[146] May 16 was 27 Floréal on the Republican calendar, but it is convenient to refer to the entire voyage and the several days of contact between the opposing fleets as the Prairial campaign. Regarding the Brest fleet's departure, see: Jeanbon Saint-André, *Journal sommaire de la croisière de la flotte de la république, commandée par le contre-amiral Villaret; tenu jour par jour par le représentant du peuple Jeanbon Saint-André, embarqué sur le vaisseau la Montagne* (Paris: Imprimerie Nationale, l'an II), p. 1 [BN 8 Le39 74]. It should be noted that only *Le Montagne* flew the new tricolour flag which Jeanbon established for the navy with his decree of February 15, 1794; AP, vol. 85, pp. 77–78. All other French ships flew the flag created early in the Revolution, a white flag with a small tricolour in the upper quarter; see Maurice Loir, "L'Adoption du Pavillon Tricolore," *Revue maritime et coloniale*, 122 (1874), 600–619.

[147] Jeanbon, *Journal sommaire*, p. 3.

[148] Ibid., pp. 4–6. Upon joining the main fleet, Captain Lucadou collided with the corvette *La Mutine* while manoeuvering under the flagship's stern. During the next seven days Lucadou demanded medicine three times and requested to leave the fleet. Villaret-Joyeuse refused; ibid., pp. 10, 16. See also: Guérin, VI, p. 27; Lévy-Schneider, II, pp. 805, 809; Bordonove, pp. 192–193, 198–200.

[149] Jeanbon, *Journal sommaire*, p. 13; see similar statements on pp. 10, 15.

[150] On May 26 the Admiral dispatched a frigate to inform ships of the rear of his displeasure at the fleet's formation and to relay his order throughout the fleet that sailors not at their posts be demoted. Jeanbon added his own message: "J'ajoutai à cet ordre celui de dire aux capitaines que j'observais avec soin le degré d'exactitude que chacun apportait à remplir ses devoirs, et d'enjoindre de tenir de notes exactes des officiers de quart qui se laisseraient arriérier, afin que ces notes, remises au représentant du peuple, il pût acquérir une connaissance détaillée du mérite de tous les officiers employés sur les vaisseaux de la République"; Jeanbon, *Journal sommaire*, pp. 15–16.

[151] Ibid., p. 17; Marine BB 4/37, f. 188.

windward position and to lead Howe away from the convoy. The British were able to close with the rear of the French line only at sunset and five ships engaged *Le Révolutionnaire* (110), inflicting sufficient damage to force her to abandon the fleet.[152] The next morning Howe tried again to bring the French to action. After heavy firing between the vanguards of both fleets, Howe tacked and cut off two ships of the French rear, *L'Indomptable* (80) and *Le Tyrannicide* (74). Villaret-Joyeuse wore ship and *Le Montagne* led the French centre and van around to rescue the two embattled ships. The Admiral's manoeuvre showed skill and audacity, but it was not well executed by all of his captains.[153] Bompard of *Le Montagnard* (74) did not obey the signal and continued west, abandoning the fleet.[154] Although Villaret-Joyeuse prevented the capture of *L'Indomptable* and *Le Tyrannicide*, both were disabled and a frigate towed *L'Indomptable* away from the fleet.[155] These losses were compensated by the arrival of Admiral Nielly and three ships of the line on the morning of

[152] Both Jeanbon and Villaret-Joyeuse were surprised to discover that *Le Révolutionnaire* was gone on the morning of May 29 and clearly had little knowledge of the evening's engagement: Jeanbon, *Journal sommaire*, pp. 17–18; Marine BB 4/37, f. 188. The British claimed that *Le Révolutionnaire* struck to *HMS Audacious* after a fierce action which disabled that ship, and in which the French captain was killed, but escaped after dark. See the copy of Howe's letter to Stephens, supplementary to that of June 2; in De Poggi (ed.), *A Narrative of the Proceedings of His Majesty's Fleet, under the command of Earl Howe, from the second of May to the second of June 1794* (London, 1796; facsimile repr. London: Cornmarket Press, 1971), pp. 36–37; see also pp. 9–10. On May 29 *Le Révolutionnaire* met *L'Audacieux* (74), separated from Nielly's squadron, which towed her to Rochefort where all of her officers were imprisoned; Marine BB 4/39, ff. 134, 225–238, 240. See also Lévy-Schneider, II, pp. 811–816.

[153] Marine BB 4/37, ff. 188–189. Jeanbon, *Journal sommaire*, pp. 19–20 praised the conduct of the captains of *L'Indomptable* and *Le Tyrannicide*, but expressed concern regarding that of others. The British praised Villaret-Joyeuse: "it is but justice to Monsieur Villaret to say, that, as far as he had gone, he showed considerable ability as a sea-officer; and by such distant and continued, though partial, cannonade, he gradually brought his fleet into practice; but his manner of recovering the two ships in question claims the admiration of his enemies and the thanks of his country"; De Poggi (ed.), p. 12; see also pp. 37–39.

[154] *Le Montagnard* was badly damaged during the opening phase of the engagement, but left the fleet without permission. She was taken in tow by *La Seine*, commanded by Cornic's son, and eventually came upon Vanstabel's convoy with which she returned to Brest. See: Lévy-Schneider, II, pp. 823, 825–826; Bordonove, pp. 211, 215–217; Warner, p. 67.

[155] *Le Tyrannicide* remained with Villaret-Joyeuse's fleet, but was taken in tow by *Le Trajan*; Bordonove, pp. 211–215. Jeanbon, *Journal sommaire*, p. 24 did not realize that *L'Indomptable* or *Le Montagnard* were gone until May 31.

11 Prairial (May 30).[156] Fog descended on the two fleets and prevented the renewal of fighting for the next two days.[157] Villaret-Joyeuse used the time to reorganize his line of battle: *Le Téméraire* (74) was placed in the van which Admiral Bouvet commanded from *Le Terrible* (110); Nielly transfered his flag from *Le Sans-Pareil* (80) to *Le Républicain* (110) and took command of the fleet's rear.[158]

On the morning of 13 Prairial (June 1, 1794) the French fleet, now numbering twenty-six battleships, was in line ahead formation, steering north-west parallel to the British line of twenty-five ships. Unlike the first two days of action, Howe had the weather gage and at 9:00 a.m. he bore up and steered towards the French line in four columns. It was his intention to break through and attack from leeward, and he was successful in cutting the French line in at least four places.[159] Firing became general and the battle developed into a confused mêlée of engagements between separate groups of ships.[160] "The battle was

[156] Jeanbon, *Journal sommaire*, pp. 21–22. Two of his ships having separated from his squadron, Nielly arrived with only *Le Sans-Pareil* (80), *Le Téméraire* (74), and *Le Trajan* (74); Lévy-Schneider, II, pp. 826–827. Bordonove, p. 217 claims that the third ship was *Le Trente-et-un Mai* (74), but it seems more likely that Captain Ganteaume's command was one of the original twenty-five ships which sailed from Brest.

[157] See: Jeanbon, *Journal sommaire*, pp. 22–23; De Poggi (ed.), pp. 13, 39; Chevalier, p. 217.

[158] See: De Poggi (ed.), p. 15; Lévy-Schneider, II, pp. 828–831; Bordonove, p. 219. There is some confusion in the sources regarding the French line on June 1, 1794. British contemporary sources include French ships which were not present on that date, including *Le Mont-Blanc* which was the name of *Le Trente-et-un Mai* before it was rebaptized: De Poggi (ed.), pp. 16, 91, attached Plan of Battle; Steel, Plan between pp. 4–5. Troude, II, pp. 328–329 also includes this ship. Villaret-Joyeuse's "Ordre de Bataille Naturel de l'Armée de la République dans le combat du 13 Prairial," Marine BB 4/37, f. 192 does not include *Le Tourville* (74), which all other sources agree took part in the battle. The best lists of the twenty-six French ships of the line present on June 1 are those in Bordonove, p. 220 and Warner, p. 175. There is also disagreement regarding the position of the ships. The initial line of battle depicted on the map included in this study, itself adapted from that in Steele, is based partly on British sources, partly on Villaret's line, and partly on the likely position of individual ships given their opponents in the ensuing mêlée.

[159] Guérin, VI, p. 33 says the French line was cut at four places; Mahan, *Influence of Sea Power upon the French Revolution*, I, p. 140 says six places as does Lévy-Schneider, II, p. 834; Bordonove, pp. 227–229 gives seven places. Regarding Howe's battle plans, see: De Poggi (ed.), p. 17; Mahan, *Influence of Sea Power upon the French Revolution*, I, pp. 136–138; Warner, pp. 35–36; Bordonove, pp. 224–226.

[160] For accounts of the Battle of 13 Prairial, and the numerous individual engagements, see: Guérin, VI, pp. 33–49; Chevalier, pp. 138–145; Mahan, *Influence of Sea Power upon the French Revolution*, I, pp. 131–147; Rouvier, pp. 155–172; Troude, II, pp. 231–237; Tramond, pp. 595–600; Lévy-Schneider, II, pp. 832–848; Jouan, pp.

horrible, the fleets were entangled and confused," observed Jeanbon from the flagship's quarter deck, "they fought each other at the range of a pistol shot, with unheard of ferocity. The whirling clouds of gunsmoke prevented one from seeing what was happening around us and our frigates reported that *Le Montagne* was invisible to them for two hours and they could only rally to the sound of its formidable artillery."[161] Howe's flagship, *HMS Queen Charlotte* (100), broke through a gap in the French line opened by *Le Jacobin* (80), the ship directly astern *Le Montagne*.[162] The *Queen Charlotte* raked Villaret-Joyeuse's flagship in passing, killing many of her crew including Flag-Captain Basire, then came about and the two ships exchanged broadsides in a fierce contest which lasted over an hour.[163] By far the most famous duel, however, was between *HMS Brunswick* (74) and *Le Vengeur-du-Peuple* (74). The *Brunswick* followed the *Queen Charlotte* toward the French line and was engaged by *Le Vengeur*. The two ships became hooked together and fired into one another at point-blank range.[164] After more than three hours of combat, *Le Vengeur* began to sink. This episode was to be distorted as a piece of Jacobin propaganda,[165] but even the factual account in Captain Renaudin's report is stirring:

185–190; Bordonove, pp. 231–237. For the British perspective, see: De Poggi (ed.), pp. 17–21, 26–28; Warner, esp. pp. 76–82, 104–122, 127–141.
[161] Jeanbon, *Journal sommaire*, pp. 26–27. See also the account of the battle from *Le Jemappes* (80) in Moreau de Jonnes, pp. 59–67.
[162] "Il [Captain Gassin of *Le Jacobin*] s'aperçut trop tard de sa faute, il mit son grand hunier sur les mât, mais il se trouvait engagé sous le vent à nous, et la vérité est qu'il ne savait plus ce qu'il faisait. L'amiral anglais, qui s'aperçut de son embarras, voulut en profiter; il laissa arriver sur *Le Montagne* dans l'intention de couper la ligne derrière ce vaisseau, ce qu'il fit en effet"; Jeanbon, *Journal sommaire*, p. 26. See also: Marine BB 4/37, f. 190; Mahan, *Influence of Sea Power upon the French Revolution*, I, pp. 139–140; Bordonove, pp. 238–241.
[163] Villaret-Joyeuse reported that during an hour's engagement, which left his flag-captain, maritime agent, and most of his officers dead, *Le Montagne* sustained fire from at least six enemy ships, but dismasted the enemy flagship; Marine BB 4/37, ff. 190–191. Jeanbon, *Journal sommaire*, p. 29 reports 300 casualties aboard *Le Montagne*. See also Howe's letter to Stephens of June 2, 1794; copy in De Poggi (ed.), pp. 26–27.
[164] Among many accounts of this action, see: Guérin, VI, pp. 40–41, 45–46; Mahan, *Influence of Sea Power upon the French Revolution*, I, pp. 140–144; Bordonove, pp. 245–254. For excerpts from British logs and eyewitness testimony, see Warner, pp 122–126.
[165] The "Legend of *Le Vengeur*" began with Barère's speech to the Convention on 21 Messidor an II (July 9, 1794) which described the loss of the ship in most dramatic terms and claimed the wounded and dying crew all chose patriotic death over dishonourable surrender: "imaginez le vaisseau le Vengeur, percé de coups de canons, s'entr'ouvrant de toutes parts, et cerné de tigres et de léopards anglais; un équipage

The flags were lowered, several English ships having launched their boats, the pumps and buckets were soon abandoned. Boats along side received all those who could throw themselves in. They had hardly pulled clear when the most frightful spectacle presented itself: those of our comrades who remained on board *Le Vengeur*, hands raised to heaven, implored with lamentable cries the help for which they could no longer hope. Soon the ship and the unhappy victims it contained disappeared. Amidst the horror which this heart-rending tableau inspired in all of us, we could not help a mixed sentiment of admiration and grief. We heard as we drew away some of our comrades raising their voices again for their *patrie*, the last cries of these unfortunates were those of *Vive la République*; . . .[166]

The outcome of the battle had been decided, however, long before *Le Vengeur* went down. *Le Montagne* made more sail and moved away from the *Queen Charlotte*, the British flagship having lost her topmasts and being unable to follow, and when the smoke cleared at 11:00 a.m., Villaret-Joyeuse found himself alone. Only Bouvet's *Le Terrible* had held her position in the van and most of the French rear was out of action. Several French vessels were dismasted and drifting slowly downwind. The Admiral managed to rally twelve of his ships and led them

composé de blessés et de mourants, luttant contre les flots et les canons; tout'à-coup le tumulte du combat, l'effroi du danger, les cris de la douleur des blessés cessent, tous montent ou sont portés sur le pont; tous les pavillons, toutes les flammes sont aborés: les cris de *vive la République! vivent la liberté et la France* se font entendre de tous côtés: c'est le spectacle touchant et animé d'une fête civique, plutôt que le moment terrible d'un naufrage. Un instant ils ont dû délibérer sur leur sort; ils voient les Anglais et la patrie; ils aimeront mieux s'engloutier que la déshonorer par une capitulation: ils ne balancent point, leurs derniers voeux sont pour la liberté et pour la République; ils disparoisent! . . ."; AP, vol. 93, pp. 31–33. The impact of Barère's propaganda can be seen in the references to *Le Vengeur* made by provincial Jacobin clubs during 1794 in their campaigns to raise funds for the navy: Marine BB 3/59, ff. 174–175; and in Marie-Joseph Chénier's "Ode au Vengeur." The image of Republican martyrdom suffered when Captain Renaudin returned to France in a prisoner exchange, but the legend persisted. See: Albert Le Roy, "Histoire et la Légend: Le Rapport de Barère et le Rapport de Renaudin sur le combat du Vengeur," *La Révolution française*, 1 (1881), 407–419; Maurice Loir, "Le 'Vengeur' d'après les documents des Archives de la marine," *Revue Bleue, Revue politique et littéraire*, 49: 22 (28 May 1892), 697–701; "Deux lettres de Pol de Courcy sur l'affaire du Vengeur (13 prairial an II – 1er juin 1794)," *Les Cahiers de l'Iroise*, 35e Année – No. 3 (Nouvelle série) (Messidor 1988), pp. 164–166; Bordonove, pp. 281–299; Henwood and Monage, pp. 229–231.

[166] "Procès-verbal des officiers du Vengeur, 1 Messidor an II"; Marine BB 4/39, ff. 405–407. The report is cited in several secondary sources, but the entire *procès-verbal* is printed in Bordonove, pp. 327–331.

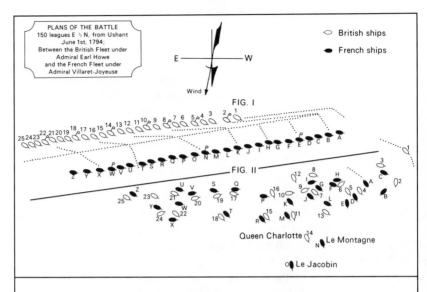

FIG. 1 Represents the British Fleet bearing down in line-of-battle. The corresponding figures 22, 18, 14, 10, 8, 5 represent the situation of the flag-ships at the commencement of the action, and the oblique dotted lines the track to their respective opponents.

FIG. II Represents the situation at approx. 10:45 A.M. Note the engagements between the opposing Fleet flag-ships Le Montagne (N) and Queen Charlotte (14), between Le Vengeur (R) and Brunswick (15), and the withdrawal of Le Jacobin (0).

Map 9. The Battle of 13 Prairial (June 1, 1794) [Accompanied by Legend giving names of ships and commanding officers]. *After [Main Map]* "Plans of the Battle, . . . June 1st 1794 . . ." in David Steel, *Steel's Naval Chronologist of the War* (London, 1802; facsimile reprint London: Cornmarket Press, 1969), p. 4. *Note*: This plan was corrected in accordance with information from French archival sources. [*Insert*: Site of battle] "The Glorious First of June" in R. Natkiel and A. Preston, *Atlas of Maritime History* (New York: Bison Books, 1986), p. 88.

French Fleet

A	Le Convention (74),	Capt. Allary
B	Le Gasparin (74),	Capt. Tardy
C	L'America (74),	Capt. Lhéritier
D	Le Téméraire (74),	Capt. Morel
E	Le Terrible (110),	Capt. Leray; Admiral Bouvet
F	L'Impétueux (74),	Capt. Douville
G	L'Eole (74),	Capt. Bertrand Keranguen
H	Le Mucius (74),	Capt. Larreguy
I	Le Tourville (74),	Capt. Langlois
J	Le Trajan (74),	Capt. Dumoutier
K	Le Tyrannicide (74),	Capt. Dordelin
L	Le Trente-et-un Mai (74),	Capt. Gantheaume
M	Le Juste (80),	Capt. Blavet
N	Le Montagne (120),	Capt. Basire; Admiral Villaret-Joyeuse
O	Le Jacobin (80),	Capt. Gassin
P	L'Achille (74),	Capt. La Villegris
Q	Le Patriote (74),	Capt. Lucadou
R	Le Vengeur du Peuple (74),	Capt. Renaudin
S	Le Northumberland (74),	Capt. Etienne
T	Le Jemappes (80),	Capt. Desmartis
U	L'Entreprenant (74),	Capt. Lefrancq
V	Le Neptune (74),	Capt. Tiphaigne
W	Le Républicain (110),	Capt. Longer; Admiral Nielly
X	Le Sans-Pareil (80),	Capt. Courant
Y	Le Scipion (80),	Capt. Huguet
Z	Le Pelletier (74),	Capt. Barrade

British Fleet

1	Caesar (80),	Capt. Molloy
2	Bellerophon (74),	Capt. Hope; Rr-Adm. Pasley
3	Leviathan (74),	Capt. Seymour
4	Russel (74),	Capt. Payne
5	Royal Sovereign (100),	Capt. Nicholls; Adm. Graves
6	Marlborough (74),	Capt. Berkeley
7	Defence (74),	Capt. Gambier
8	Impregnable (90),	Capt. Westcott; Rr-Adm. Caldwell
9	Tremendous (74),	Capt. Pigott
10	Barfleur (98),	Capt. Collingwood; Rr-Adm. Bowyer
11	Invincible (74),	Capt. Pakenham
12	Culloden (74),	Capt. Schomberg
13	Gibraltar (80),	Capt. Mackenzie
14	Queen Charlotte (110),	Capt. Curtis, Capt. Douglas; Admiral the Earl Howe
15	Brunswick (74),	Capt. J. Harvey
16	Valiant (74),	Capt. Pringle
17	Orion (74),	Capt. Duckworth
18	Queen (90),	Capt. Hutt; Rr-Adm. Gardner
19	Ramillies (74),	Capt. H. Harvey
20	Alfred (74),	Capt. Bazely
21	Montague (74),	Capt. Montagu
22	Royal George (110),	Capt. Domett; Adm. A. Hood
23	Majestic (74),	Capt. Cotton
24	Glory (90),	Capt. Elphinstone
25	Thunderer (74),	Capt. Bertie

to prevent the capture of those which were disabled.[167] Five were rescued, and later taken in tow; but, when Villaret-Joyeuse eventually bore off to the north-west, six ships of the line were abandoned to Howe.[168] On June 11 the fleet anchored outside the entrance to Brest's roadstead, and Vanstabel's convoy arrived the following day.[169] Jeanbon was thus able to report in the Convention on July 4 that despite a "military reverse," a "great political victory" had been achieved.[170]

There is some merit in Jeanbon's claim of a strategic victory. Securing the convoy's safe return was the reason the Brest fleet was ordered to sea, Villaret-Joyeuse had led Howe away from the convoy's track most effectively, and after the battle the British fleet was in no state to pursue Vanstabel's transports. It is indisputable, however, that the outcome at sea was defeat. The French lost seven ships and had over 5,000 men killed, wounded, or taken prisoner, while the British suffered fewer than 1,100 casualties and returned to Portsmouth with all their vessels.[171] Yet in regard to the greater effort to create a regenerated

---

[167] Marine BB 4/37, f. 190; Jeanbon, *Journal sommaire*, pp. 27–28. See also: Guérin, VI, pp. 44–45; Mahan, *Influence of Sea Power upon the French Revolution*, I, pp. 144–146; Lévy-Schneider, II, pp. 840–842; Bordonove, pp. 229, 255–256.

[168] Villaret-Joyeuse ordered his frigates to take disabled ships in tow, but some failed to acknowledge or were unable to obey. The ships captured by the British were *Le Sans-Pareil* (80), *Le Juste* (80), *L'America* (74), *L'Achille* (74), *Le Northumberland* (74), and *L'Impétueux* (74). See: De Poggi (ed.), pp. 21, 30; Guérin, VI, pp. 46–49. For the ultimate fate of these ships, see Warner, p. 85. The ships which were towed from the battle were *Le Mucius* (74), *Le Scipion* (80), *Le Jemappes* (80), *Le Républicain* (110), and *Le Terrible* (110) which was totally dismasted; Jeanbon, *Journal sommaire*, pp. 28–30.

[169] Marine BB 4/37, f. 202. On June 9, 1794 Villaret-Joyeuse's nineteen remaining ships sighted a British squadron off the Ile d'Ouessant. Admiral Montagu overestimated the strength of the French fleet and retreated, allowing Villaret-Joyeuse to continue to Brest unopposed. See: Jeanbon, *Journal sommaire*, p. 32; Warner, pp. 70–72; Bordonove, pp. 262–263. Although the warships were anchored on June 11, and witnessed the lights of the arriving convoy on the night of the 12th, Jeanbon reported that the fleet had not yet entered the roadstead on June 18; Marine BB 3/61, f. 52.

[170] AP, vol. 92, pp. 388–390.

[171] The following casualty figures are given in De Poggi (ed.), pp. 31–34: 1,098 seamen and marines killed or wounded in the British fleet during the actions of May 29, 30 and June 1, 1794; 62 British officers killed or wounded; p. 21 gives the figures of 690 French killed and 580 wounded in the six prizes, with an estimate of 320 lost in *Le Vengeur*. Other estimates of French casualties include: Chevalier, p. 146, "around five thousand were put out of action"; Warner, p. 87, 3,500 killed or wounded and 3,500 taken prisoner; Henwood and Monage, p. 227, 1,654 killed, 1,000+ wounded, 4,000 taken prisoner. Among these casualties were four captains who were killed or died of wounds: Basire, Douville, Desmartis, Bertrand Keranguen.

navy for the Republic, there are issues more significant than the possible failings of Villaret-Joyeuse's tactics, the superiority of British gunnery, or the inexperience of French crews.[172] The aftermath of the campaign, rather than the battle, demonstrated Jeanbon's failure to achieve unity in the navy.

Shortly after the fleet limped back into Brest, Admiral Villaret-Joyeuse reported to the Commission of Marine and Colonies[173] on why his forces were defeated on 13 Prairial. He exaggerated the strength of the British fleet (he claimed the enemy numbered thirty-four ships of which eight were first-rates), but he was accurate in judging that enemy gunnery was superior to his own.[174] The Admiral was also justified in pointing to the dearth of trained seamen in his fleet.[175] His principal explanation for the battle's outcome, however, was the inexperience or incapacity of his captains, particularly those who yielded in the face of enemy broadsides and allowed the British to break his line:

Give command of ships of the line to experienced men who have proved themselves. Courage is innate no doubt in French Republicans, but the man

---

[172] Jeanbon's analysis of the battle led him to the conclusion that the admiral's position aboard a ship of the line prevented him from gaining sufficient and immediate intelligence regarding the course of the battle and from being able to direct all units of his fleet: he was reduced to the role of commander of one vessel. Therefore Jeanbon ordered, in his *arrêté* of 24 Priarial, that admirals should direct battles from frigates; Jeanbon, *Journal sommaire*, pp. 32–33, 35–37. Virtually every account of the campaign includes analysis or explanation for the battle's outcome, and these reflect the wider interpretative bias of the historian: Guérin, VI, p. 45 blames the loss of the six ships on Jeanbon's cowardly misjudgement in ordering Villaret-Joyeuse to depart before they had been rescued; Chevalier, pp. 145–153, 162 emphasizes the superiority of British gunnery and the inexperience of French officers and men, but he judges Jeanbon to have been ultimately responsible for these weaknesses; Mahan, *Influence of Sea Power upon the French Revolution*, I, pp. 149–155 concentrates on the reasons for British success rather than French defeat, but his whole study suggests that the Revolution had fatally disregarded the immutable laws of sea power; Lévy-Schneider, II, pp. 858–861 reflects Jeanbon's assessment that the faults of particular captains, rather than the tactical leadership of Villaret-Joyeuse, were responsible for the defeat.
[173] The Committee of Public Safety, to further ensure its control of government, abolished the Provisional Executive Council and replaced the ministries with twelve Commissions on 12 Germinal (April 1, 1794); see Stewart (ed.), pp. 521–525.
[174] Marine BB 4/37, f. 204. Villaret-Joyeuse observed that thirteen French ships were dismasted as opposed to only four or five British vessels, but he was wrong to assume that British gunners were trained to aim high and he probably overestimated the importance of British employment of grape and chain shot. The Admiral also emphasized the dryness of French masts and the poor quality of cordage.
[175] Marine BB 4/37, ff. 204–205. Villaret-Joyeuse asked that greater pay or distinction be given to petty officers so that not all would demand to be made officers.

accustomed to gunfire has great advantages, and if all captains had done their duty, if without consulting tactics they had consulted the sentiment of nature to fly to the rescue of one's brother, 13 Prairial would never have been made infamous to the French navy.[176]

It was hardly a coincidence that Jeanbon issued an *arrêté* on June 23, four days later, which called for the dismissal or arrest of several captains.[177] Jeanbon ordered the Prosecutor of Brest's Revolutionary Tribunal specifically to prepare indictments against Captain Gassin of *Le Jacobin* for abandoning his post and permitting the line of battle to be cut, and against Captain Bompard of *Le Montagnard* for deserting the fleet on 10 Priarial.[178] These officers seemed destined to share the fate of Coëtnempren, Duplessis-Grénédan and Le Dall Keréon, but the political climate was about to change dramatically. Jeanbon left Brest on June 24 for Paris, and from there he was sent on mission to Toulon to supervise the mobilization of a new Mediterranean fleet.[179] His departure deprived Villaret-Joyeuse of political support and on June 30 the Admiral informed the Representative that a cabal had formed against them in the fleet.[180] He expressed far greater concern in a letter of August 30, depicting a grim situation for the port and for himself because Jeanbon could not return:

One must not mince words, my dear Jeanbon, all goes badly here and worsens day by day. There is not a chief in the workshops or the port who does not perceive a total change and a frightful relaxation. Subordination is still main-

---

[176] Marine BB 4/37, f. 205.
[177] Captains Tardy (*Le Gasparin*), Langlois (*Le Tourville*), Barrade (*Le Pelletier*), and Lieutenant Benoît, who took command of *L'Eole* following the death of Bertrand Keranguen, were dismissed. Captains Allary (*Le Convention*) and Dumoutier (*Le Trajan*) were sent before the Revolutionary Tribunal; Marine BB 4/38, f. 223. See also Marine BB 3/59, f. 146.
[178] Marine BB 4/38, f. 223. See the copy of Bompard's letter to Jeanbon of 2 Messidor (June 20, 1794) protesting his arrest; BB 4/38, f. 209. For the interrogations of Jean-Baptiste-François Bompard and Jean-André Gassin by the *accusateur-public* on June 21, 1794, see Marine BB 4/38, ff. 225–226, 246. See also the report of the commission designated to investigate the damage to *Le Montagnard*, Marine BB 4/38, ff. 235–237. Jeanbon also ordered an indictment prepared against Captain Cornic of *La Seine* which towed *Le Montagnard*. See the letters of *Contre-amiral* Cornic in response to his son's arrest and eventual release; AD Finistère 8 L 85.
[179] See: Lévy-Schneider, II, pp. 890–897, 911–1031; Ligou, pp. 174–188; Crook, *Toulon*, pp. 160–165.
[180] Marine BB 4/37, f. 211.

tained in the roadstead, but this is by awarding more punishments in a day than I inflicted in a week [*décade*]. I hope the new Representatives, that are awaited from one moment to the next, will revive the spirit of the workers and sailors. It is high time.

Think sometimes, my dear Jeanbon, of the poor Admiral of the fleet whom the intriguers torment cruelly since they learned that you must no longer return, . . .[181]

The fall of Robespierre on 9 Thermidor (July 27, 1794), which occurred between the Admiral's two letters, altered drastically the direction of the Revolution. The Terror was repudiated, and gradually the other members of the Great Committee of Public Safety were tainted with its responsibility.[182] This made Villaret-Joyeuse's relationship with Jeanbon Saint-André potentially dangerous and a letter to the Commission of Marine and Colonies, in which he reported that the navy was attached only to the Convention and not to individuals,[183] demonstrated his concern with being compromised by the reaction against the Terror.

This fear was justified. Thermidor saved Gassin and Bompard from the Revolutionary Tribunal and the guillotine, but they were still to appear before a Court Martial. In October 1794, the two captains wrote an account of the Prairial campaign to show that their conduct had been beyond reproach. More than a justification of their actions, it was a scathing attack on Villaret-Joyeuse, whom Gassin and Bompard held wholly responsible for the defeat and accused of denouncing his captains to cover his own incompetence or treachery.[184] The document was,

---

[181] Ibid., f. 225.

[182] The strong reaction against the Terror in Brest was initially directed against the members of the local Revolutionary Tribunal: Roffin, *Dénonciation de la conduite atroce du Tribunal Révolutionnaire de Brest. Roffin à ses concitoyens (Le doigt de Robespierre est ici . . .)* (Brest: Guffroy, SD); Brest "Fonds Levot" 1991 [10]. The reaction was extended to a violent denunciation of Jeanbon in April 1795 which was presented to the Convention in May: *Dénonciation des citoyens de la commune de Brest contre Prieur (de la Marne), et Jean-Bon Saint-André, déposé au Comité de Sûreté-général par les Députés extraordinaires de la même commune, le 8 Prairial, 3e année Républicaine* (Paris: Imprimerie de la veuve d'Antoine, no date) [BN Fol Lb41 4377]. Jeanbon was arrested on May 28, 1795 and spent five months in prison. See: Henwood and Monage, pp. 237–247; Ligou, pp. 188–198; Lévy-Schneider, II, pp. 968–974, 1036–1069.

[183] Marine BB 4/37, f. 223. It is ironic that Villaret-Joyeuse also claims that the fleet was entirely free of factional intrigue.

[184] Ibid., ff. 194–199. Gassin and Bompard's critique of Villaret-Joyeuse's leadership took the form of a demand that he answer questions about the campaign which he

287

however, as much a political denunciation as a critique of tactics and it condemned the Admiral as a Terrorist: "Villaret, you will reproach yourself forever for wanting to gratuitously dishonour ardent patriots. The time of Terror is passed; the terrible word of guillotine will no longer intimidate those who have long kept silent. . ."[185] Gassin and Bompard wanted to escape punishment with this Thermidorian diatribe, but it is indicative of a fundamental problem in the Republic's navy. Tréhouart and Faure, the Representatives on mission to Brest since September 1794, saw the attack on Villaret-Joyeuse as a serious threat to the discipline and unity of the fleet:

The position in which we find ourselves appears to merit all our care and yours to maintain the subordination and discipline so necessary in the fleet; above all when a party arises and wants to sow divisions among the commanders. Two ship's captains, detained by our colleague Jeanbon Saint-André after the last battle and reentry of the squadron, are the men who strive to propagate this system by publishing a denunciation against the Admiral rather than responding to the charges of which they must clear themselves; . . .[186]

The situation was all the more dangerous because the two captains had supporters in Brest,[187] and Tréhouart and Faure seized the manuscript at the printers and sent it, along with its authors, to the Committee of Public Safety.[188] Yet such a measure could no longer guarantee an end to dissent. The Prosecutor of Brest's Revolutionary Tribunal dispatched numerous pieces of evidence to Paris, but he warned that the impending trial would disorganize the navy by requiring numerous senior officers whose presence in Brest was all that prevented the spread of malevolence and insubordination. What he was really suggesting was that the Court Martial would expose the divisions in the fleet.[189]

had supposedly tried to suppress: Why did he abandon *Le Révolutionnaire* on 9 Prairial? Why did he not attack on 10 Prairial? Why, on 13 Prairial, did he not execute the manoeuvres which would have saved all the disabled French ships and captured those of the enemy? Why did he anchor on 23 Prairial, knowing a British squadron was at large, without sending support to the convoy?
[185] Marine BB 4/37, ff. 198–199. Captain Lucadou of *Le Patriote*, dismissed by Prieur, denounced not only Villaret-Joyeuse but also Jeanbon in an account of his conduct during the Prairial campaign; Marine BB 4/38, ff. 252–253. See also Lucadou's petition to Robespierre against Jeanbon and his petitions to the *Comité de Marine*; AN DXVI/3, No. 25.
[186] Marine BB 3/61, f. 217.
[187] Ibid., f. 218.
[188] Ibid., f. 221.
[189] Marine BB 4/38, ff. 212–213.

It was a year before judgement was actually passed on the two captains: a Court Martial acquitted Bompard in November 1795;[190] another found Gassin "guilty but excusable" in February 1796, and condemned him to three months suspension of pay and employment.[191] Among the numerous pieces of testimony supporting the officers,[192] the most revealing is a letter of June 15, 1794 to Jeanbon from Captain Ganteaume of *Le Trente-et-un Mai* (74). Ganteaume, one of the best officers in the fleet,[193] asked the Representative not to send Bompard before the Revolutionary Tribunal. Only a proper naval Court Martial was competent to try him: "it is a question of the facts of manoeuvre and tactics, and not of conspiracy or Counter-Revolution . . ."[194] What Ganteaume requested was an end to the politicization of naval discipline and justice. Jeanbon and the Revolutionary Government had restored order and ended local interference, which naval commanders could only applaud. Yet the Terror had neither unified the navy around the Montagnard poles of National Authority and Republican principle, nor eliminated the atmosphere wherein professional disagreement could be given ideological significance. The case of Bompard and Gassin demonstrates that naval authority remained tenuous and political invective could still determine justice, colour discipline, and decide promotions. Non-partisan loyalty to the state, the ideal of many officers who tried to serve under the Republic, remained impossible.

[190] Ibid., f. 259; see also ibid., ff. 205–209, 216–217. The captains of the ships captured by Howe were acquitted in October 1795, Marine BB 4/37, f. 447.
[191] Marine BB 4/37, f. 469; see also BB 4/37, ff. 323–468, BB 4/38, f. 218.
[192] See: "L'Etat Major du vaisseau de la République le Montagnard au citoyen Représentant Jeanbon Saint-André, 26 Prairial an II," Marine BB 4/38, ff. 227–229; Testimony of *enseigne* Crevel on the past conduct of Captain Gassin, BB 4/38, ff. 256–257. The latter praised Gassin for his actions as commander of *La Topaze* at Toulon in 1793, which is in contrast to ex-*ordonnateur* Puissant's denunciation of Gassin as a coward for failing to take the frigate out of Toulon; Puissant, *Pétition*, "Faits," p. 8.
[193] Honoré-Joseph-Antoine Ganteaume was born at La Ciotat (Bouches-du-Rhône) in 1755 into a family of merchant seamen. During the American War, he served with distinction as an *officier auxiliaire* under d'Estaing and Suffren. Made *sous-lieutenant de vaisseau* in 1786, Ganteaume commanded a ship of the *Compagnie des Indes* from 1791 until being captured by the British in 1793. He was promoted lieutenant upon his release in September and promoted *capitaine de vaisseau* in February 1794. He commanded *Le Trente-et-un Mai* during the Prairial campaign and was wounded in action. Ganteaume served in the Irish campaign, in the Mediterranean under Martin, and was wounded at the Battle of the Nile in 1798. His most famous exploit, however, was returning Bonaparte from Egypt in 1799 aboard the frigate *La Muiron*. See: Taillemite, *Dictionnaire*, pp. 132–133; Six, *Dictionnaire biographique*, I, pp. 480–481.
[194] Marine BB 4/38, ff. 230–234.

Jeanbon Saint-André's accomplishments in mobilizing a navy for the Republic were impressive. Under his direction French dockyards outfitted or repaired warships in record time. He and his colleagues located and requisitioned naval stores and construction materials with tremendous efficiency, and levied workers and sailors despite the pressures of war and civil insurrection. These enormous efforts were made possible by the restoration of strong government authority, which was a principal theme of the Terror throughout France. Central control was imposed on the naval ports and insubordination was ended in the fleet. To accomplish this, Jeanbon curbed the notion of Popular Sovereignty expressed in the direct democracy of sailors and the independence of local administrations by replacing the ambiguous "Will of the Nation" with the categorical fiat of Revolutionary Government. Yet this government, representing the dictatorship of a single faction, had ideological objectives beyond the immediate demands of wartime emergency and sought to politicize all aspects of naval service. Restoration of order did not signal a relaxation of vigilance, and subordination was to be maintained by continual denunciation and purge. If the army thrived under the Montagnards, the navy was a better reflection of French society as a whole: instead of bringing lasting unity under the banner of a democratic Republic, the Terror only perpetuated bitter divisions.

CHAPTER

10

CONCLUSION: REVOLUTIONARY POLITICS
AND THE FRENCH NAVY

Although historians of the Revolution have paid it little attention, the French navy after 1789 provides a striking illustration of the development of Revolutionary politics. There is a close connection between naval history and political history. This is not limited to the role of sea power in shaping international relations, but includes the clash of ideas and interests behind a navy's creation and maintenance. Gerald Graham argued that even in England, where the fleet became crucial to national survival, naval development did not occur outside domestic politics:

In brief, the acquisition of naval strength, and thence, naval superiority, is quite as much a political problem as one of professional naval practice. Admirals with their fleets, remarked Sir John Fortescue, "are mere weapons wielded in the hand of the statesman." Admittedly, other elements have influenced the ultimate use of the weapons: ships' design, tactics, hygiene, finance, the military situation on land, the state of public morale at home. But in the long run, statecraft has remained the most potent determinant, and naval history, so-called, is essentially political and diplomatic history.[1]

Given the cost of building and maintaining ships of war, and the complex organization required to furnish them with men and stores, navies demand sustained political will over a long period. Furthermore naval officers derive their authority from the government they serve. Thus a navy reveals the stability of a state's political institutions and the vitality of its ideas of governance. The experience of the French

[1] Gerald S. Graham, *Empire of the North Atlantic: The Maritime Struggle for North America* (Toronto: University of Toronto Press, 1950; 2nd edn, 1958), p. x. Regarding the origins of French sea power in this context, see pp. 21–40, 58–64.

291

navy from 1789 to 1794 reflects the evolution and impact of a new conception of political authority which was central to the French Revolution: Popular Sovereignty.

In 1789 the navy embodied the qualities of the Old Regime and reflected eighteenth-century society. Aristocratic privilege dominated the officer corps and few non-nobles achieved high rank. Many of those who served the fleet as auxiliary officers in wartime, but were denied permanent rank, resented the exclusive *Grand Corps*. Yet by the 1780s administrators and some members of the *Grand Corps* suggested that officer recruitment should be based more on merit. The Minister of Marine, the marquis de Castries, integrated non-noble *sous-lieutenants* into the officer corps in 1786 as part of his larger effort to modernize the navy. Thus the institution fit within the reforming climate of the age. Claims that the navy had reached a state of excellence at the end of the Old Regime, however, need to be qualified. The fleet's success during the War of American Independence concealed profound structural weaknesses. The navy's conscription system failed constantly to provide enough sailors to man the ships. For construction materials, the naval arsenals relied upon foreign sources which could be cut off in wartime. Most importantly, the financial weakness of the French state limited its naval power in absolute terms and affected all aspects of the service.

Beyond constant and vigorous infusion of state capital, the navy needed permanent and well-supplied bases. The logistical and financial support for France's widely separated naval ports required central control and management. Located in maritime provinces which did not always share the interests of the state, the naval ports depended on political stability and strong, recognized government authority. Thus the Revolution of 1789 had a profound impact on the navy. In overturning the Old Regime, Revolutionary Popular Sovereignty discredited the principle of executive power. Springing from the ideas of eighteenth-century philosophy but taking definite shape during the pre-Revolutionary struggles, this ideology claimed that ultimate authority must rest with the nation, rather than with the king. Moreover, it suggested that the government and the People must be one and the same.

The "Toulon Affair" of 1789 revealed the implications of Popular Sovereignty for the navy. Just as the National Assembly legitimized its defiance of absolute monarchy, a Revolutionary municipality overturned royal authority in Toulon on the basis of popular will. This municipal revolution occurred in the context of an economic crisis which created unrest among the port's arsenal workers. Given measures of economy in the dockyards, they directed their frustration against naval authority. Toulon's new municipality supported the workers' grievances because naval officers, whose power was derived from the distant royal executive, represented a rival concept of authority. Commandant Albert de Rioms' inflexibility exacerbated the conflict. Following a riot on December 1, 1789, the municipality imprisoned the Commandant and his senior officers. This was a direct challenge to central government as well as to the validity of naval authority. Though demanding the officers' release, the Constituent Assembly claimed to represent the nation, but would not support agents of executive power against those who justified their actions in the name of "the People." This illustrates the ambiguity of Popular Sovereignty which prevented its confinement to the decrees of the national legislature. Malouet recognized the danger this posed to the navy, indeed to the exercise of central government, but his concern went unheeded.

In 1790 a new marine Penal Code incited mutiny in the fleet outfitting at Brest. The situation escalated to a revolt against the authority of all naval commanders following the arrival of *Le Léopard* (74), which had been taken over by its crew in the West Indies. Inspired by these rebels, sailors and inhabitants of Brest accused officers of planning to crush colonial patriots. The port's Revolutionary municipality, which along with the Jacobin Club had striven to undermine officers' authority, took advantage of the disorder to assert its domination over the Commandant and squadron commander. This was done in the name of popular will, but during the Brest mutiny some sailors also claimed that their direct democracy was the true expression of Popular Sovereignty. The Constituent Assembly denounced the mutiny and the local interference initially, but again the deputies' Revolutionary principles prevented them from supporting agents of executive power. The Assembly yielded to the mutineers' demands and thanked the Brestois for helping to end the revolt. This response to the mutiny, far more than the Assembly's egalitarian naval reorganization, convinced many officers that further service was untenable.

The incidence of insubordination, mutiny, and direct attacks on naval officers rose dramatically following the events at Brest. In response to the collapse of their authority, the majority of officers from the *Grand*

Corps retired, emigrated, or otherwise abandoned their posts in 1791–1792. Yet officer absenteeism was as much a cause as an effect of Revolutionary hostility. The key was the clash of different notions of authority, and the campaign in the Legislative Assembly to impeach the Minister of Marine, Bertrand de Moleville, reveals the political nature of this conflict. The Department of Finistère accused him of concealing and abetting officer emigration, and radical deputies in Paris used these charges to attack him as part of a suspect executive. The Minister sympathized with the officers and certainly had contempt for the Constitution, but he also represented the view that central government must control the navy. Despite the animosity against Bertrand de Moleville, the majority of the divided Assembly retreated from an impeachment which attacked the basis of government under the Constitution of 1791. The destruction of royal executive power in the name of Popular Sovereignty required the second revolution of August 10, 1792.

French naval officers, both newcomers promoted to fill gaps opened by emigration and the important minority remaining from the *Grand Corps*, welcomed the declaration of the Republic. The Constitutional Monarchy had proved incapable of providing effective government and officers hoped the Republic would restore order and stability in the ports. Above all, they hoped their authority as non-partisan servants of a democratic central government would be recognized. Yet local Jacobin regimes continued to suspect naval officers. This was most apparent in Toulon where a violent municipal coup, less than two weeks before the fall of the monarchy, placed control of the city in the hands of radicals. The navy did not escape the violence, and following the murder of Commandant Flotte in September 1792 Toulon's Jacobins treated the arsenal and fleet as subordinate to local popular authority. This continued despite the Republic's declaration of war against Great Britain which made naval mobilization vital to national defence. The events surrounding the Court Martial of Captain Basterot at Toulon in May 1793 demonstrate the extent to which Revolutionary conflict had politicized French sailors, and the depth of Jacobin animosity towards aristocratic officers. Yet, despite tremendous pressure to find Basterot guilty of conspiracy and treason, the Court Martial convicted the Captain only of professional misconduct. This judgement was part of the officers' larger effort to retain legality in their duties and remain aloof from local Revolutionary politics.

The attempt to preserve the navy's autonomy was in vain. Popular Sovereignty thwarted the ideal of non-partisan loyalty to the nation. In July of 1793 political moderates overturned Toulon's Jacobin regime, justifying their action in terms of popular will, and went on to defy the rule of the National Convention in the larger context of the "Federalist Revolt." On May 31–June 2 the Montagnards and the Sections of Paris had purged the "Girondins," the outspoken opponents of the Montagnards, from the Convention. This provoked protests throughout France and many provincial administrations declared themselves to be in rebellion against the government in Paris. Threatened by internal adversaries and the advancing armies of the Convention, Toulon's revolt escalated to Counter-Revolution and an alliance with the foreign enemy: the "Federalist" rebels agreed to declare for the monarchy and surrender the port to a British fleet in return for Allied protection. At the time of this crisis the French Mediterranean fleet was bitterly divided, principally from interaction with the city's factional struggle. Despite its divisions, the navy at Toulon expressed overwhelming opposition to the treasonable alliance and wished to remain loyal to the nation: yet who represented "the Nation" was terribly unclear. Both the Jacobins and their "Federalist" opponents employed the language of Popular Sovereignty and claimed to speak for the nation. Since April the Commander of the Mediterranean fleet, Admiral Trogoff, had tried to preserve his forces for central authority despite little support and continual local interference. Far from a royalist conspirator, he sided with Toulon's "Federalists" rather than the Jacobin Republic reluctantly and only under the pressure of circumstances. Other officers, notably Admiral Saint-Julien, attempted to rally the fleet. Yet the moral dilemma regarding the location of legitimate authority made unity impossible and rendered the fleet incapable of resisting the surrender.

Popular Sovereignty produced similar confusion regarding the location of national authority in the Atlantic fleet. In September 1793 news of Toulon's treason provided a pretext for mutiny aboard the ships under Morard de Galles' command in Quiberon Bay. Sailors demanded to return to Brest and the Admiral failed to uphold his own authority or convince the crews that they must obey government orders. This mutiny reveals deep divisions in the navy. Beyond the hostility towards aristocratic commanders, Revolutionary conflict ashore had intruded into the fleet. Though without a violent, local struggle between factions, Brest and the Department of Finistère had also rebelled against the Convention in the spring of 1793. Finistère's denunciations of Montagnard extremism, and its demands for the rule of law under a constitutional Republic, echo the principles proclaimed in Toulon and support the interpretation of the "Federalist Revolt" as the work of moderate provincial Republicans. Conflict between political moderates and radical Jacobins divided the Brest fleet but, as at Toulon, the more fundamental effect of "Federalism" was to provide a conflicting claim to Popular Sovereignty. There was no consensus on the location of the Nation's Will aboard the ships under Morard de Galles' command, but a widespread belief that the fleet's direct democracy was a more legitimate expression than the Admiral's authority made mutiny unavoidable.

The Quiberon mutiny represents the culmination of political disorder in the navy, but it also marked the end of the struggle to locate the National Will. In September the Convention declared Terror to be "the order of the day" and established the Revolutionary Government, with the Committees of Public Safety and General Security functioning as a powerful executive. The reassertion of state authority was a fundamental characteristic of the Terror. In this context, the Committee of Public Safety sent its naval expert, Jeanbon Saint-André, to Brest to regain control of the navy. Hence Jeanbon imprisoned many sailors, cashiered several commanders compromised at Quiberon, and dispatched those whom he considered guilty of Counter-Revolutionary intrigue to the guillotine. The Representative also demanded a return to strict discipline and employed harsh repression to enforce it. Having restored order, Jeanbon turned his formidable energy to the navy's appalling material condition and began to mobilize a fleet capable of meeting the British in battle.

Behind all these measures lay the imposition of a new definition of Revolutionary authority. The Terror put an end to the ambiguity of Popular Sovereignty and to suggestions that either direct democracy or local popular assemblies represented the authentic voice of the People. For Jeanbon and the Montagnards, national authority resided only with the Revolutionary Government and all dissent constituted Counter-Revolution. This was particularly apparent in the Representatives' measures to crush any hint of "Federalist" sentiment in Brest. Beyond the reassertion of central authority, the Terror enforced conformity to the Montagnard vision of the Republic. Thus Popular Sovereignty now justified the absolute power of government and complete ruthlessness towards all those it considered enemies. Moreover, the Terror politicized all aspects of naval service. Along with reforming conditions in the fleet, Representatives educated sailors on Revolutionary principles. While promoting several talented commanders, notably Villaret-Joyeuse, Jeanbon scrutinized the political purity of all officers and rewarded fervent Jacobinism.

Jeanbon Saint-André accompanied the Brest fleet when it sailed in May 1794, believing his presence necessary to ensure obedience to the Admiral. The purges and politicization had not unified the officer corps. Rather than in the battle and defeat at sea, this is most apparent in the aftermath of the Prairial Campaign. The Admiral and the Representative charged several captains with criminal misconduct, yet, following 9 Thermidor, two of these officers accused Villaret-Joyeuse of Terrorism. The Montagnards had explicitly denied the ideal of non-partisan loyalty to the state and service, and consequently Revolutionary politics continued to divide the fleet.

Despite the failure to create a loyal and unified officer corps, the Montagnard Revolutionary Government had reestablished some degree of central control over the naval ports and started to rebuild the fleet as an arm of state power. Although Thermidor marked the end of the Terror, the war continued and subsequent French governments sought to use the navy in their struggle against Great Britain. The Directory, the new executive body established under the Constitution of the Year III, launched two major naval operations in the late 1790s. The first was an attempt to invade Ireland. Encouraged by Wolfe Tone and other United Irishmen in Paris, who claimed that the arrival of French troops would spark a general uprising against British rule, the Directory appointed General Lazare Hoche to command such an expedition in 1796.

Hoche attributed the difficulties and delays in outfitting the invasion force at Brest to the malevolence of naval officers and the Directory replaced Villaret-Joyeuse, who openly opposed the operation, with Morard de Galles as fleet commander. On December 16 seventeen ships of the line, thirteen frigates and six *flûtes* carrying 15,000 soldiers sailed from Brest. Things began to go wrong, however, before the expedition entered the English Channel. In heavy seas and falling darkness several ships missed Morard de Galles' signal ordering a change of course, and the following morning found the expedition scattered. Rear-Admiral Bouvet rallied most of the fleet and led it to Bantry Bay in southern Ireland, the intended site for putting troops ashore, on December 21.

Yet an easterly wind, and the inexperience of French sailors, forced Bouvet to anchor near the bay's entrance. Moreover the flagship *La Fraternité*, carrying Morard de Galles and General Hoche, never arrived. When a gale blew several vessels out to sea, Bouvet cut his cables and stood away for France. The commanders of the few warships which remained in Bantry Bay held a council of war on December 27. Given dwindling food supplies and the limited number of soldiers, they decided to abandon the invasion. Most of the expedition regained French ports by January 14, 1797, but three frigates and three ships of the line were lost including *Le Droits-de-l'homme* (74) which ran aground in Audierne Bay, north of Penmarch, following a running battle with two British frigates.[2]

The failure of this operation did not end the Directory's hopes of invading the British Isles, but the French navy's other major effort of the late 1790s was in the Mediterranean. In March 1798 General Napoleon Bonaparte, who had returned from Italy to command the Army of England, convinced the Directory that the conquest of Egypt would enable France to seize India and thus cripple British power. Consequently French Mediterranean ports, as well as dockyards in Italy and Corsica, fitted out numerous vessels to transport an army of 35,000 troops for Bonaparte's Egyptian campaign. Thirteen ships of the line, commanded by Vice-Admiral François-Paul de Brueys d'Aigalliers, would escort the armada. This battle fleet originated with Jeanbon's mission to Toulon in 1794–1795, but the navy continued to suffer from political upheaval in Toulon as well as from the shortage of supplies and trained seamen. Nevertheless the expedition sailed from Toulon on May 19, 1798, and was soon joined by convoys from other ports. The British Admiralty, fearful of a cross-Channel invasion, had dispatched only a token force under Admiral Nelson to watch Toulon, and a storm blew these ships off station. Thus the French fleet proceeded unmolested to Malta, which surrendered to it on June 12, and from there to Egypt.

Arriving at Alexandria on July 1, Bonaparte landed his army and captured the city the following day. The commander-in-chief then ordered Brueys to anchor his ships of the line in Alexandria's old port. The Admiral disliked this shallow and bottle-necked harbour, however, and instead took his fleet to Aboukir Bay fifteen miles to the east.

---

[2] For accounts of the Irish expedition of 1796–1797, see: Cornou and Jonin, pp. 69–90, 101–167; Desbrière, *Projets et tentatives*, I, pp. 135–232; Chevalier, pp. 263–316; Mahan, *Influence of Sea Power upon the French Revolution*, I, pp. 346–360.

There he anchored his battleships in a defensive line parallel to the shore. It was in this position that Nelson's fleet found them on August 1. Nelson had received reinforcements early in June and with fourteen ships of the line he raced for Alexandria, which he deduced to be the French fleet's destination. He arrived on June 28 to find no sign of the enemy. In fact he had passed Bonaparte's expedition *en route*, but Nelson feared that he had miscalculated and departed on June 29. The British fleet watered in Sicily before returning to Egypt. Although the French fleet was not at Alexandria, Nelson soon sighted it in Aboukir Bay and attacked without hesitation. Admiral Brueys assumed that an enemy would be forced to sail along his anchored line, but Nelson and his captains recognized that there was sufficient room to pass before the leading French ship and then to navigate between the line and the shore. Five British ships did so while the others enveloped Brueys' van and centre from seaward. During the night action which ensued, they subjected the French fleet to a devastating concentration of firepower. At 10:00 p.m. Brueys' flagship *L'Orient* (120) blew up, but not before the Admiral had died on his quarter deck. The morning revealed the extent of the disaster: eleven French ships of the line had surrendered or been destroyed, and 3,500 men had been killed or wounded. This action had great strategic and political significance because it trapped Bonaparte's army in Egypt and enabled Great Britain to unite a new coalition against the French Republic. Yet for the French navy, the Battle of the Nile represented simply the most crushing defeat in its history.[3]

This study has been concerned with the impact of Revolutionary politics on the navy as an institution rather than with explanations for French defeats, yet the two are not completely unrelated. A comparison with the British adversary suggests that political stability and sound ideas of governance have a direct bearing on naval superiority. It should be noted that, despite defeats in specific engagements, the French navy furthered the Republic's war aims simply by continuing to pose a threat to Great Britain. The assessment of failed invasions also should take into account the difficulties such strategy imposes on a navy as compared to merely defending coasts. Moreover, the continuation of the French

---

[3] For accounts of the French navy's Egyptian campaign, see: Acerra and Meyer, pp. 215–227; Chevalier, pp. 343–396; Mahan, *Influence of Sea Power upon the French Revolution*, I, pp. 248–278; C. de La Jonquière, *L'Expédition d'Egypte, 1798–1801*, 5 vols. (Paris: Henri Charles-Lavauzelle, 1899–1907), I and II.

navy's structural weaknesses after 1794 should not be minimized. The chronic shortage of construction materials made recovery from losses suffered during the occupation of Toulon or the Prairial Campaign terribly difficult. Defective gear and inadequate maintenance plagued French warships, while manning problems persisted. Financial woes reinforced these other weaknesses. It has been suggested that maintaining the Terror's economic controls could have given France a navy equal to Great Britain's,[4] but such commitment would have required political support along with resources. The material strength of the British navy from 1793 to 1815 resulted from years of effort and consistent policy, which constant Parliamentary support for the Navy Board's estimates made possible.[5] In both countries, building and funding the fleet tested the state's ability to rally political support over the long term.

There are factors other than material ones conducive to success at sea. The relationships between officers and crews determine morale and discipline. The Jacobin-inspired suspicion and surveillance of naval commanders was not easily forgotten, and the democratization of the French fleet never instilled the habit of confident obedience.[6] Yet given the great mutinies which paralyzed the Channel and North Sea fleets in 1797, it might appear that the British navy had more serious discipline problems. Although these threatened national security, there was a crucial difference between them and the disorders in the French navy. The mutinies of 1797 demonstrated that eighteenth-century naval discipline rested on tacit consent rather than force, but they also revealed that British sailors did not question the legitimacy of naval leadership or royal authority. At Spithead the mutineers first addressed their grievances to Admiral Howe, and the presence of "Black Dick" was instrumental in ending the mutiny peacefully. Even while demanding increased pay and better conditions, sailors assured the Admiralty that they would return to duty if the French put to sea.[7] At the Nore, however, mutineers of the North Sea fleet went so far as to intercept shipping on the Thames, placing London under blockade, in order to

[4] Hampson, *La Marine de l'an II*, pp. 128–129, 158–159, 229–230, 238–240.
[5] Paul Webb, "Construction, repair and maintenance in the battle fleet of the Royal Navy, 1793–1815," in Jeremy Black and Philip Woodfine (eds.), *The British Navy and the Use of Naval Power in the Eighteenth Century* (Leicester: Leicester University Press, 1988), pp. 207–219.
[6] Acerra and Meyer, p. 190.
[7] Manwaring and Dobrée, pp. 19–25, 36–40, 53–58, 106–118.

force acceptance of their demands. This more radical leadership provoked violent divisions among the seamen and brought about the mutiny's tragic collapse.[8] The efficiency and spirit of this same fleet at the Battle of Camperdown four months later suggest that discontent in the British navy was never as contentious, or political, as that in the French navy.

This points to a more general conclusion. Navies require effective executive power, but they also reflect the nature of the government's authority. The mounting of the Irish expedition in 1796 and the Egyptian campaign in 1798 demonstrated central control by executive power, however the inauguration of the Directory in 1795 did not establish political stability in France. The bitter divisions of 1793 remained and the government faced constant challenges from the "Right" and the "Left." The history of the Directory is that of a series of *coups d'état* in which different elements sought to consolidate the constitution through the elimination of political opponents. Each successive regime ruled in the name of the Sovereign People and equated its own survival with that of the Republic. The ambiguity of Popular Sovereignty proved antithetical to both the rule of law and the fostering of non-partisan loyalty, and it paved the way for an authoritarian solution under Bonaparte. The French navy's problems cannot be separated from this context.[9]

In contrast, the British navy was the product of the relative political stability under the British constitution. The strength of the "fiscal-military state" in Great Britain, which gave priority to a powerful navy, was built on the rule of law and on limitations to executive power.[10] The navy, unlike a professional army, enjoyed enduring public support because it posed no threat to civil government. Just as Parliamentary consent to taxation actually contributed to the superiority of the British fiscal system, constraints on the Board of Admiralty's authority did not reduce the navy's effectiveness. The Admiralty depended upon its membership in a strong ministry which would make the difficult political decisions necessary to wage a successful naval war.[11] Naval authority

---

[8] Ibid., pp. 163–169, 186–189, 214–231.
[9] I am planning a sequel to the present study which would examine political conflict during the period of the Directory, 1795–1799, through the lens of the French navy.
[10] John Brewer, *The Sinews of Power* (London: Unwin Hyman, 1989), esp. pp. 31–38, 42–45, 62–63, 126–134.
[11] Daniel A. Baugh, *British Naval Administration in the Age of Walpole* (Princeton: Princeton University Press, 1965), pp. 501–504. Limitations on the Admiralty's

was respected, both ashore and afloat, because of its constitutional basis. Even though conditions for English sailors worsened, as the 1797 mutinies revealed, the Royal Navy continued to repel threats of invasion and to defeat its French enemy at sea. Granting the fundamental importance of the French navy's structural weaknesses, it might be suggested that Nelson's victories at the Nile and Trafalgar were not merely the result of financial strength, naval logistics, or even superior seamanship. In a real sense they also represented the triumph of British Parliamentary Government over the French Revolution.

authority also did not prevent efficiency in the Royal Dockyards during the wars with Revolutionary France; Roger Morriss, *The Royal Dockyards during the Revolutionary and Napoleonic Wars* (Leicester: Leicester University Press, 1983), pp. 190–193, 195–198.

BIBLIOGRAPHY

MANUSCRIPT SOURCES

Archives de la Marine

These Archives' central depot, for pre-1870 material, is in the Archives Nationales, Paris, where the collection is referred to as the 'Fonds de la Marine.'

Série BB "Service Général"

Sous-série Marine BB 2 "Correspondance au départ":
[This sub-series contains correspondence from the Minister of Marine to Port authorities, etc.]

  BB 2/1   "Minutes, 1790"

Sous-série Marine BB 3 "Lettres reçus":
[This sub-series contains correspondence addressed to the Minister of Marine from Port authorities and other correspondents ashore.]

  BB 3/1   "Correspondance, 1790"
  BB 3/13   "Toulon. Commandant de la marine, 1792"
  BB 3/14   "Toulon. Ordonnateur, 1792"
  BB 3/17   "Brest. Autorités Départementales, Fonctionnaires divers, particuliers, 1792"
  BB 3/22   "Brest. Thévenard, Commandant des armes, 1793"
  BB 3/23   "Brest. Ordonnateur; Petits ports de Bretagne, 1793"
  BB 3/30   "Toulon. Commandant des Armes, 1793"
  BB 3/31   "Toulon. Ordonnateur, 1793"
  BB 3/38   "Représentants du Peuple en mission, 1793"
  BB 3/43   "Clubs et Sociétés populaires, 1793"
  BB 3/59   "Arrêtés du Comité de Salut public; Divers Députés; Sociétés populaires, 1794"

303

BB 3/61   "Brest. Représentants du Peuple en mission dans les ports, 1794"

Sous-série Marine BB 4 "Campagnes":
[This sub-series contains correspondence addressed to the Minister of Marine from commanders of naval forces or warships at sea or outfitting in the ports.]

BB 4/1   "Campagnes, 1790"

BB 4/3   "Station des Iles du Vent, Station des Iles sous le Vent, 1790"

BB 4/5   "Station des Iles du Vent, Expédition de la Martinique, 1791"

BB 4/8   "Armements en général; Escadre de Brest, commandant: Morard de Galles, 1792"

BB 4/9   "Escadre de la Méditerranée, commandée par le contre-amiral Truguet, 1792"

BB 4/12   "Station des Iles du Vent, 1792"

BB 4/16   "Armée navale de Brest, commandant en chef: le vice-amiral Morard de Galles, 1793"

BB 4/17   "Armée navale de Brest: vaisseaux, 1793"

BB 4/19   "Croisière de la Vendée, commandant: Villaret-Joyeuse, 1793"

BB 4/21   "Armée navale de la Méditerranée: le contre-amiral Truguet; le contre-amiral Trogoff; Autorités diverses, 1793"

BB 4/22   "Armée navale de la Méditerranée: vaisseaux, 1793"

BB 4/37   "Armée navale de Brest commandée par le contre-amiral Villaret-Joyuese: combats des 9–13 prairial, 1794"

BB 4/38   "Armée navale de Brest . . .; les commandants des bâtiments: A–N"

BB 4/39   "Armée navale de Brest . . .; les commandants des bâtiments: P–V"

Archives Nationales, Paris

Série AF "Archives du pouvoir exécutif"

Sous-série AF II "Comité de Salut Public":

Cart. 294/Registre 2463 "Missions des représentants du Peuple, Brest, 6 juillet 1793 – 29 nivôse an II"

Série D "Missions des Représentants du Peuple et Comités des Assemblées" Sous-série D XVI "Comité de Marine":
D XVI/3, No. 25 "Pétitions individuelles adressés à l'Assemblée Nationale et renvoyées au Comité de Marine, 1790 – an III"

Série W "Juridictions Extraordinaires"
W 311/No. 414 "Affaire Lebourg, Verneuil, Coëtnempren, Duplessis-Grénédan"

Archives Départementales du Finistère, Quimper

100 J "Archives de Kernuz"
- 100 J 311 "Correspondance générale et particulière de la commission administrative, 13 septembre 1793 – 23 thermidor an II"
- 100 J 312 "Correspondance particulière du secrétariat, 4 juillet 1792 – 25 juin 1793"
- 100 J 324 "Procès-verbal des séances des administrateurs du Département du Finistère, 15 novembre – 16 décembre 1791"
- 100 J 470 "Tribunal révolutionnaire à Brest, fonctionnement, an II – an III"
- 100 J 605 "Etat des jugements dressés par le greffe, 23 ventôse an II – 24 thermidor an III"
- 100 J 606 "Affiches de jugements rendus par le tribunal révolutionnaire de Brest, an II"

Série L "Documents administratifs et judiciaires de la periode révolutionnaire, 1790 – an VIII"

Sous-série 8 L "Actes des Représentants du Peuple en mission":
- 8 L 9 "Correspondance du citoyen Prieur (de la Marne) avec Jeanbon Saint-André, Représentant du Peuple dans les Départements maritimes, 7 ventôse an II – 21 vendémiaire an III"
- 8 L 13 "Arrêtés, lettres et proclamations des Représentants Defermon, Rochegude, Prieur de la Marne, Jeanbon Saint-André, Faure, en mission dans les Départements

maritimes de la République, février 1793 – fructidor an II"

8 L 16   "Arrêtés, lettres et proclamations des Représentants en mission près les côtes de Brest et de Lorient, septembre 1793 – vendémiaire an IV"

8 L 83   "Correspondance reçue: du Ministre et de la Commission de la Marine et des Colonies"

8 L 84   "Lettres de l'amiral Villaret, an II – an IV"

8 L 85   "Lettres du contre-amiral Cornic, an II & III"

8 L 87   "Journaux de bord. Pièces re. Combat de Prairial"

8 L 88   "Correspondance, ordres et arrêtés relatif à l'Armée navale du 21 septembre au 14 nivôse an II"

8 L 92 and 93   "Demands d'avancement dans la marine, an II: A–K" and ". . . L–Z"

Service Historique de la Marine, Brest

Archives de la Marine

Série A "Commandement de la marine dans le port de Brest"

Sous-série 1 A "Commandant des Armes":

1 A 102   "Lettres particulières"

1 A 127   "Correspondance de départ; officiers, février 1790 – janvier 1792"

Bibliothèque de la Marine

"Fonds Levot"

[This is a collection of published documents pertaining to Brest during the Revolution. Most pieces used are listed below with the published primary sources.]

1965 *Collection des arrêtés pris par le républicain Jean-Bon Saint-André, Représentant du Peuple, à Brest, concernant la marine de la République française, depuis le 21 vendémiaire jusqu'au 21 floréal, de l'an second de la République française, une et indivisible.* Brest: Gauchlet, An II.

Service Historique de la Marine, Toulon

Archives de la Marine

Série A "Commandement de la marine dans le port de Toulon"

Sous-série 4 A 1:

4 A 1/259   "Lettres du Chef d'escadre des armées navales, Com-

| | mandant de la Marine, 17 mai 1786 – 29 mai 1793" |
| 4 A 1/364 | "Lettres, mémoires, déclarations concernant l'affaire arrivée le 1er décembre 1789 à M. le Marquis de Riom, Commandant de la marine, et autres officiers du même corps" |

Série L "Controle de l'administration de la marine"

Sous-série 1 L:

1 L 139 (4) "Déclaration du Roi de la Grande Bretagne. Discours Prononcés à la députation du Comité Général des Sections de Toulon par leurs excellences Lord Hood, le Chevallier Gilbert Elliot, Baronet et Lord O'Hara, Commissaires Plénipotentiaires de Sa Majesté Le Roi de la Grande Bretagne, le 20 novembre 1793"

1 L 140 "Divers arrêtés des Représentants du Peuple dans les Départements maritimes, an II – an III"

Série O "Institutions de répression"

Sous-série 4 O "Cour martiale maritime":

4 O 1 "Procédures et interrogatoires, 1792 – an II" [This unsorted bundle of documents contains the dossier concerning the affair of *La Melpomène* and *La Minerve* and the Court Martial of Captain Basterot in 1793.]

Bibliothèque de la marine

"Fonds du Commandant Emmanuel Davin"

[This is a heterogeneous collection of documents, manuscripts, and typed papers.]

Sous-série 5 S "La Révolution et l'Empire":

5 S 22, liasse no. 4 "Rapport du Commodore Anglais Sidney Smith, incendiaire du port de Toulon en 1793, à l'amiral Hood"

Archives Municipales de Toulon

Série: "Révolution & Empire, 1789–1815"
Article: L 2 XIX
Objet: Periode Sectionnaire, Anti-conventionnelle
Divers: 1793–1818

L 2 XIX – 4 "Puissant, 1795–1799"

L 2 XIX – 17 Panisse, J. L. *Histoire des événemens de Toulon, en 1793, pour le rétablissement de la monarchie. Depuis la levée des Sections, jusqu' à l'époque de l'évacuation de cette ville. Par M. J. Louis PANISSE, ancien membre et secrétaire du Comité Général des Sections, émigré de Toulon,* Toulon, 12 juin 1815 [manuscript].

L 2 XIX – 18   "Précis en rade de Toulon 1793: Journal de l'enseigne Absolut du vaisseau Orion"

PUBLISHED PRIMARY SOURCES

Adresse de la Société des Amis de la Constitution, établie à Brest, aux citoyens, composant les équipages de l'Armée navale. Brest: Malassis, 1790.

Adresse de la Société des Marins de St. Malo aux citoyens du département de Saint-Malo embarqués sur l'Armée actuellement à Brest. St. Malo: Valais, 1790.

Adresse de l'Equipage du vaisseau le Superbe, en rade de Brest, à la Société des Amis de la Constitution. Séance du 4 novembre 1790. Paris: Imprimerie Nationale, [no date].

Adresse des Capitaines & officiers de la Marine Nationale de Dieppe, aux marins Dieppois employés sur la Flotte de Brest, pour le service de la Patrie. Dieppe, 1790.

Adresse et Doléances des Maîtres & autres canonniers des classes du Département de Brest, présentées au Conseil général & permanent de cette ville; et Rapport de M. Siviniant, Secrétaire de ce Conseil. Brest: Malassis, 1789.

Albert de Rioms, comte d'. *Mémoire historique et justificatif de M. le comte D'Albert de Rioms sur l'affaire de Toulon.* Paris: Desenne, 1790.

Mémoire que M. le comte d'Albert de Rioms a fait dans la prison où il est détenu. Détail de ce qui s'est passé lundi 30 novembre, et le lendemain mardi 1er décembre. [No place, no date.]

Archives Parlementaires de 1787 à 1860. 95 vols. Paris: Libraire Administrative de Paul Dupont [vols. 1–82], 1875–1913; C.N.R.S. [vols. 82bis–95], 1966–1987.

Aulard, François-Victor-Alphonse (ed.). *Recueil des Actes du Comité de salut public; avec la correspondance officielle des réprésentants en mission et le registre du conseil exécutif provisoire.* 25 vols. Paris: Imprimerie Nationale, 1889–1918.

La Société des Jacobins: recueil de documents pour l'histoire du Club des Jacobins de Paris. 6 vols. Paris: Imprimerie Nationale, 1889–1897.

Bertrand de Moleville, Antoine-François. *Compte Rendu à l'Assemblée Nationale par le Ministre de la Marine, sur les loix de détail qu'exige l'establissement de la nouvelle organisation de ce département (31 octobre 1791).* Paris: Imprimerie Nationale, 1791.

Compte Rendu par le Ministre de la Marine, à l'Assemblée Nationale, le 31 octobre 1791. Paris: Imprimerie Nationale, 1791.

Discours du Ministre de la Marine, prononcé à la séance du 5 décembre 1791. Paris: Imprimerie Nationale, 1791.

Lettre du Ministre de la Marine, à M. le Président de l'Assemblée Nationale. Paris, 20 janvier 1792. Paris: Imprimerie Royale, 1792.

Lettre du Ministre de la Marine, à M. le Président de l'Assemblée Nationale. Paris, le 10 février 1792. Paris: Imprimerie Royale, 1792.

Private Memoirs of A. F. Bertrand de Moleville, Minister of State, 1790–1791, relative to the last year of the reign of Louis the Sixteenth. 2 vols. Translated by R. C. Dallas. London, 1797; New edn, edited by G. K. Fortescue. Boston: J. B. Millet Company, 1909.

Boissauver. *Boissauver, ex-capitaine de vaisseau de la République, à la Convention Nationale et à ses concitoyens.* Brest: Malassis, [no date].

Boubennec. *Mémoire du citoyen Boubennec, capitaine de vaisseau, commandant ci-devant le vaisseau de la République, l'Entreprenant venant de Toulon, à tous mes concitoyens de Brest, Frères et Amis (6 ventôse 1794 an II).* Landernau: Havard, [no date].

Bréard, Jean-Jacques. *Décret relatif à l'organisation provisoire de la Marine militaire de la République française, des 2, 6, et 17 février 1793, l'an 2 de la République. Précédé du Rapport fait au nom du Comité de marine, par Bréard, député du département de la Charente Inférieure.* Paris: Imprimerie Nationale, [no date].

Bréard and Tréhouart. *Les Représentans du Peuple sur les côtes de Brest et de l'Orient, aux citoyens des Départemens maritimes de l'Ocean, de la Manche, et autres circonvoisins. Brest, le 17 septembre 1793.* Brest: Gauchlet, 1793.

Les Brestois à la Convention Nationale. Brest: Gauchlet, 1793.

Caron, Pierre (ed.). *Rapports des agents du ministre de l'intérieur dans les départements (1793 – An II).* 2 vols. Paris: Imprimerie Nationale, 1951.

Cavellier, Blaise. *Rapport fait à l'Assemblée Nationale, au nom du Comité de marine, par M. Cavellier.* Paris: Imprimerie Nationale, [no date].

Rapport fait à l'Assemblée Nationale, au nom du Comité de la Marine, par M. Cavellier, Député du Département du Finistère, sur la nécessité de mettre à exécution la Loi du 15 mai, concernant l'organisation de la Marine; de remplacer les officiers émigrés, ou qui ont déserté leur poste; & de réformer quelques abus relatifs aux congés. Paris: Imprimerie Nationale, 1791.

Bibliography

Rapport fait à l'Assemblée Nationale, au nom du Comité de marine, le 13 janvier 1792. Par M. Cavellier. Paris: Imprimerie Nationale, 1792.

Dalbarade, Jean. *Le Ministre de la Marine à ses concitoyens.* Paris: Patris, [no date].

Vigilance et Fermeté. Copie de la lettre écrite le 9 juillet 1793, par le Ministre de la Marine au citoyen Trogoff, Contre-amiral, commandant les Forces Navales en rade à Toulon. Toulon: Imprimerie de Rochebrun et Mazet, [no date].

Defermon. *Opinion de M. Defermon, sur l'organisation de la Marine; prononcé dans la séance du 13 avril 1791.* Paris: Imprimerie Nationale, 1791.

Dénonciation des citoyens de la commune de Brest contre Prieur (de la Marne), et Jean-Bon Saint-André, déposé au Comité de Sûreté-générale par les Députés extraordinaires de la même commune, le 8 Prairial, 3e année Républicaine. Paris: Imprimerie de la veuve d'Antoine Joseph Gorsas, [no date].

Dermigny, Louis and Gabriel Debien (eds.). "La Révolution au Antilles: Journal maritime du commandeur de Villevielle, commandant de la frégate La Didon (septembre 1790 – septembre 1792)," *Revue d'histoire de l'Amérique française,* 9 (1955), 55–73, 250–271.

"La Révolution aux Antilles. Marins et colons – Marchands et Petits Blancs. Deux documents (août 1790 – août 1792)," *Revue d'histoire de l'Amérique française,* 8: 4 (mars 1955), 496–517.

Des Robert, Ferdinand. "Correspondance de deux officiers de marine en 1789," *Académie de Stanislas: Mémoires,* Série 5, 9 (1892), 191–239.

Etat-Major de la Marine, et service des ports. Paris: Imprimerie Nationale, 1791.

Extrait du Procès-verbal de la séance de la Société des Amis de la Constitution à Brest, du 22 octobre 1790. Paris: Imprimerie Nationale, 1790.

Gualbert. *Projet de Décret sur l'organisation d'une Marine militaire. Proposé par M. de Gualbert, Major de vaisseau, Député à l'Assemblée Nationale.* Paris: Imprimerie Nationale, 1791.

Gauthier de Brécy. *La Révolution royaliste de Toulon.* Paris, 1795.

Hardman, John (ed.). *The French Revolution: The Fall of the Ancien Régime to the Thermidorian Reaction, 1785–1795.* London: Edward Arnold, 1981.

Hugues, Victor. *Acte d'Accusation contre les complices de la trahison de Toulon. Rochefort, 29 Brumaire an II.* Rochefort: R. D. Jousseront, Imprimeur du Tribunal révolutionnaire, [no date].

Jeanbon Saint-André, André. *Journal sommaire de la croisière de la flotte de la république, commandée par le contre-amiral Villaret; tenu jour par jour par le représentant du peuple Jeanbon Saint-André, embarqué sur le vaisseau la Montagne.* Paris: Imprimerie Nationale, An II.

Réponse de Jean-Bon Saint-André à la Dénonciation des citoyens de la commune de Brest. Paris, 20 Prairial an 3. Paris: Imprimerie Nationale, An III.

Rapport sur les mouvemens qui ont eu lieu sur l'escadre de la République, commandée par le vice-amiral Morard de Galles, et sur sa rentrée à Brest, fait aux représentans du peuple auprès de l'armée navale. Brest: Malassis, 1794.

Opinion et Projet de Décret, du citoyen Jeanbon Saint-André, Député du Lot, sur l'organisation de la Marine française. Paris: Imprimerie Nationale, [no date].

Rapport des représentans du peuple envoyés à Brest et auprès de l'armée navale; par Jeanbon Saint-André. Paris: Imprimerie Nationale, [no date].

Les Représentans du Peuple près les côtes de Brest et de Lorient, aux membres de la Société Populaire de Brest. [No place, no date].

Jourdan, Louis (ed.). "Journal d'un matelot de l'an II (1792)," *Bulletin de la Société de géographie de Rochefort,* 35 (1913), 77–91.

Julien (de Toulouse). *Rapport fait au nom du Comité de Surveillance et de Sûreté général, sur les administrations rebelles, 15 octobre 1793.* Paris: Imprimerie Nationale, 1793.

Kerguelen-Trémarec, Yves-Joseph de. *Relation des combats et des événements de la guerre maritime de 1778, mêlée de réflexions sur les manoeuvres des généraux et terminée par un précis des principaux événements de la guerre présente, des causes de la destruction de la marine française et des moyens de la rétablir.* Paris: Patris, 1796.

Kersaint, Armand-Guy-Simon, comte de. *Développemens du Projet de Décret sur l'organisation du service de mer, proposé par A. Gui-Kersaint, à la séance du 31 mai 1792, et imprimé par ordre du Comité de marine le 18 septembre 1792.* Paris: Imprimerie Nationale, 1792.

Lacoste, Jean de. *La Coste, à ses concitoyens.* Paris: Imprimerie Nationale, 1793.

La Coudraye, François-Célestin de Loynes, chevalier de. *Opinion de M. La Coudraye, ancien lieutenant de vaisseau, de l'Ordre Royal & Militaire de Saint-Louis, Député du Poitou; sur le nouveau projet d'organisation de la Marine militaire, proposé par le Comité de la Marine.* Paris: Imprimerie Nationale, 1791.

La Gallissonnière. *Nouvelle opinion de M. de La Gallissonnière, sur le nouveau projet d'organisation de la Marine militaire, proposé par le Comité de la Marine; prononcée le 14 avril 1791.* Paris: Imprimerie Nationale, 1791.

La Luzerne, César-Henri, comte de. *Extrait de la première partie d'un Mémoire envoyé au Comité de la Marine, par le Ministre de ce Département, sur l'instruction, l'admission, le nombre des officiers militaires, & le mode de leur avancement.* Paris: Imprimerie Royale, 1790.

311

Bibliography

Lettre de M. de La Luzerne, Ministre & Secrétaire d'Etat de la Marine, à M. le Président de l'Assemblée Nationale. A Paris, le 5 août 1790. Paris: Imprimerie Royale, 1790.

Mémoire envoyé le 18 juin 1790, au Comité des rapports de l'Assemblée Nationale, par M. de La Luzerne, Ministre & Secrétaire d'Etat. Paris: Imprimerie Royale, 1790.

Lannoy, César-Auguste de. "Mémorial de M. de Lannoy (1763–1793): Notes de voyage d'un officier de marine de l'ancien régime," *Carnet de la Sabretache: Revue militaire rétrospective* Whole series, vol. 13, 2nd series 3 (1904), 682–688, 748–765.

La Tuillerie. *Réponse du citoyen La Tuillerie, capitaine de frégate, aux calomnies du citoyen Pinsemin, lieutenant de vaisseau.* [No place, no date].

Lebret d'Imbert, Thomas, baron de. *Précis Historique sur les événemens de Toulon en 1793.* Paris: Chez Poulet, 1814.

Legg, L. G. Wickham (ed.). *Select Documents illustrative of the history of the French Revolution. The Constituent Assembly.* 2 vols. Oxford: Oxford University Press, 1905.

Lelarge, Jean-Baptiste-Amable. *Lelarge, ex-contre-amiral de la République, à la Convention nationale, et à ses concitoyens.* Brest: Gauchlet, [no date].

Lettre de MM. de la Municipalité de Brest à MM. les Membres de l'Assemblée Générale de Saint-Domingue à Paris. Brest, le 27 septembre 1790. [No place, no date].

Lettre des Commissaires envoyés à Brest par le Roi, sur la demande de l'Assemblée Nationale, pour rétablir l'ordre dans l'Escadre. Paris: Imprimerie Nationale, 1790.

Malouet, Pierre-Victor. *Deuxième opinion de M. Malouet, sur le nouveau projet de Décret du Comité de la Marine, relativement à l'organisation militaire.* Paris: Imprimerie Nationale, 1791.

Opinion de M. Malouet, sur l'organisation de la marine militaire, prononcée dans la séance du 14 janvier 1791. Paris: Imprimerie Nationale, 1791.

Mémoires de Malouet. 2 vols. Paris: Didier, 1868.

Défense du commandant et des officiers de la marine, prisonniers à Toulon. Deuxième opinion de M. Malouet. [No place, no date].

Opinion de M. Malouet sur l'affaire de M. le comte d'Albert. [No place, no date].

Mirabeau, vicomte de. *Opinion du vicomte de Mirabeau, membre de l'Assemblée Nationale, dans l'affaire de Toulon.* [No place, no date].

Les Membres de la Société Populaire et Montagnard de Brest, à la Convention Nationale. Brest: Audran, [no date].

Mémoire des officiers de mérite des Troupes de la marine au Département de Brest, à l'Assemblée Nationale. Brest: Malassis, 1790.

Monge, Gaspard. *Circulaire aux Matelots, canonniers et soldats de la Marine Française. Paris, le 15 février 1793.* Paris: Patris, [no date].

Compte Rendu à la Convention Nationale par le Ministre de la Marine, de l'état de situation de la Marine de la République, le 23 septembre de l'an premier; imprimé & envoyé aux 83 Départements & à l'Armée, par ordre de la Convention Nationale. Paris: Imprimerie Nationale, [no date].

Considérations Essentielles au service du département de la marine. Paris: Imprimerie Nationale, [no date].

Monneron, Louis. *Opinion de M. Louis Monneron, Député des Indes orientales, sur l'organisation de la Marine.* Paris: Imprimerie Nationale, 1791.

Moreau de Jonnès, Alexandre. *Adventures in the Revolution and under the Consulate.* Trans. Cyril Hammond. Paris, 1858; repr. in trans. London: Peter Davies Ltd., 1929.

Moreau de Saint-Méry. *Opinion de M. Moreau de Saint-Méry, Député de la Martinique, sur l'organisation du Ministère, et notamment sur la nécessité de ne faire qu'un seul ministère de la Marine & des Colonies, 9 avril 1791.* Paris: Imprimerie Nationale, 1791.

Nompère de Champagny, Jean-Baptiste de. *Rapport fait à l'Assemblée Nationale, au nom du Comité de marine; sur l'organisation de la Marine militaire.* Paris: Imprimerie Nationale, 1791.

Obet, Yves-Louis. *Précis de la vie militaire & politique d'Yves-Louis Obet, capitaine de vaisseau, suspendu de ses fonctions depuis treize mois, sous prétexte de nécessité de son témoignage dans l'affaire de Quiberon, intriguée par le tribunal révolutionnaire.* Brest: Audran, [no date].

Pétition de l'Equipage du vaisseau l'America, à la Société des Amis de la Constitution. Séance du 4 novembre 1790. Paris: Baudouin, [no date].

Pons, M. Z. *Mémoires pour servir à l'histoire de la ville de Toulon en 1793.* Paris: C. J. Trouvé, 1825.

Poupé, Edmond (ed.). "Journal d'un Ponantais de l'Apollon," *Revue historique de la Révolution française*, (jan.–mars 1911), 34–62.

Prisset. *Exposé de ma conduite à Nantes, en 1789, 1790, 1791 et 1792, et pendant mon séjour à Brest, dans la même année.* Brest: Gauchlet, [no date].

Mémoire justicatif du Républicain Prisset, enseigne du vaisseau, la Convention, détenu depuis deux mois, à cause des mouvemens qui eurent lieu dans l'escadre de la République, alors commandée par le vice-amiral Morard de Galle.

Confession du Républicain Prisset, enseigne du vaisseau la Convention. Brest: Gauchlet, [no date].

Projet de Décret sur l'organisation de la Marine militaire, et sur le mode d'admission et d'avancement, présenté par le Comité de la Marine. Paris: Imprimerie Nationale, 1791.

Puissant, Joseph-Maurice, de Molimont. *Pétition au Conseil des Cinq-Cents, concernant l'événement de Toulon en 1793.* Paris: Galletti, An V.

Précis de la conduite de Puissant, ordonnateur de la marine à Toulon, pendant les événemens de 1793. Paris: Galletti, An V.

Toute la France a été trompée sur l'événement de Toulon en 1793, voici la vérité. Coutances: Agnes, An V.

Raby, Thomas. *Thomas Raby aux Vétérans de la Révolution. Du Château de Brest, le 1er ventôse l'an 2e.* [No place, no date].

Réclamations des maîtres, seconds maîtres, contre-maîtres & quartier-maîtres d'équipage du Port de Brest; présentées au Conseil général & permanent de cette ville. Brest: Malassis, 1789.

Redon de Beaupréau. *Un Administrateur du Port de Brest, devenu la malheureuse victime de la tryannie, à tous les Républicains de la France, justes, honnêtes et sensibles.* Brest: Malassis, [no date].

Justification du citoyen Redon, ci-devant ordonnateur de la Marine, détenu depuis quatorze mois, tant à Carhaix qu'au Fort-la-Loi, ci-devant le Château de Brest. Brest: Malassis, [no date].

Réimpression de l'Ancien Moniteur depuis la réunion des états-généraux jusqu'au consulat (mai 1789 – novembre 1799). 31 vols. Paris: Imprimerie d'A. René et cie., 1840–1854.

Réponse de l'Assemblée Générale de la partie française de Saint-Domingue à MM. les Maire et officiers de la Municipalité de Brest. Paris, le 2 octobre 1790. [No place, no date].

Révolutions de France et Brabant. No. 45 (4 octobre 1790).

Révolutions de Paris. Vol. 5: no. 57 (7–14 août 1790), no. 63 (18–25 septembre 1790).

Ricard de Séalt. *Opinion sur un projet de décret du Comité de la Marine, et nouveau projet de décret sur l'admission & l'avancement dans le corps de la marine; par M. Ricard, Député de Toulon.* Paris: Imprimerie Nationale, 1791.

Richaud, Louis. *Mémoires de Louis Richaud sur la Révolte de Toulon et l'Emigration.* 1809; repr. edited by R. Busquet, B. Roberty and A. J. Parès. Paris: Editions Rieder, 1930.

Roffin, Michel. *Dénonciation de la conduite atroce du Tribunal Révolutionnaire de Brest. Roffin à ses concitoyens. (Le Doigt de Robespierre est ici . . .).* Brest: Guffroy, [no date].

Séance de MM. les officiers des grades intermédiaires de la Marine, assemblés extraordinairement à l'hôtel du Commandant, le 13 octobre 1790. [No place, no date].

Sévestre, J. M. F. *Rapport fait par le citoyen Sévestre, l'un des Représentans du Peuple envoyés près l'armée des côtes de Brest; Imprimée par ordre de la Convention Nationale, le 23 juin 1793, l'an 2 de la République française.* Paris: Imprimerie Nationale, [no date].

Sillery, C. A. P. Brulart de Genlis, marquis de. *Développement du projet du Comité de la Marine sur l'organisation de la Marine française, par M. de Sillery.* Paris: Imprimerie Nationale, 1791.

Opinion de M. de Sillery et projet de décret, sur l'admission des aspirans dans le corps de la marine militaire, 14 janvier 1791. Paris: Imprimerie Nationale, 1791.

Stewart, John Hall (ed.). *A Documentary Survey of the French Revolution.* New York: Macmillan, 1951; repr. 1963.

Tréhouart, Bernard-Thomas. *Projet de Décret sur l'organisation de la marine militaire, présenté au nom du Comité de la marine et des colonies par B. Tréhouart, Deputé du Département d'Ille-et-Vilaine.* Paris: Imprimerie Nationale, An IV.

Turner, Frederick J. (ed.). *Correspondence of the French Ministers to the United States, 1791–1797,* Vol. II: *Annual Report of the American Historical Association, 1903.* Washington: United States Government Printing Office, 1904.

Valous, marquis de (ed.). *Avec les Rouges aux Iles du Vent: Souvenirs du chevalier de Valous (1790-1793) pendant la Révolution française.* Paris, 1930; repr. Paris: Editions Caribéennes, 1989.

Villeon, Jean-Baptiste-François. *Villeon, contre-amiral, à la Convention Nationale. A l'Abbaye, 6 janvier de l'an second de la République.* Paris: N. H. Nyon, 1793.

SECONDARY SOURCES

Acerra, Martine, José Merino, and Jean Meyer (eds.). *Les Marines de guerre européennes, XVII–XVIIIe siècles.* Paris: Presses de l'Université de Paris – Sorbonne, 1985.

Acerra, Martine and Jean Meyer. *Marines et Révolution.* Rennes: Editions Ouest-France, 1988.

Aman, Jacques. *Les Officiers Bleus dans la marine française au XVIIIe siècle.* Geneva: Librairie Droz, 1976.

Asher, Eugene L. *The Resistance to the Maritime Classes: The Survival of Feudalism in the France of Colbert.* Berkeley and Los Angeles: University of California Press, 1960.

Aulard, F. V. A. *The French Revolution: A Political History, 1789–1804.* 4 vols. Trans. Bernard Miall. Paris, 1901; repr. London: T. Fisher Unwin, 1910.

Baker, Keith Michael. *Inventing the French Revolution.* Cambridge: Cambridge University Press, 1990.

Baker, Keith Michael (ed.). *The Political Culture of the Old Regime.* Oxford: Pergamon Press, 1987.

Bamford, Paul Walden. *Forests and French Sea Power, 1660–1789.* Toronto: University of Toronto Press, 1956.

Fighting Ships and Prisons: The Mediterranean Galleys of France in the Age of Louis XIV. Minneapolis: University of Minnesota Press, 1973.

Baugh, Daniel A. *British Naval Administration in the Age of Walpole.* Princeton: Princeton University Press, 1965.

Bertaud, Jean-Paul. *The Army of the French Revolution. From Citizen-Soldiers to Instrument of Power.* Trans. R. R. Palmer. Paris, 1979; repr. Princeton: Princeton University Press, 1988.

Bien, David. "La Réaction aristocratique avant 1789: l'exemple de l'armée," *Annales: Economies, Sociétés, Civilisations*, 39 (1974), 23–48.

Black, Jeremy and Philip Woodfine (eds.). *The British Navy and the Use of Naval Power in the Eighteenth Century.* Leicester: Leicester University Press, 1988.

Bluche, François. *La vie Quotidienne de la noblesse français au XVIIIe siècle.* Paris: Hachette Littérature, 1973.

Bonnel, Ulane (ed.). *Fleurieu et la Marine de son temps.* Paris: Economica, 1992.

Bordonove, Georges. *Les marins de l'an II.* Paris: Editions Robert Laffont, 1974.

Bosher, J. F. *French Finances 1770–1795: From Business to Bureaucracy.* Cambridge: Cambridge University Press, 1970.

Boudriot, Jean. *The Seventy-Four Gun Ship: A Practical Treatise on the Art of Naval Architecture.* 4 vols. Trans. David H. Roberts. Paris and Grenoble, 1973; repr. Annapolis: Naval Institute Press, 1986.

Boulaire, Alain. "Le Comte Hector, commandant de la Marine à Brest en 1789," *Les Cahiers de L'Iroise*, 35e Année – No. 3 (Nouvelle série) (Messidor 1988), 134–137.

Bouloiseau, Marc. *The Jacobin Republic, 1792–1794.* Trans. Jonathan Mandelbaum. Paris, 1972; repr. Cambridge: Cambridge University Press, 1983.

Brewer, John. *The Sinews of Power. War, Money and the English State, 1688–1783.* London: Unwin Hyman, 1989.

Bibliography

Brun, Vincent-Félix. *Guerres maritimes de la France: Port de Toulon. Ses armements, son administration, depuis son origine jusqu'à nos jours.* 2 vols. Paris: Henri Plon, 1861.

Cabantous, Alain. *La Vergue et les fers: Mutins et déserteurs dans la marine de l'ancienne France (XVIIe–XVIIIe s.).* Paris: Tallandier, 1984.

Le ciel dans la mer: Christianisme et civilisation maritime XVIe–XIXe siècle. Mesnil-sur-l'Estrée: Fayard, 1990.

Cameron, John B. *The Revolution of the Sections of Marseilles: Federalism in the Department of the Bouches-du-Rhône in 1793.* Ph.D. Thesis. University of North Carolina, 1971.

"Federalism in Marseilles." *The Consortium on Revolutionary Europe, 1750–1850. Proceedings,* 13 (1984), 99–104.

Capp, Bernard. *Cromwell's Navy: The Fleet and the English Revolution 1648–1660.* Oxford: Clarendon Press, 1989.

Castries, René de La Croix, duc de. *Le maréchal de Castries (1727–1800).* Paris: Flammarion, 1956.

Censer, Jack Richard. *Prelude to Power: The Parisian Radical Press, 1789–1791.* Baltimore and London: Johns Hopkins University Press, 1976.

Chaussinand-Nogaret, Guy. *The French Nobility in the Eighteenth Century: From Feudalism to Enlightenment.* Trans. William Doyle. Cambridge: Cambridge University Press, 1985.

La Bastille est prise. La Révolution française commence. Paris: Editions Complexe, 1988.

Chevalier, Edouard. *Histoire de la marine française sous la première République.* Paris: Hachette, 1886.

Christianson, Paul. "Patterns of Historical Interpretation." Paper presented to the Philosophy Colloquium at Queen's University, 4 February 1988.

Christie, Ian R. *Wars and Revolutions. Britain, 1760–1815.* Cambridge, Mass.: Havard University Press, 1982.

Cobban, Alfred. *A History of Modern France. Volume 1: 1715–1799.* Harmondsworth: Penguin, 1957; repr. 1979.

In Search of Humanity: The Role of the Enlightenment in Modern History. London: Jonathan Cape, 1960.

Aspects of the French Revolution. London, 1968; repr. Frogmore: Paladin, 1973.

Cornou, Jakez and Bruno Jonin. *L'Odyssée du vaisseau "Droits de l'homme" & l'expédition d'Irlande de 1796.* Quimper: Editions DUFA, 1988.

Cottin, Paul. *Toulon et les Anglais en 1793, d'après des documents inédits.* Paris: P. Ollendorff, 1898.

Bibliography

Coulet, Eugène. *Le Comité général des sections de Toulon (13 juillet – 17 décembre)*. Toulon: Imprimerie Gallinari, 1960.

Crook, Malcolm. "Federalism and the French Revolution: The Revolt of Toulon in 1793," *History*, 65: 215 (1980), 383–397.

"Le mouvement sectionnaire à Toulon en juillet–août 1793," in François Lebrun and Roger Dupuy (eds.), *Les résistances à la Révolution: Actes du Colloque de Rennes (17–21 septembre 1985)*. Paris: Editions Imago, 1987.

Toulon in war and revolution: From the ancien régime to the Restoration, 1750–1820. Manchester and New York: Manchester University Press, 1991.

De Poggi (ed.). *A Narrative of the Proceedings of His Majesty's Fleet, under the command of Earl Howe, from the second of May to the second of June 1794*. London, 1796; facsimile repr. London: Cornmarket Press, 1971.

Desbrière, Edouard. *1793–1805: Projets et tentatives de débarquement aux îles britanniques*. 4 vols. Paris: Librairie Militaire R. Chapelot et cie., 1900–1902.

Le Blocus de Brest de 1793 à 1805. Paris: Librairie Militaire R. Chapelot et cie., 1902.

Doyle, William. "Was there an Aristocratic Reaction in Pre-Revolutionary France?" *Past and Present*, 57 (November 1972), 97–122.

Origins of the French Revolution. Oxford: Oxford University Press, 1980; 2nd edn, 1989.

The Oxford History of the French Revolution. Oxford: Clarendon Press, 1989.

Duchatellier, Armand. *Histoire de la Révolution dans les départements de l'ancienne Bretagne*. 6 vols. Nantes: Mellinet, 1836.

Dugan, James. *The Great Mutiny*. London: Andre Deutsch, 1966.

Dull, Jonathan R. *The French Navy and American Independence: A Study of Arms and Diplomacy, 1774–1787*. Princeton: Princeton University Press, 1975.

"Why Did the French Revolutionary Navy Fail?" *The Consortium on Revolutionary Europe, 1750–1850. Proceedings*, 18: 2 (1989), 121–137.

Dupont, Amiral Maurice, *L'Amiral Willaumez*. Paris: Editions Tallandier, 1987.

Edmonds, W. D. " 'Federalism' and Urban Revolt in France in 1793," *Journal of Modern History*, 55 (March 1983), 22–53.

"A Jacobin Debacle: The Losing of Lyon in Spring 1793," *History*, 69 (1984), 1–14.

Jacobinism and the Revolt of Lyon, 1789–1793. Oxford: Clarendon Press, 1990.

Egret, Jean. "The Origins of the Revolution in Brittany (1788–1789)," in Jeffry Kaplow (ed.), *New Perspectives on the French Revolution.* New York: John Riley and Sons, Inc., 1965.

Evans, H. V. "The Nootka Sound Controversy in Anglo-French Diplomacy – 1790," *Journal of Modern History,* 46 (1974), 609–640.

Ferrier, Jacques. "Les singuliers successeurs de Malouet à Toulon (1792–1797)," *Bulletin de l'Académie du Var* (1979), 131–154.

"L'événement de Toulon du 28 août 1793," *Bulletin de l'Académie du Var* (1985), 129–176.

Fleury, E. J. and J. T. Viaud. *Histoire de la ville et du port de Rochefort.* Rochefort: Honorine Fleury, 1845.

Fontaine de Resbecq, H. "L'Administration Centrale de la marine avant 1793," *Revue maritime et coloniale,* 61 (1879), 148–154.

Forrest, Alan. *Society and Politics in Revolutionary Bordeaux.* Oxford: Oxford University Press, 1975.

Conscripts and Deserters. The Army and French Society during the Revolution and Empire. Oxford and New York: Oxford University Press, 1989.

The Soldiers of the French Revolution. Durham: Duke University Press, 1989.

Furet, François. *Interpreting the French Revolution.* Trans. Elborg Forster. Paris, 1978; repr. Cambridge: Cambridge University Press, 1985.

Furet, François and Mona Ozouf (eds.). *A Critical Dictionary of the French Revolution.* Trans. Arthur Goldhammer. Cambridge, Mass.: Belknap Press of Harvard University Press, 1989.

Garrett, Clarke. "Religion, Revenge, and the Reign of Terror in Montauban," *Proceedings, Western Society for French History,* 15 (1988), 190–197.

Geggus, David Patrick. *Slavery, War, and Revolution: The British Occupation of Saint-Domingue, 1793–1798.* Oxford: Clarendon Press, 1982.

Gill, Conrad. *The Naval Mutinies of 1797.* Manchester: Manchester University Press, 1913.

Goodwin, Albert. "The Federalist Movement in Caen during the French Revolution," *Bulletin of the John Rylands Library,* 42 (1960), 313–344.

Graham, Gerald S. *Empire of the North Atlantic: The Maritime Struggle for North America.* Toronto: University of Toronto Press, 1950; 2nd edn, 1958.

Greer, Donald. *The Incidence of the Emigration During the French Revolution.* Cambridge, Mass.: Harvard University Press, 1951.

Griffiths, Robert. *Pierre-Victor Malouet and the "Monarchiens" in the French Revolutoin and Counter-Revolution.* Ph.D. Thesis. University of British Columbia, 1975.

Bibliography

Le Centre Perdu. Malouet et les "monarchiens" dans la Révolution française. Grenoble: Presses Universitaires de Grenoble, 1988.

Guérin, Léon. *Histoire maritime de France.* 6 vols. Paris: Dufour, Mulat et Boulanger, 1851–1856.

Guès, André. "La marine de la Révolution française," *Itinéraires; chroniques et documents,* 203 (1976), 72–84.

Guibal, Georges. *La Mouvement fédéraliste en Provence en 1793.* Paris: Plon-Nourrit et cie., 1908.

Guttridge, Leonard F. *Mutiny. A History of Naval Insurrection.* Annapolis: Naval Institute Press, 1992.

Guyon, Marcel. "Les Officiers de la marine royale et la Révolution," *Revue maritime* (octobre 1922), 443–466.

Hahn, Roger. "L'Enseignement scientifique des gardes de la marine en XVIIIe siècle," in R. Taton (ed.), *Enseignement et diffusion des sciences en France au XVIIIe siècle.* Paris: Hermann, 1964.

Hampson, Norman. "Une mutinerie anti-bellliciste aux Indes en 1792," *Annales historiques de la Révolution française,* 22 (1950), 156–159.

"The 'Comité de Marine' of the Constituent Assembly," *The Historical Journal,* 2 (1959), 130–148.

La Marine de l'an II: Mobilisation de la Flotte de l'Océan, 1793–1794. Paris: Libraire Marcel Rivière et Cie., 1959.

"Les Ouvriers des arsenaux de la marine au cours de la Révolution française (1789–1794)," *Revue d'histoire économique et sociale,* 39 (1961), 287–329, 442–473.

A Social History of the French Revolution. Toronto: University of Toronto Press, 1963; repr. 1979.

Hanson, Paul R. *Provincial Politics in the French Revolution: Caen and Limoges, 1789–1794.* Baton Rouge and London: Louisiana State University Press, 1989.

Harris, Robert D. "French Finances and the American War, 1777–1783," *Journal of Modern History,* 48 (June 1976), 233–258.

Havard, Oscar. *Histoire de la Révolution dans les ports de guerre.* 2 vols. Paris: Nouvelle Libraire Nationale, 1911–1913.

Hayet, Armand. "Officiers Rouges, Officiers Bleus," *Revue maritime* (avril 1960), 444–456.

Henry, D. M. J. *Histoire de Toulon depuis 1789 jusqu'au Consulat, d'après les documents de ses archives.* 2 vols. Toulon: Eugène Aurel, 1855.

Henwood, Philippe and Edmond Monage. *Brest. Un port en Révolution, 1789–1799.* Rennes: Editions Ouest-France, 1989.

Higonnet, Patrice. *Class, Ideology and the Rights of Nobles During the French Revolution.* Oxford: Clarendon Press, 1981.

Hood, Ronald Chalmers (III). *Royal Republicans: The French Naval Dynasties Between the World Wars.* Baton Rouge and London: Louisiana State University Press, 1985.

Horn, Daniel. *Mutiny on the High Seas: The Imperial German Naval Mutinies of World War One.* London: Leslie Frewin, 1973.

Hunt, Lynn. *Revolution and Urban Politics in Provincial France: Troyes and Reims, 1786–1790.* Stanford: Stanford University Press, 1978.

Politics, Culture and Class in the French Revolution. Los Angeles and Berkeley: University of California Press, 1984.

Hutt, Maurice. *Chouannerie and Counter-Revolution. Puisaye, the Princes and the British Government in the 1790s.* Cambridge: Cambridge University Press, 1983.

Jackson, Melvin H. *Privateers in Charleston, 1793–1796; an account of a French Palatinate in South Carolina.* Washington: Smithsonian Institution Press, 1969.

Jenkins, E. H. *A History of the French Navy. From its Beginnings to the Present Day.* London: Macdonald and Jane's, 1973.

Jenkins, H. J. K. "Admiral Laforey and the St. Pierre Raiders, 1790," *Mariner's Mirror*, 71 (1985), 218–220.

"The Leeward Islands Command, French Royalism and the *Bienvenue*; 1792–93," *Mariner's Mirror*, 71 (1985), 477–478.

Jordan, David P. *The Revolutionary Career of Maximilien Robespierre.* Chicago: University of Chicago Press, 1985; repr. 1989.

Joret, Eric. *Absentéisme des officiers de la marine à Brest pendant la Révolution, 1789–1793.* 2 vols. Mémoire de maîtrise. Université de Bretagne Occidentale, 1985.

Jouan, René. *Historie de la marine française.* Paris: Payot, 1950.

Jourdan, Louis. "Le Remplacement des officiers après l'insurrection de l'escadre à Quiberon," *Bulletin de la Société de géographie de Rochefort*, 34 (1912), 137–147.

Jurien de la Gravière, Jean-Pierre-Edmond. *Guerres maritimes sous la République et l'Empire.* 2 vols. Paris: Charpentier, 1847.

Keegan, John. *The Price of Admiralty: The Evolution of Naval Warfare.* London, 1988; repr. Harmondsworth: Penguin Books, 1990.

Kennedy, Michael L. *The Jacobin Clubs in the French Revolution: The First Years.* Princeton: Princeton University Press, 1982.

The Jacobin Clubs in the French Revolution: The Middle Years. Princeton: Princeton University Press, 1988.

Bibliography

Kennedy, Paul M. *The Rise and Fall of British Naval Mastery*. London: Allen Lane, 1976.

The Rise and Fall of the Great Powers. Economic Change and Military Conflict from 1500 to 2000. London: Unwin Hyman, 1988.

Kimbrough, Mary A. "The Revolutionary French Navy." Paper delivered at the Seventh International Congress on Enlightenment, Budapest, Hungary, 1987.

Kuscinski, Auguste. *Dictionnaire des conventionnels*. Paris: Société de l'histoire de la Révolution française, 1916.

Labroue, Henri. *Le Club Jacobin de Toulon, 1790–1796*. Paris: Félix Alcan, 1907.

Lacour-Gayet, Georges. *La Marine militaire de la France sous le règne de Louis XVI*. Paris: Honoré Champion, 1905.

La Jonquière, C. de. *L'Expédition d'Egypte, 1798–1801*. 5 vols. Paris: Henri Charles-Lavauzelle, 1899–1907.

Lajuan, A. "La mutinerie de *la Cybèle* en 1792," *Annales historiques de la Révolution française*, 26 (1954), 74–75.

Lavery, Brian. *Nelson's Navy. The Ships, Men and Organization, 1793–1815*. Annapolis: Naval Institute Press, 1989.

Lefebvre, Georges. *The Coming of the French Revolution*. Trans. R. R. Palmer. Paris, 1939; Princeton: Princeton University Press, 1947; repr. 1979.

The French Revolution: From Its Origins to 1793. Trans. Elizabeth Moss Evanson. Paris, 1962; repr. New York: Columbia University Press, 1967.

The French Revolution: From 1793 to 1799. Trans. John Hall Stewart and James Friguglietti. Paris, 1964; repr. New York: Columbia University Press, 1967.

The Great Fear of 1789: Rural Panic in Revolutionary France. Trans. Joan White. Princeton: Princeton University Press, 1973; repr. 1982.

Le Gallo, Yves (ed.). *Histoire de Brest*. Toulouse: Privat, 1976.

Le Goff, T. J. A. "Naval Recruitment and Labour Supply in the French War Effort, 1755–59," in *Naval History Symposium*. Annapolis: Naval Institute Press, 1981.

"Offre et productivité de la main-d'oeuvre dans les armements français au XVIIIème siècle," *Histoire, économie et société*, 2 (1983), 457–473.

"Les origines sociales des gens de mer français au XVIIIe siècle," *La France d'Ancien Régime: Etudes réunies en l'honneur de Pierre Goubert* (1985), pp. 367–380.

"Les gens de mer devant la système des classes (1755–1763): résistance ou passivité?" in A. Lottin, J. Hocquet, and S. Lebecq (eds.), "Les hommes et la mer dans l'Europe du Nord-Ouest de l'Antiquité à nos jours." *Revue du Nord* (extra number), 1986.

Leith, James A. *Media and Revolution*. Toronto: CBC Publications, 1968; repr. 1974.

Le Roy, Albert. "L'Histoire et la Légende: Le Rapport de Barère et le Rapport de Renaudin sur le combat du Vengeur," *La Révolution française*, 1 (1881), 407–419.

Levot, Prosper-Jean. *Histoire de la ville et du port de Brest pendant la Terreur, avec un plan de la prison des administrateurs du Finistère*. Brest, 1870; repr. Brionne (Eure): le Portulan, 1972.

Lévy-Schneider, Léon. *Le conventionnel Jeanbon Saint-André*. 2 vols. Paris: Félix Alcan, 1901.

Ligou, Daniel. *Jeanbon Saint-André, membre du grand Comité de salut public (1749–1813)*. Paris: Messidor/Editions sociales, 1989.

Loir, Maurice. "L'Adoption du pavillon tricolore," *Revue maritime et coloniale*, 122 (1874), 600–619.

La Marine royale en 1789. Paris: Armand Colin et Cie., 1892.

"Le 'Vengeur' d'après les documents des Archives de la marine," *Revue Bleue. Revue politique et littéraire*, 49: 22 (28 mai 1892), 697–701.

Jean-Gaspard Vence, corsaire et amiral (1747–1808). Paris: Librairie Militaire de L. Baudoin, 1894.

"La Marine et la proclamation de la première République," *Revue maritime et coloniale*, 127 (1895), 257–271.

Etudes d'histoire maritime. Révolution – Restauration – Empire. Paris et Nancy: Berger-Levrault et Cie., 1901.

Lynn, John A. *The Bayonets of the Republic. Motivation and Tactics in the Army of Revolutionary France, 1791–94*. Chicago and Urbana: University of Illinois Press, 1984.

Mahan, Alfred Thayer. *The Influence of Sea Power upon History, 1660–1783*. Boston: Little, Brown and Co., 1890.

The Influence of Sea Power upon the French Revolution and Empire, 1793–1812. 2 vols. Boston: Little, Brown and Co., 1898.

Manwaring, G. E. and Bonamy Dobrée. *The Floating Republic*. London, 1935; repr. London: The Cresset Library, 1985.

Martray, Joseph. *La destruction de la marine française par la Révolution*. Paris: Editions France Empire, 1988.

Mathiez, Albert. *The French Revolution*. Trans. Catherine Alison Phillips. London, 1928; repr. New York: Russell and Russell Inc., 1962.

Bibliography

Meyer, Jean. *La Noblesse Bretonne au XVIIIe siècle.* 2 vols. Paris: S.E.V.P.E.N., 1966.

Michel, Jacques. *Du Paris de Louis XV à la marine de Louis XVI. L'oeuvre de M. de Sartine,* Vol. II: *la Reconquête de la liberté des mers.* Paris: Editions de l'Erudit, 1984.

Mills, Herbert Elmer. *The Early Years of the Revolution in San Domingo.* Ph.D. Thesis. Cornell University, 1889.

Mitchell, C. J. "Political Divisions within the Legislative Assembly of 1791," *French Historical Studies,* 13 (1984), 356–389.

Mitchell, Harvey. *The Underground War against Revolutionary France: The Missions of William Wickham, 1794–1800.* Oxford: Clarendon Press, 1965.

Morriss, Roger. *The Royal Dockyards during the Revolutionary and Napoleonic Wars.* Leicester: Leicester University Press, 1983.

Nicolai, Martin. "Bougainville, Louis-Antoine de Bougainville, Comte de," in Allan Gallay (ed.), *Encyclopedia of the Colonial Wars of America.* New York: Garland, forthcoming.

Nicolas, Michel. *Jean-Bon Saint-André. Sa vie et ses écrits.* Paris: Imprimeurs-Unis, 1848.

Nicolle, P. "Le mouvement fédéraliste dans l'Orne en 1793," *Annales historiques de la Révolution française,* 25 (1938), 12–53.

Paillé, Marc. "Les Destitutions d'officiers nobles dans la marine de l'an II: un arrêté du Comité de Salut public du 10 frimaire (30 novembre 1793)," *Université de Nantes. Centre de recherches sur l'histoire de la France Atlantique. Enquêtes et documents,* 3 (1975), 105–126.

Palmer, R. R. *Twelve Who Ruled. The Year of the Terror in the French Revolution.* Princeton: Princeton University Press, 1941; repr. 1973.

Parès, A. J. "Le tribunal populaire martial de Toulon, juillet–décembre 1793," *Bulletin du comité des travaux historiques et scientifiques* (1925), 75–130.

Patrick, Alison. *The Men of the First French Republic.* Baltimore and London: Johns Hopkins University Press, 1972.

Patterson, Alfred Temple. *The Other Armada: The Franco-Spanish Attempt to Invade Britain in 1779.* Manchester: Manchester University Press, 1960.

Pluchon, Pierre (ed.). *Histoire des médecins et pharmaciens de marine et des colonies.* Toulouse: Privat, 1985.

Pol de Courcy. "Deux lettres de Pol de Courcy sur l'affaire du Vengeur (13 prairial an II – 1er juin 1794)," *Le Cahiers de l'Iroise,* 35e Année – no. 3 (Nouvelle série) (Messidor 1988), 164–166.

Poupé, Edmond. "L'Affaire de la Minerve et de la Melpomène, avril–mai 1793," *La Revue historique de Provence* (juin–août 1902), 5–47.

"Les fédérés varois du 10 août," *Révolution française* (1904), 305–325.

Pritchard, James. *Louis XV's Navy, 1748–1762: A Study of Organization and Administration.* Kingston and Montreal: McGill–Queen's University Press, 1987.

Prudhomme, Auguste. *Fédéralisme dans l'Isère et François de Nantes.* Grenoble, 1907.

Reinhard, Marcel. *La Chute de la Royauté.* Paris: Gallimard, 1969.

Richard, Hélène. *Une grande expédition scientifique au temps de la Révolution française: Le Voyage de d'Entrecasteaux à la recherche de Lapérouse.* Paris: Editions du Comité des Travaux historiques et scientifiques, 1986.

Rodger, N. A. M. *The Wooden World: An Anatomy of the Georgian Navy.* London: Collins, 1986; repr. Fontana, 1988.

Ropp, Theodore. *The Development of a Modern Navy. French Naval Policy, 1871–1904.* Edited by Stephen S. Roberts. Annapolis: Naval Institute Press, 1987.

Rose, J. Holland. *Lord Hood and the Defence of Toulon.* Cambridge: Cambridge University Press, 1922.

Rostu, Loïc du. *Histoire extérieure et maritime des guerres de Vendée.* Artigues-près-Bordeaux: Le Cercle d'Or, 1987.

Rouvier, Charles. *Histoire des marins français sous le République (de 1789 à 1803).* Paris: Arthus Bertrand, 1868.

Rudé, George. *The Crowd in the French Revolution.* Oxford: Oxford University Press, 1959; repr. 1972.

Saintoyant, J. *La Colonisation française pendant la Révolution (1789–1799).* 2 vols. Paris: La Renaissance du Livre, 1930.

Saul, Norman E. *Sailors in Revolt: The Russian Baltic Fleet in 1917.* Laurence: Regents Press of Kansas, 1978.

Savina, J. "Les Fédérés du Finistère pour la garde de la Convention (décembre 1792 – mai 1793)," *La Révolution française,* 65 (1913), 193–224.

Schama, Simon. *Citizens. A Chronicle of the French Revolution.* Toronto: Random House, 1989.

Schurman, D. M. *The Education of a Navy: The Development of British Naval Strategic Thought, 1867–1914.* London: Cassell, 1965.

Scott, Samuel F. *The Response of the Royal Army to the French Revolution. The Role and Development of the Line Army, 1787–93.* Oxford: Oxford University Press, 1978.

Scott, William. *Terror and Repression in Revolutionary Marseilles.* London: Macmillan, 1973.

Six, Georges. *Dictionnaire biographique des généraux et amiraux français de la Révolution et de l'Empire, (1792–1814).* 2 vols. Paris: Georges Saffroy, 1934.

Soboul, Albert. *The Sans-Culottes: The Popular Movement and Revolutionary Government, 1793–1794*. Trans. Rémy Inglis Hall. Paris, 1956; repr. Princeton: Princeton University Press, 1980.

Les Soldats de l'an II. Paris: le club français du livre, 1959.

The French Revolution, 1787–1799. Trans. Alan Forrest and Colin Jones. Paris, 1962; repr. New York: Vintage Books, 1975.

Solé, Jacques. *La Révolution en questions*. Paris: Editions du Seuil, 1988.

Spate, O. H. K. *Paradise Found and Lost: The Pacific since Magellan, Vol. III*. Minneapolis: University of Minnesota Press, 1988.

Steel, David. *Steel's Naval Chronologist of the War, From its commencement in Feb. 1793, to its conclusion in 1801*. London, 1802; facsimile repr. London: Cornmarket Press, 1969.

Sutherland, D. M. G. *France 1789–1815. Revolution and Counterrevolution*. London: Fontana Press, 1985.

Sydenham, Michael J. *The Girondins*. London, 1961; repr. Westport, Conn.: Greenwood Press, 1976.

The French Revolution. London, 1965; repr. Westport, Conn.: Greenwood Press, 1985.

The First French Republic, 1792–1804. Berkeley and Los Angeles: University of California Press, 1973.

"The Republican Revolt of 1793: A Plea for Less Localized Local Studies," *French Historical Studies*, 12 (1981), 120–138.

"The Republican Revolt of 1793 in Widening Perspective," *The Consortium on Revolutionary Europe, 1750–1850. Proceedings*, 13 (1984), 116–123.

Taillemite, Etienne. *Dictionnaire des marins français*. Paris: Editions Maritimes et d'Outre-Mer, 1982.

L'Histoire ignorée de la marine française. Paris: Librarie Académique Perrin, 1988.

Thompson, Eric. *Popular Sovereignty and the French Constituent Assembly, 1789–91*. Manchester: Manchester University Press, 1952.

Thompson, J. M. *The French Revolution*. Oxford, 1943; repr. New York: Oxford University Press, 1966.

Tramond, Joannès. *Manuel d'histoire maritime de la France des origines à 1815*. Paris, 1916; repr. Paris: Société d'Editions Géographiques Maritimes et Coloniales, 1947.

Troude, O. *Batailles navales de la France*. 4 vols. Paris: Challamel, 1867–1868.

Vergé-Franceschi, Michel. *Les officiers de marine d'origine Provençale à Toulon au XVIIIème siècle*. Mémoire de la maîtrise. Nice, 1973.

"Les Officers Généraux de la Marine Royale en 1715," *Revue historique*, 273: 1 (1985), 131–157.

Les Officiers généraux de la marine royale (1715–1774). Origines – conditions – services. Thèse en vue de l'obtention du Doctorat d'Etat. Paris, 1987.

Villiers, Patrick. *La Marine de Louis XVI, Vol. I: de Choiseul à Sartine.* Grenoble: J. P. Debbane, 1985.

Vovelle, Michel. "Une champ de bataille de la Révolution (1789–1815)," in Maurice Agulhon (ed.), *Histoire de Toulon.* Toulouse: Privat, 1980.

Wallon, H. A. *La Révolution du 31 mai et le fédéralisme en 1793.* 2 vols. Paris, 1886.

Warner, Oliver. *The Glorious First of June.* London: Batsford, 1961.

White, John Charles. *Pierre Victor Malouet: Administrator and Legislator (1740–1792).* Ph.D. Thesis. Duke University, 1964.

"Aspects of Reform of the French Navy under Castries: A Case for Humanity and Justice," *The Consortium on Revolutionary Europe, 1750–1850. Proceedings*, 4 (1975), 59–67.

Wismes, Armel de. *La vie quotidienne dans les Ports Bretons aux XVIIe et XVIIIe siècles (Nantes, Brest, Saint-Malo, Lorient).* Paris: Hachette, 1973.

Zysberg, André. "Galley Rowers in the Mid-Eighteenth Century," in Orest Ranum and Robert Forster (eds.), *Deviants and the Abandoned in French Society: Selections from the Annales ESC.* Baltimore: Johns Hopkins University Press, 1978.

INDEX

328

Index

Index

Index

343

DATE DUE

FEB 2 5 1998		
MAR 2 4 1998		
OCT 1 5 2001		